CW00701550

Trump Fiction

Trump Fiction

Essays on Donald Trump
in Literature, Film, and Television

Edited by Stephen Hock

LEXINGTON BOOKS
Lanham • Boulder • New York • London

Published by Lexington Books
An imprint of The Rowman & Littlefield Publishing Group, Inc.
4501 Forbes Boulevard, Suite 200, Lanham, Maryland 20706
www.rowman.com

6 Tinworth Street, London SE11 5AL, United Kingdom

Copyright © 2020 by The Rowman & Littlefield Publishing Group, Inc.

All rights reserved. No part of this book may be reproduced in any form or by any
electronic or mechanical means, including information storage and retrieval systems,
without written permission from the publisher, except by a reviewer who may quote
passages in a review.

British Library Cataloguing in Publication Information Available

Library of Congress Cataloging-in-Publication Data Available

ISBN 978-1-4985-9804-0 (cloth)
ISBN 978-1-4985-9806-4 (pbk)
ISBN 978-1-4985-9805-7 (electronic)

Contents

List of Illustrations

FIGURES

TABLE

Acknowledgments

This book had its genesis in the summer of 2016. One of the rising senior English majors at Virginia Wesleyan, Justin FitzGerald, had submitted a proposal that spring to write his senior thesis that fall on *American Psycho*, and I was rereading the novel in preparation for serving as the second reader for Justin's project. Rereading *American Psycho* reminded me of just how often that novel invokes Donald Trump as a signifier of the excesses of the 1980s, and as Patrick Bateman's idol. Excited, I wrote to Justin and suggested that his thesis might address Trump's role in the novel in terms of the 2016 presidential campaign. Sensibly, Justin stuck with his own plans for his thesis, though he did kindly add a few words on Trump, both in the thesis itself and in his presentation at our department's senior conference that December. So, the first person I must thank is Justin FitzGerald.

Gavin Pate, my colleague in the Virginia Wesleyan English Department, was the primary advisor for Justin's thesis, and much of the initial conception of this project was hashed out in conversation with Gavin. Leslie Caughell, Kellie Holzer, and Kathy Merlock Jackson, fellow members of the Virginia Wesleyan faculty, provided valuable help at key stages of the project. I owe particular thanks to Stephen Leist, interlibrary loan coordinator at Virginia Wesleyan, for his work assembling sources.

Earlier versions of several of the essays in this collection were presented at the 2018 Northeast Modern Language Association convention in Pittsburgh, so this project owes a debt to NeMLA for providing a venue for that scholarship. Thanks also to Richard Schumaker and Chris McComb for their work spearheading Trump scholarship at NeMLA.

I am deeply grateful to the contributors to this volume, for the quality of their work and for their gracious responses to my editorial requests. I could not have asked for a better group to work with.

Judith Lakamper at Lexington Books has been a wonderful editor to work with, and I am indebted to her for her guidance of this project from my initial inquiry through publication. Along with Judith, assistant editor Shelby Russell offered tremendous help as the project came to fruition.

Finally, as always, my greatest thanks and appreciation go to my wife, Dawn Richardson, for her endless patience and understanding when it came to the time and attention this project required.

Introduction

Reading Trump

Stephen Hock

In his essay "The Year in Trump Novel Pitches: An Agent's Lament," Erik Hane (2018) notes a curious phenomenon of his experience as a literary agent in 2017, namely, "an overwhelming number of aspiring novelists started writing about Trump." What his essay does not mention, however, is that novelists, screenwriters, cartoonists, and other writers (and not just aspiring ones) had been writing about Donald Trump for years before he became the forty-fifth president of the United States, often in terms that uncannily prefigure the discourse that has since grown to surround his presidency. This unexplored history is, in one sense, unsurprising. After all, Trump was a public figure long before he became president of the United States, one who became familiar to American audiences through his appearances in a wide variety of media over a period of several decades, so it is only natural that depictions of or references to Trump turn up in any number of cultural artifacts that predate his presidency.[1] In this respect, as in so many others, Trump differs radically from many of his predecessors as president. Barack Obama, for instance, does not feature as an object of hero worship for the protagonist of any novel published twenty-five years before he was elected president, as Trump does for Patrick Bateman in Bret Easton Ellis's *American Psycho* (1991).

Moreover, Trump himself has obviously long recognized the power of texts of various stripes to cultivate his persona in the body politic, and has sold an image of himself in a multitude of branded productions that have identified him as their author or producer, ranging from books such as *Trump: The Art of the Deal* (1987) to his reality TV *Apprentice* franchise (2004–2015). Many of these productions devote themselves to establishing not only the personal brand of Donald Trump but also the brand of the Trump family, a practice that the other members of his family have likewise taken up. As Arwa Mahdawi (2018) observes in a piece for *The Guardian* on Donald Trump Jr.'s proposal to write a book of his own, "The man hails from a famously literary family. His father has 'written' almost 20 books. His sister, Ivanka, has published two. Ivana, Donald Jr's mother, released a memoir in 2017. Even Eric has been published; he wrote the foreword to Newt Gingrich's book *Understanding Trump*, which came out last year. Donald Jr, it would seem, is the Branwell Brontë of the Trump clan." Donald Trump *père* has even tried his hand at Broadway, claiming a producer's credit for putting up half the money to stage a production of the (admittedly Trump-content-free) play *Paris Is Out!* in 1970, entering into discussions to turn *The Apprentice* into a Broadway musical in 2005, and exploring the idea of "producing a revue, using songs from the Irving Berlin catalog, with 'The Trump Follies' as the working title" in 2007 (Paulson 2016). At each stage, self-aggrandizement, blurring if not demolishing the line between fact and fiction, has been a hallmark of Trump the impresario, culminating in a presidential administration that has come to resemble a reality TV series. As Amy Chozick (2018) writes for the *New York Times*, "Flip comparisons of Mr. Trump's White House and his years on 'The Apprentice' abound, but behind the 'You're fired!' jokes is a serious case study in mass viewing habits and a president who has made up for his lack of experience in governing with an uncanny grasp of must-see TV." This experience with self-promotion that turns his life into a fiction and a spectacle has, obviously, served Trump well in his political career.[2] As Trump's political career has grown, so, too, has academic attention to Trump from scholars of language, literature, and culture, and apropos of Chozick's description of Trump's presidency as "a serious case study" of political persuasion through the logic and rhetoric of television, the nascent body of academic work on Trump has often focused on studying Trump's rhetoric.[3] Such studies of Trump's fashioning of his rhetorical appeals constitute the first major branch of Trump cultural studies scholarship that has emerged to date.

The second branch of cultural analysis of Trump focuses on reading—or, frequently, *rereading*—texts "in the age of Trump." The earliest published example of this mode of scholarship that I have been able to identify is Michael Dowdy's (2016) "Ascendance and Abjection: Reading Latina/o Poetry in the Summer of Trump." Published in an issue of the *American Poetry Review* dated September/October 2016, the essay's very title conjures a moment when it might have been possible to imagine that the country was experiencing a mere "summer of Trump." In the essay itself, however, Dowdy offers a pointed reflection on the longer history that term obscures: "'The Summer of Trump' was meant to denote a season that passes. In the U.S., however, it has been an endless summer, from early-nineteenth century dreams of Latino autonomy in what is now Texas to the undocumented

'Dreamers' seeking the right to pursue college educations free of the fear of deportation" (7). With this, Dowdy gives an early statement of what will become one of the key refrains of academic studies of Trump, namely, the degree to which Trump must be understood within larger cultural, historical, and political contexts. As Yogita Goyal (2017) will later put it, "It is . . . crucial to not treat Trump as an exception rather than the culmination and continuation of previous policies by democrats and republicans alike. . . . The reminder to think not just about Trump the man but Trumpism as a product of history remains valuable" (471). In reminding us of that longer history that Trumpism is a product of, Dowdy's essay likewise anticipates how quickly analysis will turn from "the summer of Trump" to broader framing that evokes "the age of Trump." Indeed, Dowdy's readers in the fall of 2016 had already experienced not one but two "summers of Trump," as his essay reminds them by opening with a reading of Trump's expulsion of journalist Jorge Ramos from a press conference in August 2015 (7).[4] Following Dowdy, a number of critics have taken up reading texts "in the age of Trump," likewise following Goyal's "reminder to think not just about Trump the man but Trumpism as a product of history," drawing out elements of earlier texts that come to new light "in the age of Trump." Notably, Joseph Valente's (2018) "Reading Joyce in the Age of Trump" bears a title that marks the recognition that Trump's era has lengthened from a "summer" to an "age." This branch of Trump scholarship likewise shows every sign of continuing to flourish through many more "summers of Trump."[5]

Another early scholarly work that touches on Trump, James I. Deutsch's (2017) "Folklore, Politics, and Fake News in the Reception of *Rogue One*," serves as a hinge text that connects this second branch of Trump scholarship with the third. Deutsch begins with "one of the more bizarre but intriguing rumors related to the United States presidency in 2016," namely, "that the makers of the film *Rogue One: A Star Wars Story* (2016) had rewritten and reshot scenes to make it seem explicitly opposed to the policies and personality of President-elect Donald J. Trump" (109). Deutsch proceeds to offer what, for my purposes, constitutes a meta-analysis: not a reading of a text in light of Trump but rather a reading of a popular reading of a text in light of Trump. In tracing the spread of the rumor that *Rogue One* had been rewritten in response to Trump, Deutsch implicitly points to the expectation that the culture will address Trump: in a time when our politics is cultural, we take it for granted that the products of our culture will likewise be political.

Hence, the third (and, for purposes of the present study, final, though there are surely more to come) branch of Trump scholarship in literary and cultural studies, namely, scholarship that focuses on texts that address themselves to Trump, whether more or less directly. Victoria McCollum's forthcoming (as of this writing) anthology *Make America Hate Again: Trump-Era Horror and the Politics of Fear* might serve as a foundational example of this mode of scholarship, moving from rereading earlier texts anew in light of "the age of Trump" to reading texts that are themselves products of—and, implicitly or explicitly, written in response to—"the era of Trump."

The present anthology focuses on a particular subset of these texts: not just texts that take up issues pertinent to "the age of Trump," but rather texts that directly depict or refer to Trump, texts in which Trump, specifically, figures as a signifier. This category of texts includes both those earlier works, like *American Psycho*, that took up Trump the public figure before his successful presidential campaign and the "Trump novels" that have begun to appear in the wake of Trump's election, the proliferation of which Hane laments. The contention of the present volume, however, is that such works of what I am terming "Trump fiction" can open up new avenues for understanding not just (or even necessarily primarily) Trump himself, but rather those larger cultural, historical, and political structures ordering life in the United States, of which Trump stands as an effect, in which he is a willing participant, and for which he functions in these texts as a figure.[6]

In describing these texts as "Trump fiction," I do not mean to refer narrowly to fiction as a genre that would exclude, for instance, poetry. Rather, I use the term "fiction" more broadly, drawing on the roots of the term in the Latin *fingĕre*, meaning "to fashion or form" (*Oxford English Dictionary Online* [1989] n.d.). Fiction, in this broader sense, comprises a range of textual fashionings and formations, whether prose narrative, poetry, visual art, or other modes. My aim in referring to these collectively as "Trump fiction" is to draw attention to the "fictional" as a category whose distinctiveness from the "nonfictional" the discourse surrounding Trump continues to erode. For example, after an investigation into available tax records from 1985 to 1994 by *New York Times* reporters Russ Buettner and Susanne Craig (2019) showed that "year after year, Mr. Trump appears to have lost more money than nearly any other individual American taxpayer," Tony Schwartz, Trump's ghostwriter on the ostensibly nonfiction book *The Art of the Deal*, tweeted, "Given the Times report on Trump's staggering losses, I'd be fine if Random House simply took the book out of print. Or recategorized it as fiction" (2019). Schwartz's tweet reminds us that Trump's presentation of himself has always relied on fictions. This phenomenon has in turn been recognized as a key element of the present "post-truth" climate that, as several of the contributors to this volume note, poses challenges to both writers and readers of fiction (broadly defined). As such, Trump fiction prompts the work of thinking through the questions that Trump and the larger structures for which he serves as a figure pose for the very work of fashioning and forming texts of all stripes.[7]

"IF THE DONALD EVER BECOMES PRESIDENT"

As noted above, a number of works of Trump fiction, like Ellis's *American Psycho*, predate Trump's successful presidential campaign. These texts offer a range of models of Trump fiction, both for their own time (what in retrospect can be read as the cultural prehistory of President Trump) and for our own "age of Trump." Robert Crumb's 1989 five-page comic book story "Point the Finger," for instance, originally published in the third issue of *Hup*, directly targets Trump, but, in its focus on Trump the personality, falls into an ahistorical Trumpian logic of misogyny. In doing so, this text demonstrates the dangers of forgetting Goyal's "reminder to think not just about Trump the man but Trumpism as a product of history." The narration in the first panel of Crumb's story seems to set the stage for a broader consideration of Trump's role in American life, intoning, "now it's time to shake our fist at the injustices of the system" ("'Point the Finger': R. Crumb Takes on Donald Trump" [1989] 2016).[8] Discussion of "the system" quickly drops out of the story, however, as Crumb himself appears in the second panel, speaking directly to the reader, to introduce the "crass and venal character [who] is so arrogant he seeks out the spotlight and publicly boasts of his disgusting exploits" that the story will "point the finger" at. Questions of "the system" are immediately reframed in terms of personal "character" and morality, and the absence of any discussion of Trump's place within the larger American culture persists throughout the story. Trump is dragged into the story in its fourth panel by Tracy and Marny, a pair of women allied with Crumb in his efforts to take down Trump, but Crumb can barely begin to "point the finger" at Trump before Trump fires back, literally pointing his own finger at Crumb and dismissing Crumb as "poisoned by jealousy for anyone who's successful and attractive to women" in the third panel of the story's second page. Over the remainder of the story's second page and into its third, Trump charms the two women, offering to fly them to "a humongous banquet" at Mar-a-Lago that he describes with such decadence that Crumb sputters, "You're—you're Trimalchio from Petronius's 'Satyricon'!!" As Trump leaves with his arms around Tracy and Marny, Crumb is left to stew not just in his own personal impotence but rather an impotence reframed as unchanging fact. "It's just like th' fuckin' Roman Empire! Nothing's changed in 2,000 years," he mutters, effacing any historical specificity to Trump's position, as well as any possibility of agency that could effect change.

A glimmer of the larger social context in which Trump operates appears in the final panel of the story's third page, where a defeated, slumping Crumb is surrounded by a pair of policemen, guns drawn and pointed at him, shouting, "Freeze!!" and "You gonna come along quietly?!?" The appearance of the police here, allied with Trump and prepared to punish his enemies, resonates with the advertisement headed "Bring Back the Death Penalty. Bring Back Our Police!" that Trump took out the same year this story was published, as part of his involvement in the case of the Central Park Five (Laughland 2016).[9] That hint of context is quickly obliterated, however, as the story's fourth and fifth pages metafictionally reset the narrative with a "new ending," granting Crumb a revenge that sees Tracy and Marny giving Trump a swirly at Crumb's command, a humiliated Trump crying his way out of the story, and the two women indulging Crumb's sexual fantasies, even as Crumb confides, "th' first ending was more realistic." Realistic, maybe, but not meaningfully so: Trump's wealth and power come across as products of his sheer personal magnetism. Crumb does mention on the story's final page that his "irreverent" comics work gets "ice[d] . . . out of th' market place," but there is no attempt to situate Trump's position within that market, and the story devolves into a sexual competition between two men, in which the women appear to have no agency of their own. This is not a terribly surprising result for a Crumb comic,[10] but more disturbing is the degree to which the story's narrative logic fits with Trump's own self-fashioning. This, then, is one of the dangers in crafting Trump fiction: the possibility that, in focusing on Trump, the text will fall into the trap of playing by Trump's rules, a mug's game if ever there was one. As Hane (2018) argues in his lament over the onslaught of Trump novel pitches, "It is one of fascism's goals to monopolize our attention. It would like to shrink our imagination; it would like for us to peer wide-eyed at its harsh restrictions and be able to think of nothing else."[11]

In fact, surveying the works of Trump fiction that appeared before Trump's presidency suggests that it is not the works where Trump occupies a central role that resonate the most productively with our present "age of Trump," but rather those where Trump's position in the text is more marginal or even tangential, allowing room to avoid a blinding focus on Trump the individual and instead do the contextualizing and historicizing work that Goyal calls for. For works that predate Trump's presidency, that context is amplified by the irony of historical perspective, namely, the fact that the texts' references to Trump are resignified by our knowledge of Trump's presidency. Trump's presence in such texts functions as a kind of Barthesian *punctum*, "that accident which pricks me" (Barthes 1981, 27). Such might be the case with, for instance, Ari Bach's *Valhalla* (2014), a young adult dystopian novel set in the early twenty-third century that includes a scene in which one character, a would-be theocrat, makes a passing reference to Trump in a discourse on the history of the Inquisition: "'Its CEO, Thomas De Torquemada, was a true genius of the era. Centuries before Trump'—he genuflected—'Thomas established systems that made use of any means to seek out people who didn't believe or didn't comply'" (276). Bach is, to be sure, painting in broad historical strokes (though not as broad as Crumb's), but this text offers an intriguing gesture of placing Trump within a lineage of repressive ideologies, one that resonates within *Valhalla*'s LGBTQ+ context, and, apropos of the *punctum*, pricks us with our knowledge of the path Trump's career has taken since the novel's publication. As Bach (n.d., ca. 2016) wrote in a blog post in response to a reader who brought up this passage,

> I'm actually sort of sad that Trump is now known for his political debacle. That line was written in 2005 when Trump was best known for going bankrupt over and over again but still somehow being incredibly rich. So the joke is that the religiously corporate future of 2230 sees him as a holy figure. But I have no clue how that joke will read after this, now that he'll be known for egregious racism and general political debacle. I guess we'll find out.

Trump's presence in the text, "this wound, this prick," as Barthes notes of the *punctum*, "also bruises me, is poignant to me" (1981, 26, 27).[12]

This quality of the *punctum* can pertain even to works of Trump fiction that foreground Trump, even works of Trump fiction authorized by Trump himself. Jeffrey Robinson's novel *Trump Tower* (2012) follows the lives of various residents and members of the staff of Trump Tower, and Trump is mentioned throughout the novel, though his role in the narrative is mostly limited to emailing a few directives to his staff. Todd Van Luling (2016) notes that *Trump Tower* was originally announced as a novel by Trump himself, though by the time the novel was actually published, Robinson was listed as the sole author. Van Luling suggests that the novel may have grown out of Trump's (as yet) unrealized plans for a television series set in Trump Tower:

> Trump has worked on a "Trump Tower" project since at least the late 1990s, when he tried to make it a television show. "We hired a writer out of Los Angeles and developed a pilot with Showtime," Bob Frederick of the Canadian production company MVP Entertainment explained to HuffPost. "And Donald was happy with it because it was more of a 'Dallas,' 'Dynasty,' 'Upstairs, Downstairs,' kind of concept. And although he had no creative say in the series, we did write him a check for his rights."

Indeed, the novel reads like a novelization of the first season of a nighttime soap opera in the Trump style, filled as it is with sexual hijinks, misogyny, scenes of high-end luxury, and reams of celebrity cameos. A little over halfway through the novel, one such celebrity caps off a joking exchange about lying about golf handicaps with a quip about Trump: "Yeah, well . . . if The Donald ever becomes president, he'll claim to play to fifteen. It's what we do" (Robinson 2012, 238). The uncanny prick of the *punctum* is only enhanced by the fact that the celebrity who makes this joke is Bill Clinton.[13]

"YOU DIDN'T MENTION TRUMP BY NAME ONCE, BUT THAT'S WHAT THE CLASS WAS ABOUT"

The more productive works of Trump fiction open fissures, like these *punctum* moments, through which the texts can speak to the larger contexts of Trumpism. This is true not only of the Trump fiction that predates Trump's presidency but also of the Trump fiction that has appeared since his election. By way of a counterexample, consider Gary Shteyngart's *Lake Success* (2018). Gareth Watkins (2019) suggests that "Trump is evoked enough in Gary Shteyngart's *Lake Success* that he ought to feel integral to the book, and yet nothing of substance is ever said about him," largely because the novel is narrated by a character, Barry Cohen, who obstinately refuses the work of contextualizing and historicizing.[14] The portrait the novel sketches of Barry's vapid self-absorption may hold more value when it comes to examining the United States "in the age of Trump" than Watkins acknowledges, but his point that the novel's references to Trump are out of proportion to its insights is well taken: it would be better to lance the text with a *punctum* that could open up a more engaged treatment of Trump and Trumpism. That said, the novel does offer one moment that gestures toward its position as a Trump fiction manqué. After sitting in on a lecture that his old girlfriend Layla Hayes, a college professor, gives to her class on the Holocaust, Barry can think only of sex, and, in an attempt at seduction, gives Layla what he thinks is a compliment, "'Look, I thought you were amazing as a teacher,' he said, once they were lying in bed. 'You didn't mention Trump by name once, but that's what the class was about'" (Shteyngart 2018, 238). This formula surely offers a better model than *Lake Success*'s mode of mentioning Trump by name repeatedly, but, as Watkins has it, saying nothing. Even more productive, though, would be a model of Trump fiction that mentions Trump in order to say something *more*: not texts that don't mention Trump but are about him, but rather texts that mention him as an avenue to address the contexts of Trumpism. Such texts might open up possibilities for agency and action more meaningful than Barry's performance of a midlife crisis against the backdrop of the 2016 presidential election.

The poems collected in *Resistance, Rebellion, Life: 50 Poems Now*, edited by Amit Majmudar (2017), for instance, collectively frame their resistance to Trump within a number of political contexts, even as the majority of the poems do not mention Trump by name. So, a poem like Eduardo C. Corral's (2017) "Border Patrol Agent," which ends, "Sometimes only body parts remain. / They're buried / in baby caskets" (lines 48–50), insists on bluntly showing the consequences of the xenophobic strain of American politics that Trump has tapped into. Corral's poem then resonates with the treatment of the Syrian refugee crisis in A. E. Stallings's (2017) "Aegean Blues" from her larger "Refugee Fugue," which asks, "Why would a kid lie in the sand, and not take off his shoes? / Why would he lie there face down, the color of a bruise?" (lines 16–17).[15] The notes on contributors at the end of *Resistance, Rebellion, Life* frame Stallings's poem in the context of activism: "She has been active volunteering in Athens with the refugee crisis in Greece since November 2015" (Majmudar 2017, 104). The title of another poem in the collection, Cody Walker's (2017a) "Sitting on a Sofa in a 1925 Bungalow in Ann Arbor, Michigan," suggests a less obviously engaged posture, but turns that fact back on its speaker, as its final line reads, "I have wasted my life" (line 13). Walker's poem also appears in his chapbook *The Trumpiad* (2017b),[16] which appears to want to redress that waste, as, in lieu of an epigraph or dedication, it begins with a notice that "all proceeds from this book will be donated to the American Civil Liberties Union."

A model of poetry as activism likewise underlies the anthology *Resist Much/Obey Little: Inaugural Poems to the Resistance* (Boughn et al. 2017), whose cover announces, "50% of proceeds donated to Planned Parenthood." This collection is similar to *Resistance, Rebellion, Life*, only much larger, running over 700 pages in length. Its poems, too, situate Trump and Trumpism within a range of discourses and contexts, even as most of them do not mention Trump by name. One that does is Luis J. Rodriguez's "Same Morning in America" (2017), which, as its title suggests, presents Trump as only the latest in a lineage that includes Richard Nixon, Ronald Reagan, George W. Bush, and Bill Clinton. Ultimately, however, the "Same" of the poem's title yields, in its final lines, to a call to action that includes lines such as "Let's trump Trump with class knowledge," "Let's trump Trump with unity," and "Let's trump Trump with organization" (lines 65, 70, 71), the anaphora emphasizing not only the continuity of Trump with the history of the United States but also the ongoingness of the work of resistance.

Donald Trump would surely reject the picture that is painted by these and the many other resistant works of Trump fiction that have already appeared. Nonetheless, new works of Trump fiction appear on a regular basis, and will just as surely continue to appear as "the age of Trump" continues to unspool. As such, the present volume can only begin to address the emerging cultural response to Trump and Trumpism. The essays collected here likewise demonstrate a commitment to taking Trump as only the starting point of investigations into the cultural contexts out of which Trumpism grows, and into which it feeds.

The essays in this collection are organized into two parts. Part I, "The Cultural Prehistory of President Trump," examines treatments of Trump in literature, film, and television from the years before his successful presidential campaign. Rereading those texts in "the age of Trump" offers the

uncanny recognition that Trump has long figured in the discourses of racialized violence, paranoid conspiracy theories, and xenophobic nationalism that
have since become central to discussions of his presidency, and shows how
these texts both critique and reify Trump's self-presentation as an avatar of
masculine power, neoliberalism, gentrification, and white privilege.

The first four essays in part I focus on the most prominent work of Trump
fiction published before Trump's turn to a political career, Bret Easton Ellis's
American Psycho. David Markus's essay begins by going back to Trump's
emergence in the public eye in the early 1980s and reading closely the way
Trump Tower was marketed to prospective residents, in order to develop a
theorization of Trumpspace as a construction common to Trump's work in
real estate and to his political career. Drawing on the work of Giorgio Agamben, Markus demonstrates how Trumpspace reflects and drives "the fantasies
governing the supposedly 'normal' lives of the professional-managerial class
under late capitalism," including *American Psycho*'s protagonist, Patrick
Bateman.

Caitlin R. Duffy investigates Trump as a father figure not only to *American
Psycho*'s Patrick Bateman but, more broadly, to two generations of supporters, both the yuppies of the 1980s and the alt-right of the 2010s. Duffy's
reading of Trump's "daddy power" examines two key features of that power,
"the activation of privatized violence and surface-level masks," that recur
throughout *American Psycho* and Trump's political career. These elements of
Trump's power, Duffy argues, are crucial to understanding Trump's appeal
not only to upper-class men like Bateman but also to the white working-class
men and women who have joined "the cult of Trump."

In line with Duffy's argument that "the activation of privatized violence
and surface-level masks" is key to Trump's power, Clinton J. Craig offers a
close reading of scenes of Patrick Bateman's violence in *American Psycho*,
informed by both Lacanian psychoanalysis and the reader-response theory
of Norman Holland, to show how that violence is wrapped up in a "fixation
on surface, the outward appearance of things which can be most easily recognized through branding." As Craig demonstrates, this dynamic governing
Bateman's violence informs fantasies of not just the self but also the nation,
as in the case of the Trumpian "United States of Make America Great Again."

William Magrino wraps up the collection's consideration of *American
Psycho* with a reflection on the swirl of commodity fetishism and celebrity
culture at work in Ellis's treatment of Trump. Drawing out the ways in which
the rise of Trump to the presidency casts a new light on the existing critical
discussion of Ellis, Magrino demonstrates how *American Psycho*'s "positioning the ubiquitous image of Trump alongside reports of violence emphasizes
Bateman's fetishistic impulses" and highlights the degree to which that
violence is an inherent part of the consumer culture in which Bateman lives.

Moving to other works of Trump fiction, my essay reads Amy Waldman's *The Submission* (2011) as a novel whose portrait of American politics and culture following the September 11 attacks revolves around a series of discourses (Islamophobia, anti-immigrant xenophobia, politics as media spectacle, and a white working-class resentment of liberal elites that is often figured in gendered terms) that will come to shape discussion of Trump's political career. I read Trump's presence in *The Submission*, in a roman-à-clef-style cameo based on the real-world Trump's offer to buy the site of the so-called Ground Zero Mosque, to link the novel's concern with memorialization to Trump's infamous weighing-in on the August 2017 Unite the Right rally in Charlottesville, Virginia.

Further exploring texts that function both as 9/11 fiction and as Trump fiction, Joseph M. Conte builds on the references to Trump in Thomas Pynchon's *Bleeding Edge* (2013) to show how that novel anticipates Trump's America. Pynchon's characteristic paranoid mode, in Conte's reading, serves as an apt foundation for a reflection on the means by which "paranoid conspiracy has been injected into mainstream culture—as the poison of controlled demolition, a forged birth certificate, crisis actors, and the Deep State—with the syringe now wielded by a president who acts as Conspirator-in-Chief." At the same time, however, Conte argues that Pynchon offers a vision of paranoia as a more productive search for truth that remains particularly apt in our era of "fake news."

William G. Welty likewise examines *Bleeding Edge*, to show how its references to Trump, when considered in light of Pynchon's treatment of Richard Nixon in *Gravity's Rainbow* (1973), can "shift how we think about the post-45 period: not only post-1945, but also post-Trump, president #45." Ultimately, by demonstrating "that we can't do literary history without attending to the ways fiction theorizes and portrays the activity of reading," Welty's essay leads to a reconsideration of postmodernism not as purely ironic and apolitical but rather in terms of its political engagement.

Turning from the literary to examine depictions of Trump in film and television, Ashleigh Hardin examines a range of Trump's film and TV cameos, spanning the years from 1990 through 2004, to trace their depictions of Trump from beneficent to villainous. Hardin argues that, "in the relative incoherency of his star persona and in the anti-narrativizing tendency of the cameo as vehicle, the outline of Trump's candidacy and presidency becomes legible." Ultimately, Hardin argues, examination of Trump's cameos, including those that were cut from the films in which they were supposed to appear, suggests the degree to which Trump's rise to power was fueled by a complicit popular culture.

Peter Kragh Jensen focuses on Trump's 1994 cameo appearance in *The Fresh Prince of Bel-Air*, in which he appears as a potential buyer for the

Banks family home. Drawing on Nell Irvin Painter's analysis of the role Trump's whiteness played in his presidential campaign, Jensen argues that Trump's *Fresh Prince* cameo exemplifies the ways in which "Trump's star persona has been constructed in a manner that casts him as a member of a benign, pseudo-royal white elite, both with respect to his appearances with black actors and in terms of an aesthetic tradition that presupposes the global centrality of the European/American white male." Jensen then turns to the opening sequence of *The Celebrity Apprentice* to demonstrate how it reinforces that persona, framing Trump as the dominant figure of the entire urban landscape of New York City.

Susan Gilmore concludes part I of this collection with an examination of *Sesame Street*'s parody of Trump, Ronald/Donald Grump, who has appeared three times in the show's history. Gilmore analyzes *Sesame Street*'s parodic depiction of Grump in the context of the program's pedagogical mission, particularly in comparison to the "celebratory" approach taken by Joanne Mattern's biography of Trump for Scholastic's Rookie Biographies Series. Each time Grump appears on *Sesame Street*, he challenges the values that the program aims to nurture in its young viewers, ultimately leading to lessons in how to "contend with seemingly unmitigable executive power."

The essays in part II of this collection, "Trumpocalypse Now," examine works that have appeared during Trump's presidency, to detail the emerging cultural response to the full-blown Trump phenomenon. The texts that these essays examine offer reflections on a range of crises, including the devolution of American politics, Trump's marginalization of the LGBTQ+ community, and the threat of war. At the same time, these essays collectively demonstrate the need for new modes of fiction that can more fully engage the contemporary post-truth moment.

This part begins with Tim Lanzendörfer's reading of Howard Jacobson's *Pussy* (2017) as a text that, in offering an imprecise allegory of Trump and the cast of characters surrounding his political rise, "reflects, too, on the allegorical mode itself." Lanzendörfer argues that *Pussy*'s position in the literary marketplace as a literary hot take responding to Trump's presidency is fundamental to its allegorical quality, rendering it "an accidental allegory: an allegory whose full force stems from what we may suggest is the fundamentally rushed working through that it provides."

Related to the questions of allegory that Lanzendörfer addresses, questions of the efficacy of satire as a response to Trumpism emerge in Bruce Krajewski's reading of Mark Doten's *Trump Sky Alpha* (2019), for instance, in the novel's treatment of internet humor and in Doten's precise mimicry of Trump's presentation of himself on social media. Krajewski argues that

Trump Sky Alpha suggests "a way satire can offer more than an all-or-nothing prospect, either a form of performance able to shame politicians into conformity or a delusional and futile, if entertaining, exercise in significant political reform" insofar as it "expands the audience that should be fed up, that wants its hate to energize change before Trump's hate achieves its goals."

Steven Rosendale and Laura Gray-Rosendale argue that, by contrast, the first season of the satirical television program *Our Cartoon President* (2018) "does the president's work for him." *Our Cartoon President* seems to mount a harsh critique of Trump, characteristic of Juvenalian satire. However, the satire slides into over-the-top caricatures, and even winds up humanizing Trump and his family in a way that yields a gentler Horatian satire. As such, *Our Cartoon President* "may perform a task that the real Trump seems to be unable to accomplish—to lessen by some increment the outrage of those opposed to him."

Meredith James examines a more productive treatment of Trump on television, reading the first season of *Pose* (2018) in terms of its juxtaposition of 1980s-vintage Trump with New York City drag ball culture. James argues that *Pose* marginalizes Trump's world as the dangerous other against which the series' LGBTQ+ protagonists attempt to carve out lives that affirm domestic and middle-class values. In doing so, *Pose* "succeeds in uplifting the communities which Trump is currently vilifying," as well as in "calling Trump World out as the inauthentic pose that it is."

Shannon Finck examines Olivia Laing's adoption of the voice and techniques of Kathy Acker in her novel *Crudo* (2018) as a means of conveying the atmosphere of distraction that arises from social media, particularly the tweets of Donald Trump. Against Trump's mode of engaging with the world through Twitter, Laing's novel, in Finck's reading, affirms a politics grounded in an Ackerian "deliberate engagement with a diverse range of texts" that "must now be reworked and reworked again to include new and fleeting forms of minutiae—the texts, tweets, and Instagrams through which we attend to the world's bedlam and its beauty."

Finally, Jaclyn Partyka reads Salman Rushdie's *The Golden House* (2017), in its treatment of not one but two fictionalized avatars of Trump, as an attempt to grapple with different modes of realism in the contemporary post-truth moment. Partyka argues that Rushdie's novel calls its readers to "take into account how discussions of genre and fictionality have become much more significant within a post-truth moment," to ultimately conclude that "when many of our knowledge institutions seem less reliable as representatives of truth and facts, recognizing fiction for what it is—a way to shape a world—may be one of the best balms for our insecure times," an especially apt note on which to end this collection's study of Trump fiction.

NOTES

1. That said, it should be remembered that, well before Trump's ultimately successful 2016 presidential campaign, he teased the possibility of running for president on multiple occasions, beginning as early as 1987, and formally explored running for the presidential nomination of the Reform Party in the 2000 campaign.

2. As Benjamin ([1936] 1969) observed:

Radio and film not only affect the function of the professional actor but likewise the function of those who also exhibit themselves before this mechanical equipment, those who govern. Though their tasks may be different, the change affects equally the actor and the ruler. The trend is toward establishing controllable and transferable skills under certain social conditions. This results in a new selection, a selection before the equipment from which the star and the dictator emerge victorious. (247n12)

3. See, for instance, Ivie (2017), Bostdorff (2017), and Johnson (2017).

4. Dowdy's essay itself first appeared immediately following that first "summer of Trump": it was originally delivered as a talk at Eastern Illinois University on October 14, 2015 (Dowdy 2016, 12n).

5. For other early examples of this branch of Trump scholarship, see Reza and Nessa (2016), Ward (2018), Martinez (2018), Rose (2018), and Ventura (2018).

6. Previously published examples of this strain of Trump scholarship include Weinhold and Bodkin (2017), Goyal (2017), Wally (2018), and Burlingame (2019).

7. For an example of scholarship on a Trump fiction working primarily in a nonverbal and nonnarrative mode that makes a similar point about "fiction," see Tony Perucci's (2018) discussion of Alison Jackson's staged photographs of a Trump lookalike. "By staging simulation's deterrence machine," Perucci argues, "the photos show Trump's presidency to function as a simulation on the order of Baudrillard's examples of Disneyland or Watergate. As with those instances, the 'scandal' of Trump's corruption and deception supports the collective delusion that capitalism can produce otherwise" (195), even as Trump's "'post-truth' campaign succeeded by blurring the boundary between the 'seeming real' and the 'in fact a fiction' because it addressed what Clinton could not: neoliberalism cannot trump the very rage it has produced" (197).

8. The five pages of "Point the Finger" can be read on a variety of websites as of this writing, including the Imgur post cited here.

9. For discussion of Trump's involvement in the Central Park Five case, see Caitlin Duffy's chapter in the present volume.

10. As Edward Shannon (2012) notes of Crumb's work, "Crumb's experience of gender allows him to assume a privileged position, making clearly misogynist statements" (641), while his work demonstrates that "Crumb rebels against totalitarian power while envying the ability to wield it" (642). Shannon ultimately reads Crumb's larger body of work more as more politically engaged, concluding, "Crumb's confessions urge the reader to consider the artist as a survivor not just of his personal demons but of a culture crippled by its own materialism, racism, bigotry, and neuroses" (647), a statement that could likewise apply to "Point the Finger."

11. For discussion of Hane and the politics of attention, see Shannon Finck's chapter in the present volume.

12. My thanks to Melissa Fisher for directing me to *Valhalla*'s reference to Trump.

13. The chapter in which Bill Clinton makes this statement is set at a Clinton Foundation benefit for Haiti, and is particularly stuffed with celebrity cameos (Robinson 2012, 235–45). Hillary Clinton does not appear in the chapter, though Bill does refer to her at one point (237).

14. My thanks to Shannon Finck for bringing Watkins's essay to my attention.

15. The referent is Nilüfer Demir's photograph of the body of three-year-old Syrian refugee Alan Kurdi lying on a beach in Turkey after he drowned in his family's attempt to reach Greece. See "Alan Kurdi" (n.d.).

16. Not to be confused with Martin Rowe's *The Trumpiad: Book the First* (2018). Rowe has since published a second book of his *Trumpiad*.

REFERENCES

"Alan Kurdi." n.d. *Time*. Accessed June 23, 2019. http://100photos.time.com/photos/nilufer-demir-alan-kurdi.

Bach, Ari. 2014. *Valhalla*. Tallahassee: Harmony Ink.

———. n.d., ca. 2016. "Facts, I Was Reading *Valhalla* b/c It Was Free for . . ." *Facts I Just Made Up* (blog). Accessed June 23, 2019. https://facts-i-just-made-up.tumblr.com/post/134079880968/i-was-reading-valhalla-bc-it-was-free-for.

Barthes, Roland. 1981. *Camera Lucida: Reflections on Photography*. Translated by Richard Howard. New York: Hill and Wang.

Benjamin, Walter. (1936) 1969. "The Work of Art in the Age of Mechanical Reproduction." In *Illuminations*, edited by Hannah Arendt, translated by Harry Zohn, 217–51. New York: Schocken Books.

Bostdorff, Denise M. 2017. "Obama, Trump, and Reflections on the Rhetoric of Political Change." *Rhetoric & Public Affairs* 20 (4): 695–706.

Boughn, Michael, John Bradley, Brenda Cárdenas, Lynne DeSilva-Johnson, Kass Fleisher, Roberto Harrison, Kent Johnson et al., eds. 2017. *Resist Much/Obey Little: Inaugural Poems to the Resistance*. N.p.: Dispatches Editions.

Buettner, Russ, and Susanne Craig. 2019. "Decade in the Red: Trump Tax Figures Show over $1 Billion in Business Losses." *New York Times*. May 8, 2019. https://www.nytimes.com/interactive/2019/05/07/us/politics/donald-trump-taxes.html.

Burlingame, Christopher. 2019. "Social Identity Crisis? Patrick Bateman, Donald Trump, and the Hermeneutic Maelstrom." *Journal of Popular Culture* 52 (2): 330–50.

Chozick, Amy. 2018. "Why Trump Will Win a Second Term." *New York Times*. September 29, 2018. https://www.nytimes.com/2018/09/29/sunday-review/trump-2020-reality-tv.html.

Corral, Eduardo C. 2017. "Border Patrol Agent." In Majmudar 2017, 37–38.

Deutsch, James I. 2017. "Folklore, Politics, and Fake News in the Reception of *Rogue One*." *New Directions in Folklore* 15 (1–2): 109–20.

Dowdy, Michael. 2016. "Ascendance and Abjection: Reading Latina/o Poetry in the Summer of Trump." *American Poetry Review* 45 (5): 7–13.

Goyal, Yogita. 2017. "Third World Problems." *College Literature* 44 (4): 467–74.

Hane, Erik. 2018. "The Year in Trump Novel Pitches: An Agent's Lament." *Literary Hub*. March 30, 2018. https://lithub.com/the-year-in-trump-novel-pitches-an-agents-lament/.

Ivie, Robert L. 2017. "Rhetorical Aftershocks of Trump's Ascendancy: Salvation by Demolition and Deal Making." *Res Rhetorica*, no. 2, 61–79.

Johnson, Paul Elliott. 2017. "The Art of Masculine Victimhood: Donald Trump's Demagoguery." *Women's Studies in Communication* 40 (3): 229–50.

Laughland, Oliver. 2016. "Donald Trump and the Central Park Five: The Racially Charged Rise of a Demagogue." *Guardian*. February 17, 2016. https://www.theguardian.com/us-news/2016/feb/17/central-park-five-donald-trump-jogger-rape-case-new-york.

Mahdawi, Arwa. 2018. "Donald Trump Jr Is Hawking a Book. *The Art of the Plea Deal*, Anyone?" *Guardian*. June 13, 2018. https://www.theguardian.com/commentisfree/2018/jun/13/donald-trump-jr-is-hawking-a-book-the-art-of-the-plea-deal-anyone.

Majmudar, Amit, ed. 2017. *Resistance, Rebellion, Life: 50 Poems Now*. New York: Alfred A. Knopf.

Martinez, Inez. 2018. "Trump's Base, Ahab, and the American Dream." *Journal of Jungian Scholarly Studies* 13 (1): 3–17.

McCollum, Victoria, ed. Forthcoming. *Make America Hate Again: Trump-Era Horror and the Politics of Fear*. Routledge.

Oxford English Dictionary Online. (1989) n.d. S.v. "fiction."

Paulson, Michael. 2016. "For a Young Donald J. Trump, Broadway Held Sway." *New York Times*. March 6, 2016. https://www.nytimes.com/2016/03/07/theater/for-a-young-donald-j-trump-broadway-held-sway.html.

Perucci, Tony. 2018. "Sordid Ironies and the Short-Fingered Vulgarian: Alison Jackson's *Mental Images*." *TDR: The Drama Review* 62 (1): 191–200.

"'Point the Finger': R. Crumb Takes on Donald Trump." (1989) 2016. Imgur post. Bastoid. June 24, 2016. https://imgur.com/gallery/X01BI.

Reza, Fouzia, and Vikarun Nessa. 2016. "Reading *Lord Jim* in the Twenty-First Century: The Context, the Immigrant, and the Lord." In *Joseph Conrad*, edited by Jeremiah J. Garsha, 99–113. Ipswich: Grey House.

Robinson, Jeffrey. 2012. *Trump Tower*. New York: Vanguard.

Rodriguez, Luis J. 2017. "Same Morning in America." In *Resist Much/Obey Little: Inaugural Poems to the Resistance*, edited by Michael Boughn, John Bradley, Brenda Cárdenas, Lynne DeSilva-Johnson, Kass Fleisher, Roberto Harrison, Kent Johnson et al., 540–42. N.p.: Dispatches Editions.

Rose, Arthur. 2018. "Mining Memories with Donald Trump in the Anthropocene." *MFS: Modern Fiction Studies* 64 (4): 701–22.

Rowe, Martin. 2018. *The Trumpiad: Book the First*. Independently published.

Schwartz, Tony (@tonyschwartz). 2019. "Given the Times report on Trump's staggering losses, I'd be fine if Random House simply took the book out of print. Or recategorized it as fiction." Twitter, May 8, 2019. https://twitter.com/tonyschwar tz/status/1126233571696492544.

Shannon, Edward. 2012. "Shameful, Impure Art: Robert Crumb's Autobiographical Comics and the Confessional Poets." *Biography: An Interdisciplinary Quarterly* 35 (4): 627–49.

Shteyngart, Gary. 2018. *Lake Success*. New York: Random House.

Stallings, A. E. 2017. "From 'Refugee Fugue.'" In Majmudar 2017, 58–61.

Valente, Joseph. 2018. "Reading Joyce in the Age of Trump." *Éire-Ireland* 53 (3–4): 221–41.

Van Luling, Todd. 2016. "The Incredibly Sexist Book Once Mysteriously Billed as Trump's 'Debut Novel.'" *HuffPost*. October 31, 2016. https://www.huffpost.com/ entry/donald-trump-novel_n_580a62bce4b0cdea3d874ca9.

Ventura, Patricia. 2018. "Dystopian Eating, Queer Liberalism, and the Roots of Donald Trump in HBO's *Angels in America*." *Journal of Popular Culture* 51 (2): 317–36.

Walker, Cody. 2017a. "Sitting on a Sofa in a 1925 Bungalow in Ann Arbor, Michigan." In Majmudar 2017, 64.

———. 2017b. *The Trumpiad*. Oxfordshire, UK: Waywiser.

Wally, Johannes. 2018. "The Return of Political Fiction? An Analysis of Howard Jacobson's *Pussy* (2017) and Ali Smith's *Autumn* (2016) as First Reactions to the Phenomena 'Donald Trump' and 'Brexit' in Contemporary British Literature." *AAA: Arbeiten aus Anglistik und Amerikanistik* 43 (1): 63–86.

Ward, Maggie. 2018. "Predicting Trump and Presenting Canada in Philip Roth's *The Plot against America*." *Canadian Review of American Studies/Revue canadienne d'études américaines* 48 (1): 17–37.

Watkins, Gareth. 2019. "The Disappointing Trump Novel." *Commune*. Spring 2019. https://communemag.com/the-disappointing-trump-novel/.

Weinhold, Wendy M., and Alison Fisher Bodkin. 2017. "Homophobic Masculinity and Vulnerable Femininity: *SNL*'s Portrayals of Trump and Clinton." *Feminist Media Studies* 17 (3): 520–23.

Part I

THE CULTURAL PREHISTORY OF PRESIDENT TRUMP

Chapter 1

A Truly "Free" Psychopathology

Notes on Trumpspace

David Markus

The emergence of Donald Trump as a major public figure is announced in a mostly laudatory 1980 *New York Times* profile titled "Trump: The Development of a Manhattan Developer" (Blum 1980). The article features a photograph of Trump, then thirty-four, standing behind a model of Trump Tower (figure 1.1). Architecture has always relied on mythmaking, and this image follows a hallowed convention of depicting the male "genius" architect or doer alongside his creation. It is the same convention highlighted by Paul B. Preciado (2014, 14–16), who takes the similarities between a photograph of Hugh Hefner with an architectural model of the first Playboy Club and images of Le Corbusier in his studio as a jumping-off point for an analysis of the role of Playboy and modern architecture in the production of new forms of masculinity in mid-century America. Preciado argues that, as a case study in heteronormative culture under capitalism, "*Playboy* is for the contemporary critical thinker what the steam engine and the textile factory were for Karl Marx in the nineteenth century" (2014, 10). Although the scope of the investigation that follows can hardly do justice to the comparison, I would venture that Trumpspace—by which I mean to suggest the vision of dwelling and being-in-the-world promoted by Trump as both a real estate developer and politician—is no less elucidating an object of study for our present neoliberal age than Playboy is for the mid-twentieth century.

Architect and writer Michael Sorkin (2016) has written that Trump is Hefner's "virtual twin" in terms of his relationship to architecture, "leisure-oriented consumption," and women. And it is true that, as the 1970s expired, the form of dwelling that Trump refers to as "super-luxury" ("History: Trump Tower, New York," n.d.)—one of his many coinages—was in some ways an extension of Hefner's monumental project. This can be gleaned from a brief side-by-side examination of the marketing language for the

Figure 1.1   Trump with Model of Trump Tower Site, 1980. Photograph by Don Hogan Charles. In Thomas de Monchaux, "Seeing Trump in Trump Tower," *New Yorker*, October 6, 2016. The *New Yorker* article, which exemplifies the interest in Trump Organization architecture ignited by the 2016 presidential election, reprints the original photograph from Howard Blum's August 26, 1980, *New York Times* article "Trump: The Development of a Manhattan Developer." *Credit*: Don Hogan Charles/*The New York Times*/Redux.

Playboy penthouse and the original Trump Tower. In both advertisements the residence in question is described, in the first few lines, as catering to the "elegant" and "sophisticated" lifestyles of its would-be inhabitants. Both ads ask their readers to envision themselves arriving home in the evening and enjoying the sparkling views of the city from their exclusive perches. "It is just after dark," the marketing copy for Playboy's penthouse apartment reads, "Coming down the hallway, we . . . see the terrace and the winking towers of the city beyond." The Trump Tower advertisement echoes: "You turn the key and wait a moment before clicking on the light. A quiet moment to take in the view. . . . Thousands of tiny lights are snaking their way through Central Park." Both ads also describe an array of amenities, while emphasizing the cutting-edge technology behind the various domestic conveniences at their prospective owner's disposal ("Playboy's Penthouse Apartment" [1956] 1996, 54–67; "Yap of Luxury" [1982] 2017, 43). Both promise would-be clients the rarefied opportunity—in the famous words of Rem Koolhaas, describing the program of "Manhattanism"—"to live *inside* fantasy" (1994, 10). Indeed, the most memorable passage from the Trump Tower advertisement is quite explicit in this regard: "Your diamond in the sky. It seems a fantasy. And you are home" ("Yap of Luxury" [1982] 2017, 43).

The parallels, however, only extend so far. First of all, the Playboy penthouse was, in Preciado's terms, a "male electronic boudoir" (2014, 83), which explicitly deployed its numerous apparatuses (a turning cabinet bar, a reclining couch, a bed with headboard-mounted light dimmers) in the service of its owner's seduction routine. By contrast, the long list of apparatuses on offer at Trump Tower—"Maid service, valet, laundering and dry cleaning, stenographers, interpreters, multilingual secretaries, Telex and other communications equipment, hairdressers, masseuses, limousines, conference rooms"—is geared not toward the production of sexual pleasure, but rather toward the demands of professional life in an increasingly globalizing world ("Yap of Luxury" [1982] 2017, 43). Whereas the Playboy penthouse—for all its outrageously misogynistic underpinnings—was essentially forward-looking in its conception, a space whose high-tech appliances and futuristic Saarinen-designed furniture were geared toward reshaping the "sexually inexperienced middle-class American male" and producing a "postdomestic" alternative to the single-family suburban home (Preciado 2014, 87, 84), the vision of dwelling offered by Trump Tower is one tinged with nostalgia for a bygone era. The building's elite aura is derived from its geographic proximity to the former Gilded Age family residences clustered around Fifth Avenue near Central Park. "It's been fifty years at least since people could actually live at this address," the Trump Tower advertisement informs us, "They were Astors. And the Whitneys lived just around the corner. And the Vanderbilts across the Street" ("Yap of Luxury" [1982] 2017, 43). Finally, for the Playboy penthouse owner—"a man" who "dreams of his own domain, a place that is exclusively his" ("Playboy's Penthouse Apartment" [1956] 1996, 56)—exclusivity was linked to privacy and personal space. For the resident of Trump Tower, by contrast, exclusivity means being surrounded by subordinates and having one's private life perforated by managerial considerations: "You approach the residential entrance—an entrance totally inaccessible to the public—and your staff awaits your arrival. Your concierge gives you your messages. . . . Your elevator man sees you home" ("Yap of Luxury" [1982] 2017, 43).

Obviously, many of these differences are owing to the singular nature of the Playboy enterprise, which emerged from a specific sociohistorical configuration within the postwar United States. There's nothing surprising about the lack of reference to specially designed seduction apparatuses in the marketing copy for Trump Tower. What is perhaps noteworthy, however, is the way in which the Trump advertisement breathlessly reiterates Playboy's language of seduction in unveiling for us a dream home that seems designed for those with little time to dream of anything beyond their next business appointment: "If you can think of any amenity, any extravagance or nicety of life, any service that we haven't mentioned, then it probably hasn't been invented yet" ("Yap of Luxury" [1982] 2017, 43). Stenographers? Telex? Multilingual secretaries? As a high-tech bachelor pad disguised as an office, the Playboy penthouse already aimed at a new intimacy between work and leisure. Yet it emphatically privileged sexual conquest as the sine qua non of male sovereignty. Trump Tower, which, one assumes, was not designed exclusively with male consumers in mind, reflects the outright dissolution of boundaries between the private and professional spheres, and the ascent, in the neoliberal era, of a new constellation of desire and self-affirmation, one inextricable from the possibility of attaining stratospheric, Vanderbiltian, levels of wealth. With the right address and job title comes access to not only the latest array of cutting-edge business and consumer technology but an empowering sense of exclusivity, entitlement, and autonomy. As we will see, this can very easily open onto forms of living "inside fantasy" in contrast to which the mid-century Playboy lifestyle seems charmingly innocent.

Trumpspace, as it figures in the remarks that follow, exemplifies two salient aspects of neoliberal culture: its constrictive hyperprofessionalism, on the one hand, and its obscene fantasies of unrestrained excess on the other. It is, I propose, a privileged arena within which to observe how these two seemingly contradictory tendencies overlap and become indistinguishable. Among the numerous commentators to have considered the significance of Trump-branded real estate in the wake of the 2016 election is artist and writer Liam Gillick (2016), who discusses the architectural vernacular of Trump Tower within the context of mid-1970s and early 1980s postmodernism, among other aesthetic regimes. In this essay, I follow Gillick in returning to some of Fredric Jameson's (1991) seminal insights into postmodernism, arguing for their newfound relevance in the era of Trump's presidency. Prompted by an allusion in Gillick's text to J. G. Ballard's *High-Rise* ([1975] 2012),

I then turn to a brief analysis of how the exclusive dwelling space figures, in Ballard's novel, as a prototype for Trumpspace. I conclude with a discussion of Trump's shadowy presence within Bret Easton Ellis's *American Psycho* (1991). As a paradigmatic figure within the period Ellis describes, a period that saw the rise, in New York City and elsewhere, of what Samuel Stein (2019) calls "the real estate state," Trump was instrumental, I suggest, in affirming the relationship between the exclusive dwelling space and a pathological conception of individual freedom that continues to haunt the American psyche.

ALWAYS ON

"A Building on Fifth Avenue" is how Gillick (2016) refers to Trump Tower, highlighting not only the surprising mundaneness of this structure freighted with so much symbolic weight but also the manner in which it *"takes its place politely within the existing power structure"* despite its supposed *"bad taste."* Gillick likens the building to the Bonaventura Hotel analyzed by Fredric Jameson (1991) in his classic account of postmodernism, observing how all pretenses to the utopian-modernist project of transforming the city around it have been abandoned. Rather, like the aviator shades of disgraced alt-right icon Milo Yiannopoulos, the "phenomenon of reflection" as utilized by Trump Tower "repels the city outside," as Jameson says of the Bonaventura, instituting a scopic regime designed to "achieve a certain aggressivity toward and power over the Other" (quoted in Gillick 2016). In its very surface reflectivity, the building, no less than Milo's *Top Gun*-era aviators, reflects an *"aesthetic regime"* and *"a particular value system"* that, as Gillick notes, are *"more than thirty years old,"* and that were ushered in by the last president who came to power under promises to "Make America Great Again."[1] The minimalistic incorporation of glass, granite, brass, and stainless steel, all of it polished to produce distortive mirror-like effects, summons *"the values of car production and kitchen design,"* both of which Gillick associates with *"individual desire."* Stepping into the funhouse lobby through one of the *"excessive"* number of entrances that make up the *"postmodernist double-revolving-doors-around-central-double-doors arrangement,"* one glimpses a *"confusion"* of glossy signifiers, a complex interlacing of commerce and consumption, business, tourism, and luxury living, all of it bound together somehow by the ubiquitous master signifier of the letter T, which appears gilded on glass windows or stamped into plates of brass (Gillick 2016). If the Bonaventura's lobby anonymously enacts what Jameson (1991, 43) describes as a spatial "vengeance" on the confused and bewildered guests passing through it, the vengeance enacted by the lobby of Trump Tower is of a more personalized origin. Everywhere we look, we are made to know who owns this space. In this sense, the environment figures as a microcosm of the post-2016 world around us: a world in which Trump's name seems all but inescapable.

Developing ideas he first published around the start of Reagan's second term as president, Jameson (1991) characterized "postmodern hyperspace" by its production of an "alarming disjunction point between the body and its built environment," a disjunction ultimately analogous to "the incapacity of our minds, at least at present, to map the great global multinational and decentered communicational network in which we find ourselves caught as individual subjects" (44). What "hyperspace" presents us with, he wrote, is the "imperative to grow new organs, to expand our sensorium and our body to some new, yet unimaginable, perhaps ultimately impossible, dimensions" (39). Thirty years onward there can be little doubt that built environments have become only more complex and confounding as material technologies have advanced, new virtualities have been spawned, and urban "smart space" has begun to crisscross the globe. If our sensoriums have expanded in the meantime, it is only to the extent that we have become increasingly reliant upon the technological prostheses we carry around with us in our pockets today. Within this context, Trump's buildings inhabit a privileged position. In a video that accompanies the online version of his article "Fool's Gold: The Architecture of Trump," Ian Volner (2016) describes the Trump Organiza-tion's architectural portfolio and program as "completely lacking in order . . . a kind of horrifying asymptote or lacuna in the middle of capital . . . a kind of a black hole," before going on to observe how this aberration seems analo-gous to Trump's political operations. Volner not only affirms the hyperspa-tiality of Trumpspace, at least at the level of its radically disjunctive totality, but also posits it as no less than a bend in the space-time continuum itself. But what of the organs and sensorium of the man responsible for engendering this vacuum-like singularity within both the architectural sphere and the spatio-temporality of contemporary politics?

Among the many things Trump appears to embody is the fantasy of a sen-sorial system or apparatus voracious and hypertrophied enough to extend its mutant proboscides into every unseemly crevasse of our increasingly system-atized, but mindbogglingly chaotic, contemporary global reality. This fan-tasy is as potent for the rural white conservatives who praise the president's multinational business know-how (while somehow forgiving his membership among the distrusted global elite) as it is for certain paranoiac corners of the left, which became convinced after the election that for all of his ineptitude, Trump (or at least his Steve Bannon-led team of advisers) was, as certain of his supporters have suggested, playing an elaborate game of geopolitical 3-D chess. Such viewpoints may be largely confabulatory; but there can be none so tragic in its delusions as that of a Democratic Party that failed to recognize the extent to which Trump's sensorium is, by virtue of whatever horrifying mutation, far more attuned than that of his professional political-class opponents to the perpetually shifting, multi-surfaced, hyper-networked spaces of our current reality. Trump, in his unceasing self-promotion and convulsive, self-styled managerialism, exposes something like the perverse core of the neoliberal subject. He both embodies and explodes the post-Fordist understanding of professionalism as, in the words of Paolo Virno, "a *subjective property*, a form of know-how inseparable from the individual person" (2007, 44). Difficult as it has been for liberal technocrats to accept, Trump is president not despite but because he is the kind of person who sends out tweets at 3 a.m. His days are filled with unceasing, obsessional media consumption and self-promotion. Like the lights that adorn the front of Trump Tower, which Gillick (2016) suggests were "*learned from Las Vegas*" and give the impression that "*time has been taken for a ride*," the building's owner and sometime resident is *always on*.

Numberless commentators have pointed to the ways in which Trump has ushered in an unprecedented realignment of established social, political, institutional, and mediatic orders. However, one could just as easily assert that Trump's presidency is no more—nor less—than the consummation of an "aesthetic regime" and "system of values" that has been around for at least three decades. In this sense, Jameson's analysis of the "alarming disjunction" he felt back in the 1980s can be understood—as his own text seems to encourage—more as a prophecy of things to come than a diagnosis of his contemporary moment. At the same time, the disorientation so many now feel within the social and political architecture of Trump's America appears less a symptom of historical rupture than of postmodernism's belated vengeance.

ZONES OF INDISTINCTION

At the conclusion of his text on Trump Tower, Gillick (2016) points us to a passage from J. G. Ballard's *High-Rise* in which the luxury tower at the center of the novel is described as "a model of all that technology had done to make possible the expression of a truly 'free' psychopathology" (Ballard [1975] 2012, 47). Let us briefly consider the significance of Ballard's work for our present concerns. It is a fitting coincidence that the film version of *High-Rise* was released in theaters the same year Trump was elected president: the novel on which it is based is an extended inquiry into the relationship between psychopathology and the built environment. Published in 1975, at the edge of the neoliberal era, the book explores the perverse underside of the professional social order with startling foresight. Gillick is coy about the connections between his detailed analysis of Trump Tower and Ballard's narrative. But what seems relevant to our investigation is the way in which the insomniatic mayhem of the characters in *High-Rise* is tied to the near total identification with professional status that the building enables. Each of the "virtually homogeneous . . . well-to-do professional people" that comprise the book's cast of characters inhabits an apartment whose floor, size, and decor is a direct expression of their social rank (17). Surrounded by luxurious amenities, isolated from the rest of urban life, and left entirely to their own devices, what emerges is a Social Darwinian dystopia in which the well-heeled gradually give themselves over to the frantic exploration of "any deviant or wayward impulses" (47).

Within the context of Ballard's life and work, one important reference point for understanding this paradigm, which emerges repeatedly in the author's books, is the terrifying exhilaration and paradoxical sense of freedom experienced by the protagonist of *Empire of the Sun* ([1984] 2005). The young boy at the center of that autobiographical novel lives out a portion of his youth, as Ballard himself did, inside the walls of a World War II-era internment camp in Japanese-occupied Shanghai—that is, within a space in which "the normal order," to quote Giorgio Agamben (1998, 174), "is de facto suspended." Agamben, of course, has dedicated a significant portion of his work to articulating the relationship between the concentration camp and the biopolitical structures of contemporary existence—those instituted under twenty-first-century American Empire among them. His work is therefore well suited to an analysis of Ballard's fiction in the context of our present concerns. Agamben argues that the camp should be regarded "not as a historical fact and an anomaly belonging to the past . . . but in some way as the hidden matrix and *nomos* of the political space in which we are still living" (1998, 166). The relevance of such assertions to contemporary American politics was made strikingly apparent under the George W. Bush administration, with the latter's post-9/11 institution of a "state of exception" as justification for flouting civil liberties, along with international law and conventions, en route to the full-scale destruction of Iraq.[2] During the Obama years, Agamben's philosophy was invoked in response to the extrajudicial assassination of suspected terrorists, some of them American citizens.[3] And under Trump, Agamben has again become a common reference point for commentators, particularly amid the horrific accounts that have emerged from the immigration camps along the US-Mexico border, and with the president's declaration of a national emergency in a transparent ploy to ensure the construction of his much-hyped security wall. As the global immigration crisis worsens and right-wing movements proliferate across Europe, the suspension of "the normal order" of western democracy threatens to become increasingly normalized. But, as Ballard helps us to see, the infiltration of the camp paradigm into the *nomos* of contemporary existence is by no means exclusive to the properly political realm of quasi-authoritarian governance. Rather, there would appear to be a troublingly intimate relationship between the logic of the exception and the fantasies governing the supposedly "normal" lives of the professional-managerial class under late capitalism.

Given the connection in Ballard's work between the conditions of the camp and the conditions to which the hyper-professionalized community in *High-Rise* descends, it is noteworthy that Agamben concludes his decades-long *Homo Sacer* project (or at least did so chronologically speaking) with a study that implicates, within our modern matrix, "the paradigm of the office," or what he also calls "duty" or "operativity" (2013, xii). Agamben's chief focus in this more recent work (titled *Opus Dei: An Archeology of Duty*) is on the collapse of boundaries between "what a human does and what a human is" (2013, xii). He makes no direct mention of the camp, and he even leads us to wonder if "operativity" has not effectively displaced "the camp" as his new paradigm for modernity. One does, however, find traces of material addressed in previous works, notably in the references to Hannah Arendt's remarks on Adolf Eichmann—the consummate functionary—and the links between Kantian ethical duty and "the execution of the Final Solution" (122–23). In describing "office or duty" as a collapse between "being and praxis," Agamben also alludes to what he terms the "zone of indistinction" (xii). This is the same label he elsewhere reserves for the camp qua "space of exception," or the space in which the rules of law governing human behavior give way, as they do in Ballard's nightmarish imagination, to a condition in which "everything is possible" (Agamben 1998, 169–70). If Agamben nevertheless remains reticent about the links between operativity and the camp as a space in which the inhumane exception becomes the rule, *High-Rise* would appear to fill in the blanks rather starkly. As much as the space of pure operativity represents the total victory, over social life, of the existing capitalist order, it also suggests the collapse of order itself—or rather, the emergence of an order in which absolute domination is the only operative principle. In short, when human beings no longer distinguish between themselves and their business titles, between their self-worth and their earning power, between their place in the world and the floor number of their luxury condo, the conditions are in place for a holocaust.

Returning to our initial object of analysis, we can observe how the collapse of the personal and the professional, the private and the public, the night and the day, which defines the psychogeography of Trump's "Building on Fifth Avenue," subtly reflects a more troubling "zone of indistinction." As *High-Rise* appears to anticipate, the perverse allure of the neoliberal project—signaled, at the political level, by the fixation on deregulation and regulatory reform, on the passage of *laws suspending laws*—at least partially lies in the fantasy of achieving a state of ultimate lawlessness, which must always find its space of (paradoxical, because inherently restricted) localization.[4] "Secure within the shell of the high-rise," Ballard writes of the professional climbers that inhabit his novel, "like passengers on board an automatically piloted airliner, they were free to behave in any way they wished, explore the darkest corners they could find" ([1975] 2012, 47). We have yet to discover the videotapes of Trump's alleged sexual deviances, but for a contemporary permutation of the space Ballard envisions, one need look no further than the private island of billionaire financier and sex offender Jeffrey Epstein, whose private jet—dubbed "Lolita Express" by the tabloids—played host to both Trump and former president Bill Clinton, each a fine case study in Agamben's conception of "office." Spaces of luxurious exception seem to work wonders on otherwise docile brains. Through a perverse internalization of the German proverb, "the house shows the owner," exclusivity reinforces the sense that one is, often quite literally, *above* the "normal order" ("German Proverb" 2017, 81). To make a "diamond in the sky" one's home is to find oneself elevated to the ultimate state of exception: the status of the star. And "when you're a star," as Trump has reminded us, "you can do anything" (Jacobs, Siddiqui, and Bixby 2016).

I FEEL FREE

The notion of a "truly 'free' psychopathology," which is conjured by the infamous words quoted above, hangs about another remark that emerged in the heat of Trump's quest for the White House—that is, for a still more prestigious address than that of his Fifth Avenue penthouse. "I could stand in the middle of 5th Avenue and shoot somebody, and I wouldn't lose any voters," he told a group of supporters in Iowa before going on to clinch the Republican nomination and the presidency (East 2016). In the context of the preceding discussion, one is reminded of a scene from *American Psycho*, Bret Easton Ellis's early 1990s exercise in "the poetics of deregulation" (Godden 2011). Toward the end of the novel, which is set in the waning years of the Reagan era, Patrick Bateman finds himself on Fifth Avenue, "look[ing] up, admiringly, at Trump Tower, tall, proudly gleaming in the late afternoon sunlight." A moment later he has to "fight the impulse" to "blow . . . away" two black teenagers he observes standing in front of the building (Ellis 1991, 385).

It is ironic that Ellis, the onetime literary "brat pack" star, has received perhaps the worst critical drubbing of his career for his commentary on the Trump era. His provocatively titled work of nonfiction, *White*, has been derided as a lazy, reactionary screed that has more to say about the privilege and narcissism of its author than about our contemporary moment.[5] Ellis has downplayed the repeated references to Trump in *American Psycho*

(Grow 2016), but the novel offers a prescient vision of the position occupied by the future president within the structure of late-capitalist American fantasy. Set to the soundtrack of Belinda Carlisle's "I Feel Free" (Ellis 1991, 52)—along with, more famously, the corporate rock of Huey Lewis and the News (352–60)[6]—the narrative unfolds within a New York in which seemingly "everything is possible." And yet Bateman, who pursues any and all forms of deviance with impunity, is a figure defined as much by his crushing sense of insecurity as by his smug entitlement. The detailed inventories of designer attire and the menu items of upscale restaurants that occur with suffocating regularity in the book are not merely the self-satisfied descriptions of someone with the means to partake of luxury culture's finer things. They reflect a pervasive anxiety about what it means to be somebody, to make a name for oneself, in the purely transactional world Bateman inhabits.

The central male characters in Ellis's novel, for all their elitism, mostly appear as interchangeable—slightly better or less well-dressed—iterations of one another. They are expensive non-entities, nobodies, who are perpetually confusing the names of their colleagues, and being mistaken for one another by those same colleagues. If there is one exception it is Paul Owen, manager of the coveted Fisher account, whose ability, in Mary Harron's film adaptation of the novel (2000), to score a Friday night reservation at Dorsia is a marker of *true* freedom.[7] But even toward Owen the attitude is less one of reverence than astonishment and contempt. Within this world of flimsy selfsame semblances, of interchangeable Madisons and Turnballs and Ebersols and Halberstams, *Trump* signifies the ultimate: he is the real McCoy, the unimpeachable authority on all things luxury, the man elevated to ubiquitous brand, the totally sovereign figure. Bateman will end up hacking Paul Owen's face in half with an ax for having a slightly better tan and professional profile than he does. But he won't dare to contradict Trump's glowing assessment, in a magazine interview, of the pizza at "Pastels"—even though Bateman admits he personally finds the crust a bit too "brittle" (Ellis 1991, 46).

But then, as Lauren Berlant notes in a short text published in the wake of the 2016 election, it's not so much Trump's "taste" that his followers share with the man, as his "intensity of appetite and his commitment to a shameless life" (2017). In our era this shamelessness is bound up with white America's desire, in the wake of the Obama years, to feel comfortable in its skin again, or, in other words, to indulge its casually supremacist inclinations. For Trump's part, it involves the embrace of his own orange-headed cartoonishness, which is perhaps the true and final testament to the man's lust for grandiosity. As Berlant reminds us, "Cartoon characters never die" (2017). In the late 1980s, fragile whites may have been less threatened by "politically correct" discourse, but Trump's public shows of racism and weaponization of uppermiddle-class fear—expressed most blatantly in his response to the Central

Park Five case[8]—were no less a part of his identity and appeal.[9] At the same time, the Trumpian *"glitter"* and *"glare"* that Edgar Allan Poe long ago associated with the American "aristocracy of dollars," and that now seems almost as cartoonish as the man's hair, was à la mode (Poe [1840] 2015, 158, 157, 155). Still, the core of what the "Big Man," as Berlant calls him, was selling, was the same—namely, "Big Man-style sovereign sovereignty." Except that here we should understand "sovereignty" not in the properly political sense intended by Berlant but in a discursive, mediatic, and fantasmatic dimension that is, itself, not without political consequences.[10]

To put it another way, among the band of feuding finance bros that inhabit Ellis's book, Trump is—for Bateman, at least—the Big Poppa. Like the father of the primal horde in Freud's *Totem and Taboo*, who hoards all the women to himself, he represents the exception to the rule of limited enjoyment. He is what Jacques Lacan calls the *"au moins un"* or "homoinzun"—that figure outside the law who fantasmatically assures those subjected to it that there is such an outside, that *"au moins un"* (at least one) has access to total satisfaction or jouissance. Although he never appears in person in Ellis's book, at the level of signification his name stands for something more tangible than the mostly interchangeable cast of male characters. To quote Kenneth Reinhard's (2005, 53) treatment of Lacan's concept, Trump is the "signifier that is not subject to [the signifier's] laws," he is, "an 'exception,' the singular signifier that remains rigid, intransigent, and around which all other signifiers revolve." At the level of material belongings, what Trump embodies, in his own phrasing from *Trump: The Art of the Deal*, is "the biggest and the greatest and the most spectacular" that advanced consumer culture has to offer (Trump 1987, 40). He is the star, the nonpareil, the one. And yet, the very existence of Trump's 1987 bestselling guide to success should remind us that he also represents something else within the realm of the popular imagination: a figure who ostensibly wants to aid others in attaining the same exceptional status that he has. In other words, in keeping with Lacan's conception of the myth of the primal father, he is not a figure who simply hoards his enjoyment so much as one who institutes the notion that total enjoyment is possible.

This logic can be mapped onto Trump's political persona. It is not that his seeming magnanimity renders him any less hierarchical a figure. Mark Fisher writes that "one of the successes of the current global elite has been their avoidance of identification with the figure of the hoarding Father, even though the 'reality' they impose on the young is *substantially harsher* than the conditions they protested against in the 60s" (2009, 14). But this statement, which was made in the late aughts, can hardly be applied to the numerous "Big Man-style sovereign" leaders that have emerged since. It is far more the case that the inability of a less traditionally paternal order of "third-way" technocrats to prove their beneficence has conditioned the atavistic emergence of a new breed of strongmen who, if nothing else, are living testaments to the stunning potential for wealth and power accumulation under the prevailing political economic system. Yet it would also be foolish to assert that "The Great God Trump," as Mike Davis (2017) has called him, is not in crucial ways a God who giveth.

This is as true for the high-earners who stand to benefit the most from the president's trillion-and-a-half-dollar tax giveaway as it is for poorer Americans. Among Trump's unwavering base of supporters, it would appear that many experience the outlandish grandiosity of his personhood and presidency as itself a kind of generosity. His excesses can be thought of in terms of what Georges Bataille (1985, 126) called "sumptuary processes," forms of spectacular expenditure along the lines of the potlatch. Foremost among these must certainly be the proudly wasteful monument to racism that the president has endeavored to build along the 1,954-mile US border with Mexico. Trump, it seems, has never ceased to be a real estate guy. The vision he is offering, of an entire country transformed into a gated community, is little more than a mass-marketed right-wing populist version of exclusive dwelling—the product upon which he built his fame and fortune. This brings us back to Bateman standing in front of Trump Tower with a murderous look in his eyes.

As perhaps the most notorious developer during a period in which the largest city in the United States was handed over to financiers and transformed into the gleaming capital of capital that it is today, Trump is a paradigmatic figure. Trump Tower is his signature achievement of the 1980s. By the time Bateman arrives in front of the building, in the final pages of Ellis's novel, he has left a trail of wreckage across Manhattan. Thomas Heise has argued that Bateman is "a psychotic subject who embodies neoliberal theory and performs it through his repeated acts of disembowelment" (2011, 135). Standing before a shining emblem of the city's sterile future, sneering at the blacks and the homeless, he might just as fittingly be described as "the Angel of Death . . . that gluttonous ravager of humans—capital" (Stein 2019, 1). The quote, from a 1911 editorial by Abraham Cahan, is the one that Samuel Stein places at the start of *Capital City: Gentrification and the Real Estate State*, a book that analyzes how capital under neoliberalism ravages the urban landscape, "rushing in and out of spaces with abandon in search of profit and growth" (2). Even more than the collapse of boundaries between "what a human does and what a human is" it is, perhaps, finally, the total identification of oneself with capital, conceived in its most ruthless, alienating, and exploitative dimension that constitutes a "truly 'free' psychopathology." The genius of Trump has been not just to embody the fantasy that such a total identification is possible, by, among other things, making himself over as a brand, but to sell this fantasy as something you can own and occupy—literally "live *inside* of."

While Bateman does not live in Trump Tower, he does live among the stars (Tom Cruise owns the penthouse in his building), and he has clearly bought into the fantasy that Trumpspace exemplifies. No less essential than clothes and food to the inventory of luxury things that he unceasingly details in *American Psycho* are the attributes of his apartment: its flooring, and carpet, and furniture, and art, and high-end consumer electronics. In the most extensive description we're offered of the space, a five-page-long paragraph that begins the book's second chapter (Ellis 1991, 24–29), Bateman transitions seamlessly between his description of luxury objects and his description of himself as he goes about his morning routine. He is keenly aware, of course, that not everything he possesses is "the biggest and the greatest and the most spectacular." While his appropriately named "Duntech Sovereign 2001 speakers in Brazilian rosewood" (25) may well be the best that money can buy, his "Wurlitzer 1015 jukebox" is "not as good as the hard-to-find Wurlitzer 850" (24). Likewise, he still can't get a reservation at Dorsia. But he has "vowed" to get one before his thirtieth birthday, just like he's vowed to get himself "invited to the Trump Christmas party aboard their yacht" (225, 177). In the meantime, his apartment suffices to reinforce a sense of his place in the world. It is, after all, an elegant and sophisticated space, tailored to the needs of the young professional accustomed to carrying out "murders and executions" on Wall Street by day, and who knows what else after work (206). And should someone at the office mistake him for Halberstam or McDonald—no matter. Patrick Bateman, after all, is only "an idea . . . some kind of abstraction . . . something illusory. . . . fabricated, an aberration" (376–77). At the end of the evening, he'll "say good night to a doorman [he doesn't] recognize (he could be anybody) and then dissolve into [his] living room high above the city" (24). It seems a fantasy. And you are home.

NOTES

1. The reference is to Ronald Reagan. Matt Taibbi (2015) calls the slogan "a backbone" of Reagan's 1980 presidential campaign.

2. See Giorgio Agamben (2005). In his sequel to *Homo Sacer*, Agamben addresses the Bush administration's actions within a wider history of totalitarian violence.

3. See Adam Kotsko (2013).

4. For discussion of lawlessness in terms of Trump as a Deleuzian sadistic father in the context of neoliberalism, see Caitlin Duffy's chapter in the present volume.—Ed.

5. See, for example, Andrea Long Chu (2019), *"Psycho Analysis."*

6. Perhaps no scene in Hollywood cinema expresses the odd mixture of conformity and freedom that defines neoliberal subjectivity so well as the famous scene

from Mary Harron's adaptation of *American Psycho* (2000) in which Bateman murders his colleague while the sounds of Huey Lewis's "Hip to Be Square" blast from his high-end sound system.

7. The name of the Owen character in Harron's film is Paul Allen.

8. For further discussion of Trump's involvement in the Central Park Five case, see Caitlin Duffy's chapter in the present volume.—Ed.

9. See, among others, Jelani Cobb (2019), "The Central Park Five, Criminal Justice, and Donald Trump."

10. Berlant is rightly critical of the facile manner in which political and personal (or *practical*) sovereignty are often collapsed by various thinkers. She emphasizes the merely partial applicability that the concept holds outside the domain of absolute power. See Lauren Berlant, *Cruel Optimism* (2011, 95–100).

REFERENCES

Agamben, Giorgio. 1998. *Homo Sacer: Sovereign Power and Bare Life*. Translated by Daniel Heller-Roazen. Stanford: Stanford University Press.

———. 2005. *State of Exception*. Translated by Kevin Attell. Chicago: University of Chicago Press.

———. 2013. *Opus Dei: An Archaeology of Duty*. Translated by Adam Kotsko. Stanford: Stanford University Press.

American Psycho. 2000. Directed by Mary Harron. Santa Monica: Lionsgate.

Ballard, J. G. (1984) 2005. *Empire of the Sun*. New York: Simon & Schuster.

———. (1975) 2012. *High-Rise*. New York: Liveright.

Bataille, Georges. 1985. "The Notion of Expenditure." In *Visions of Excess: Selected Writings, 1927–1939*, edited by Allan Stoekl, translated by Allan Stoekl, Carl R. Lovitt, and Donald M. Leslie Jr., 116–29. Minneapolis: University of Minnesota Press.

Berlant, Lauren. 2011. *Cruel Optimism*. Durham: Duke University Press.

———. 2017. "Big Man." *Social Text*. January 19, 2017. https://socialtextjournal.org/big-man/.

Blum, Howard. 1980. "Trump: The Development of a Manhattan Developer." *New York Times*, August 26, 1980.

Chu, Andrea Long. 2019. "*Psycho* Analysis." *Bookforum*. April/May 2019. https://www.bookforum.com/print/2601/bret-easton-ellis-rages-against-the-decline-of-american-culture-20825.

Cobb, Jelani. 2019. "The Central Park Five, Criminal Justice, and Donald Trump." *New Yorker*. April 19, 2019. https://www.newyorker.com/news/daily-comment/the-central-park-five-criminal-justice-and-donald-trump.

Davis, Mike. 2017. "The Great God Trump and the White Working Class." *Jacobin*. February 7, 2017. https://www.jacobinmag.com/2017/02/the-great-god-trump-and-the-white-working-class/.

de Monchaux, Thomas. 2016. "Seeing Trump in Trump Tower." *New Yorker*. October 6, 2016. https://www.newyorker.com/culture/cultural-comment/seeing-trump-in-trump-tower.

East, Kristen. 2016. "Trump: I Could 'Shoot Somebody' and I Wouldn't Lose Voters." *Politico*. January 23, 2016. https://www.politico.com/story/2016/01/donald
-trump-shooting-vote-218145.
Ellis, Bret Easton. 1991. *American Psycho*. New York: Vintage Books.
Fisher, Mark. 2009. *Capitalist Realism: Is There No Alternative?* Winchester, UK:
Zero Books.
"German Proverb." 2017. *Lapham's Quarterly* 10 (1): 81.
Gillick, Liam. 2016. "A Building on Fifth Avenue." *E-flux*, no. 78. December 2016.
http://www.e-flux.com/journal/78/83040/a-building-on-fifth-avenue/.
Godden, Richard. 2011. "Fictions of Fictitious Capital: *American Psycho* and the
Poetics of Deregulation." *Textual Practice* 25 (5): 853–66.
Grow, Kory. 2016. "'American Psycho' at 25: Bret Easton Ellis on Patrick Bateman's Legacy." *Rolling Stone*. March 31, 2016. https://www.rollingstone.com/
movies/movie-news/american-psycho-at-25-bret-easton-ellis-on-patrick-bateman
s-legacy-175227/.
Heise, Thomas. 2011. "*American Psycho:* Neoliberal Fantasies and the Death of
Downtown." *Arizona Quarterly* 67 (1): 135–60.
"History: Trump Tower, New York." n.d. TrumpTowerNY.com. Accessed June 6,
2019. https://www.trumptowerny.com/trump-tower-new-york.
Jacobs, Ben, Sabrina Siddiqui, and Scott Bixby. 2016. "'You Can Do Anything':
Trump Brags on Tape about Using Fame to Get Women." *Guardian*. October 8,
2016. https://www.theguardian.com/us-news/2016/oct/07/donald-trump-leaked-re
cording-women.
Jameson, Fredric. 1991. *Postmodernism, or, the Cultural Logic of Late Capitalism*.
Durham: Duke University Press.
Koolhaas, Rem. 1994. *Delirious New York: A Retroactive Manifesto for Manhattan*.
New York: The Monacelli Press.
Kotsko, Adam. 2013. "How to Read Agamben." *Los Angeles Review of Books*. June
4, 2013. https://lareviewofbooks.org/article/how-to-read-agamben/.
"Playboy's Penthouse Apartment." (1956) 1996. In *Stud: Architectures of Masculinity*, edited by Joel Sanders, 54–67. New York: Princeton Architectural Press.
Poe, Edgar Allan. (1840) 2015. "The Philosophy of Furniture." In *The Annotated Poe*,
edited by Kevin J. Hayes, 155–62. Cambridge: Harvard University Press.
Preciado, Beatriz [Paul B.]. 2014. *Pornotopia: An Essay on Playboy's Architecture
and Biopolitics*. New York: Zone Books.
Reinhard, Kenneth. 2005. "Toward a Political Theology of the Neighbor." In Slavoj
Žižek, Eric L. Santner, and Kenneth Reinhard, *The Neighbor: Three Inquiries in
Political Theology*, 11–75. Chicago: University of Chicago Press.
Sorkin, Michael. 2016. "The Donald Trump Blueprint." *Nation*. July 26, 2016. https
://www.thenation.com/article/the-donald-trump-blueprint/.
Stein, Samuel. 2019. *Capital City: Gentrification and the Real Estate State*. London:
Verso.
Taibbi, Matt. 2015. "Donald Trump Claims Authorship of Legendary Reagan Slogan; Has Never Heard of Google." *Rolling Stone*. March 25, 2015. https://www.

rollingstone.com/politics/politics-news/donald-trump-claims-authorship-of-lege
ndary-reagan-slogan-has-never-heard-of-google-193834/.

Trump, Donald J. 1987. *Trump: The Art of the Deal*. With Tony Schwartz. New York:
Random House.

Virno, Paolo. 2007. "Post-Fordist Semblance." Translated by Max Henninger. *Sub-
Stance* 36 (1): 42–46.

Volner, Ian. 2016. "Fool's Gold: The Architecture of Trump." *Artforum*. November 2016. https://www.artforum.com/print/201609/fool-s-gold-the-architecture-of-
trump-64212.

"Yap of Luxury." (1982) 2017. *Lapham's Quarterly* 10 (1): 43.

Chapter 2

Trump as "Daddy"

American Psycho *and Hero Worship in the Neoliberal Era*

Caitlin R. Duffy

Near the end of Bret Easton Ellis's (1991) novel *American Psycho*, serial killer and wealthy investment banker Patrick Bateman takes a moment to admire the Manhattan skyline: "I look up, admiringly, at Trump Tower, tall, proudly gleaming in the late afternoon sunlight." In the next sentence, the euphoric atmosphere of his daydream shatters as Bateman spies two teenagers ripping off tourists in front of the glorious tower and suddenly must "fight the impulse to blow them [the teenagers] away" (Ellis 1991, 385). This violent outburst can be at least partly attributed to Bateman's hero worship of the Donald Trump of his era—the 1980s. Throughout the novel, Patrick Bateman eagerly seeks to meet and impress Trump, going to such lengths as attending a U2 concert and dining at restaurants frequented by his idol. Although he never actually appears in the novel, Donald Trump, his family, and his real estate are mentioned a staggering twenty-seven times in *American Psycho*, which is obsessively narrated by its monster/protagonist, Patrick Bateman. The macabre and mundane acts of worship performed by Bateman at the altar of Trump and yuppiedom all follow the market logic of neoliberalism. As trolling white nationalists like Milo Yiannopoulos and Richard Spencer continue to view Trump as a "daddy" figure, the worship enacted by the yuppies of 1980s New York City who inspired Bret Easton Ellis to write *American Psycho* continues and mutates, now growing to allow white working-class men and women into the cult of Trump.

Trump's appeal to the seemingly disparate populations of the wealthy elite and the white working class at first glance appears as an anomaly. Bret Easton Ellis, the writer of *American Psycho*, seems unable to figure out where his fictional character's allegiance would lie because of Trump's strange appeal.

In 2016, Ellis told *The Guardian* that Patrick Bateman would feel "embarrassed" by Trump's connection with "white, angry, blue-collar voters" (Cain 2016). In the same year, however, Ellis told the *New York Post* that Bateman would vote for Trump because "Trump would be a father figure for him. He would see a kindred spirit in the Donald Trump of today: Somebody who calls out bulls—t when he sees it" (Kaplan 2016). Of course, the hypothetical vote of a fictional character is not what's important here. Instead, I want to use Ellis's novel *American Psycho* and the character of Patrick Bateman to better understand Trump's ability to present himself as a father figure for two generations and classes of supporters.

DONALD TRUMP AS A FATHER FIGURE

In a recent interview, Bret Easton Ellis explained that he included references to Donald Trump in *American Psycho* because for almost all of the Wall Street yuppies who Ellis interviewed while conducting research for the book, Donald Trump was an "aspirational figure" (Grow 2016). In the 1980s, Trump was a hero of the age after he "started to buy up derelict buildings in New York and . . . announced that he was going to transform them into luxury hotels and apartments. But in return, he negotiated the biggest tax break in New York's history, worth $160 million." Trump "began to transform New York into a city for the rich" (Curtis 2016), a benefit which Patrick Bateman also supplies through his violent suppression of the lower class.

During the 2016 presidential election, by contrast, Donald Trump targeted white working-class voters by appealing to conservative populism. Of course, Trump is not the first Republican to use the rhetoric and imagery of the white blue-collar population. Rather, "class-based political language and appeals to blue-collar identity" have been popularized and used by conservative politicians ever since the 1970s (Lombardo 2018). According to Timothy J. Lombardo (2018), what he terms "blue-collar conservatism" has its foundations in the 1970s, when blue-collar white populations felt threatened by the civil rights movement and worked to defend their culture and social standing by avoiding overt discussions of race and instead "invok[ing] a blue-collar cultural identity that championed pride, tradition and a loosely defined reverence for hard work." In the 1980s, when Donald Trump and the yuppies that inspired the creation of Patrick Bateman stalked the streets of Manhattan, President Reagan exploited blue-collar conservatism rhetoric by denigrating the populations that supposedly threatened the white working class. One such target was the so-called welfare queen, a heavily "racialized and gendered" term that allowed Reagan to take a stance against the supposedly lazy, immoral, and undeserving poor in favor of the blue-collar white population (Lombardo 2018). While the policies touted by politicians like Reagan and Trump may appeal to the white working class, they typically favor the wealthy elite and materially hurt the very voters who supported them.

Part of Donald Trump's ability to appropriate white working-class language and identity is due to his self-presentation as a father figure. In the 1980s, Donald Trump described his own business practices as representative of his ability to "escape" his father, Fred C. Trump, by surpassing his real estate success (Bender 1983). By the early 1980s, Donald Trump had managed to take control of the Trump Organization by pushing the business past his father's "empire of middle-class apartment houses" in the outer boroughs by developing properties in prime spots in Manhattan, causing the *New York Times* to refer to the company as "unquestionably a Donald Trump extravaganza" (Bender 1983). For every new property he purchased and developed, Donald Trump would decorate it with the family name in gold. He suddenly not only became the face of the family business but also took control of the family name. This usurpation of his father's empire, along with his loud and showy personality, is what first attracted the interest of the 1980s yuppies on whom Bret Easton Ellis based his novel. It was through conversations with these men that Ellis first decided that Bateman would not only be obsessed with Trump but also "aspire to be Donald Trump" (Cain 2016).

Deleuze's description of the father figure in relation to sadism is helpful to consider here. For Deleuze, "The father can only be a father by overriding the law" while sadism represents "an exaltation of the father who is beyond all laws" (Deleuze 1989, 60). Trump's fatherly appeal is deeply tied to his performed "authentic outlaw" persona, allowing him to speak his mind, bully his opposition, and ignore the traditional presidential rules of decorum. Anything he does wrong only helps to increase the support he receives rather than hurt his status, due to this public persona. During his 2016 presidential campaign, Trump famously bragged to a crowd in northwest Iowa that he could "stand in the middle of Fifth Avenue and shoot somebody, and I wouldn't lose any voters" (Johnson 2016). This outlandish and violent claim not only reeks of Patrick Bateman but also resulted in an anonymous member of the crowd proclaiming love and admiration for the presidential candidate, while the rest of the audience cheered in agreement (Johnson 2016). Throughout the campaign, Trump made numerous crass and misogynistic attacks against Hillary Clinton, which included claims that she was "crooked" and "weak," and that "the only card she has is the woman's card. She's got nothing else going" (Smith et al. 2016). In eerie celebration of Trump's behavior, supporters donned shirts, pins, and hats that mimicked their favorite candidate's anti-Hilary Clinton stance. At the 2016 Republican National Convention, merchandise tables sold shirts and pins emblazoned with slogans like "Life's a bitch, don't vote for one" among the swarm of red "Make America Great Again" baseball caps (Mahdawi 2016).

Trump perfectly fits the role of the father as defined by Deleuze, as he repeatedly flaunts his ability to ignore traditional rules of decorum which his female opposition, Hillary Clinton, insists upon. This is very important to the power and fatherly image of Donald Trump. The admittedly problematic book *Kill All Normies*, by Angela Nagle (2017), explains how conformity is often tied to femininity, while rebellion is viewed as a masculine trait: the "rebel imagination" as described by Reynolds and Press in *The Sex Revolts* views women as part of the "castrating conformity" plaguing America; Philip Wylie's 1942 *Generation of Vipers* expresses anxiety surrounding "momism," a trend degenerating America through its focus on materialism and consumer culture; and the so-called Red Pill community found on Reddit and 4chan views marriage and domesticity as a trap that places men within the clutches of the female "counter-revolutionary enforcers of suburban mediocrity" (Nagle 2017, 112–13).

Of course, Donald Trump's successful performance as the fatherly outlaw working against so-called momism is due in part to the fact that he is an actual father. His adult children are heavily involved in his presidency, delivering speeches at rallies, advertising Trump merchandise on their social media accounts, and posing for manicured family portraits. Although a lot of focus has been placed on Ivanka Trump, Donald Trump Jr. is a particularly interesting figure to examine in relation to his father. According to Don Jr.'s mother, Trump originally didn't want to give his name to anyone, arguing that "You can't do that! . . . What if he's a loser?" As Don grew up, Trump began to call his son "Donny," a name which Trump hated and proclaimed that he would never want to be called. Although Don Jr. is now one of the most fervent defenders of President Trump, their relationship has been troubled; for an entire year, Don Jr. refused to speak to his father and namesake (Ioffe 2018).

Today Don Jr. seems to work for his father's approval through constant trolling on social media: posting memes on Instagram and insulting President Trump's critics on Twitter with a healthy mix of emoticons and sarcastic verbal attacks. On February 2, 2019, Don Jr. posted a meme to his Instagram account depicting his father above a wall of text stating that "grown adults are acting like children about President Trump . . . because he's stepped up and has acted like the 'strict parent' . . . in a Government that has been in need of a true Father figure for a long time!!!!!" Don Jr. captioned this meme, "This!!! We all need a disciplinarian parent once in a while . . . some more than others" (2019b; ellipsis in the original). Despite Don Jr.'s over-the-top support of his father and use of hashtags like #MAGA and #Dad, President Trump has never publicly responded to his son's Instagram posts since the

2016 presidential campaign. Many of the photos Don Jr. posts that feature both himself and his father demonstrate their strange cold relationship, as the two rarely touch.[1] Patrick Bateman shares a similarly strained relationship with his father that is briefly referenced in *American Psycho*. While visiting his mother at a sanatorium named Sandstone, Bateman glances at two framed family photos near her bed, one depicting Bateman and his brother Sean as teenagers listlessly wearing tuxedos, and the other showing his apparently deceased father (Ellis 1991, 366). Bateman experiences greater photographic distance from his father than Don Jr., as Bateman and his brother do not even exist in the same frame as their father.

NEOLIBERALISM AND "DADDY POWER"

Besides serving as a means to curate his public persona and gain enough support to be elected president of the United States, Trump's recurrent status as a father figure is also deeply tied to his standing within the neoliberal state. Similarly, Patrick Bateman's position as a successful yuppie serial killer, as well as his obsession with Donald Trump, can be attributed to neoliberal structures. Neoliberalism is a difficult word to define as it has come to be overused and overextended within the academic community, often becoming a synonym for "bad." That being said, as privatization, financialization, deregulation, and welfare cuts continue to pervade American thinking, it remains important for scholars to critically approach representations of neoliberalism and late capitalism. Throughout this essay, I've adopted Wendy Brown's compelling definition of neoliberalism, which she views as a "governing rationality" that "disseminates the *model of the market* to all domains and activities—even where money is not at issue—and configures human beings exhaustively as market actors, always, only, and everywhere as *homo oeconomicus*" (2015, 30, 31).

As defined in Linnie Blake and Agnieszka Soltysik Monnet's edited volume on the subgenre, neoliberal gothic texts "are unified by a will to interrogate the ways in which neoliberal economics has impacted the modern world, has pervaded our very consciousness and, in so doing, has refashioned the very subjectivities we inhabit" (2017, 3). Neoliberal gothic fiction works to make monstrous much of the behavior and thinking which Donald Trump and other neoliberals normalize. Although Donald Trump's presidency does not always align with neoliberal ideology, I find it helpful to examine both *American Psycho* and the idolization of Donald Trump through the lens of the neoliberal gothic. *American Psycho* satirically twists economic competition and consumption into life-or-death scenarios. Bret Easton Ellis's controversial novel can therefore be easily understood as a commentary on the neoliberal era and has, in fact, already been written about as such by academics like Robert Zaller (1993), Carla Freccero (1997), and Thomas Heise (2011). Patrick Bateman's overwhelming appetite for consumption is matched only by his less obvious desire to defend New York City from the economically undesirable.

Patrick Bateman furiously reproduces his hero's behavior, allowing him to become a truly competitive bit of human capital within the neoliberal mecca of 1980s Manhattan. Bateman's private acts of violence serve to protect the interests of the wealthy by removing undesirable individuals from the system, while his ability to maintain his yuppie veneer and expensive taste allows Bateman to maintain his own personal success. Donald Trump continues this work today, though in a slightly different form. As both a presidential candidate and president, Trump has worked to appeal to white blue-collar workers through his self-branding as a tough-talking father figure who has achieved the American dream, all while pushing forward policies that benefit corporations and the wealthy elite. In order to explore both the sources and results of what I call Trump's "daddy power," I focus on two of its characteristics as they appear in *American Psycho* and Trump's presidency: the activation of privatized violence and surface-level masks.

PRIVATIZED VIOLENCE

In 1989, a privately funded advertisement appeared in the four major New York newspapers. The advertisement asked:

> What has happened to our City over the past ten years? . . . What has happened is the complete breakdown of life as we knew it. . . . I want to hate these muggers and murderers. They should be forced to suffer and, when they kill, they should be executed for their crimes. They must serve as examples so that others will think long and hard before committing a crime or an act of violence. . . . I am looking to punish them. . . . I no longer want to understand their anger. I want them to understand our anger. I want them to be afraid.

Although this language may sound like it belongs in a violent 1980s vigilante action film, these words were written by the real estate mogul Donald Trump. He was hoping to encourage the institution of the death penalty in New York City in reaction to the so-called Central Park Five. These five teenaged boys were accused of raping a woman in Central Park. As a result of these advertisements, which cost him $85,000, the five young men of color, who were all aged sixteen and younger at the time of the incident, were sentenced to jail time ranging from five to fifteen years. Twelve years later, a convicted serial rapist confessed that he was the one who actually committed the crime, and a DNA test further proved the innocence of the Central Park Five (Laughland 2016).

During his presidential campaign, however, Trump not only refused to acknowledge their innocence and his mistake but used his involvement in the "Central Park Five" case as evidence of his tough stance on crime. As a result, these men have not only spent their formative years in jail but faced considerable harassment from private individuals who agreed with Trump's anger. According to Yusef Salaam, one of the Central Park Five, Trump was "the fire starter," and shortly after the ads appeared, Salaam's family received death threats, a female audience member at a daytime talk show called for their castration and execution, and Pat Buchanan called for the oldest member of the Central Park Five to be "tried, convicted and hanged in Central Park by June 1." As Trump's ads appeared a mere two weeks after the attack, and before the boys even stepped foot inside a courtroom, it's quite possible that Trump's violent rhetoric also influenced the outcome of the trial itself. Through the use of his well-known name and considerable wealth, Trump managed to activate others (or, as the Central Park Five's lawyer put it, "He poisoned the minds of many people who lived in New York") in order to help him enact his own version of racially inflected vigilante justice (Laughland 2016).

As a resident of New York City in 1989 and a massive Donald Trump fanatic, Patrick Bateman is particularly susceptible to the violent rhetoric of these ads. Although the Central Park Five are never explicitly named in Ellis's novel, there are moments when Bateman performs labor either in Trump's honor or in an attempt to ghoulishly mimic his hero. As Thomas Heise (2011, 154) describes it, Bateman's "serial killing efficiently disposes of surplus populations that strain limited resources" and diminish the cool, glossy look of the city's plastered advertisements, metallic skyscrapers, and storefronts. Upon finding a homeless beggar and his emaciated dog in front of an abandoned antique shop on Twelfth Street, Bateman manically asks him why he doesn't just get a job (Ellis 1991, 129). In doing this, Bateman engages in the belief that it is the lower class's own fault that they are unable to thrive in the conditions which neoliberalism promotes as equal (Spade 2015, 28). In reality, according to Wendy Brown, states operating under neoliberal rationality do away with the liberal promise of equality and instead create a new hierarchy of "winners and losers" (2015, 41). This is certainly the case in Patrick Bateman's world, where success is measured in material displays of wealth as opposed to genuine relationships or accomplishments gained from actual hard work.

During his presidential campaign, Donald Trump promised to run the country "like his business" (Associated Press 2016). Operating under a business structure instead of a democracy, the neoliberal state encourages ruthless competition among its citizens, who are now configured as bits of human capital. Anyone who fails to strengthen the state's economic standing can and will be left for disposal (Brown 2015, 37). For neoliberal states such as 1980s Manhattan or the United States under President Donald Trump, welfare programs are not efficient means to solve issues of poverty and homelessness. Rather, it's far more efficient to allow these undesirable populations to fend for themselves and, eventually, disappear. Patrick Bateman offers the even speedier solution of killing those who fail to contribute to the constant production of capital. He stabs the bum repeatedly, popping both of the man's eyeballs out of their sockets, slices his nose in two, tosses a quarter in his face, and leaves him to die (Ellis 1991, 131). Bateman's methods are certainly brutal; however, it's important to consider the fact that his work simply speeds up the punishments of death and shame which the poor and homeless already experience under neoliberal rationality.

SURFACE, SURFACE, SURFACE

The second characteristic of Donald Trump's "daddy power" is his hyper-focus on and use of surface-level masks and values. Similarly, the power placed by Patrick Bateman and his fellow yuppies on surface-level value is rendered absurd through its absolute enormity. Indeed, the most famous joke within *American Psycho* is the fact that Bateman and the other bankers are so interchangeable that they are rarely correctly addressed. This focus on surface is not limited to Patrick Bateman and the nonfictional yuppies who inspired his creation. It is also helpful in considering Donald Trump's supporters today. Most of Trump's popularity can be attributed to the Trump brand. His self-presentation as both an outlaw figure and creator of wealth and success has allowed him to resonate with a considerable number of American voters. He appears authentic due to his refusal to obey traditional laws of decorum in politics. His often questionable behavior is reinterpreted as representative of his complete freedom and independence from restraint.

Trump's ability to execute a powerful surface-level persona rather than focus on the content of his beliefs or plans (e.g., his purposefully vague comments regarding how he would "Make America Great Again") is repeated by many of his present-day admirers. For example, the leader of the white nationalist think tank known as the National Policy Institute, Richard Spencer, is well aware of the importance of branding and marketability. Both the name of his think tank as well as his term "alt-right" were created to purposefully attach a less-monstrous face to policies and beliefs more accurately labeled as Nazism, racism, and/or white nationalism. At a 2016 alt-right conference in Washington, DC, his proclamation, "Hail Trump, hail our people, hail victory," was met with cheers and Nazi salutes (Lombroso and Appelbaum 2016). In their questionable 2016 coverage of the alt-right, news outlets such as *Mother Jones* and the *Los Angeles Times* were criticized for their presentation of Spencer as the "dapper" white nationalist. This "dapper" identity and clean-cut dress is particularly dangerous because it works to integrate white supremacist thought into the mainstream—one of Spencer's primary objectivies. Because they don't look or act dangerous, Spencer and his followers are more likely to spread their ideas of "peaceful ethnic cleansing" (Silman 2016).

For Patrick Bateman and his fellow yuppies, human worth is largely determined by "surface, surface, surface" (Ellis 1991, 375). In order to gain human capital for oneself in this excessive neoliberal world, characters within *American Psycho* must practice an extreme form of consumerism. Everything they wear, the restaurants at which they dine, and the new techno-gadgets they purchase all work toward forming a surface-level identity. The interior—an individual's personality, beliefs, behaviors—has no bearing on a person's goodness or worth. Therefore, no matter how many times Bateman confesses his crimes or espouses his love of torture, nobody ever views him as a criminal. He remains interchangeable from the other male investment bankers who live uptown, so long as he continues to wear Oliver Peoples glasses and Valentino suits. At the end of the novel he admits that "there is an idea of Patrick Bateman," but he is "something illusory . . . *simply . . . not there*" (Ellis 1991, 376–77).

In *American Psycho*, Donald Trump is also "something illusory," and "*simply . . . not there*." Despite the fact that he is mentioned twenty-seven times, Trump never actually appears in the same physical space as Bateman. In searching constantly for his idol, Bateman only imagines that he sees members of the Trump family in person, stares lovingly at Trump Tower, or feels comforted by the presence of Trump's image on magazines, posters, and newspaper articles. Similarly, Donald Trump has become a constant spectral presence for both his supporters and his detractors due to his bombastic Twitter presence and self-promotional rallies, as well as the disastrous consequences of his presidency. Although he is not physically present in most American homes, for most Americans, Trump is all too "there." President Trump's ubiquity has confronted America with truths that many citizens would prefer to forget. For example, while President Barack Obama was in office, the false belief that America had entered into a post-racial era was common. Trump's growing popularity across his campaign and beyond has brutally proven that racism is alive and well by giving voice to the "silent majority" who now feel free to vocalize and take action on their racist beliefs. Trump's presence provides Patrick Bateman with a similar sort of freedom.

Immediately before Bateman decides to murder a stranger near Central Park West, he admires "faded posters of Donald Trump" and is filled with "new-found confidence" (Ellis 1991, 163). Trump and his inflammatory rhetoric have radicalized racist and psychotic individuals in the real world, as well. In 2018, Cesar Altieri Sayoc Jr., a passionate supporter of President Trump, delivered explosive packages to more than a dozen of Trump's critics (Rash-baum, Feuer, and Goldman 2018). In early 2019, a gunman in New Zealand murdered fifty people at two mosques. He wrote a manifesto which included a description of Donald Trump as "a symbol of renewed white identity and common purpose" (Reuters 2019). The White House immediately separated Trump from these two individuals, allowing the president to continue spout-ing hateful rhetoric and encouraging violence without any consequences.

Today, devotees of Donald Trump follow the flickering signifier of his Twitter profile and the Trump brand, which they view as symbols of Ameri-can exceptionalism, truth, and freedom. Trump's work toward making his brand stand for freedom is particularly interesting. According to Angela Nagle (2017), "freedom" has recently become a buzzword for the alt-right, whose members use it as a mask to cover their threatening, racist, and misog-ynistic views. For example, the 2017 "Unite the Right" rally in Charlottes-ville was able to claim the protection of the First Amendment despite the fact that protestors carried semi-automatic rifles, Confederate battle flags, swasti-kas, and riot gear. Aligning his brand with freedom, Trump described these protestors as "very fine people" (Thrush and Haberman 2017), without losing too much support. According to David Harvey, buzzwords like "freedom" are also often deployed by neoliberals in order to grow support for their policies; however, these words also mask nefarious ideology (2005, 183). In this case, "freedom" is applied to corporations, while the only freedoms individuals seem to gain are the freedom to consume and to not receive public assistance.

At this point, it's helpful to turn to Henry Giroux's use of Renana Brooks's term "empty language," which Giroux defines as "statements that are so abstract as to be relatively meaningless, except to reinforce in simplistic terms an often reactionary ideological position" (2004, 23). Donald Trump's insistence that there were "very fine people on both sides" of the Charlot-tesville "Unite the Right" rally and the alt-right's obsessive defense of "freedom" certainly both fit under Giroux's view of empty language. Trump refuses to go beyond a simplistic view of the rally, choosing to not take sides instead of speaking out against neo-Nazism, while the alt-right defends an incredibly simplistic view of freedom that refuses to acknowledge the danger-ous potential of hate-speech and the freedom of their opposition to respond.

Early in *American Psycho*, while at a dinner party, Patrick Bateman rattles off a list of seemingly compassionate and liberal beliefs, claiming them as his own political stances; he expresses a desire to end racial apartheid, to "provide food and shelter for the homeless" and "training and jobs for the unemployed" (Ellis 1991, 15–16). In the same breath, however, Bateman also inserts his disdain for people who are "abusing the welfare system" and illegal immigration, as well as his desire for "a return to traditional moral values" in popular culture (Ellis 1991, 16). Although Bateman's statements aren't necessarily "abstract" here, they are contradictory to both his actions and words, demonstrating that Bateman probably doesn't believe most of what he says. Trump, too, often doesn't seem to agree with what he says; a common criticism of the president is that he repeatedly contradicts himself. In 2016, for example, Donald Trump told *60 Minutes* that he would be "very restrained" on Twitter (Superville 2018); however, ever since he was elected president, a day rarely goes by when he doesn't tweet an insult toward his opponents, or a bit of nonsense such as "covfefe" (Flegenheimer 2017). Additionally, Trump has flipped on many of the people who have worked for him. While Trump once raved about George Papadopoulos, his campaign foreign policy adviser, calling him an "excellent guy," just one year later, Trump claimed that "few people knew" Papadopoulos, "who has already proven to be a liar" (Superville 2018). This ability to drastically depart from past statements of beliefs without any sort of explanation is an important aspect of the surface-level masks that fuel Trump's "daddy power" and Bateman's psychotic power. Patrick Bateman furiously builds his own identity through the surface-obsessed Manhattan of 1980s by consuming expensive products and bodies. Bateman never stops moving and shifting, something which Ellis effectively demonstrates in the very structure of *American Psycho*, as it unceasingly mutates into different genres, from fiction, to advertisement, to music review, to pornography, to exploitation horror, to self-help guide, to restaurant review, to shopping list, and beyond. These shifts refuse any sort of deeper knowledge of Patrick Bateman to the reader, despite the fact that the novel is entirely narrated by him.

CODA

Reexamining *American Psycho* is essential to understanding Trump's fatherly appeal to two generations of worshippers. The continuous flashes of Trump worship within *American Psycho*, as well as public moments enacted by Trump in the 1980s, allow the violence and absurd horror inherent within the cult of Trump today to be traced and analyzed. Patrick Bateman is partly dangerous because of his ability to mask the violence and hatred festering beneath his yuppie surface. Readers of Ellis's book may also fall prey to Bateman's brand of hyper-normalization, as dismemberment, torture, and cannibalism are presented with the same eerily apathetic yet obsessive tone as his descriptions of waiting for a machine at the gym and dropping off clothes at the dry cleaners. Donald Trump, like some of his major supporters today like Richard Spencer, uses a similar tactic. White supremacy, redistribution of wealth to the rich, and "locker-room banter" (Fahrenthold 2016), among other topics, are currently being normalized within our national consciousness mainly under the guise of "freedom." Gothic literature, particularly neoliberal gothic literature, such as Bret Easton Ellis's *American Psycho*, can allow readers to pry open this dangerous mask of supposed freedom and normalcy to find the monster festering beneath.

NOTE

1. Some examples of this include Don Jr.'s Instagram posts "Great time with @realdonaldtrump on Air Force 1" (2019a), "Thanks Dad!" (2018c), "Riding with @realdonaldtrump on Marine One" (2018b), and "Cool pic leaving The White House with @realdonaldtrump" (2018a).

REFERENCES

Associated Press. 2016. "Donald Trump Says He'll Run America Like His Business." *Fortune.* October 27, 2016. http://fortune.com/2016/10/27/donald-trump-hillary -clinton-business-management/.
Bender, Marylin. 1983. "The Empire and Ego of Donald Trump." *New York Times.* August 7, 1983. https://www.nytimes.com/1983/08/07/business/the-empire-and-e go-of-donald-trump.html.
Blake, Linnie, and Agnieszka Soltysik Monnet. 2017. "Introduction: Neoliberal Gothic." In *Neoliberal Gothic: International Gothic in the Neoliberal Age*, edited by Linnie Blake and Agnieszka Soltysik Monnet, 1–18. Manchester: Manchester University Press.
Brown, Wendy. 2015. *Undoing the Demos: Neoliberalism's Stealth Revolution.* New York: Zone Books.
Cain, Sian. 2016. "Bret Easton Ellis Still Stuck with *American Psycho* after 25 Years." *Guardian.* April 1, 2016. https://www.theguardian.com/books/2016/apr/01 /bret-easton-ellis-american-psycho-25-years.
Curtis, Adam, director. 2016. *HyperNormalisation.* London: BBC.
Deleuze, Gilles. 1989. *Coldness and Cruelty.* In *Masochism*, translated by Jean McNeil, 7–138. New York: Zone Books.
Ellis, Bret Easton. 1991. *American Psycho.* New York: Vintage Books.
Fahrenthold, David A. 2016. "Trump Recorded Having Extremely Lewd Conversation about Women in 2005." *Washington Post.* October 8, 2016. https://ww w.washingtonpost.com/politics/trump-recorded-having-extremely-lewd-conversa

tion-about-women-in-2005/2016/10/07/3b9ce776-8cb4-11e6-bf8a-3d26847eee
d4_story.html?utm_term=.54f508f5e0cc.

Flegenheimer, Matt. 2017. "What's a 'Covfefe'? Trump Tweet Unites a Bewildered
Nation." *New York Times*. May 31, 2017. https://www.nytimes.com/2017/05/31/
us/politics/covfefe-trump-twitter.html.

Freccero, Carla. 1997. "Historical Violence, Censorship, and the Serial Killer: The
Case of *American Psycho*." *Diacritics* 27 (2): 44–58.

Giroux, Henry A. 2004. *The Terror of Neoliberalism*. Boulder: Paradigm.

Grow, Kory. 2016. "'American Psycho' at 25: Bret Easton Ellis on Patrick Bateman's
Legacy." *Rolling Stone*. March 31, 2016. https://www.rollingstone.com/movies/
movie-news/american-psycho-at-25-bret-easton-ellis-on-patrick-batemans-leg
acy-175227/.

Harvey, David. 2005. *A Brief History of Neoliberalism*. Oxford: Oxford University
Press.

Heise, Thomas. 2011. "*American Psycho*: Neoliberal Fantasies and the Death of
Downtown." *Arizona Quarterly* 67 (1): 135–60.

Ioffe, Julia. 2018. "The Real Story of Donald Trump Jr." *GQ*. June 21, 2018. https://
www.gq.com/story/real-story-of-donald-trump-jr.

Johnson, Jenna. 2016. "Donald Trump: They Say I Could 'Shoot Somebody' and
Still Have Support." *Washington Post*. January 23, 2016. https://www.washingt
onpost.com/news/post-politics/wp/2016/01/23/donald-trump-i-could-shoot-some
body-and-still-have-support/?utm_term=.a926ee5dc40a.

Kaplan, Michael. 2016. "'American Psycho' Author: Patrick Bateman Would Vote
for Trump." *New York Post*. April 24, 2016. https://nypost.com/2016/04/24/ameri
can-psycho-author-patrick-bateman-would-vote-for-trump/.

Laughland, Oliver. 2016. "Donald Trump and the Central Park Five: The Racially
Charged Rise of a Demagogue." *Guardian*. February 17, 2016. https://www.the
guardian.com/us-news/2016/feb/17/central-park-five-donald-trump-jogger-rape
-case-new-york.

Lombardo, Timothy J. 2018. "Why White Blue-Collar Voters Love President
Trump." *Washington Post*. September 16, 2018. https://www.washingtonpost.com
/outlook/2018/09/17/why-white-blue-collar-voters-love-president-trump/.

Lombroso, Daniel, and Yoni Appelbaum. 2016. "'Hail Trump!': White Nationalists
Salute the President-Elect." *Atlantic*. November 21, 2016. https://www.theatlantic.
com/politics/archive/2016/11/richard-spencer-speech-npi/508379/?utm_source=a
tlfbcomment.

Mahdawi, Arwa. 2016. "The Bill Clinton Rape Shirt: What Anti-Hillary Merch Says
about This Election." *Guardian*. July 20, 2016. https://www.theguardian.com/us
-news/2016/jul/20/bill-clinton-rape-shirt-republican-convention-hillary-merch.

Nagle, Angela. 2017. *Kill All Normies: The Online Culture Wars from Tumblr and
4chan to the Alt-Right and Trump*. Winchester, UK: Zero Books.

Rashbaum, William K., Alan Feuer, and Adam Goldman. 2018. "Outspoken Trump
Supporter in Florida Charged in Attempted Bombing Spree." *New York Times*.
October 26, 2018. https://www.nytimes.com/2018/10/26/nyregion/cnn-cory-bo
oker-pipe-bombs-sent.html.

Reuters in Washington. 2019. "White House Dismisses Trump mention in Christ-church Shooter Manifesto." *Guardian*. March 17, 2019. https://www.theguardian.com/world/2019/mar/17/trump-christchurch-shooter-manifesto.

Silman, Anna. 2016. "For the Alt-Right, Dapper Suits Are a Propaganda Tool." *The Cut*. November 23, 2016. https://www.thecut.com/2016/11/how-the-alt-right-u ses-style-as-a-propaganda-tool.html#_ga=2.246256452.1134985096.1553182 289-1300104812.1553182289.

Smith, David, Lauren Gambino, Ben Jacobs, and Sabrina Siddiqui. 2016. "Trump Attacks Clinton as Victories Set Stage for Brutal Election." *Guardian*. April 27, 2016. https://www.theguardian.com/us-news/2016/apr/27/donald-trump-hillary-c linton-primaries-results-general-election-sanders-delegates.

Spade, Dean. 2015. *Normal Life: Administrative Violence, Critical Trans Politics, and the Limits of Law*. Revised and expanded edition. Durham: Duke University Press.

Superville, Darlene. 2018. "He Said-He Said: 10 Times That Trump Has Contradicted Trump." *AP News*. January 19, 2018. https://www.apnews.com/495269c1760c 4268b6fa3162dffd1eb3.

Thrush, Glenn, and Maggie Haberman. 2017. "Trump Gives White Supremacists an Unequivocal Boost." *New York Times*. August 15, 2017. https://www.nytimes.com/2017/08/15/us/politics/trump-charlottesville-white-nationalists.html.

Trump, Donald, Jr. (@donaldjtrumpjr). 2018a. "Cool pic leaving The White House with @realdonaldtrump earlier today. Great to be with him for the day. Really miss seeing him on a regular basis." Instagram, July 5, 2018. https://www.instagra m.com/p/Bk3uMDhnhCa/.

———. 2018b. "Riding with @realdonaldtrump on Marine One earlier this year. Such an amazing experience to be able to take part in. ususus." Instagram, November 29, 2018. https://www.instagram.com/p/BqyBje2lC1R/.

———. 2018c. "Thanks Dad!" Instagram, December 31, 2018. https://www.instagra m.com/p/BsEXf4iA05f/.

———. 2019a. "Great time with @realdonaldtrump on Air Force 1 and at the border in Tx yesterday. Amazing turnout with lots of youth and enthusiasm present. Amazing experience except for the 2:30 am landing time back in DC." Instagram, February 12, 2019. https://www.instagram.com/p/BtyKiGwAkGm/.

———. 2019b. "This!!! We all need a disciplinarian parent once in a while...some more than others." Instagram, February 2, 2019. https://www.instagram.com/p/Bt ZzH6NgqQn/?hl=en.

Zaller, Robert. 1993. "*American Psycho*, American Censorship, and the Dahmer Case." *Revue française d'études américaines*, no. 57, 317–25.

Chapter 3

Nation Surface Mirror *Psycho*

A Fantasy of Coherence

Clinton J. Craig

Bret Easton Ellis's novel *American Psycho* (1991) presents a model of identity-building as established in Lacan's description of the mirror stage, in which, upon first beholding one's reflection, a subject fantasizes himself as whole and coherent. Patrick Bateman, who happens to be a sociopath/murder, carries this fantasy of identity into his interpretation of the virtual complex around him—the United States, thus presenting a view of nationhood that can only be interpreted through name brands and whiteness. For Bateman, who can make no meaning beyond surface, it is impossible to comprehend the identity of those who are different from him racially and socioeconomically. They do not cohere with the identity-fantasy of America that Bateman would like to see in himself, making empathy impossible for him.

Oddly, presciently, fittingly, Donald Trump—who is also a brand that Bateman uses to manufacture his coherence—exists in *American Psycho* as a measuring stick and a distraction that perpetuates a fantasy of individual and national identity. As an assertion of "American values" which encourage both capitalism in its most savage possible form and absolute racial and class homogeneity, Ellis's novel foretells a climate of identity-building nostalgia for an America that never existed, a climate in which a slogan such as "Make America Great Again" can thrive.

To Lacan (2002), the mirror stage, in which a child first comes into psychic contact with their own reflection, is a necessary step in the formulation of a gestalt identity, an "ideal-I" (4) that is fantasized as whole and coherent. As important as the visualization of the child's own body and mind are in this genesis of identity, Lacan also points to the world around the infant, the environment which is reflected in the mirror, as formative. He describes the event of a child first encountering their reflection as such: "This act . . . immediately gives rise in a child to a series of gestures in which he playfully experiences the relationship between the movements made in the image and the reflected environment, and between this virtual complex and the reality it duplicates— namely, the child's own body, and the persons and even the things around him" (3). The child's interactions with the world around them, when represented in a reflection that simulates a third-person model with which the child identifies, help to build a fantasy of coherence that will remain unescapably embedded in the child's psyche even into adulthood. I would argue that this process of identification and fantasizing coherence repeats itself every time a subject reads a text, especially if we think of the process of meaning-making through the lens of Norman Holland's "Unity Identity Text Self" (1980). According to Holland's model, the unity one finds in any text (its meaning) is determined by the identity of the self that encounters it. In an inescapable cycle, the subject (or reader) must integrate interpretations of a text with their own gestalt-self: "That is, all of us, as we read, use the literary work to symbolize and finally to replicate ourselves. We work out through the text our own characteristic patterns of desire and adaptation. We interact with the work, making it part of our own psychic economy and making ourselves part of the literary work—as we interpret it. For, always, this principle prevails: identity re-creates itself" (124). Therefore, the process which Lacan describes becomes the foundational mimesis for future mimeses. The "duplicated reality" the child perceives in the mirror sets the stage for that same duplication in the future reading of texts as "identity re-creates itself" over and over again.

However, what if no identity is formed? What if the surface of the reflection is never penetrated, meaning never made? What would the subject then make of the ideal-I and the virtual complex that warps itself around them? These are, perhaps, the questions that Bret Easton Ellis's novel *American Psycho* sets to answer. I posit table 3.1.

In the first two columns, I have listed terms taken from Lacan's "The Mirror Stage as Formative of the *I* Function" as I see them corresponding to those that make up the title of Holland's essay on reader-response theory. In the third column, I have listed terms to represent how I see these relationships corresponding to the reading of America performed by Patrick Bateman, *American Psycho*'s narrator. The child/self/psycho Bateman, whose identity is formed through reflection and *identifies* through surface, makes meaning of a virtual complex—a supposed unity that is the United States—to read its reality, its text, through a mirror that continues to mutually reflect. In this essay, I will trace this process as it occurs throughout the novel, arguing that Bateman and America, as Ellis crafts them in *American Psycho*, are an ever *faithful* reflection of one another.

The child, the self, the psycho that is Patrick Bateman is not a typical narrator. As the novel opens, the reader does not immediately realize that this will be a first-person account, focused as the narrator is on graffiti, other

Table 3.1   Mapping of Ellis's *American Psycho* and Bateman's Fantasy of Coherence

"Mirror Stage as Formative of the I Function" (Lacan)	*Theory of "Unity Identity Text Self" (Holland)*	*Fantasy of Coherence*
Virtual complex	Unity	Nation
Reflection	Identity	Surface
Reality it duplicates	Text	Mirror
Child	Self	Psycho

Source: Clinton J. Craig.

characters' appearances, and other characters' dialog. It is in this dialog that the narrator is first addressed, even before he introduces himself or makes any judgments about his surroundings. Gradually, Bateman, the narrator, comes more and more into focus, until his ego dominates the construction of the novel's world. This escalation tellingly picks up the first time he notices his reflection at a party with other New York socialites—he has entered Lacan's mirror stage: "I catch a glimpse of my reflection on the surface of the table. . . . I notice how good the haircut I got at Gio's last Wednesday looks" (Ellis 1991, 12). Just as Lacan argues that the subject first recognizes himself as whole and coherent (a fantasy) upon seeing his reflection, Bateman's narration has taken the reader from an unstable notion of identity into the prelude to full self-absorption. From the reflection on the table Bateman has formed an identity based on surface. Brand names, such as Gio's, are social markers that Bateman uses to create a coherence; they are the bedrock of making meaning of identity for himself and others.

Identity formation through surface alone is not for everyone. Carla Freccero (1997) writes that critics have mostly panned Ellis for his focus on the surface in *American Psycho*, that they "explicitly reject the MTV-style postmodernist aesthetics of surface adopted by Generation X (for which Ellis has been dubbed a spokesperson)" (51). Freccero adds, "The aesthetic critique of the absence of a formal or stylistic surface/depth model in the novel is echoed by a critique of the absence of a metaphorical surface/depth model in Ellis's character portrayal. What critics reproach Ellis for is that he precisely does not provide a psychologized narrative of origins, a comforting etiology for his killer's illness" (51). I would argue that a fixation on surface, the outward appearance of things which can be most easily recognized through branding, *is itself* the etiology for Bateman's violence (I personally hesitate to use the term "illness"). Close-reading Bateman's murder of his ex-girlfriend Bethany—one of the only times where one of Bateman's acts of violence seems *personal* (as in it matters that he is killing Bethany specifically, rather than any other woman)—helps reveal how Bateman forms his identity as surface.

Bateman begins the chapter where he meets Bethany for lunch uncharacteristically anxious, worrying about his hair, blaming his nervousness on the new Italian mousse he has switched to. After meeting her at the restaurant, he first pointedly asks Bethany about his hair, which she assures him is fine (Ellis 1991, 232). One actual source of Bateman's apprehension could be that Bethany seems to know him more deeply, or at least *know more about him*, than anyone else in his life. However, the possibility of knowing someone at all is alien to Bateman, as he demonstrates when the conversation moves to relationships and who Bateman is "seeing": "Does anyone really *see* anyone else? Did *you* ever see *me*? *See*? What does that mean? Ha! *See*? Ha! I just don't get it. Ha!" (238). This outburst is interesting in that Bateman specifically conflates two meanings of "see": *to be in a relationship with someone* and *knowing someone*. That the more common definition of *to see*, using your eyesight, also corresponds with these meanings is no accident, as Bateman makes meaning through looking at the surface of things. What may be most telling of all is that Bateman's philosophical treatise on *seeing* follows shortly after Bethany fails to identify the brand name of his suit, asking if it is a Henry Stuart (232). After Bethany's misrecognition of branding, the main building block of his identity, Bateman purposefully misbrands himself, saying that the suit is by Garrick Anderson, even though it is actually a third brand (something that will come into play later). Misrecognized by Bethany, Bateman himself has put his identity in flux.

As the conversation with Bethany progresses, Bateman's inadequacies are revealed to be sourced in branding. It turns out that the man Bethany is currently seeing is Robert Hall, a mutual acquaintance from Harvard, and currently a chef at Dorsia. This trendy restaurant is particularly pertinent to Bateman as he has tried and failed on multiple occasions to make a reservation at Dorsia—this is a brand name that has been denied him. Additionally, Bethany's nonchalant description of her boyfriend's workplace betrays the fact that she does not realize the symbolic importance of the brand to Bateman. Furthermore, at Bateman's apartment, Bethany points out that a painting, an Onica (an important brand to Bateman), is hanging upside down (Ellis 1991, 244–45). He discovers he has visually misinterpreted a marker of his own identity, failed to read adequately the surface of the painting, thus implicating Bethany as destabilizing to his own self-coherence. All of these revealed inadequacies, misrecognitions, and negations of brand-based identity lead to what is perhaps the most drawn-out and gratuitous violence in the novel.

Throughout the grisly process of Bethany's murder, the roles of vision and gaze stand out. Seeing is so important to Bateman that he controls Bethany's visual awareness throughout the process of her torture. As Bateman nails her to wood, Maces her repeatedly, cuts and bites her flesh away, and rapes her, he also deliberately sets up a camera to film the gruesome spectacle (Ellis 1991, 246). The Mace temporarily blinds Bethany, seemingly a way for him to correct her vision of him. Later, when it is unclear whether or not Bethany is capable of vision anymore, Bateman remarks, "Her eyes, dull with horror, close, then open halfway, her life reduced to nightmare" (247). Finally, upon this complete control of Bethany's field of vision, Bateman corrects her mistake in suit-branding from earlier in the day, screaming, "The suit is by *Armani! Giorgio* Armani" (247). Brand name recognition is so important to Bateman that he emphasizes *Giorgio*, presumably to make sure Bethany understands which Armani he is talking about. Ultimately, he destroys utterly any representation of Bethany's capacity for seeing, beating her face with a severed limb until it is completely smashed (252).

Violence that seems chaotic and gratuitous serves Bateman's purposes of methodically correcting (as he sees it) his own reflection. Alone in his apartment with what is left of Bethany, many loose threads of the novel come together: "There was so much of Bethany's blood pooled on the floor that I could make out my reflection in it while I . . . watched myself make a haircut appointment at Gio's" (Ellis 1991, 252). This ending to the Bethany saga mirrors the opening of their encounter, when he was unsure of his hair, in addition to mirroring, with the mentioning of Gio's, the novel's initial establishment of Bateman's identity in the table's reflection. In order to reassert his identity, he has re-performed Lacan's mirror stage. Seeing his reflection in the gore he has caused, he has become sure of himself, his identity, decisively making the appointment to get a haircut. In the surface of a pool of blood, in gore, in the emptiness of a mutilated corpse, Bateman sees his identity reflected and reformed.

Bateman's horror at the instability of his identity and its violent reassembly evokes Julia Kristeva's (1982) theory of abjection, in which a subject's selfhood is violated by a confrontation with a misrecognition between self and other, particularly when "other" is a product of the self. Kristeva writes, "The body's inside, in that case . . . compensate[s] for the collapse of the border between inside and outside. It is as if the skin, a fragile container, no longer guaranteed the integrity of one's 'own and clean self' but, scraped or transparent, invisible or taut, gave way before the dejection of its contents" (53). As Bateman lacks an identity associated with his inner self, when he is misbranded by Bethany, he feels the abjection of nearly comprehending a vision of selfhood that is almost, but not quite, what he knows. His surface rendered a "fragile container," and lacking his own inner contents, Bateman resorts to vicious acts to reassert his identity. Furthermore, a subject reacts to abjection, according to Kristeva, by seeking to cast off what threatens: "The abjection of those flows from within suddenly become the sole 'object' of sexual desire—a true 'ab-ject' where man, frightened, crosses over the horrors of maternal bowels and, in an immersion that enables him to avoid coming face to face with an other, spares himself the risk of castration" (53). As

Bateman feels castrated of identity, he lashes out, castrating Bethany, wielding her limb as a prosthetic phallus in order to kill her. This cycle of identity assertion, abjection, and reassembly through violence recurs throughout the novel, not just to create an isolated self in Bateman, but to read a vision of his environment—the United States of the 1980s.

As the first part of this essay focused on the *Psycho*, half of the title to Ellis's novel, I turn now to *American*, an equally integral ideal in the analysis of the text. *American Psycho*, though Ellis might disguise this fact, is an extremely political novel. Colin Hutchinson (2008) perceives in the presentation of the novel's Reagan-era Wall Street setting that "the 1960s dream of individual emancipation has been traduced by its outcome within the context of capitalism reconstructed according to its own interpretation of that dream: a behavioural nexus between social libertarianism and economic liberalism, the apotheosis of which is the . . . domination of one physical body by another" (40). Therefore, according to Hutchinson's model, Bateman's violence, his domination of physical bodies with his physical body, is a manifestation in the most literal sense of the symbolic order of capitalism, and his body count might mirror his bank account in determination of self-worth. While this is a compelling analysis for how identity is formed through capitalism—and *perhaps* exaggerated in *American Psycho*—it is not the only form of identity Bateman re-creates in his vision of his surroundings. America is the virtual complex Bateman perceives around himself, and he makes meaning of nationhood by projecting his own fantasy of coherence through surface established during his mirror stage. Bateman repeatedly asserts a lack of coherence with those around him who are different racially and socioeconomically. Furthermore, their difference is imposed upon the vision of the United States that Bateman fantasizes, thus creating a disharmony with the virtual complex Bateman perceives. Black people and the poor do not look like him, nor do they wear the brands such as Armani into which he invests himself; therefore, they are incoherent with Bateman's fantasy of American identity.

While Bateman's reflection of himself in Bethany might be somewhat coded, he is much more explicit in how he sees himself through the eyes of the black people he encounters. In the novel's first manifestation of violence, Bateman comes across a homeless black man, and after taunting him both with insults and by pretending that he will give him money, he finally admits his inability to sympathize as a disharmony of reflection, declaring, "I don't have anything in common with you" (Ellis 1991, 131). Beholding the surface of the man, Bateman sees nothing of himself reflected, and as a result cannot assemble any selfhood in relation to the other. As a mirror, the man reflects blankly in Bateman's eyes. If others' ability to see him is what symbolizes the mirror function according to Bateman, he smashes the mirror that is the homeless black man, dispassionately describing sinking a serrated knife into the man's retina (131). Later, after stabbing him in the stomach and hands several times, Bateman finishes the blinding by removing the man's other eye. Unable to create identity in the gaze of the other, Bateman destroys the other's capacity to gaze. When Bateman admires his handiwork, he finds satisfaction in the new surface of his surroundings, lingering and laughing at the scene (132). The surface, or tableau, that is the homeless man's ruined face and body, so removed from humanity as to become setting, no longer reflects anything other than violence, and, to Bateman, becomes a pleasing reflection of his identity.

If the poor and the black cannot cohere with Bateman's American identity, only rich white men can form what he perceives as a positive reflection, and perhaps the most appropriate exemplification of rich white male privilege Bateman could possibly cling to would be Donald Trump. Bateman decorates his office with art bought at Trump Tower in an attempt to replicate a culture vaguely bohemian and American (Ellis 1991, 65). Yet he can only comprehend the surface of it, failing to discern artistic meaning, focusing solely on its association with the Trump name brand. When discussing what women look for in a man, one of Bateman's colleagues (he has no friends) posits that women might be seeking someone who is "a close personal acquaintance of Donald Trump" (54). Here, "close personal acquaintance" seems an appropriate oxymoron, focused as it is on the *semblance* of knowing, penetrating toward identity. However, perhaps the most insidious presence of Trump initiating identity formation comes following an argument about pizza crust at the restaurant Pastels. Bateman denigrates the pizza crust at Pastels as "brittle" (46), a power play that silences one of his associates who has just suggested ordering the pizza. Days later, the same colleague presents Bateman with an article on Donald Trump, a figure the coworker correctly asserts is Bateman's "hero" (110). Infuriated, Bateman scans the article, unable to discern meaning, to which his colleague points out that Pastels serves Trump's favorite pizza. The colleague asks, "What do you think of the pizza at Pastels *now*, Bateman?" (110). In an attempt to maintain the fantasy of his coherence, Bateman does not hold to his original opinion. His first reaction is to reform his identity around Trump's, saying, "I think I have to go back and *re*taste the pizza," ultimately concluding, "if the pizza at Pastels is okay with Donny . . . it's okay with me" (110). Presented with a mirror that threatens his identity, Bateman, in an effort to remain whole and coherent, clings to the American brand he most trusts: Donald Trump.

Later, the Trump brand acts as a distraction, covering beneath it Bateman's acts of violence. While making plans for dinner with his girlfriend Evelyn, Bateman seems to attempt to compulsively confess (as he often does throughout the novel), even blurting out that he has her neighbor's head in his freezer (Ellis 1991, 118), yet Evelyn does not acknowledge his admission.

Later, at dinner, after he rambles about posters on the subway, Bateman leans in, hopeful that Evelyn has seen him, his "character." However, the source of Evelyn's distraction becomes clear as she gazes over Bateman's shoulder and asks, "Is that . . . Ivana Trump?" (121; ellipsis in the original). The moment passes, and even Bateman scrambles to recognize Ivana Trump (it is not her). At a point where there is a real possibility of Bateman being recognized as a sociopath, his crimes revealed and addressed, the Trump name is enough to distract both him and his peers from the inherent violence of his lifestyle.

If Bateman is ultimately a cipher, America is an ever *faithful* reflection of him through the presentation of an ideology where those whose surfaces do not cohere with a fantasy of homogeneity are excised. Through notions of identity formation, politics spill uncannily from the novel into the present day. At a party, Bateman paints a complicated portrait of American politics in which contradictions overlap into an attempt at a coherent agenda. In a single comma-less breath, he enumerates a long list of America's objectives such as "protect[ing] existing American jobs from unfair foreign imports" (Ellis 1991, 15). In addition, Bateman focuses on civil rights policy in which Americans must paradoxically maintain "equal rights for women," "the right to life," and "women's freedom of choice" (16). Finally, a desire to identify a coherent American identity and morality is expressed when Bateman concludes by segueing from describing a national imperative to limit "the influx of illegal immigrants" to articulating an American desire to "return to traditional moral values" which are degraded by popular national media permeated with "graphic sex and violence" (16). Though Bateman so acutely sums up the problems, paradoxes, and hypocrisies of American politics, the only response to his speech is the party's host's banal declaration that it is time for dessert (16). American politics, in all its messy contradiction, is presented as acutely *incoherent*. The denizens of Bateman's Trump-infused far-upper-class New York crave simplicity and wholeness, and when presented with the paradoxes of policy, retreat to what makes sense to them, that is, class, race, and social markers.

Thus: "Make America Great Again." When Donald Trump declares that undocumented people from Mexico are "bringing drugs. They're bringing crime. They're rapists" (quoted in Peoples 2015), he very clearly simplifies an issue that would threaten the identity of white Americans. Violent crime and drugs are other, alien, and extractable—they complicate a fantasy of coherence. When Trump proposes that he would "build a great, great wall on our southern border . . . and I will have Mexico pay for that wall, mark my words" (quoted in Burnett 2015), he reinforces a fantasy of wholeness in which it is easy to define "America" and "not America." *American Psycho*, through Patrick Bateman's self-mimesis based on his view of Donald Trump, presents a nascent identity-investment in the Trump brand—all in the name of coherence. This is an eerie precursor to what so many Americans would do in 2016: attempt to maintain a fantasy of wholeness and coherence in a world that continuously presents challenges in empathy and identity.

Is it fair to reread Donald Trump's presence in *American Psycho* in light of his rise to the presidency? It is certainly a deliberate political act, and one that people seem to be performing today as Ellis has been interrogated regarding his apathetic view of politics. In an interview, Ellis was asked if Patrick Bateman would have voted for Donald Trump, and the author admitted that, yes, his character probably would have ("Bret Easton Ellis Interview" 2017). Even so, Ellis seems to be unconcerned with the present. Of current political trends, he notes that controversies sell. Fascism in today's America? Not a "tidal wave," but "maybe a puddle or two" ("Bret Easton Ellis Interview" 2017). More recently, in a *New Yorker* interview about his first book of non-fiction, *White*, which examines "liberal outrage" toward politics in 2019, Ellis rationalizes the existence of President Trump as reality without considering its meaning: "I just think that there is a man that got elected President. He is in the White House. He has vast support from his base. He was elected fairly and legally. And I think what happened is that the left is so hurt by this that they have overreacted to the Presidency" (quoted in Chotiner 2019). Most appropriately of all, in this same interview, Ellis says of his reaction to the 2016 election, "I am not that interested in politics. . . . What I was interested in was the coverage." To Ellis, the spectacle—the visual surface of Trump's election—is the fascinating thing, uninterested as he is by the implications of a "puddle or two" of fascism. Ellis cannot escape Trump's role in the genesis of his novel, noting that "Patrick Bateman sees [Trump] as the father he never had" (quoted in Chotiner 2019), and that Trump was "someone to aspire to for an entire generation of men who [he] kind of based Bateman on" ("Bret Easton Ellis Interview" 2017). In describing Trump's pseudo-paternal influence on Bateman and his capitalist Wall Street colleagues, Ellis seems to be talking about Trump's ability to enforce a transmittable fantasy of coherence.[1] It just so happens that the generation Ellis is talking about is one that escalated a disastrous and racist "war on drugs," exacerbated the AIDS crises, and initiated political trends that move wealth upward—a generation that faithfully enabled and reflects Patrick Bateman in addition to being a generation commonly evoked by the nostalgia of "Make America Great Again."

Novels of the recent past have a unique ability to shock as their subject matter, close as it is to the present, takes on redefined meanings. However, what is most apparent rereading *American Psycho* as a piece of Trump fiction is the degree to which it is not shocking. One of the novel's contemporary reviewers notes that the sentences of *American Psycho*, especially those that describe vicious acts of violence, are "flat and realistic," resulting in a dulling of the reader's senses (Silverblatt 1993). As the novel progresses, the violence becomes commonplace, part of a pattern of describing what was on *The Patty Winters Show* and essays on pop music. Ellis evokes a world where violence and depravity intertwine with popular culture and the news, mirroring a present-day world where the rage sparked in the novel's initial reception is barely remembered, a present-day world where separation of migrants and their children at the southern border becomes "policy." Under a barrage of rhetoric from the president equating white supremacists with those who would protest them, describing African and Caribbean nations as "shithole countries" (quoted in Dwyer 2018), and bragging about sexual assault, the language of the text that is America becomes ever more numbing, meaning swept under the surface of making America "great" again. And the text that is America becomes more and more similar to a novel about an unrepentant murderer.

At the end of the novel, Patrick Bateman describes himself as an "abstraction," an "illusory" being, noting that there is nothing *real* in his identity (Ellis 1991, 376). The virtual complex he beholds around himself is as equally devoid of meaning, "colossal and jagged" (375), a "crater" (374), in which "surface, surface, surface was all that anyone found meaning in" (375). Bateman's identity (surface) reflects back upon this landscape around him perpetually, creating the experience of self (psycho) and unity (nation). The result is a text (mirror), that when held up to the United States of Make America Great Again, creates a most appropriate reflection.

NOTE

1. For discussion of Trump as a "daddy" figure, see Caitlin Duffy's chapter in the present volume.—Ed.

REFERENCES

"Bret Easton Ellis Interview: Donald Trump and *American Psycho*." 2017. YouTube video. *Channel 4 News*. February 5, 2017. https://www.youtube.com/watch?v=wUH9UZlLSzA&.
Burnett, John. 2015. "How Realistic Is Donald Trump's Immigration Plan?" *National Public Radio*. August 20, 2015. https://www.npr.org/sections/itsallpolitics/2015/08/20/432934599/how-realistic-is-donald-trumps-immigration-plan.
Chotiner, Isaac. 2019. "Bret Easton Ellis Thinks You're Overreacting to Donald Trump." *New Yorker*. April 11, 2019. https://www.newyorker.com/news/q-and-a/bret-easton-ellis-thinks-youre-overreacting-to-donald-trump.
Dwyer, Colin. 2018. "'Racist' and 'Shameful': How Other Countries Are Responding to Trump's Slur." *National Public Radio*. January 12, 2018. https://www.npr.org/

sections/thetwo-way/2018/01/12/577599691/racist-and-shameful-how-other-coun tries-are-responding-to-trumps-slur.

Ellis, Bret Easton. 1991. *American Psycho*. New York: Vintage Books.

Freccero, Carla. 1997. "Historical Violence, Censorship, and the Serial Killer: The Case of *American Psycho*." *Diacritics* 27 (2): 44–58.

Holland, Norman. 1980. "Unity Identity Text Self." In *Reader-Response Criticism: From Formalism to Post-Structuralism*, edited by Jane P. Tompkins, 118–33. Baltimore: Johns Hopkins University Press.

Hutchinson, Colin. 2008. "Cult Fiction: 'Good' and 'Bad' Communities in the Contemporary American Novel." *Journal of American Studies* 42 (1): 35–50.

Kristeva, Julia. 1982. *Powers of Horror: An Essay on Abjection*. Translated by Leon S. Roudiez. New York: Columbia University Press.

Lacan, Jacques. 2002. "The Mirror Stage as Formative of the *I* Function, as Revealed in Psychoanalytic Experience." In *Écrits: A Selection*, translated by Bruce Fink in collaboration with Héloïse Fink and Russell Grigg, 3–9. New York: W. W. Norton.

Peoples, Steve. 2015. "Hispanic Leaders Urge GOP Hopefuls to Condemn Trump." *PBS*. July 4, 2015. https://www.pbs.org/newshour/politics/hispanic-leaders-urge-reluctant-gop-hopefuls-condemn-trump-comments.

Silverblatt, Michael. 1993. "Shock Appeal: Who Are These Writers, and Why Do They Want to Hurt Us? The New Fiction of Transgression." *Los Angeles Times*. August 1, 1993. https://www.latimes.com/archives/la-xpm-1993-08-01-bk-21466-story.html.

Chapter 4

"Is That Donald Trump's Car?"

On the Trail of the Original American Psycho

William Magrino

As a reflection of his immediate environment, Wall Street executive and serial killer Patrick Bateman appropriates and reproduces the discourse of the capitalist icons of his time in Bret Easton Ellis's 1991 novel, *American Psycho*. Albeit clearly a work of fiction, this text accurately documents an era in the United States when, reminiscent of the robber barons of the nineteenth century's Gilded Age, people gained immense notoriety for amassing vast wealth. The moment in history depicted by this novel, New York City in the mid-1980s, was marked by a bourgeoning media obsession with celebrity culture. These latter-day captains of industry, of which Donald Trump was a main constituent, stood firmly at the center of this confluence of finance and fame. While the popular press lauded them as paragons of the American Dream, the media coverage largely obscured the economic realities they represented. In this way, their public profile facilitated their pernicious actions and allowed correlated government policies to be implemented unchecked. In hindsight, the maneuvers of these corporate icons, and the ideologies they represented, clouded by their widespread notoriety, have had real, and equally damaging, effects upon world markets and precipitated the current vast inequalities of wealth, the insidious and far-reaching impacts of which are only beginning to be realized. The present political moment of Donald Trump's presidency, however, may provide some clarity in terms of the prescience of Ellis's work.

The mass media of the mid- to late 1980s, empowered by the advent of the twenty-four-hour news cycle, perpetuated a narrative in which corporate figures such as Donald Trump were elevated as representatives of the male archetype of the age. As an integral part of the prevailing discourse, Trump and others of his ilk have come to be known as *masters of the universe*, raised to celebrity status because of their alleged business acumen. The supposed shroud of mystery, and the narrative that it presupposed, surrounding how such large amounts of money could be amassed through trading of stocks and commodities and purchasing of real estate only amplified the image of the Wall Street wizard. As Gordon Gekko, Hollywood's fictionalized composite alpha male of this era, famously boasts in Oliver Stone's 1987 film *Wall Street*, "I create nothing. I own." This type of bombast proclaimed by the leaders of the private sector has found resurgence in this new millennium through the rise of Donald Trump as a viable political figure in the early twenty-first century. Ellis frequently acknowledges the influence of the Wall Street crowd with whom he was acquainted in the late 1980s while researching and writing *American Psycho*. In a recent interview, speaking about the banking executives with whom he became familiar while working on his novel, Ellis recalls, "They loved *The Art of the Deal*. They loved Trump. He was an aspirational figure" ("Bret Easton Ellis on 'American Psycho'" 2018). As a master self-promoter and provocateur, Trump's reemergence was in no small part due to the media-constructed image he has cultivated for the last forty years.

The media-generated interest in the mogul-as-celebrity coincided with a fledgling 1980s literary movement of which Bret Easton Ellis has been often identified as a leading figure, first termed as *blank generation fiction* by Elizabeth Young and Graham Caveney (1993). A graphically violent, psychological social satire presented almost entirely through the interior monologue of its first-person narrator, *American Psycho*, Ellis's third novel, documents roughly a year in the life of Patrick Bateman, described by Jeff Sipe (1999) as "a Wall Street broker who frequently ends his nights of expensive dining . . . drinking and snorting coke in nightclub toilet stalls with cold-hearted sexual encounters and vicious murders" (8). In turn, this novel encapsulates the largest of Ellis's major themes: isolation, self-absorption, and reduction of all to mere surface. As Ellis illustrates in his presentation of Patrick Bateman, a discourse of violence is deeply engrained in the contemporary capitalist system. In many ways, Bateman's actions are the physical manifestation of the trite business phrase, *making a killing*.

THE RISE AND RESURGENCE OF *THE DONALD*

Decades before recasting himself as the working-class billionaire, in time for the 2016 presidential election, Donald J. Trump was *the* yuppie icon of the 1980s. Even before he became a household reality television personality on *The Apprentice* in 2004, Trump was a persistently, and publicly, polarizing figure. Manifest in the tabloid headlines throughout the 1980s and 1990s, *The Donald*, as many in the press anointed him, was met with as much affection as he was derision. A master of branding of both his name and himself, Trump was, and still is, able to parlay his media-constructed image into a supremely marketable product. In *American Psycho*, the future forty-fifth president of the United States ubiquitously appears as an illusory image, and by extension, a vital element of the culture that serves to construct Patrick Bateman's subjectivity. To a large extent, Bateman attempts to carve out his own identity in response to the media's depiction of Trump. While never actually encountering him, Bateman's New York milieu is punctuated by headlines, possible glimpses, and, in keeping with one of the major themes of the novel, occasions of misrecognition of the billionaire. In turn, the language that contributes to Bateman's identity is rooted in Trump's discourse of fear and division, primarily along class lines. As President Trump famously stated at a rally in mid-2018, "They always call the other side 'the elite.' Why are they elite? I have a much better apartment than they do" (Lyons and Levin 2018). Similarly, at the end of the text, when he reaches the nadir of his psychosis, Bateman confesses, "I'm left with one comforting thought: I am rich—millions are not" (Ellis 1991, 392). In the current political culture, when masculinity is largely demarcated by a discourse of debasement and violence, in terms of race, ethnicity, social class, gender, and disability, Ellis's text, through its interrogation of what Julia Kristeva (1982) identifies as the *abjection*, or *casting-off*, of the *Other*, as a means to attempt to construct an autonomous *self*, is even more salient today than it was when first published.

The revelation of the magnitude of the misdeeds of recent figures such as Bernie Madoff only emphasizes the pervasiveness of the societal ills precipitated by the economic policies of the era represented in *American Psycho*. However, the pathology that Bateman exemplifies runs much deeper than the actions of any lone rogue Wall Street trader or the policies of any individual political administration. The fact that Patrick Bateman is never held accountable for his deeds, nor does Ellis provide substantial motivation for his crimes, which are often cited by critics among the most problematic facets of this novel, precisely illustrates the author's indictment of a culture that privileges a media-constructed image and perpetuates a narrative of surface over substance. As a product of his environment, Bateman is beyond reproach precisely because of his perceived social position. However, much like his fictional, idealized representation of Donald Trump, Bateman has no identity outside of the cultural signs that encircle and define him. As Bateman searches for agency among these recycled images, his subjectivity becomes increasingly fractured. Subsequently chasing and attempting to apprehend these signs, of which the Trump brand is paramount, in the form of commodities, Bateman ensures his own erasure.

PURSUING THE ULTIMATE IMAGE

American Psycho takes place in a society completely engulfed in consumerism. Ellis presents a mid-1980s New York milieu that his intended readers would find eerily familiar. In the novel, there are clear demarcations among social strata, reflected in the trappings of the respective classes. While Patrick Bateman does not associate with individuals outside of his social circle, except for the purposes of belittling or terrorizing them, even those within his insular world, in his eyes, are completely interchangeable. In the sphere of his lived experience, social relations are represented only as commodities. Patrick Bateman is unable to recall the name of a close colleague, yet can easily recite a sixteen-digit model number on a piece of camera equipment. This contingency of identity operates throughout *American Psycho*, with characters unable to recognize each other and, at times, even themselves. As James Annesley (1998) points out in an early analysis of this literary trend popularized by Ellis and a number of his contemporaries, "Blank fiction does not just depict its own period, it speaks in the commodified language *of* its own period" (7). For Bateman, designer brands, status symbols, social stereotypes, and the other trappings of the postmodern lifestyle have supplanted names and, in turn, serve to challenge identity. As he is progressively subsumed into this environment, Bateman's inability to distinguish the subject from its context, permeated by the image of Trump, becomes more apparent.

Bateman's existence is exclusively dependent upon the signs of his culture—represented by designer clothing labels, luxe goods, and other trappings of his contemporary bourgeois culture. The value imbued within these cultural signs, particularly in Bateman's incessant listing and repetition of them, at times with fetishistic intensity, serves as a stand-in for social relations. As a paragon of late capitalism, Bateman is unable to exist outside of the signs of the dominant discourse. Upon being challenged at a lunch reuniting him with his college girlfriend, Bateman assuages his visible distress with a fabrication about having returned from Washington earlier that day aboard the Trump shuttle (Ellis 1991, 232). Here, Bateman attempts to assert his position by patronizing, and endorsing, an emblem of the Trump brand. In line with the fragility of Bateman's existence, however, the Trump label is as insubstantial as any of the brands that populate Bateman's world: Ellis's mention of the airline is an anachronistic reference to one of the many resounding Trump-branded failures of the late 1980s, whose short-lived run would not have begun until a few years after the purported action of the novel.

Despite failures like the Trump shuttle, Trump's image of infallibility, circulated by the popular press for the better part of the last four decades, has largely protected him from significant scrutiny. In turn, he has been able to construct and reconstruct this image and recast himself as real estate magnate, television celebrity, and, eventually, president of the United States. As both an artifact and record of the era it documents, the textual world of *American Psycho* is replete with references to Donald Trump, as both mise-en-scène and a mark of the standard-bearer of its protagonist. Emphasizing the alignment of his desires with the image of Donald Trump, Bateman frequently punctuates his narration with Trump-sightings throughout New York, particularly when he feels challenged or insecure. Early in the novel, when Bateman becomes concerned about being able to eat in what he would consider to be an acceptable restaurant with Courtney, the woman with whom he is having an affair, he asks, half-rhetorically, "Is that Donald Trump's car?" (Ellis 1991, 93). Bateman's anxiety concerning not having a proper reservation, which, as a status symbol, serves to document his existence, is assuaged by the potential proximity of Trump. The recurring references to Donald Trump, in the form of possible sightings and media reports of his preferences and partialities, serve to shape, while simultaneously challenge, Bateman's gradually fragmenting identity. According to Elizabeth Young, in "The Beast in the Jungle, the Figure in the Carpet," from her seminal collection with Graham Caveney, "Ellis manages to take his obsession with deindividualization in consumer society to its extreme and demonstrate that Patrick, in his role of ultimate consumer, someone who is composed entirely of inauthentic commodity-related desires *cannot* exist as a person. He is doomed to fragmentation and disintegration" (1993, 121). With a subjectivity that is completely based upon the signs of his culture, Bateman's potential for agency relies upon the images that surround him, with Trump as the masculine ideal.

CHASING THE ULTIMATE TASTEMAKER

The image of Donald Trump and his entrepreneurial contemporaries, emblematic of a new world order in the 1980s, was shaped and insulated by an economic policy that allowed for unregulated growth of financial markets as well as a social policy that successfully hid a concomitant scourge of poverty and homelessness. In *Bret Easton Ellis: Underwriting the Contemporary*, Georgina Colby (2011) claims, in reference to *American Psycho*, "Ellis here shows the effect of the reactionary politics of the Reagan administration on the consumer choices of the public, and points to the influence that the measures taken in the culture war period had on American society" (70). It is equally vital to discuss this novel in terms of the popular discourse of masculinity, ascribed to abjection and perpetuated by Trump through the 1980s, and the segment of society that anointed him their tacit representative. Additionally, it is important to examine how this discourse, permeating bourgeois

American culture in the 1980s remained intact, if not exacerbated, leading up to the 2016 presidential election and beyond.

In *American Psycho*, the discourse perpetuated by Trump, demarcated by the values he represented, is perpetuated through his presence, and the media coverage of it, in New York at that time. When Bateman becomes anxious about potentially being interviewed by Donald Kimball, a detective investigating the murder of Paul Owen, for which Bateman is actually responsible, he attempts to ingratiate himself with his interlocutor by invoking Trump's bestselling book *The Art of the Deal* (Ellis 1991, 276). Bateman's explicit approval of the book, as a cultural artifact of the moment, as well as a believed blueprint for success, serves as an initiation for the detective. On the one hand, unsurprisingly, Trump's ghostwritten text commands center stage on the desk of the quintessential executive. On the other, it is also a means by which he attempts to disarm the detective—a point of reference Bateman believes they should share. In terms of his frame of mind while writing *American Psycho*, Ellis, himself, admits in an interview with *The Paris Review*, "I was pursuing a life—you could call it the *Gentleman's Quarterly* way of living—that I knew was bullshit, and yet I couldn't seem to help it" (Ellis 2012, 180). In this novel, Ellis takes on the inherently difficult task of satirizing a culture in its own time and in its own dominant discourse. Accordingly, the distance provided by the last three decades, particularly in light of the concurrent rise of Trump, provides a perspective previously unattainable. An interrogation of the present political moment, and the larger culture that informs it, requires a careful rereading of Ellis's novel.

Our current political rhetoric, directly contributing to a precipitous increase in racial tension and violence in the United States, is rooted in the dominant discourse of *American Psycho*. This language of difference and oppression reached an apex in New York City, the hub of the financial services industry, with the policies of Rudolph Giuliani. Elected to the office of mayor in the early 1990s, in response to the disillusionment of the previous decade, Giuliani campaigned on a *quality of life* platform that pushed the homeless and petty criminals out of public spaces and led to what has since been termed as a *Disneyfication* of tourist centers such as Times Square. In turn, New York regained its reputation as a popular destination and shopping mecca, replete with the upscale stores and restaurants patronized by the elite, which the media dutifully covered. When asked to elucidate his position on a restaurant to which he refers as "hip," Bateman emphasizes his point by stating, "Donald *Trump* eats there" (Ellis 1991, 283). For Bateman, Trump's endorsement provides the unnamed establishment with a panache suggesting an immediacy of the moment. The reemergence of New York as an epicenter for the rich, and the associated fleeting nature of its au courant restaurants, boutiques, and their respective neighborhoods is clearly reflected and, at times, lampooned in *American Psycho*, as an obvious metaphor for Bateman's tenuous subjectivity. In this way, Ellis magnifies the reactionary views which served as the cornerstone of Giuliani's two terms of office from the mid-1990s to the cusp of the twenty-first century. In hindsight, and to Trump's political fortune, in our post-9/11 world, these conservative policies have become indelibly ingrained into American political culture. Interestingly, Giuliani has made his own reemergence into public life in the current political and media spheres, now as Trump's principal defender and apologist following the 2017 inauguration. While the neoliberal policies of the Giuliani administration, guided by the now largely discredited, and implicitly racist, Broken Windows Theory, were lauded at the time for their subsequently immediate decrease in visible crime, there was something much more insidious taking place in the financial markets that were housed amid the newly gentrified streets. In depicting his protagonist as a Wall-Street-executive-cum-serial-killer, on the brink of psychosis, Ellis aggressively portrays Patrick Bateman as representative of the cannibalistic aura of 1980s capitalist America. Patrick Bateman is not an aberration. He is not an anomaly. He is the natural product of his environment—inseparable from his surroundings.

GETTING AWAY WITH IT?

The impact of *American Psycho* resides in its lack of a moral center. While Bateman believes, and frequently fantasizes, that a higher authority is hunting him, intent on bringing him to justice, his crimes go unnoticed. Ellis challenges his readers to accept the fact that Bateman's offenses are without consequence. Not only is no one attempting to bring him to justice, his actions seem to attract little attention. Bateman's social status serves to insulate him. In some ways, this is largely a reversal from the traditional representation of the blue-collar serial killer. However, as David Schmid (2010) confirms, "Acutely aware of their status as nonentities, the murderous methods of serial killers become their way of asserting both their identity and their ability to exert some kind of control over their environment" (36). Ellis's representation of Bateman as a serial killer is not simply a metaphor for the violence of capitalism. Through this character, Ellis identifies a deeper relationship between the mass media's depiction of masculinity and anti-social behavior. The ubiquitous images of figures like Trump resulted in their veneration and status as cultural icons, becoming celebrities in their own right and desensitizing America's consciousness to their transgressions. In his construction of Patrick Bateman, Ellis is confronting us with a composite of our collective latter twentieth-century values. The level of privilege that cloisters Bateman and his misdeeds eerily echoes Trump's now-famous boast on the campaign

trail in 2016: "I could stand in the middle of Fifth Avenue and shoot somebody, and I wouldn't lose any voters" (Dwyer 2016). The challenges that
Ellis faced in presenting his critique are now overcome with the distance of
almost thirty years. Through the privileged point of view of the current political moment, one can begin to see how the discourse that created Bateman has
fully permeated the fabric of America.

Bateman and the others of his ilk have no language of their own. As indicated earlier, they simply regurgitate the signs of the mass media. As Elizabeth Young (1993) asserts, "Patrick *is* a cipher; a sign in language and it is
in language that he disintegrates, slips out of our grasp" (119). The headline,
the sound bite, and the brand name constitute the vocabulary of the culture
Bateman represents. Georg Lukács (1971), in *History and Class Consciousness*, contends that among the tendencies of capitalism are "the fetishistic
character of economic forms, the reification of all human relations," as well
as "the constant expansion and extension of the division of labour" (6). In
terms of class consciousness, the subjects that comprise Bateman's society
are unified not by virtue of any actual accomplishment but by the trappings
of their collective privilege. Only through his psychosis, however, does
Bateman become gradually, but intensely, aware of the tenuous nature of
his existence. Bateman's invocation of Trump throughout the novel provides
him with a purpose. As Bateman adamantly states, "'We're going to a party
Donald Trump's having,' I lie" (Ellis 1991, 229). Bateman's object choice is
always the pursuit of Trump—never actually Trump, himself.

Bateman's society is negotiated through status symbols, primarily the
clothing and accessories that adorn him and his colleagues. As is Bateman's
custom, he identifies people both inside and outside of his social circle predominantly by their clothing. However, unlike the labels that embellish Bateman's clothing, stereo equipment, and personal care products, which possess
a built-in obsolescence, the Trump brand provides a stable point of reference
for success, or at least the image of success. The recycled signs of Bateman's
status are appropriated through this dominant signifier. This is apparent when
Bateman corrects a colleague who is discussing a benefit at the Plaza Hotel:
"'That's the *Trump* Plaza,' I note absently, while finally opening the Perrier
bottle" (Ellis 1991, 312). Subsequently, Evelyn, Patrick's girlfriend, learns
to invoke the Trump name in an attempt to garner his attention: "'Listen,'
she says. 'The Young Republican bash at the Pla . . .' She stops herself as if
remembering something, then continues, 'at the *Trump* Plaza is next Thurs-
day'" (336; ellipsis in the original). In Bateman's mind, the Trump name
elevates the sign, and therefore, has consequence.

Bateman attempts to rewrite his subjectivity in the signs that contribute
to the banality of his everyday life. When, as usual, listing the highlights of
one of his days, Bateman emphatically states, "Best of all, *The Patty Winters*

Show this morning was in two parts. The first was an exclusive interview with Donald Trump, the second was a report on women who've been tortured" (Ellis 1991, 256). Aside from the obvious connection between capitalism and violence in this description of the television segment, Ellis also reinforces his overall theme of the horrific as commonplace. As Sonia Baelo-Allué (2011) observes, "This insistence on juxtaposing the banal with the serious is also reflected in the descriptions of the murders and becomes a way of laying bare their brutality and our own attitude towards them in real life" (121). Positioning the ubiquitous image of Trump alongside reports of violence emphasizes Bateman's fetishistic impulses. The fetishization of the image of evil produced by this dichotomy makes Bateman's existence as horrifying as it is inevitable. Normalizing terror through his depiction of Bateman, Ellis forecasts the trajectory of Trump's public persona. From his carefully constructed indictment, and vitriolic call for the execution, of a group of African American teenagers accused of the brutal rape and assault of a white, female jogger in New York in 1989, through his current outcries for racialized and misogynistic violence against those who challenge his worldview, Donald Trump has flourished in his valorization of degradation and hatred. Trump's involvement in the high-profile case of the Central Park Five, as the media had designated them, set the stage for the Trump campaign and presidency in which the *Other* is publicly exploited and metaphorically cannibalized for political gain.[1]

In reading *American Psycho* through the lens of the *commodity fetish*, the goals of Ellis's project become increasingly apparent in terms of the relationship he identifies between consumer culture and systemic violence. In *American Psycho*, this fetishism results in the reification of the subject. Bateman's connections with objects produce a concurrent detachment from other people. In *The Contemporary American Novel in Context*, Dix, Jarvis, and Jenner (2011) state, "Bateman collects and counts with a fetishistic intensity" and contend that his "clearly compulsive consumerism cannot be reduced to the simple possession of serial objects since it also involves the magical aura of specific brands" (43). These designer names, as fetish objects, stand in for connections with other human beings. "There . . . is a definite social relation between men," Marx ([1867] 1967) states, "that assumes, in their eyes, the fantastic form of a relation between things" (72). The logic that draws Bateman to the image of Trump is a consequence of his specific time and place. Consequently, Bateman's negotiations with this image, as a commodity, supplant interpersonal relations.

As Bateman takes pains to distinguish himself from his environment, he becomes increasingly subsumed into the milieu. Ellis's use of misrecognition as a narrative function intensifies the disruption of continuity experienced by the reader. Bateman's ritual of repeating the names of labels, brands, and characters, as well as his residual misrecognition of these signs, amplifies the futility of identification and ownership in *American Psycho*. Michael P. Clark (2011) claims, "The failure of language both as denotation and as expression profoundly disorients the characters and leaves them incapable of meaningful relationships with others" (27). These existential disruptions experienced by Bateman, contributing to his reification, frequently elicit a comedic response from the reader. As Clark states, "Characters are constantly calling each other by the wrong names; even Patrick's fiancée has trouble telling him apart from his friend Timothy. Those pervasive misnomers are matched by equally frequent errors of attribution" (26). In a running joke throughout the novel, Bateman adopts one of the monikers unwittingly thrust upon him. Paul Owen, Bateman's nemesis throughout the text, constantly refers to him as Marcus Halberstam. When Bateman is finally able to secure a long-awaited face-to-face meeting with Owen, Bateman attempts to document his presence by making the reservation under Halberstam's name. Fearing being bested by his rival, Bateman again invokes the image of Trump, asking, "Is that Ivana Trump over there?" (Ellis 1991, 215). Here, the inconsequentiality of recognition extends even into Bateman's frenetic pursuit of Donald Trump.

As evidenced by Bateman's listing of brand names as a narrative function, fashion and accoutrement are the features that serve to approximate recognition. As Elana Gomel (2011) tells us, "Fashion in the novel becomes the only stable discourse underpinning the postmodern flux of identities and desires" (52). Consumption is Bateman's only function. Gomel goes on to assert, "The discourse of the body—dead or alive, lost or found—is slippery, unstable, and provisional. It is the discourse of fashion, with its clear-cut rules, epistemological procedures, and hierarchies of expertise that provides the foundation of the social reality-picture" (55). Toward the end of the novel, when Bateman is no longer able to separate himself from his environment, with the Trump name looming large as his only potential source of solace, he reports, "I move away from the bum, noticing, instead, a little girl smoking a cigarette, begging for change outside Trump Tower" (Ellis 1991, 386). Like a cathedral to capitalism, Trump Tower provides the appropriate contrast between his fantasies of grandeur and the realities that precipitate his disgust. The cultural signs of New York in the 1980s litter, literally and figuratively, the cityscape presented in *American Psycho*. Bateman's juxtaposition of the cultural signs of class distinction, as he does in his description of Trump Tower, is rooted in his abjection of the *Other*. As Julia Kristeva (1982) states, "In this struggle, which fashions the human being, the *mimesis*, by means of which he becomes homologous to another in order to become himself, is in short logically and chronologically secondary. Even before being *like*, 'I' am not but do *separate, reject, ab-ject*" (13). This rejection of the *Other* in an effort to construct an autonomous *self* ensures a subsequent interpellation into the dominant symbolic order. Bateman's inability to function as a speaking subject relegates him to languishing in his Trump-saturated culture. As Bateman describes, "Faded posters of Donald Trump on the cover of *Time* magazine cover the windows of another abandoned restaurant, what used to be Palaze, and this fills me with a newfound confidence" (Ellis 1991, 163). Despite abundant evidence to the contrary, the Trump name signifies a sense of economic and social stability for Bateman. Not only does this image, albeit faded, serve to obscure reality, it provides a competing discourse from the tabloid newspaper headlines of economic and social despair.

At the precipice of psychosis toward the end of the novel, Bateman offers the following: "I look up, admiringly, at Trump Tower, tall, proudly gleaming in the late afternoon sunlight" (Ellis 1991, 385). Aside from the obvious phallic implications, this is a clear example of the accepted prestige associated with the Trump name and the potential in Bateman's pursuit of it. Opening its doors in 1983, Trump Tower etched an indelible mark on the city with which Bateman identifies. As an icon of the dominant social order, Bateman's identification with Trump Tower facilitates his abjection of what remains outside of its doors.

AT THE CROSSROADS OF THE
FINANCIAL AND THE POLITICAL

In the *era of Trump* and its prevailing discourse of the derision of the *Other*, the language that frames Ellis's satire of the late 1980s has saturated the contemporary political rhetoric. In the current climate, marked by the intersection of Wall Street and Washington, an assiduous examination of the signs that construct our collective consciousness is warranted. As Bateman boasts in reference his personal hero, "Donald's a nice guy. You should meet him" (Ellis 1991, 229). In actuality, our American culture has intimately met Donald Trump over and over again throughout the past four decades. A contemporary reading of Ellis's *American Psycho* through the eyes of Trump's America elucidates the pernicious and insidious nature of the discourse that now shapes national and global policy. The 2016 election was a wakeup call to those who conveniently wrote Trump off as a fringe element among the polyphony of voices in our media-saturated culture. In hindsight, the present political moment should come as little surprise to those who have been paying attention to the values pervading not only today's political rhetoric but also the postmodern American culture as a whole. Only through a careful analysis of the deleterious language that permeates our body politic may one be able to respond to this discourse in a meaningful, and equally powerful, way.

NOTE

1. For discussion of Trump's involvement in the Central Park Five case, see Caitlin Duffy's chapter in the present volume.—Ed.

REFERENCES

Annesley, James. 1998. *Blank Fictions: Consumerism, Culture and the Contemporary American Novel*. New York: St. Martin's Press.
Baelo-Allué, Sonia. 2011. *Bret Easton Ellis's Controversial Fiction: Writing between High and Low Culture*. London: Continuum.
"Bret Easton Ellis on 'American Psycho,' Hollywood Hypocrisy, and the Excesses of #MeToo." 2018. YouTube video. *ReasonTV*. August 22, 2018. https://www.you tube.com/watch?v=CeCOSuh0XBk.
Clark, Michael P. 2011. "Violence, Ethics, and the Rhetoric of Decorum in *American Psycho*." In *Bret Easton Ellis*, edited by Naomi Mandel, 19–35. London: Continuum.
Colby, Georgina. 2011. *Bret Easton Ellis: Underwriting the Contemporary*. New York: Palgrave Macmillan.
Dix, Andrew, Brian Jarvis, and Paul Jenner. 2011. *The Contemporary American Novel in Context*. London: Continuum.
Dwyer, Colin. 2016. "Donald Trump: 'I Could...Shoot Somebody, and I Wouldn't Lose Any Voters.'" *National Public Radio*. January 23, 2016. www.npr.org/sections/thetwo-way/2016/01/23/464129029/donald-trump-i-could-shoot-someb ody-and-i-wouldnt-lose-any-voters.
Ellis, Bret Easton. 1991. *American Psycho*. New York: Vintage Books.
———. 2012. "The Art of Fiction No. 216." Interview by Jon-Jon Goulian. *Paris Review*, no. 200, 168–96.
Gomel, Elana. 2011. "'The Soul of This Man Is His Clothes': Violence and Fashion in *American Psycho*." In *Bret Easton Ellis*, edited by Naomi Mandel, 50–63. London: Continuum.
Kristeva, Julia. 1982. *Powers of Horror: An Essay on Abjection*. Translated by Leon S. Roudiez. New York: Columbia University Press.
Lukács, Georg. 1971. *History and Class Consciousness: Studies in Marxist Dialectics*. Translated by Rodney Livingstone. Cambridge: MIT Press.
Lyons, Kate, and Sam Levin. 2018. "Eight Things We Learned from Trump's Minnesota Speech." *Guardian*. June 21, 2018. https://www.theguardian.com/us-news /2018/jun/21/eight-things-we-learned-from-trumps-minnesota-speech.
Marx, Karl. (1867) 1967. *Capital*. Vol. 1. Translated by Samuel Moore and Edward Aveling. Edited by Frederick Engels. New York: International.
Schmid, David. 2010. "A Philosophy of Serial Killing: Sade, Nietzsche, and Brady at the Gates of Janus." In *Serial Killers – Philosophy for Everyone: Being and Killing*, edited by S. Waller, 29–40. Malden: Wiley-Blackwell.
Sipe, Jeff. 1999. "Blood Symbol." *Sight and Sound*, July 1999, 8–10.

Wall Street. 1987. Directed by Oliver Stone. Los Angeles: Twentieth Century Fox.

Young, Elizabeth. 1993. "The Beast in the Jungle, the Figure in the Carpet." In *Shopping in Space: Essays on America's Blank Generation Fiction*, edited by Elizabeth Young and Graham Caveney, 85–122. New York: Atlantic Monthly Press.

Young, Elizabeth, and Graham Caveney, eds. 1993. *Shopping in Space: Essays on America's Blank Generation Fiction*. New York: Atlantic Monthly Press.

Chapter 5

Memorializing the Future of Donald Trump in Amy Waldman's *The Submission*

Stephen Hock

In April of 2019, it was reported that US president Donald Trump, while on a guided tour of George Washington's Mount Vernon estate the previous April with Melania Trump, French president Emmanuel Macron, and Brigitte Macron, was baffled by the fact that Washington had not named the estate after himself. "If he was smart, he would've put his name on it," Trump is reported to have remarked, "You've got to put your name on stuff or no one remembers you" (Johnson and Lippman 2019). According to the story, "The VIPs' tour guide for the evening, Mount Vernon president and CEO Doug Bradburn, told the president that Washington did, after all, succeed in getting the nation's capital named after him. Good point, Trump said with a laugh" (Johnson and Lippman 2019). Whether the story is true or not,[1] it works as a story because it seems to confirm something we think we already know about Trump, namely, his obsession with putting his name on things, ranging from buildings to steaks. Trump's reported comment, however, recasts his habit of putting the Trump name on everything in sight not merely as a matter of building and capitalizing on a brand name, but as a question of crafting one's place in memory. Branding and memory are linked, of course: the point of building up a brand name is to get it to stick in consumers' memories. The context of Trump's comment, though, coming as it did in a tour of a historical site, implicitly raises the stakes, taking the act of "put[ting] your name on stuff" into the realm of cultural memory.

Cultural memory lies at the heart of the work of Trump fiction this essay will examine, Amy Waldman's *The Submission* (2011). Waldman's novel is primarily set two years after the September 11 terrorist attacks. Drawing on the controversy surrounding Maya Lin's winning the competition to design the Vietnam Veterans Memorial, as well as the so-called Ground

Zero Mosque controversy, the novel imagines a blind competition to design a memorial to the victims of the attacks that is won by a Muslim American architect named Mohammad Khan, an event that sets off bitter debates about the work of memorialization. As it addresses questions of cultural memory, *The Submission* insists on the chronologically multifaceted function of memorialization, as a process that reflects our present understanding of the past and also shapes the discourse of the future. As such, any given memorial might come to take on different meanings as understandings of history change over time. Analogously, *The Submission*, as a literary memorial of the process of memorializing the trauma of September 11, lends itself to rereadings in light of subsequent history and shifting understandings of the attacks and their consequences. One such consequence, as rereading Waldman's novel today makes clear, is the cultural environment that led to the political rise of Trump. Waldman refers to Trump only once in *The Submission*, and not even by name, but the novel's roman-à-clef-style treatment of Trump situates him in the context of a number of discourses that have become central to discussions of his presidency, including narratives of Islamophobia, xenophobic anxieties about immigration, a vision of politics conducted as media spectacle, and a white working-class resentment of liberal elites that is often figured in gendered terms. Moreover, Waldman's central narrative of the role memorialization plays in American culture can inform our understanding of a key episode of Trump's political life: his wading into questions of how to understand another terrorist attack, namely, the murder of Heather Heyer during the August 2017 Unite the Right rally in Charlottesville, Virginia, an event that was itself ostensibly organized around a concern with memorialization. In all these respects, *The Submission* exemplifies the power of cultural artifacts to memorialize not only the past but also the future.

"MAYBE IT'S JUST HIS NAME"

Before turning to the central question of memorialization, I'd like to give a brief sketch of those discourses central to both Trump's political life and *The Submission* outlined above: Islamophobia, anti-immigrant xenophobia, politics as media spectacle, and white working-class resentment of liberal cultural elitism frequently cast in gendered terms. The first of those discourses, Islamophobia, provides the initial driving force of the novel's plot. *The Submission* opens with the final deliberations of the jury tasked with selecting the design for the memorial to the victims of the September 11 terrorist attacks.[2] Notably, though, as Laura Frost (2014) reminds us, "Waldman never names the attack as September 11," even as "her descriptions leave no doubt" (212). This choice on Waldman's part gestures toward the importance that the act of naming holds both for memorialization and for the plot of this novel: the blind competition comes to a surprising end when the name of the architect behind the design chosen by the jury is revealed to be Mohammad Khan. Readers of the novel quickly learn that he prefers to go by the nickname Mo, but in the initial revelation of his name, "Mohammad" is what the jurors fixate on. One juror cautions, "We don't know. Maybe it's just his name," in response to which another juror replies, "I think we need to assume the worst—I mean, that he's a Muslim," while another proclaims, "The families [of the victims of the attacks] will feel very offended. This is no time for multicultural pandering" (Waldman 2011, 18). The one representative of the victims' families on the jury, Claire Burwell, points out to another juror, "Bob, you voted for the Garden [Mo's winning memorial design]. That was the design you wanted," to which the other juror, Bob, responds, "Well, I'll be honest here. . . . I'm not sure I want it with the name Mohammad attached to it. It doesn't matter who he is. They'll feel like they've won. All over the Muslim world they'll be jumping up and down at our stupidity, our stupid tolerance" (19–20). Beyond the general tone, which prefigures the raft of Islamophobic rhetoric that characters will spout throughout the novel as well as Trump's many Islamophobic statements and actions,[3] Bob's particular language resonates interestingly with Trump's rhetoric. As Philip Bump (2017) notes in a *Washington Post* article titled "Trump's Pledge to Keep the World from Laughing at Us Hits Another Setback,"

> Trump's campaign rhetoric repeatedly centered on the idea that America was being laughed at internationally. His evidence for this claim was lacking, but it was a point he raised repeatedly.
> During his campaign launch, he said Mexico was "laughing . . . at our stupidity" on the border. In a speech before the Iowa caucuses, Trump claimed that the Islamic State was laughing at our leaders, a claim he repeated in a March debate. (Ellipsis in the original)

Ironically enough, given the echoes between Bob's concern and Trump's rhetoric, Bob is a member of the jury by virtue of being the representative of the governor of New York, and in *The Submission*'s alternate version of history in the wake of the September 11 attacks, that governor, Geraldine Bitman, is a thinly veiled version of Trump's opponent in the 2016 presidential election, Hillary Clinton.[4]

Closely aligned with Islamophobia is the anti-immigrant sentiment that forms another of *The Submission*'s motifs that resonate with Trump's political career. The key figure here is Asma Anwar, the widow of a man who worked as a janitor in the World Trade Center and who died in the September 11 attacks. Both Asma and her husband are undocumented immigrants from

Bangladesh, a fact that comes to public attention after Asma asserts her right, as a relative of a victim of the attacks, to speak at a hearing on the memorial design. Asma's powerful speech attracts media attention, a development that disturbs her friend Nasruddin, who fears "that she would draw the government's attention to her illegality" (Waldman 2011, 277). Nasruddin's fear is realized when he sees the cover of the next day's newspaper, which features "a photograph of Asma—laughing, head reared back and teeth exposed, as if she found hilarious the word written in huge capital letters across her face. ILLEGAL" (278). Later, we read, "In the days since her exposure as an alien, politicians had whipped the public into a frenzy of fear over the thousands of untracked Bangladeshi Muslims in New York, starting with Asma's own dead husband. 'I'll ask it, even if no one else will,' Lou Sarge [a radio host] proclaimed on his show. 'What was her husband doing in those buildings, anyway?'" (283). Trump's anti-immigrant rhetoric, which often links immigrants to crime and terrorism, is well known, as in his July 28, 2017, speech to law-enforcement officials on Long Island, where he said:

> We're also working . . . on a series of enforcement measures . . . to keep our country safe from crime and terrorism—and in particular, radical Islamic terrorism. . . . That includes cracking down on sanctuary cities that defy federal law, shield visa overstays, and that release dangerous criminals back into the United States' communities. That's what's happening. They're releasing them. So many deaths where they release somebody back into the community, and they know it's going to end that way. ("Remarks by President Trump to Law-Enforcement Officials on MS-13" 2017)

As we will see, this language of "so many deaths" will resonate with the resolution of Asma's story in *The Submission*, but ironically so: not a death that happens when an immigrant is released into the community, but a death that occurs when an immigrant is forced out of the community.

The third of those themes common to *The Submission* and Trump's political career is the picture the novel paints of American politics being conducted as media spectacle. Indeed, like many contemporary texts, the novel presents a portrait of a culture that takes for granted the effacement of any boundary between reality and media image, such that people live their lives and conduct their politics according to images and scripts drawn from the mass media. At one point, the novel presents an anti-Muslim protest that follows "tight scripting" and seems crafted more for how it will look on television than for anything else (Waldman 2011, 170). Later, Governor Bitman relishes the prospect of being sued by Mo for violating his constitutional rights, "imagining herself on the stand, in a trial covered by every news outlet in the country, defending her defense of the memorial site, of America itself, from the Islamist threat. Even if the state lost, she would win. Every time she had gone on the offensive against Khan she had risen in the polls" (281). In presenting politics as an activity carried out according to media scripts and designed for maximum media coverage, Waldman's novel again anticipates Trump, whose political appeal is founded in no small part on the skills he honed as a reality TV entertainer. As Robert L. Ivie (2017) notes in a study of Trump's rhetorical techniques, "Trump was a perfect fit for the new media culture's politics of spectacle and seduction" (64), a politics that, *The Submission* reminds us, was in place well before Trump became president.

The final of the four elements I'd like to highlight that *The Submission* shares with the discourse surrounding Trump's presidency is the theme of the white working class's resentment of the presumed cultural superiority of liberal elites, a resentment that Trump and the novel often figure in gendered terms. Waldman develops this narrative primarily through Sean Gallagher, a white, working-class man who loses his brother Patrick in the September 11 attacks. Like Trump, who was born and raised in Queens, Sean comes from the outer boroughs, in his case, Brooklyn. Also like Trump, who is widely believed to nurse a grudge against the Manhattan cultural elites, Sean deeply feels his exclusion from the circles of power frequented by the wealthy cultural liberals, like Claire Burwell, who are guiding the process of choosing the design for the memorial to the victims of the attacks. When Sean meets with Paul Rubin, the chair of the jury tasked with selecting the design, to confront him about his exclusion from the process, we read that Sean "felt himself in the camp of the enemy—not Muslims but the people born with silver sticks up their asses, the people who had made Manhattan a woman too good to give Sean her phone number" (Waldman 2011, 142). Michael Kruse (2017) likewise identifies a sense of cultural inferiority in relation to Manhattan elites as one of the strands of Trump's identity that explains his appeal to white working-class voters:

> To most of New York's elite, whose acceptance he sought, Trump was far too brash and gauche. He was an outer-borough outsider, bankrolled by his politically connected father. He wanted to be taken seriously, but seldom was. "He's a bridge-and-tunnel guy, and he's a daddy's boy," Lou Colasuonno, a former editor of the *New York Post* and the *New York Daily News*, said in a recent interview. "There were people who laughed at him," former CBS anchor and current outspoken Trump critic Dan Rather told me. While his loose-lipped, in-your-face approach appealed to blue-collar types in spots in Brooklyn, Staten Island and Queens, many in Manhattan, Rather says, considered him "repulsive."

Ironically enough, the focus of Sean's misogynistic resentment, Claire, does not live in Manhattan. Instead, in another of the historical ironies that litter

The Submission, she lives in Chappaqua (Waldman 2011, 94), a signifier that links her to Hillary Clinton.

The misogyny and implicit threat of sexual violence in Sean's perspective, which views "a woman too good to give Sean her phone number" as "the enemy," likewise echoes Trump's own rhetoric, most infamously, Trump's private comments recorded in the 2005 *Access Hollywood* tape. Among other boasts of sexual assault, Trump declared, "You know, I'm automatically attracted to beautiful—I just start kissing them. It's like a magnet. Just kiss. I don't even wait" ("Transcript: Donald Trump's Taped Comments about Women" 2016).[5] In similar terms, at the end of an evening in which Claire invites Sean to have a drink with her, in the interest of securing his support for her position as the representative of the victims' families on the memorial jury, "he leaned and planted a kiss on her just to prove he could. She didn't resist, simply withstood it, taut, even then wanting to keep his goodwill," a moment that feeds into Sean's sexual fantasies about Claire (Waldman 2011, 96). In figuring Sean's sense of marginalization at the hands of a liberal cultural elite in gendered terms, *The Submission* mirrors an element that Paul Elliott Johnson (2017) identifies as key to Trump's rhetorical appeals:

> Trump's rhetorical form functions through a toxic, paradoxically abject masculine style whose incoherence is opaque to his critics but meaningful to his adherents, for it helps them imagine themselves as victims of a political tragedy centered around the displacement of "real America" from the political center by a feminized political establishment. Trump's attacks on one supposed institutional matrix of power—"the Washington establishment"—bolster another power structure: White masculinity. (230)

Framed in these terms, Sean's gendered resentment of Manhattan elites renders him as exactly the type of voter Trump's rhetoric would appeal to.

In framing its narrative in terms of bigotry directed against Muslims, anti-immigrant xenophobia, a political culture driven by media images and scripts, and an often gendered resentment by members of the white working class against liberal elites, *The Submission* reminds us that Trump's successful presidential campaign and the resulting presidency were never the unprecedented and unpredictable events they are sometimes portrayed as, but rather all too logical outgrowths of long-standing strains in American culture and politics that gained new currency in the wake of the September 11 attacks. The discourses examined in *The Submission* are the discourses of Trumpism, a fact that becomes clear in retrospect. As Andreea Paris (2017) writes of the role literature plays in cultural memory, "The literary canon is part of the active cultural memory of a society, as long as it can achieve the function of keeping the past as present by means of repeated re-readings, ongoing interpretations and analyses, comments and stagings of literary works" (102). Already a part of the emerging canon of 9/11 fiction, *The Submission* becomes resignified, in the time of Trump, as part of the emerging canon of Trump fiction.

"HIS OWN MEMORIAL DESIGN COMPETITION"

In turning to *The Submission*'s central question of memorialization, I'd like to bring in the moment that seals *The Submission*'s place in the canon of Trump fiction, the novel's specific reference to Trump. As noted earlier, Waldman refers to Trump only once in *The Submission*. The reference comes a little over halfway through the novel, as the controversy over Mo's design for the memorial continues to rage. Among a "cacophony" of voices rising against Mo's design, we read, "A flamboyant real estate mogul with a toupee and an inestimable fortune was vowing to sponsor his own memorial design competition, then underwrite construction of the winner, although no one was sure he had the liquidity to do it" (Waldman 2011, 188). The reference is glancing but unmistakable, and impossible to miss post-2016.

The specific real-world intertext of this barely veiled reference is Trump's offer, reported in September of 2010, to buy the site proposed for the so-called Ground Zero Mosque, an Islamic community center that was planned to be built two blocks from the site of the World Trade Center. The proposal incited the same sort of controversy that *The Submission* presents through its depiction of the backlash against Mo's memorial design after his identity as a Muslim becomes known. Philip Sherwell (2010) reports that Trump

> offered Hisham Elzanaty, an Egyptian-born New York businessman, a 25 per cent premium over the $4.8 million price that his investment consortium paid for the site, which is just two blocks from ground zero.
> "I am making this offer as a resident of New York and citizen of the United States, not because I think the location is a spectacular one (because it is not), but because it will end a very serious, inflammatory, and highly divisive situation," Mr Trump wrote in his letter to Mr Elzanaty. . . . There was no immediate response from Mr Elzanaty. But the imam and property developer both insisted that the plan for the mosque and community centre would go ahead as planned. And a lawyer for another investor, Wolodymyr Starosolosy, dismissed Mr Trump's bid as "a cheap attempt to get publicity and get in the limelight."

The logic of Trump's offer to buy the contested site, according to his letter, is that doing so "will end a very serious, inflammatory, and highly divisive situation." A similar logic seems to be at work in Waldman's unnamed Trump's vow to build his own memorial: the design submitted by Mohammad Khan is too controversial to build, and the entire process of building the memorial has become tainted by that controversy, so it would be better to scrap the plans and begin a new memorial process altogether. As Wolodymyr Starosolosy, as quoted in Sherwell's story, notes, the idea that Trump would work in good faith to resolve an inflammatory and divisive situation must, of course, be taken ironically, insofar as Trump's entire public persona is predicated on inflaming divisive situations—for instance, apropos of those four themes of *The Submission* sketched out earlier, by using his talents as a showman to whip up the resentment of members of the white working class against immigrants, particularly Muslims, as a way to advance his political fortunes.

Indeed, Waldman's unnamed Trump immediately draws opposition. After we learn of the fictionalized Trump's vow "to sponsor his own memorial design competition, then underwrite construction of the winner," the next sentence reads, "Hearing this, a liberal hedge-fund billionaire of Paul's acquaintance had called to say he would underwrite a hefty chunk of the cost of the Garden [Khan's design]" (Waldman 2011, 188). Instead of defusing the situation, the fictional Trump only further inflames it, in a manner typical of the real Trump's political career. Lee Pierce (2014) argues that the real-world Ground Zero Mosque controversy "marked a point of emergence for an increasingly hegemonic *rhetoric of traumatic nationalism*" (55), which Pierce describes as "an exemplary rhetorical configuration through which victimage has emerged as the dominant political logic of post-9/11 U.S. national identity" (72). Pierce is writing before the beginning of Trump's presidential campaign, and does not mention Trump, but the model of the "rhetoric of traumatic nationalism," like *The Submission*, anticipates Trump's presentation of the United States as a nation that no longer can be anything but a victim. As Trump said in a post-election interview with the *New York Times*, "We don't win, we can't beat anybody, we don't win anymore. At anything. We don't win on the border, we don't win with trade, we certainly don't win with the military" ("Donald Trump's *New York Times* Interview" 2016). Recalling Paul Elliott Johnson's identification of a particularly masculine victimhood as a key element of Trump's appeal, we might suppose that this victimization of the nation occurs, at least in part, as a result of what Trump would present as the incompetent stewardship of the "feminized political establishment" (Johnson 2017, 230), an establishment that leaves the nation vulnerable to traumatic woundings that must then be memorialized.

Early in *The Submission*, Mo says that his memorial design "felt like it had the right balance between remembering and recovering" (Waldman 2011, 70). This raises the question of what sort of recovery the memorial will spur. What healing or new growth will follow the traumatic memory being memorialized, and how will that growth shape the future character of the nation?

This language of recovery highlights the orientation of memorialization toward the future, something *The Submission* further emphasizes by ending with an epilogue, set twenty years after the main narrative, that shows how the novel's characters' experience with the process of memorialization shapes their futures.

The rhetoric of an aggrieved, victimized nation whose wounds must be memorialized likewise characterizes another controversial undertaking that the real-world Trump inserted himself into early in his presidency, namely, the August 2017 Unite the Right rally in Charlottesville, Virginia. The rally, which took place over two days, August 11 and 12, was ostensibly organized to protest plans to remove a statue of Robert E. Lee from its place in a park in Charlottesville, part of the widespread efforts in recent years to rethink the ways in which the Civil War and the Confederacy have been memorialized. These efforts, too, testify to the chronologically multifaceted quality of memorialization, looking back to the past from our present position in a way that shapes the discourse of the future. If it were a simple matter of remembering the past, the stakes of memorialization would be much lower. As a means to shape the narrative we tell future generations about who we are as a people, however, memorialization becomes a flashpoint of controversy. In a *New York Times* story published in the aftermath of the Unite the Right rally, Jacey Fortin (2017) notes that the Lee statue had in fact generated considerable local controversy for years preceding the rally, a debate that culminated in the vote by the Charlottesville City Council in February of 2017 to remove the statue. While the city was unable to remove the statue because of a lawsuit alleging that state law prohibited its removal, it did, that June, rename the park in which the statue stands, from Lee Park to Emancipation Park, and this act of renaming likewise served as one of the factors cited by organizers of the rally.

So, here we have another controversial memorial, what Trump might call, in the language of his Ground Zero Mosque letter, "a very serious, inflammatory, and highly divisive situation." Moreover, just as the so-called Ground Zero Mosque was claimed by some of its opponents to be a memorial to the terrorists who perpetrated the September 11 attacks[6]—a claim that is likewise made in *The Submission* by opponents of Mo's memorial design[7]—the Lee statue is a memorial to a man who waged war against the United States. Indeed, a local news story covering a rally in March of 2016 that advocated for removing the statue quotes the president of Charlottesville's branch of the NAACP as saying, "They look at that statue, they think that was a gallant person that saved us, but he was a terrorist" ("People Show Support for, Opposition to Lee Statue in Charlottesville" 2016). The connection between the statue and terrorism becomes even stronger when we remember that the statue was erected in 1924 (Fortin 2017), nearly sixty years after the end of the Civil War and over fifty years after Lee's death. The Southern Poverty

Law Center's report "Whose Heritage? Public Symbols of the Confederacy" (2019) explains the historical context of such belated memorialization:

> The dedication of Confederate monuments and the use of Confederate names and other iconography began shortly after the Civil War ended in 1865. But two distinct periods saw significant spikes.
>
> The first began around 1900 as Southern states were enacting Jim Crow laws to disenfranchise African Americans and re-segregate society after several decades of integration that followed Reconstruction. It lasted well into the 1920s, a period that also saw a strong revival of the Ku Klux Klan. Many of these monuments were sponsored by the United Daughters of the Confederacy. The second period began in the mid-1950s and lasted until the late 1960s, the period encompassing the modern civil rights movement.

This context suggests that the Lee statue has been, from the start, not really a Lee memorial at all, but rather a memorial celebrating the terror of segregation, lynching, and the Klan in the decades after the Civil War, what Bailey J. Duhé (2018) identifies in her commentary on the successful effort earlier in 2017 to take down Confederate monuments in New Orleans as "domestic terrorism and systematic oppression" (121).

As with any memorial, the valence of the Lee statue can shift as understandings of history change with new perspectives. So, a statue that, during the era that gave rise to the Lost Cause mythologization of the Confederacy, might be celebrated for its commemoration of white supremacy and the terroristic violence that sustained it can come to be condemned for the same reason in the era of Black Lives Matter protests. As Richard M. Leventhal (2018) observes in his reflections on recent protests against Confederate monuments,

> Such protests create context and meaning for monuments in the present. Even those monuments with a deep historical context do not have any real and fixed meaning. They are viewed differently by different groups of people in different times and in different contexts. In the United States, any conversation about monuments must take into account an entire range of groups and communities, and comprehend that each of these groups will bring a different view, a different context, and a different set of meanings for the monuments. (134)

Or, as Eric Gable (2018) has it, "memory, in societies such as ours, is always emerging from a contested landscape that includes official history and selective readings of current or past versions of that official history" (133). This "contested landscape" of cultural memory is the terrain shared by *The Submission*, the Ground Zero Mosque controversy, and the Unite the Right rally in Charlottesville.

Into this "contested landscape" strides Trump, not only in Waldman's novelistic treatment of him in *The Submission*, or in the offer to buy the site of the

Ground Zero Mosque site that inspired Waldman, but also in the case of the Unite the Right rally in Charlottesville. Choosing this time to stand with the supporters of controversial memorials, Trump opposed the efforts to remove the Lee statue and other memorials to the Confederacy and the decades of domestic terrorism that followed, for instance, in a tweet on August 17, 2017: "Sad to see the history and culture of our great country being ripped apart with the removal of our beautiful statues and monuments" (Trump 2017b). By extension, then, Trump stood with those at the Unite the Right rally who were protesting in support of the Lee statue. This sense seemed to be confirmed in Trump's remarks to the press on August 15. When he was asked about "the neo-Nazis [who] started this" when "they showed up in Charlottesville to protest," Trump replied, "You had some very bad people in that group, but you also had people that were very fine people, on both sides" ("Remarks by President Trump on Infrastructure" 2017), a statement that quickly became notorious for the moral equivalence Trump seemed to be drawing.

"PILGRIMS AT THE GRAVES OF SAINTS"

As mentioned earlier, Waldman never refers to the September 11 attacks by name in *The Submission*, nor does she refer to Trump by name. To note this parallel is not to imply an equivalence between the two. Leaving the attacks unnamed marks their status as a wound that might still be too raw to address directly. Sonia Baelo-Allué (2016) reads *The Submission* as "providing a new way forward for 9/11 fiction which has often been trapped in narrowing conceptions of trauma and the impossibility of its articulation" (169), but something of that impossibility of articulation lingers in the text's refusal to name the attacks. By contrast, we might suppose that the fact that Trump remains unnamed in the novel signifies nothing more than his relative unimportance to the novel's plot—or, for that matter, his relative unimportance to the world at the time the novel was written. Unlike Hillary Clinton, who was so significant as a political figure (not just in New York, but in the nation as a whole) at the time in which the novel is set that the text can easily draw on elements of her public persona for its characterization of Governor Bitman, Trump had not yet become a political figure. Indeed, he doesn't even seem to rate on the same level as the celebrities who, Karolina Golimowska (2016, 101) reminds us, show up in the novel as supporters of Mo's cause, and who Waldman identifies by name, a list that includes Susan Sarandon and Tim Robbins, as well as Robert De Niro, Rosie O'Donnell, and Sean Penn (Waldman 2011, 140, 173–74). Unlike these celebrities, Trump remains recognizable in *The Submission*, but unnamed.[8] Interestingly, the same page of *The Submission* that presents its unnamed version of Trump among the "cacophony" of voices weighing in on Mo's design mentions that "the House minority leader, also a presidential aspirant, had labeled the jury Islamist sympathizers and vowed to sponsor legislation to block the construction of Khan's design" (188). This "House minority leader," like the "flamboyant real estate mogul with a toupee and an inestimable fortune," remains unnamed, as if a mere feature of the background. Trump might have been a mere feature of the background at the time in which the novel was set, and at the time in which it was written, but his presence, in juxtaposition with the similarly anonymous congressperson, highlights that even those unnamed background features can come to play important roles, as they emerge out of the structures of Islamophobia, xenophobia, mass-mediated politics, and resentment that *The Submission* identifies as central to the United States in the early twenty-first century.

Whether or not to name somebody or something, as well as what name to use, is, after all, an important question. Mo's name, Mohammad Khan, marks him as a Muslim ("the most obviously Muslim name you could have," Mo's father reflects [Waldman 2011, 219]), and therefore suspect in the eyes of the jury that chooses his design to memorialize the victims of the attacks. Similarly, the chapter in *The Submission* in which readers first see Mo begins, "His name was what got him pulled from a security at LAX as he prepared to fly home to New York" (26). Here, being identified by name signifies subjection to official narratives of suspicion and condemnation. However, *The Submission* also reminds us of the role naming plays in more reverent acts of memorializing, not only by virtue of the fact that Mo's memorial design includes the names of the victims of the attacks (4), but also through smaller acts of memorialization. Near the end of *The Submission*, after Asma is exposed by the press as an undocumented immigrant, she decides not to fight deportation, and prepares to return to Bangladesh. A crowd gathers outside her building on the day of her departure, and as the crowd presses on Asma, she is murdered, apparently with a knife. No one can tell who did it. Ironically, just before she's killed, we read, "As soon as Asma came out of her building a crowd surrounded her, women reaching out to touch her in a way that reminded Nasruddin of pilgrims at the graves of saints" (Waldman 2011, 286). In the novel's epilogue, set twenty years later, we see Nasruddin again, "polishing a brass memorial plaque. Affixed to the side of the Brooklyn building where she had lived, it bore her name in English and Bengali, and her image" (328–29). This bilingual memorial to an undocumented Muslim immigrant killed as she was forced out of America, one that insists on naming her, resonates deeply in the United States of Donald Trump.

Just as Waldman refers to Trump, but not by name, Trump likewise notably referred to a specific individual, Heather Heyer, but not by name, in the same question-and-answer session with the press in which he refused to condemn the "very fine people" protesting in support of the Lee statue among the white supremacists at Charlottesville. Heyer came to the rally as a counterprotester against the white supremacists, and was killed when one of the protesters drove his car into a crowd, killing Heyer and injuring many more. Trump first mentioned Heyer when he referred to "the young woman, who I hear was a fantastic young woman." Later, a member of the press asked, "Mr. President, have you spoken to the family of the victim of the car attack?"[9] Neither Trump nor the reporter referred to Heyer by name ("Remarks by President Trump on Infrastructure" 2017). The following day, Trump did name Heyer in a tweet: "Memorial service today for beautiful and incredible Heather Heyer, a truly special young woman. She will be long remembered by all!" (Trump 2017a). Indeed, that process of remembering and memorialization had already begun, outside of the narrative that Trump directs as president of United States. Two days earlier, a sign reading "Heyer Mem. Park" was placed at the base of the Lee statue (Amatulli 2017), resignifying the memorial and suggesting a desire to create a future built on different values than those the Lee statue represented. Later that year, in a more official capacity, the city of Charlottesville renamed part of a street "Heather Heyer Way" (Dodson 2017). If *The Submission*, as Lucy Bond (2014) argues, presents Mo's proposed memorial as "a means of rehabilitating the topography of New York and regaining control of the narrative of American history" (28), then these and other memorials to Heather Heyer demonstrate the same dynamic at work in Charlottesville, the need to identify by name the people and values we as a culture wish to memorialize in order to shape our national narrative.

As these cases show, the process of memorialization is an ongoing one, revising our understanding of the past and renaming it for the future as new perspectives continue to emerge. The Charlottesville park where the Lee statue continues to stand, as of this writing, has been renamed again, from Emancipation Park to Market Street Park, following a petition that argued that "the name Emancipation Park [was] offensive due to its juxtaposition with the Lee statue" ("Charlottesville City Council Changes the Names of Two Renamed Parks" 2018). Confederate monuments continue to serve as flashpoints for controversy, demonstrating the persistent relevance of *The Submission*'s portrayal of "the cultural trauma of a nation trying to close its wound by choosing a fitting Memorial, which, rather than bringing closure and healing the nation, opens a new wound in the country's social fabric" (Baelo-Allué 2016, 170). Heather Heyer continues to be remembered, as at a memorial event on the first anniversary of her death, at which her mother said, "Focus on the issues—that's exactly what Heather would say. 'Quit looking at me, look at the issues'" (Grinberg and Hartung 2018), reminding us that while naming individuals is important, naming the larger values and structures at work is what will ultimately effect change.

Donald Trump, too, continues to instigate controversy in the aim of securing political advantage, modeling the same sort of behavior he did in his remarks to the press in which he defended the "very fine people, on both sides" at Charlottesville. Earlier in those remarks, Trump commented, "So this week it's Robert E. Lee. I noticed that Stonewall Jackson is coming down. I wonder, is it George Washington next week? And is it Thomas Jefferson the week after? You know, you really do have to ask yourself, where does it stop?" ("Remarks by President Trump on Infrastructure" 2017). Indeed, the reevaluation of our cultural memory will not stop. Here, too, the question of naming is important. The beginning of this essay, for instance, referred to Trump's visit to "George Washington's Mount Vernon estate." Another name for "estate" in this context would be "plantation," which is, in the end, another name for "slave labor camp."[10] And as anybody who has ever heard a politician decry the evils of "Washington" as a metonym for the federal government can attest, even having the capital of an entire nation named after you is no guarantee that the site of memorialization will always be revered. Likewise, our cultural memory of Trump will inevitably be a site of contestation for years to come. That struggle will doubtless be carried out not only (or even primarily) through official Trump-branded memorials but also in our literature and other artifacts of our culture, even those that, like *The Submission*, choose not to name Trump at all.

NOTES

1. After the initial version of their story on Trump's visit to Mount Vernon was published, Eliana Johnson and Daniel Lippman (2019) note, "The Mount Vernon Ladies' Association released a statement saying, in part, that 'third-party accounts of the Trump-Macron visit released by several media outlets today do not correctly reflect the events that transpired nearly a year ago.' The statement added: 'Comments pulled from sources who were not present for the tour do not properly convey the tone and context in which they were delivered.'"

2. For a discussion of the jury process in *The Submission* in comparison to the actual process of choosing the design for the National September 11 Memorial, see Baelo-Allué (2016, 173).

3. See, for instance, Liptak and Shear's (2018) story on the Supreme Court's decision to uphold Trump's so-called Muslim ban.

4. In the novel's description, "She was New York's first female governor, a first that led her to think of others. She wanted to be president" (Waldman 2011, 114). By the time of the novel's epilogue, set in or about 2023, Bitman has become vice president (325).

5. Language that strangely evokes fantasies of sexualized violence likewise shows up in Trump's public rhetoric as president, for instance, in his response to a question about following through on his promise to donate $1 million to charity

if Senator Elizabeth Warren took a DNA test to substantiate her claims of Native American ancestry: "I'll only do it if I can test her personally. That will not be something I enjoy doing, either," a statement that Warren described as one of Trump's characteristic "creepy physical threats" (Kellman 2018).

6. See Pierce (2014, 54, 66, 69–70).

7. See Waldman (2011, 130, 146, 205, 213, 236, 250).

8. For discussion of a similar tension between naming and not naming contemporary figures in Howard Jacobson's *Pussy*, see Tim Lanzendörfer's chapter in the present volume.

9. Trump answered that he had not spoken to Heyer's family, but that he would "be reaching out" ("Remarks by President Trump on Infrastructure" 2017). Tim Teeman (2017) reports that Trump apparently tried to call Heyer's mother, Susan Bro, during her daughter's funeral, but did not get through. Bro later indicated that she was not interested in speaking to Trump, explaining:

You can't say there were good people coming into town with their fists taped prepared to draw blood and do harm. That's not good people. Nazis: *bad people*. White supremacists: *bad people*. And I don't see that you can call it any other way. If you choose to align yourself with those people, and you choose to call them "good," then you've told me what sort of person you are. So now I have your number and now I know how I choose to respond to you. And in his case, that means: "I'm not responding to you, you don't get my time of day." (Teeman 2017)

10. As Peter H. Wood (1999) comments on the need to face up to the history of slavery, "I would be both surprised and pleased to see *slave labor camp* become an occasional synonym for *plantation*" (231).

REFERENCES

Amatulli, Jenna. 2017. "Touching Sign Renames Charlottesville Park 'Heyer Memorial' after Woman's Death." *HuffPost*. August 14, 2017. https://www.huffingt onpost.com/entry/charlottesville-heather-heyer-memorial_us_5991d7d4e4b08a24 72764855.

Baelo-Allué, Sonia. 2016. "From the Traumatic to the Political: Cultural Trauma, 9/11 and Amy Waldman's *The Submission*." *Atlantis: Journal of the Spanish Association of Anglo-American Studies* 38 (1): 165–83.

Bond, Lucy. 2014. "From the Stricken Community to the Solitary Night Mind: The Politics of Time, Space, and Otherness in American Fiction after 9/11." In *Political Fiction*, edited by Mark Levene, 21–41. Ipswich: Grey House.

Bump, Philip. 2017. "Trump's Pledge to Keep the World from Laughing at Us Hits Another Setback." *Washington Post*. June 28, 2017. https://www.washingtonpos t.com/news/politics/wp/2017/06/28/trumps-pledge-to-keep-the-world-from-laug hing-at-us-hits-another-setback/?utm_term=.73036fe4f42d.

"Charlottesville City Council Changes the Names of Two Renamed Parks." 2018. *Daily Progress*. July 16, 2018. https://www.dailyprogress.com/news/local/city/

charlottesville-city-council-changes-the-names-of-two-renamed-parks/article_9ac
64d52-8963-11e8-853a-a3864982745e.html.

Dodson, Tim. 2017. "City Dedicates Part of Fourth Street as Heather Heyer Way."
Cavalier Daily. December 20, 2017. http://www.cavalierdaily.com/article/201
7/12/city-dedicates-part-of-fourth-street-as-heather-heyer-way.

"Donald Trump's *New York Times* Interview: Full Transcript." 2016. *New York
Times*. November 23, 2016. https://www.nytimes.com/2016/11/23/us/politics/tru
mp-new-york-times-interview-transcript.html.

Duhé, Bailey J. 2018. "Decentering Whiteness and Refocusing on the Local: Reframing Debates on Confederate Monument Removal in New Orleans." *Museum
Anthropology* 41 (2): 120–25.

Fortin, Jacey. 2017. "The Statue at the Center of Charlottesville's Storm." *New York
Times*. August 13, 2017. https://www.nytimes.com/2017/08/13/us/charlottesville-r
ally-protest-statue.html.

Frost, Laura. 2014. "Archifictions: Constructing September 11." In *Transatlantic
Literature and Culture after 9/11: The Wrong Side of Paradise*, edited by Kristine
A. Miller, 198–220. Basingstoke: Palgrave Macmillan.

Gable, Eric. 2018. "When the Monuments Came Down, Where Was Anthropology?"
Museum Anthropology 41 (2): 130–34.

Golimowska, Karolina. 2016. *The Post-9/11 City in Novels: Literary Remappings of
New York and London*. Jefferson: McFarland.

Grinberg, Emanuella, and Kaylee Hartung. 2018. "Heather Heyer's Mom Visits
Memorial in Charlottesville: 'It's Not All about Heather.'" *CNN*. August 12, 2018.
https://www.cnn.com/2018/08/12/us/charlottesville-anniversary-heather-heyer/
index.html.

Ivie, Robert L. 2017. "Rhetorical Aftershocks of Trump's Ascendancy: Salvation by
Demolition and Deal Making." *Res Rhetorica*, no. 2, 61–79.

Johnson, Eliana, and Daniel Lippman. 2019. "Trump's 'Truly Bizarre' Visit to Mt.
Vernon." *Politico*. April 10, 2019. https://www.politico.com/story/2019/04/10/don
ald-trump-mount-vernon-george-washington-1264073.

Johnson, Paul Elliott. 2017. "The Art of Masculine Victimhood: Donald Trump's
Demagoguery." *Women's Studies in Communication* 40 (3): 229–50.

Kellman, Laurie. 2018. "Doing It His Way: Warren Emulates Trump as She Taunts
Him." *AP News*. October 16, 2018. https://www.apnews.com/2ec18ce518db4f24a
0827f38dd27f78b.

Kruse, Michael. 2017. "How Gotham Gave Us Trump." *Politico Magazine*. July/
August 2017. https://www.politico.com/magazine/story/2017/06/30/donald-tr
ump-new-york-city-crime-1970s-1980s-215316.

Leventhal, Richard M. 2018. "Protests and Meaning: Monuments in the Twenty-First
Century." *Museum Anthropology* 41 (2): 134–37.

Liptak, Adam, and Michael D. Shear. 2018. "Trump's Travel Ban Is Upheld by
Supreme Court." *New York Times*. June 26, 2018. https://www.nytimes.com/2
018/06/26/us/politics/supreme-court-trump-travel-ban.html.

Paris, Andreea. 2017. "Literature as Memory and Literary Memories: From Cultural
Memory to Reader-Response Criticism." In *Literature and Cultural Memory*,

edited by Mihaela Irimia, Dragoş Manea, and Andreea Paris, 95–106. Leiden: Brill Rodopi.

"People Show Support for, Opposition to Lee Statue in Charlottesville." 2016. *Nbc29. com.* March 22, 2016. http://www.nbc29.com/story/31536897/people-show-su pport-for-opposition-to-lee-statue-in-charlottesville.

Pierce, Lee. 2014. "A Rhetoric of Traumatic Nationalism in the Ground Zero Mosque Controversy." *Quarterly Journal of Speech* 100 (1): 53–80.

"Remarks by President Trump on Infrastructure." 2017. *Whitehouse.gov.* August 15, 2017. https://www.whitehouse.gov/briefings-statements/remarks-president-trum p-infrastructure/.

"Remarks by President Trump to Law-Enforcement Officials on MS-13." 2017. *Whitehouse.gov.* July 28, 2017. https://www.whitehouse.gov/briefings-statements/ remarks-president-trump-law-enforcement-officials-ms-13/.

Sherwell, Philip. 2010. "Donald Trump Offers to Purchase Site of Ground Zero Mosque." *Telegraph.* September 10, 2010. https://www.telegraph.co.uk/news/wo rldnews/northamerica/usa/7993347/Donald-Trump-offers-to-purchase-site-of-Gr ound-Zero-mosque.html.

Teeman, Tim. 2017. "Heather Heyer's Mom: I Have to Hide Her Grave from Neo-Nazis." *Daily Beast.* December 14, 2017. https://www.thedailybeast.com/heath er-heyers-mom-im-starting-to-hold-trump-responsible-for-her-murder-in-charl ottesville.

"Transcript: Donald Trump's Taped Comments about Women." 2016. *New York Times.* October 8, 2016. https://www.nytimes.com/2016/10/08/us/donald-trump -tape-transcript.html.

Trump, Donald J. (@realDonaldTrump). 2017a. "Memorial service today for beauti-ful and incredible Heather Heyer, a truly special young woman. She will be long remembered by all!" Twitter, August 16, 2017. https://twitter.com/realDonald Trump/status/897834894822342656.

———. 2017b. "Sad to see the history and culture of our great country being ripped apart with the removal of our beautiful statues and monuments. You....." Twitter, August 17, 2017. https://twitter.com/realdonaldtrump/status/898169407213645824.

Waldman, Amy. 2011. *The Submission.* New York: Picador.

"Whose Heritage? Public Symbols of the Confederacy." 2019. *Southern Poverty Law Center.* February 1, 2019. https://www.splcenter.org/20190201/whose-heritage-public-symbols-confederacy.

Wood, Peter H. 1999. "Slave Labor Camps in Early America: Overcoming Denial and Discovering the Gulag." In *Inequality in Early America*, edited by Carla Gar-dina Pestana and Sharon V. Salinger, 222–38. Hanover: University Press of New England.

Chapter 6

The Deep Web of Conspiracies

Under the Shadow of Trump Tower in Thomas Pynchon's Bleeding Edge

Joseph M. Conte

It would seem impossible to write a novel that turns on the many unsubstantiated theories of the 9/11 attacks and the deep state of paranoia into which the country was plunged in their aftermath without reference to Donald J. Trump.[1] As the president might say in a Tweet, "Sad!" Trump's own indulgence in conspiracy theories after 9/11, during his campaign for the presidency and as a pervasive feature of his administration, is intimately of a piece with Thomas Pynchon's *Bleeding Edge* (2013), which not only looks back on 2001 but, published in 2013, also anticipates the present political moment of Trump's presidency. The direct references to Trump in the novel are admittedly few, but the zeitgeist of paranoia, resurgent nationalism, Russian interference, and the Muslim Scare takes a page from major elements of Trump's political persona. His Islamophobia, his extreme anti-immigration policies toward nonwhite asylum seekers, his plutocratic self-dealing, nepotism and corruption, and his baiting of Russian cyberintrusion into the electoral process ("Russia, if you're listening, I hope you're able to find the 30,000 emails [from Hillary Clinton's private server] that are missing. . . . I think you will probably be rewarded mightily by our press." [Schmidt 2018]) all arise out of strains in American politics that were energized in the wake of 9/11. Like any historiographic metafiction and, really, all other novels by Pynchon from *V.* (1963) to *Inherent Vice* (2009), the novel places plausible and otherwise highly colorful characters in the historical moment immediately prior to and after 9/11, investigates the intricate weaving of that plot beyond mere "cause and effect," and projects the future that is ours, Trump's America.

Donald J. Trump's checkered career as a real estate developer and his self-inflated ratings as a sometime reality TV star on NBC's *The Apprentice* do not seem to have prepared him very well for management of one of the world's largest bureaucracies and its only remaining superpower as president of the United States. Rather, Trump was schooled, not at the Wharton School and certainly not in the eponymous Trump University, in the halls or perhaps underground shelters of conspiracy theory, preceding and continuing through his campaign for the presidency. Beginning in 2010, Trump actively promoted the "birther" conspiracy that claimed his predecessor, Barack Obama, was not born in Honolulu, Hawaii, on August 4, 1961, but rather in Kenya, the native country of his father, and thus would be ineligible to hold the office of the president under Article 2 of the Constitution. This claim of illegitimacy, observers might speculate, only serves to mask Trump's deeply felt sense that the traditional nexuses of power, the Republican establishment, and the smart money would consider *him* to be an illegitimate, unfit candidate with no experience in elected office. To be fair, the claim originated with fringe theorists and was advanced by an assortment of right-wing radio talk show hosts, but Trump directed his now imprisoned personal lawyer, Michael Cohen, to intercede with the *National Enquirer* and its publisher David Pecker to run stories in the tabloid that questioned the legitimacy of Obama's birth certificate while simultaneously promoting the possibility of a Trump candidacy.[2] Note that the conspiratorial strategy of politicking is essentially disestablishmentarian, such that questioning the legitimacy of a known party as secretly pernicious becomes the leading recommendation for one's own notoriety. Such a strategy of derogation has been lustily employed by populists such as Huey Long and his "Share Our Wealth" campaign of the 1930s, Charles Lindbergh and his America First Committee of 1940, and Joseph McCarthy and the Red Scare of the 1950s. Trump would repeat his "birther" accusation in various media, at one point insinuating that Obama's reluctance to release his long-form birth certificate was because he had something to hide, such as his religion if not his birthplace.[3] These baseless accusations comport with Trump's later attempts as president to ban by executive order all Muslim immigration into the United States and his attack on the Constitution's Fourteenth Amendment, which establishes birthright citizenship. He would eventually renounce his claims regarding Obama's citizenship in September 2016 as the Republican presidential nominee, only to assert falsely that his Democratic opponent, Hillary Clinton, was responsible for instigating the controversy during her unsuccessful bid for the 2008 Democratic presidential nomination. For Trump there is never an admission of fault; only, in the spirit of Roy Cohn (who was McCarthy's lawyer and political fixer before he was Trump's personal lawyer and mentor), every charge must be met with an obfuscating counstercharge.

Beyond birtherism, Trump has breathed life into other conspiracy theories: that Antonin Scalia, the Supreme Court justice who died in his sleep while at a remote West Texas hunting resort, was murdered; that, as reported on the cover of the *National Enquirer*, Rafael Cruz, Ted Cruz's Cuban-born father, was photographed with Lee Harvey Oswald, the assassin of President John F. Kennedy; that between three and five million illegal votes were cast during the presidential election, many by undocumented migrants and more than Hillary Clinton's margin in the popular vote count; that Clinton aide and confidant Vincent Foster did not commit suicide; and that vaccines may be the cause of autism and other ailments (Cillizza 2018). And yet, the most egregious of such claims are those having to do with the national tragedy of 9/11. At the time that "low-energy" Jeb Bush was still Trump's main competition for the Republican presidential nomination, Trump attacked Jeb's assertion that his brother, President George W. Bush, had kept America safe. Trump countered that not only had W. failed to stop the September 11 attacks, Bush had known that the 2001 attacks were coming and did nothing. In an appearance on CNN's *New Day* on October 20, 2015, Trump claimed, "His brother could have made some mistakes with respect to the actual hit because they did know it was coming and George Tenet, the head of the CIA, told them it was coming. . . . So they did have advanced notice and they didn't really work on it" (Greenberg 2015). Among the conspiracy theories that swirl around 9/11, foreknowledge of the attacks nefariously suggests that the Bushes and the CIA stood to benefit in their domestic politics or foreign policy objectives, or worse, that the catastrophe was a "false flag" operation conducted by rogue elements within the US government and planted on Osama bin Laden and his poorly resourced Islamist al Qaeda network.

In Pynchon's *Bleeding Edge*, Maxine Tarnow, a censured Certified Fraud Examiner, interviews Chandler Platt, a high-powered New York attorney, regarding video recording of armed rooftop spotters on or before the morning in question, to which Platt replies that he has heard "something . . . peculiar. Not out loud, or in so many words, but as if [. . .] they know already what's going to happen" (Pynchon 2013, 284).[4] Maxine's ex-husband, Horst Loeffler, a commodities trader with sublet offices on the top floors of the World Trade Center, observes that the week before the attacks there were an inordinate number of put options on United and American airlines, whose planes were then hijacked, and that the last trading days before Tuesday, September 11, saw a series of suspicious stock transactions involving firms located in the World Trade Center, indicating "foreknowledge" of the attacks (324). Theories that 9/11 was an inside job, of course, can be counterfactual; but Maxine's old-lefty father, Ernie Tarnow, proposes, "The chief argument against conspiracy theories is always that it would take too many people in on it, and somebody's sure to squeal. But look at the U.S. security apparatus, these guys are WASPs, Mormons, Skull and Bones, secretive by nature. Trained, sometimes since birth, never to run off at the mouth" (325). One less distinguished inductee into the Skull and Bones secret society at Yale University was George W. Bush, arguably groomed from birth for membership by his father, President George H. W. Bush, also an alumnus. Skull and Bones has been linked to conspiracy theories of world domination (the phrase New World Order comes to mind), and because James Jesus Angleton, the chief of CIA Counterintelligence from 1954 to 1975, was also a Bonesman, there is the suggestion that the CIA has long been under the control of Skull and Bones.

Even so, it's astounding that a major-party candidate for president would endorse the claim that the US government had known in advance about the 9/11 plot. And once elected, President Trump, according to Julie Hirschfeld Davis and Maggie Haberman (2018), writing in the "failing" *New York Times*, continued to promote "new, unconfirmed accusations to suit his political narrative." He is a "president who has for decades trafficked in conspiracy theories [and] brought them from the fringes of public discourse to the Oval Office. Now that he is president, Mr. Trump's baseless stories of secret plots by powerful interests. . . . have fanned fears that he is eroding public trust in institutions, undermining the idea of objective truth and sowing widespread suspicions about the government and news media that mirror his own" (Davis and Haberman 2018). Trump's paranoid style of politicking is a carry-over from his approach to management, or the art of the deal, throughout his career in business. A hallmark of conspiracy theory is the assertion that someone, somewhere is in supreme control, which nevertheless masks a deep anxiety of underlying chaos. Trump's paranoid management style is both an overweening assertion of control, "Nobody knows the system better than me, which is why I alone can fix it" ("Transcript: Donald Trump at the G.O.P. Convention" 2016), and the deliberate provocation of chaos that sends rivals and underlings into the swirling waters of Charybdis. Politically motivated conspiracy theories tend to coagulate into two separate but ultimately related camps. One emanates from sources exogenous to government, which may share the goal of exposing covert consolidations of power against the people's will, or theories of a government that is secretly, powerfully in control of the body politic. Trump's assault on the fourth estate as "fake news" serves his political narrative by attempting to delegitimize any reporting that he perceives to be critical, unflattering, or an exposé of the emoluments of the office to which he feels entitled. Like Kellyanne Conway's apparently unironic proposal of "alternative facts" (the other side of the "fake news" coin), such charges rise to the level of conspiracy theory because, as Davis and Haberman (2018) point out, they undermine the very idea of objective truth by positing that observable facts are not to be believed.[5] As Trump stated explicitly in one of his rambling speeches, "Just remember, what you are seeing and what you are reading is not what's happening. . . . Just stick with us, don't believe the crap you see from these people, the fake news" (Tornoe 2018).[6] Trump's charge of "fake news" expresses a paranoid politics, reminiscent of Richard M. Nixon's hatred of the press and the *Washington Post* in particular during the Watergate scandal, in which mainstream news media conspire to tear down the presidency by false accusation.

The second source of conspiracy theories in Trump's brain is endogenous to government. The chief culprit is the "Deep State," an unelected alliance of the national security apparatus and the career bureaucrats resistant to the change that Trump promised, who conspire to sabotage his political career. It's worth recalling that Deep Throat, the anonymous informant who was responsible for providing Bob Woodward and Carl Bernstein of the *Washington Post* with information that implicated Nixon in the Watergate break-in, was ultimately revealed to be Mark Felt, the associate director of the FBI. No wonder that Trump demanded loyalty from FBI Director James Comey and that the investigation by Special Counsel Robert Mueller included the potential charge of obstruction of justice (one of the articles of impeachment against Nixon) relating to Comey's dismissal. As Trump exclaimed to Russia's foreign minister, Sergey V. Lavrov, and Russia's ambassador to the United States, Sergey I. Kislyak, in the Oval Office, "I just fired the head of the F.B.I. He was crazy, a real nut job. . . . I faced great pressure because of Russia. That's taken off," adding, "I'm not under investigation" (Apuzzo, Haberman, and Rosenberg 2017). Endogenous conspiracies, including in Trump's mind the Mueller investigation into collaboration between his campaign and the Kremlin, likewise seek to bring down the presidency by false accusation, engaging in a "witch hunt."

Cultivating an unhealthy disbelief lies at the heart of conspiracy theory. Such speculation obstinately casts doubt on the consensus explanations for a host of historical events, while advancing extremist positions that invariably claim to uncover unacknowledged nexuses of power. Like the sinking of the *Lusitania* in 1915, the attack on Pearl Harbor in 1941, or the assassination of John F. Kennedy in 1963, 9/11 has attracted its share of conspiracy theories from across the political spectrum. From the paranoid-countercultural Left, 9/11 raised the specter of a "false flag" attack meant to promote a neoconservative agenda of war in the oil-rich Middle East and a Pax Americana; while from the populist-extremist Right arose the ugly visage of global anti-Semitism, that the Mossad or its American moles had engineered a controlled demolition of the towers to, again, foment war with Israel's enemies. Or, that banking and multinational corporate interests, evidenced by a spike in suspicious trading on the Wall Street Stock Exchange shortly before the attacks, conspired to advance a globalist New World Order. Maxine's brother-in-law, Avram "Avi" Deschler, freshly returned from business in Israel, fumes, "'Every Jew hater in this town [. . .] is blaming 9/11 on Mossad. Even a story going around about Jews who worked down at the Trade Center all calling in sick that day, warned away by Mossad through their'—air quotes—'secret network'" (Pynchon 2013, 325). To which his wife, Brooke, adds with only a touch of sarcasm, "The Jews dancing on the roof of that van over in Jersey, [. . .] watching it all collapse, don't forget that one" (325). In the polymorphism of conspiracy theory, the supposed exultations of the Jews are transformed in the Islamophobic mind of Trump into the celebration of Arab-Americans from the vantage of Jersey City. At a campaign rally in Birmingham, Alabama, on November 21, 2015, Trump asserted, "I watched when the World Trade Center came tumbling down. . . . And I watched in Jersey City, N.J., where thousands and thousands of people were cheering as that building was coming down. Thousands of people were cheering" (Carroll 2015). When challenged on the factuality of this claim, because Trump could not have observed these celebrations from his apartment in Trump Tower in Midtown Manhattan, he told George Stephanopoulos, "It was on television. I saw it. . . . It was well covered at the time, George. Now, I know they don't like to talk about it, but it was well covered at the time. There were people over in New Jersey that were watching it, a heavy Arab population, that were cheering as the buildings came down. Not good" (Carroll 2015). Considering that 9/11 was the most widely viewed event in real time in human history, no archival television coverage or newspaper reports of American Muslim celebrations have been found. And yet, the lack of corroboration in the "fake news" is no obstacle to the conspiring mind; rather, it's evidence of a cover-up of whatever "they" don't want you to know.

Regardless of denomination, conspiracy theory is an expression of incredulity with respect to any rationale delivered by mainstream media or the institutions of the administered state, such as the Warren Commission or the 9/11 Commission. In his classic essay, "The Paranoid Style in American Politics," Richard Hofstadter observes that obsessive pedantry is a characteristic common to all stripes of conspiracy theorists: "One of the impressive things about paranoid literature is the contrast between its fantasied conclusions and the almost touching concern with factuality it invariably shows. It produces heroic strivings for evidence to prove that the unbelievable is the only thing that can be believed" (1964, 85). A conspiracy theory—if it were truly credible—would assume a level of factuality and the perpetrators of such conspiracy would be, as Pynchon writes of Tyrone Slothrop in *Gravity's Rainbow*, "positively identified and detained" (Pynchon [1973] 1995, 712). In which case, such a conspiracy is no longer theory but truth. Where is the body of Osama bin Laden, if he ever existed? Where is the second gunman who fires from the grassy knoll in Dealey Plaza? The essence of conspiracy theory is that it exploits a form of unpresentability; it is an attack on the dominant forms of representation. If it can be *shown*, it's not the viral insinuation of terror in the body politic. We can't show you the body, because *they* will never allow their secrets to be revealed; and therefore, since you cannot have the body, such secrets must lie recondite within the bowels of power. No longer relegated to dark crevices and crackpots, paranoid conspiracy has been injected into mainstream culture—as the poison of controlled demolition, a forged birth certificate, crisis actors, and the Deep State—with the syringe now wielded by a president who acts as conspirator-in-chief.

No doubt the magus of the paranoid style of literature is Thomas Pynchon. *Bleeding Edge* is perhaps more Pynchonesque than any of his novels in that it recapitulates conspiracy theories alluded to in earlier works, involving, for example, international cartels (IG Farben manufactures the aromatic polymer Imipolex G for use as rocket insulation in *Gravity's Rainbow*; its subsidiary produced the cyanide-based pesticide, Zyklon B, for use at Auschwitz); secret societies (the Trystero, as in a tryst or clandestine meeting, in *The Crying of Lot 49*); Freemasons, Illuminati, and Jesuits (featured in the eighteenth-century setting of *Mason & Dixon*); and the totalitarian surveillance state (the malignant Brock Vond, from the Old Norse *vándr*, evil, in *Vineland*). *Bleeding Edge* begins on the first day of spring, the vernal equinox, March 20, 2001, as the rising sun fills the Callery Pear trees on the Upper West Side in Manhattan with unnaturally bright light, and it ends with those same pear trees blooming again one year later. On a similarly bright morning in September of that year, a few days before the autumnal equinox, the sun slants between the twin towers of the World Trade Center shortly before they were turned into pillars of fire. On this astronomical calendar the twin towers are a modern Stonehenge, marking the turn not of the millennium, feared by programmers and their binary digit calendars, but in the social order that was remade in the aftermath of September 11, 2001.[7] The novel spans the period from the collapse of the dot-com bubble to the initial forays of the war on terror, and in that solar year suggests that, had we paid more attention to the details, we might have predicted the pillars' collapse.

While *Bleeding Edge* only briefly tarries on the day of the attacks, the novel strongly implies that the calamity of September 11, 2001, should not have been thoroughly unexpected, but neither was it unprovoked, as the rules of engagement between Islamists and market capitalists had already been drawn up. Nor is the country innocent of conspiring in an assault on legitimate foreign governments. The first assignment of one of the book's villains, a rogue CIA agent named Nicholas Windust (i.e., covering his fingerprints), was as a field operative in the assassination of the democratically elected, Marxist president of Chile, Salvador Allende, "on 11 September 1973" (Pynchon 2013, 108). An adviser in "the infamous School of the Americas" promoting neoliberal privatization and the armed overthrow of leftist states (109), Windust is the novel's representative of the Deep State that surreptitiously acts on US foreign policy and intervenes as necessary in its domestic affairs. Windust is now investigating Gabriel Ice's computer security firm hashslingrz for the illegal transfer of millions of USD via *hawala* to the Dubai account of a known Islamist paymaster. He shares the hashslingrz file with Maxine, knowing of her investigation into irregularities in the company's books. The question is why would Ice, who is an American Jew, be providing aid and comfort to the existential enemies of the state of Israel? While this information may come courtesy of the Mossad, Windust warns Maxine about some of the informants in her own investigation: "You've heard of the Civil Hackers' School in Moscow?" (264). Why yes, the Civil Hackers' School is an internet security firm in Moscow that may have been used by Russian military intelligence to recruit an elite team of computer hackers for its cyberwarfare program and, in particular, its assault on the servers of the Democratic National Committee in 2016 (Kramer 2016). Windust informs her: "According to some of my colleagues, it was created by the KGB, it's still an arm of Russian espionage, its mission statement includes destroying America through cyberwarfare. Your new best friends Misha and Grisha are recent graduates, it seems" (264). Although the Russian torpedoes will later deny having any such diplomas, claiming they're only "*chainiki*" (371), dumb as teakettles, the novel's emphasis on Russian cyberespionage uncannily prefigures the conspiracy theories that have seized the popular imagination in Trump's America. Reflecting on 9/11 conspiracies, it's possible that Ice is funneling money to the jihadists on behalf of the neoconservative Deep State in its conduct of an operation that will prompt US intervention in the Middle East. Pynchon's acuity with regard to all things conspiratorial, however, also points forward to the 2016 presidential elections, the *kompromat* on Donald Trump supposedly contained in Christopher Steele's dossier, and Trump's later protestations at the Helsinki summit that he didn't "see any reason why" Russia would interfere in the American elections because, you know, "President Putin was extremely strong and powerful in his denial" (Diamond 2018), thus publicly rebuking the US intelligence community. Windust is an a priori agent of the Deep State in what will become Trump's "Russia thing" (Griffiths 2017).

Bleeding Edge doggedly pursues the conspiracy theories behind 9/11 without appearing to validate any one of them. Pynchon prods his gullible reader, as he does in *Gravity's Rainbow*, "You will want cause and effect. All right" (Pynchon [1973] 1995, 663). As Igor Dashkov, an affiliate of the Russian mafia in Brighton Beach, tells Maxine, regarding the putative funding of anti-jihadists by Vladimir Putin's FSB, "You want secular cause and effect, but here, I'm sorry, is where it all goes off books" (Pynchon 2013, 376). Pynchon's narrative is an exercise in the paranoid style of literature, but he advisedly holds the unpresentability of conspiracy theory to account: you will want the body of evidence; you will want the bodies of the nineteen hijackers whose Arabic names were variously misreported, but that cannot be found.

The leads in Maxine's fraud case, following the hashslingrz money, come in the form of videotapes in plain manila envelopes from a documentary film-maker/pirater, Reg Despard, and on flash drives from a codebreaker named Eric Outfield. From Watergate's Deep Throat to Wikileaks' Julian Assange and Edward Snowden's revelations of domestic surveillance at the NSA, whistleblowers have signaled penalties within the political, military, and security apparatus. All trails in the investigation lead to Gabriel Ice, the CEO of hashslingrz, one of the few firms in Manhattan's Silicon Alley to survive the technology bust. Consistent with Pynchon's anti-realist penchant for daffy double-entendre, Ice's surname conjures either the "intrusion counter-measures electronics" of William Gibson's cyberpunk classic, *Neuromancer* (1984, 28), or Immigration and Customs Enforcement, which suggests that this avenging angel may either be operating to secure American interests abroad or exploiting the "back doors" of the surveillance packages he codes for his own financial benefit. Ice's firm is either some form of electronic "*hawala*" that is moving money to jihadist groups in the Emirates without interest charges or transaction histories (Pynchon 2013, 81); or, it gains foreknowledge of the attacks and profits on the "leading indicator[s]" of the conspiracy (452). In which case, he is either a patriot or a traitor; or, more than likely, he is a self-dealing agent who defies ideological alignments. Ice may be descended from Immanuel Ice, the ferryman who leads the surveyors Charles Mason and Jeremiah Dixon across the Big Yochio Geni (Youghiogheny) River in Maryland in August 1767 in Pynchon's *Mason & Dixon* (1997, 659). Perhaps like his ancestor, the only survivor of an Indian Massacre, Gabriel is the Charon whose dealings lead Maxine across the Styx into the oblivion of the Deep Web.

Not coincidentally, Ice's home out in Montauk, Long Island, fitted with "four-figure showerheads as big as pizzas, marble for the bathtubs special-ordered from Carrara, Italy, custom glaziers for gold-streaked mirror glass" emulates the gauche taste of "tabloid figure Donald Trump's" Manhattan tower. Like the bankrupt developer, "Ice is now applying the guiding prin-ciple of the moneyed everywhere—pay the major contractors, blow off the small ones" (Pynchon 2013, 188). The parallels between Ice and Trump extend beyond the penchant for wealthy developers to stiff contractors, though that was a recurrent theme of Trump projects such as the failed Trump Taj Mahal Casino in Atlantic City, Trump National Doral Miami golf club, the Mar-a-Lago estate in Palm Beach, Florida, and of course, Trump Tower in Manhattan. Miscreant real estate developers of the 1980s such as Trump became a model for miscreant dot-commers of the 1990s, as represented by Ice. Just as Ice, at bare minimum, is under fraud investigation for laundering money overseas from his computer security firm, so we know that Trump "received at least $413 million in today's dollars from his father's real estate empire, much of it through tax dodges in the 1990s," and that he and his siblings "participated in dubious tax schemes during the 1990s, including instances of outright fraud, that greatly increased the fortune he received from his parents," according to a lengthy exposé in the *New York Times* (Barstow, Craig, and Buettner 2018).[8] As a result of his six bankruptcies, Trump was unable to secure capital loans for his projects from American banks, so he sought loans from Deutsche Bank and, if his tax returns are ever made public, it may be revealed that he is deeply indebted to Russian oligarchs as well. The references to Trump's career as a real estate developer in *Bleeding Edge* suggest that his avariciousness, litigiousness, bullying of his competitors and contractors, and his flouting of the law, for which he may still be indicted after leaving office, schooled the virtual entrepreneurs of the dot-com bubble of 1994 to 2000 such as Gabriel Ice. March Kelleher, long-time activist and regretful mother-in-law of Ice, makes the connection crystal clear over a cholesterol-soaked brunch with Maxine at the Piraeus Diner on Columbus Avenue: "Central Park itself isn't safe, these men of vision, they dream about CPW to Fifth Avenue solid with gracious residences. [. . .] At the same time, here's all these greedy fuckin dotcommers make real-estate developers look like Bambi and Thumper" (116). Or Bambi and Trumper. More than just the gentrification of the "Yupper West Side" (166), where Mr. Pynchon is said to have a residence, the Trump Tower at 725 Fifth Avenue, New York, NY 10022, which houses not only the Trump Organization's offices but Donald and Melania Trump's gauchely decorated apartments, fails to approach the concentration of excess capital that Silicon (V)alley entrepreneurs and venture capitalists have amassed.

An earlier reference to Trump occurs when Maxine conducts an informal interview with a venture capitalist in SoHo named Rockwell "Rocky" Slagiatt. Rocky's firm has a stake in Ice's operations, including a failed dot-com called hwgaahwgh that appears to have been used as a shell company through which Ice inconspicuously moves funds. Rocky affects a "disingenuously ethnic" schtick in this scene that winks at stereotypes of the Italian-American mafia (Pynchon 2013, 61), which is interesting in the context of Maxine's fraud investigation. When pressed, Rocky admits that he has not only dined with Ice in upscale restaurants on the Upper East Side but also crossed paths with him near his home in Montauk (63–64). Rocky offers Maxine a $5,000 retainer, but she corrects him, "Five hundred, jeez all right I'm impressed, but it's only enough so I can start a ticket. Next invoice you can be Donald Trump or whatever, OK?" (65). It's hard to say whether Rocky's largesse is some sort of a bribe, possibly for Maxine to look the other way rather than pursue the trail of Ice's shell companies. It's no secret that Donald Trump's alleged ties to New York and Philadelphia mob families were "extraordinarily extensive," involving both his Atlantic City casino and Trump Tower, a skyscraper built from concrete rather than steel, for which Trump employed the concrete company S&A, controlled by the Genovese and Gambino crime families (Frates 2015). Ice may be involved in the virtual underworld of the Deep Web, while in the gloves-off world of New York real estate development Trump has had to make friends with various mobbed-up characters.

As any mob movie will relate, crossing the boss on the receipts of a job, or siphoning the vigorish (Russian выигрыш, winnings) on a loan, will usually be fatal. Such is the case with Lester Traipse, the former owner of hwgaah-wgh.com, who has embezzled money from Ice's suspect funds transfers and turns up dead by the rooftop pool of The Deseret luxury apartment building on the Upper West Side. On the night before his "departure," Traipse leaves a long message on the cellphone of Igor Dashkov to the effect that he is in fear for his life and that "Only choice I have left is DeepArcher," a virtual space where he can seek "sanctuary" (Pynchon 2013, 376). Later, Maxine encounters the avatar of Lester there, or perhaps a "bot preprogrammed with dialogue" to respond to her questions (427). Also to be found in DeepArcher is a virtual city fashioned by her sons Ziggy and Otis, christened Zigotisopolis, composed of "graphics files for a version of NYC as it was before 11 September 2001" (428). The boys have rendered a more benevolently hued Manhattan, one seen the in silver-gelatin prints of Berenice Abbott's and Alfred Stieglitz's photographs or even Woody Allen's *Manhattan* (1979): "Somebody somewhere in the world, enjoying that mysterious exemption from time which produces most Internet content, has been patiently coding together these vehicles and streets, this city that can never be. The old Hayden Planetarium, the pre-Trump Commodore Hotel, upper-Broadway cafeterias that have not existed for years" (428). The Commodore Hotel was a Beaux Arts hotel that opened in 1919 on Forty-Second Street near Grand Central Terminal, named after the "Commodore" Cornelius Vanderbilt, railroad baron and one of the wealthiest men in American history. In 1975, Donald Trump was a relatively small player in real estate development from the outer boroughs who saw an opportunity to develop the dilapidated property cheaply. He received an unprecedented forty-year tax abatement from the city through the intercession of Mayor Abe Beame, a close friend of Fred C. Trump. But the Donald did not have the quarter of a million dollars needed to secure an option agreement with the bankrupt Penn Central, which owned the Commodore. "Instead, he bluffed. He falsely announced to the press that the option was a done deal and tricked the city government" by sending an unsigned copy of the agreement to City Hall (Rosenthal 2016). It was a crooked deal. Trump's acquisition of the Commodore exemplifies his shady business practices in the service of gentrification and crony capitalism. And yet, Pynchon's evocation of a kinder, gentler pre-Trump Manhattan (or, for that matter, before his father's postwar redlining of the Trump housing projects in the boroughs) uncannily prefigures how greed, corruption, and divisiveness will come to define Trump's America. Perhaps as an affirmation of this vision of a better New York in the virtual space of DeepArcher, the New York City Council resolved "that despite president-elect Donald Trump's senseless threats, NYC will remain a Sanctuary City for immigrant residents," on December 6, 2016 ("The New York City Council," n.d.).

Maxine's widening investigation of Ice's computer security firm takes her over the side, from the surface Web with all its banal chatter and cheap transactions into the Deep Web, beyond tracking software and Google-bot indexing, to the virtual space of DeepArcher. Here on the "bleeding edge" there may yet be sanctuary (Pynchon 2013, 78), including for the avatars of 9/11's casualties, "brought here by loved ones so they'll have an afterlife" (357), or conversely, "all kinds of deep encryption" put there by Ice, the feds, terrorists, or other forces unknown to protect their assets and illicit dealings (354). The duplicity of information is like a two-way mirror that presents an image of factuality to the party on its bright side while concealing the secretive existence of the party on its dark side. Maxine's father, Ernie, channeling his old-lefty sensibilities and possibly Pynchon's as well, reminds us that what looks like freedom on the Web is really "based on control. Everybody connected together, impossible anybody should get lost, ever again. Take the next step, connect it to these cell phones, you've got a total Web of surveillance, inescapable" (420). Maxine jokes with Reg Despard that "paranoia's the garlic in life's kitchen, right, you can never have too much" (11). In the era of paranoiac politics, in which every symbol is a false flag, incredulity is the best and only defense.

Donald Trump has been writing his own false narratives for years. Let's call it Trump fiction. His typical rhetorical ploys include extravagant hyperbole, categorical rejoinders to any charge (e.g., "I am the least racist person that you have ever met" [Scott 2018]), belittling nicknames, and a conspiracist's attribution that "they say" whatever outrageous claim he has neither the facts nor the sources to corroborate. So, the tabloid style of the *National Enquirer* has taken over the Twitter feed of the office of the president. Trump's fiction is an amalgam of lies, deceit, and indecent attacks on individuals and classes of people. By contrast, Thomas Pynchon's *Bleeding Edge* takes up the paranoid style in its salutary, recuperative, and inclusive form. As a fraud investigator, Maxine Tarnow is in pursuit of the truth of Gabriel Ice's clandestine financial dealings, of Lester Traipse's murder, and of the attacks on September 11, 2001. She is the Skeptical Inquirer who pursues the leads and weighs the evidence presented by the novel's conspiracists, including March

Kelleher, Ernie Tarnow, Reg Despard, Eric Outfield, Nicholas Windust, and Ice himself. Like Agent Mueller, she believes that the Truth is out there.

NOTES

1. A portion of this chapter will appear in my book *Transnational Politics in the Post-9/11 Novel*, forthcoming from Routledge. Reprinted with permission.

2. "In 2010, at Cohen's urging, the *National Enquirer* began promoting a potential Trump presidential candidacy, referring readers to a pro-Trump website Cohen helped create. With Cohen's involvement, the publication began questioning President Barack Obama's birthplace and American citizenship in print, an effort that Trump promoted for several years, former staffers said" (Horwitz 2018).

3. See Bump (2019). Here again, Trump's insinuations only serve to underscore his own reluctance to release his tax returns, his academic transcripts, or his standardized test scores.

4. Ellipses in quotations from *Bleeding Edge* are Pynchon's, except where indicated by brackets.

5. See also Blake (2017).

6. The address was to the Veterans of Foreign Wars Convention in Kansas City, Missouri.

7. Pynchon joins the British novelist Martin Amis (see "September 11," in *The Second Plane: September 11: Terror and Boredom* [2008]) in refusing to use the numerical acronym of 9/11 because it denotes a parochial American exceptionalism.

8. The authors won the 2019 Pulitzer Prize for Explanatory Reporting for this investigation.

REFERENCES

Amis, Martin. 2008. "September 11." In *The Second Plane: September 11: Terror and Boredom*, 193–204. New York: Alfred A. Knopf.

Apuzzo, Matt, Maggie Haberman, and Matthew Rosenberg. 2017. "Trump Told Russians that Firing 'Nut Job' Comey Eased Pressure from Investigation." *New York Times*. May 19, 2017. https://www.nytimes.com/2017/05/19/us/politics/trump-russia-comey.html.

Barstow, David, Susanne Craig, and Russ Buettner. 2018. "Trump Engaged in Suspect Tax Schemes as He Reaped Riches from His Father." *New York Times*. October 2, 2018. https://www.nytimes.com/interactive/2018/10/02/us/politics/donald-trump-tax-schemes-fred-trump.html.

Blake, Aaron. 2017. "Kellyanne Conway Says Donald Trump's Team Has 'Alternative Facts.' Which Pretty Much Says It All." *Washington Post*. January 22, 2017. https://www.washingtonpost.com/news/the-fix/wp/2017/01/22/kellyanne-co

nway-says-donald-trumps-team-has-alternate-facts-which-pretty-much-says-it-all/?noredirect=on&utm_term=.2fe8bfa87f2e.

Bump, Philip. 2019. "Another Trump Birther Conspiracy Debunked with a Birth Certificate. This Time: His Father." *Washington Post*. April 3, 2019. https://www.washingtonpost.com/politics/2019/04/03/another-trump-birther-conspiracy-debunked-with-birth-certificate-this-time-his-father/?utm_term=.c357cdf26089.

Carroll, Lauren. 2015. "Fact-Checking Trump's Claim that Thousands in New Jersey Cheered When World Trade Center Tumbled." *PolitiFact*. November 22, 2015. https://www.politifact.com/truth-o-meter/statements/2015/nov/22/donald-trump/fact-checking-trumps-claim-thousands-new-jersey-ch/.

Cillizza, Chris. 2018. "A Running List of Donald Trump's Conspiracy Theories." *CNN*. September 13, 2018. https://www.cnn.com/2018/09/13/politics/donald-trump-conspiracy-theories/index.html.

Davis, Julie Hirschfeld, and Maggie Haberman. 2018. "With 'Spygate,' Trump Shows How He Uses Conspiracy Theories to Erode Trust." *New York Times*. May 28, 2018. https://www.nytimes.com/2018/05/28/us/politics/trump-conspiracy-theories-spygate.html.

Diamond, Jeremy. 2018. "Trump Sides with Putin over US Intelligence." *CNN*. July 16, 2018. https://www.cnn.com/2018/07/16/politics/donald-trump-putin-helsinki-summit/index.html.

Frates, Chris. 2015. "Donald Trump and the Mob." *CNN*. July 31, 2015. https://www.cnn.com/2015/07/31/politics/trump-mob-mafia/index.html.

Gibson, William. 1984. *Neuromancer*. New York: Ace Books.

Greenberg, Jon. 2015. "Donald Trump Says CIA Warned George W. Bush of Sept. 11 Attacks." *PolitiFact*. October 21, 2015. https://www.politifact.com/truth-o-meter/statements/2015/oct/21/donald-trump/trump-says-cia-warned-president-bush-9-11-attacks/.

Griffiths, James. 2017. "Trump Says He Considered 'This Russia Thing' before Firing FBI Director Comey." *CNN*. May 12, 2017. https://www.cnn.com/2017/05/12/politics/trump-comey-russia-thing/index.html.

Hofstadter, Richard. 1964. "The Paranoid Style in American Politics." *Harper's*. November 1964, 77–86.

Horwitz, Jeff. 2018. "*National Enquirer* Hid Damaging Trump Stories in a Safe." *AP News*. August 23, 2018. https://www.apnews.com/143be3c52d4746af8546ca6772754407.

Kramer, Andrew E. 2016. "How Russia Recruited Elite Hackers for Its Cyberwar." *New York Times*. December 29, 2016. https://www.nytimes.com/2016/12/29/world/europe/how-russia-recruited-elite-hackers-for-its-cyberwar.html.

"The New York City Council—File #: Res 1321-2016." n. d. New York City Council Legislative Research Center. Accessed April 16, 2019. https://legistar.council.nyc.gov/LegislationDetail.aspx?ID=2900211&GUID=B85E5DB4-4E57-40A1-8CE5-03183261CFC6.

Pynchon, Thomas. (1973) 1995. *Gravity's Rainbow*. New York: Penguin.

———. 1997. *Mason & Dixon*. New York: Henry Holt.

———. 2013. *Bleeding Edge*. New York: Penguin.

Rosenthal, Max. 2016. "The Trump Files: How Donald Tricked New York into Giving Him His First Huge Deal." *Mother Jones*. July 11, 2016. https://www.motherjo nes.com/politics/2016/07/trump-files-how-donald-tricked-new-york-huge-deal/.

Schmidt, Michael S. 2018. "Trump Invited the Russians to Hack Clinton. Were They Listening?" *New York Times*. July 13, 2018. https://www.nytimes.com/2018/07/13/ us/politics/trump-russia-clinton-emails.html.

Scott, Eugene. 2018. "Six Times President Trump Said He Is the Least Racist Person." *Washington Post*. January 17, 2018. https://www.washingtonpost.com/news /the-fix/wp/2018/01/17/six-times-president-trump-said-he-is-the-least-racist-per son/?utm_term=.39e6bac2e1a3.

Tornoe, Rob. 2018. "Trump to Veterans: Don't Believe What You're Reading or Seeing." *Philly.com*. July 24, 2018. https://www.philly.com/philly/news/politics/ presidential/donald-trump-vfw-speech-kansas-city-what-youre-seeing-reading-n ot-whats-happening-20180724.html.

"Transcript: Donald Trump at the G.O.P. Convention." 2016. *New York Times*. July 22, 2016. https://www.nytimes.com/2016/07/22/us/politics/trump-transcript-r nc-address.html.

Chapter 7

From Faithful Readers to Fake News

Thomas Pynchon, Trump, and the Return of the Postmodern

William G. Welty

POST-POST-POST(?)MODERNISM

If we live in a post-postmodern world, as Jeffrey Nealon has claimed, then the 2016 election marked a return of the repressed of postmodernity (Nealon 2012, ix).[1] While Jacques Lacan argued that truth is structured like a fiction, we now have Rudy Giuliani claiming that "Truth isn't truth" (Lacan 2007, 684; Kenny 2018). Furthermore, "fake news," "alternative facts," and "post-truth" all contain a resonance with a vulgar understanding of the postmodern, with its "incredulity towards" or deconstruction of objective narrative truths.[2] Several commentators linked the election to David Foster Wallace's novel *Infinite Jest* and its obsession with reality TV and "post-shame" celebrity culture (White 2016, Masciotra 2017). Curiously, though, many overlooked the parallels between Donald Trump and the fictional President Johnny Gentle, the germaphobe B-list celebrity turned politician who swears during his inaugural address, throws a tantrum against Canada, and threatens to nuke his own country as revenge. (And, of course, President Gentle is represented in the novel as a literal puppet.) In a post-election piece, I looked to another postmodern writer, Ishmael Reed, in order to understand Trump's ascent to the presidency (Welty 2018). The dictator in Reed's first novel, *The Free-Lance Pallbearers*, is a former used-car salesman who issues all of his official decrees from the toilet, since he hasn't left his bathroom in decades. Just days before the election, the *New Yorker* published a profile of self-professed online troll and "mastermind of the alt-right" Mike Cernovich, who remarks, "If everything is a narrative, then we need alternatives to the dominant narrative. . . . I don't seem like a guy who reads Lacan, do I?" (Marantz 2016).

Such a forceful return of the postmodern raises the question whether it had ever even left at all.

And yet, if 2016 marked a return of postmodernity, it also marked its inadequacy to understand the contemporary. When Sean Spicer, Rudy Giuliani, and Sarah Huckabee Sanders (or whoever they have been replaced with by the time you read this) daily make claims about the relative, subjective nature of the truth that would make Derrida or Foucault blush, any assumption that postmodern theories are predominantly leftist or amenable to a radical politics crumbles.[3] More troubling, and more to our present concerns here, the synergy between postmodern thinking and the Trump administration calls into question the usefulness of those theories for critiquing or even understanding Trump, his politics, and his relationship to contemporary literature. Thus, Trump demands a rethinking of what postmodernism was and has been, in order to provide a better narrative of the late twentieth and twenty-first centuries. In order to tell this story, I turn to Thomas Pynchon.

In this essay, I will connect Thomas Pynchon's *Gravity's Rainbow* (1973) to his later work *Bleeding Edge* (2013). The basis for this connection is the role that Richard Nixon and Donald Trump play in those novels.[4] Brian McHale has claimed that "without Pynchon's fiction, there might never have been such a pressing need to develop a theory of literary postmodernism in the first place" (McHale 2012, 97). Then, perhaps, Pynchon also can help us reconceptualize postmodernism in the time of Trump. He can do so precisely because he has addressed Trump in his fiction. Briefly, I will argue that Pynchon consistently connects an understanding of history to the activity of reading books. While that understanding of history is connected to a precise understanding of material facts, like twentieth-century genocide or the twenty-first-century Dot Com Bubble, Pynchon likewise uses his portrayal of reading to create anachronous histories. That is, Pynchon's narrative imagination is always shifting both backwards and forwards, anachronously joining the imagined future to the historical past. Pynchon grounds his sense of anachronous history and reading in the real historical figures of Richard Nixon and Donald Trump. Pynchon's knotting together of reading, global history, and Trump helps us to see his work as materially and politically engaged, rather than "merely" ironic or concerned with aesthetic experimentation. This reframing, in turn, shifts our understanding of postmodernity and its potentialities. And, just maybe, shifts our understanding of Trump too.

Those who are familiar with Pynchon's work, even in passing, know that it is next to impossible to give a thumbnail sketch of the plots of novels like *Bleeding Edge* or *Gravity's Rainbow*. For the purposes of this essay, it's enough to know that *Gravity's Rainbow* follows a seemingly global conspiracy during the Second World War, centered on an American army lieutenant named Tyrone Slothrop, who seems to get an erection whenever he's near a

German rocket. *Bleeding Edge* follows a fraud investigator named Maxine Tarnow as she investigates another potentially global conspiracy centered around tech tycoon Gabriel Ice, in the months around the 2001 Dot Com Bubble and the 9/11 terrorist attacks.

Before delving into those texts, however, it is necessary to clarify some of the above remarks about postmodernism. *Bleeding Edge* is a treasure trove of pop culture references and pastiches, ranging from *Dragonball Z* to *The Simpsons*. While *Bleeding Edge* features an episode where Homer masquerades as a detective in an old movie called *D.O.H.* (Pynchon 2013, 316), a different real-world episode of the show demonstrates that postmodernism is a notoriously difficult movement to define. The character Moe settles for just explaining the postmodern as "weird for the sake of weird" (2001).[5] Whether we buy this definition or not, I highlight Moe's example because I am not interested in a singular definition of the postmodern. Such a definition would be impossible in this space, and moreover, a singular definition would be at odds with postmodernism itself. To return to McHale, he proposes understanding postmodernism as "multiple, overlapping and intersecting inventories and multiple corpora; not *a* construction of postmodernism, but a plurality of constructions" (McHale 1992, 3). My own sense of postmodernism includes such overlapping inventories. In thinking of the aesthetics of postmodernism, I draw on both Fredric Jameson and Linda Hutcheon: Pynchon's postmodern artistic productions are defined by irony, parody, pastiche, and a tendency toward metafiction (Jameson 1991, 16–25; Hutcheon 1989, 14). In tracing out the ideology of postmodernism, I draw on Jean-François Lyotard, who has famously defined the postmodern as an "incredulity toward metanarratives" (Lyotard 1984, xxiv). While this inventory helps us to understand a writer like Pynchon, I likewise don't want to limit us to even that narrative of the postmodern. Thus, drawing on Moe's Raymond Williams-esque sentiment from *The Simpsons*, I understand postmodernism here as a structure of feeling (Williams 1977). It is characterized by a sense of weirdness and difference, of time and space "out of joint," of pervasive irony and skepticism that can lead equally to opportunities for play and for anxiety.[6] While such a structure of feeling emerges out of a specific set of material historical conditions in the last half of the twentieth century, understanding postmodernism this way allows us to also perceive that structure of feeling in earlier moments (*Don Quixote, Tristram Shandy*) and also in later moments (post-2016).

In triangulating Trump, Pynchon, and postmodernism, I will accomplish three things. First, I will show that Pynchon's postmodernism is not a-political, paralyzed by irony and only invested in linguistic play. Indeed, several contemporary Pynchon scholars are beginning to show just how politically and historically committed Pynchon's work is (Witzling 2008; Freer 2014).[7] For example, Luc Herman and Steven Weisenburger's book *"Gravity's*

Rainbow", Domination, and Freedom (2013) provides the perfect terms for thinking about contemporary politics under Trump. But, their book is about a novel from a political moment over forty-five years ago, which leads me to my second point. Pynchon's career ranges from the beginnings of the postmodern in the United States to the contemporary moment. By connecting *Gravity's Rainbow* to *Bleeding Edge*, I will show the historical repetitions and continuities between these two moments. This, in turn, enables an understanding of the contemporary *through* the postmodern, rather than *opposed* to it. Lastly, my arguments can shift how we think about the post-45 period: not only post-1945 but also post-Trump, president #45. In particular, my readings of Pynchon and Trump can help us to reframe some of the narratives of that time period, in particular the critiques of close reading made by thinkers like Franco Moretti, Amy Hungerford, and Heather Love.[8] Trump as a historical figure shows us what it looks like when we don't closely read texts. But Trump as part of Pynchon's oeuvre show us that we can't do literary history without attending to the ways fiction theorizes and portrays the activity of reading. In other words, Pynchon shows how the two 45s—the year and the president—bookend and bring into focus a consistent set of issues, which gives us a way of periodizing and thus understanding the contemporary.

"I WAS ELECTED TO LEAD, NOT TO READ"

Trump is mentioned three times in *Bleeding Edge*, compared to the single mention of Hillary Clinton, a fact I'm sure he'd be glad to know.[9] In two of these instances, Trump's name is linked to dishonest financial dealings. About halfway through the novel the narrator relates a story about the tech tycoon Gabriel Ice and his crooked business practices: "Everybody in the room chimes in with a story like this. As if at some point having had a fateful encounter with tabloid figure Donald Trump's cost accountants, Ice is now applying the guiding principle of the moneyed everywhere—pay the major contractors, blow off the small ones" (Pynchon 2013, 188). Trump here is a figure of narrative: someone out of the tabloids, and a source for understanding "a story" that is common to "everybody." His invocation here suggests relationality, how different stories can be "like" each other. Trump's "populism"—the way "everybody" can relate to him—also recalls the final line of *Gravity's Rainbow*: "Now everybody—" (Pynchon [1973] 1995, 760). In *Bleeding Edge*, however, he's a populist figure, but only as a popularly known grifter and B-list celebrity from the tabloids.

While Trump's name creates a network of relations—of stories that are "like this"—his presence here also seems deeply unnecessary. "Cost accountants" are the ones doing the acting, not Trump himself. Furthermore, the "guiding principle" of "blow[ing] off" contractors is attributed to "the moneyed everywhere," and not Trump specifically. In other words, we don't need Trump to understand that rich people are cheap. Indeed, the whole sentence is rendered as a rather tangled simile which further displaces Trump's presence. Gabriel Ice is cheap "as if" he has encountered Trump (or at least his accountants), but the fact that Ice is already one of the "moneyed" renders that encounter unnecessary from the beginning. Donald Trump thus exists in this simile as an absent signifier; he seems to stabilize the meaning of the sentence and the network of "stories" that it refers to, all the while becoming effaced from those very stories. That effacement is true of *Bleeding Edge* itself; Trump is never actually present in the narrative of the novel.

If Trump's name seems to stabilize Pynchon's simile even while deconstructing it, it likewise highlights how absence is central to the novel's narrative strategies. "Stories like this" establishes a simile, but that simile functions through deixis. Understanding what kind of story "this" is depends on the reader's own encounter with the text, since the narrator doesn't directly describe any of the secondary stories that are "like" the first one. Deixis also highlights the importance of space: stories like "this" as opposed to "that." That formal emphasis is repeated in the scene's content, since the stories of fraud being described are about stiffing contractors for spatial renovations. Trump's name signifies a network of stories about fraud, but it also suggests that his name is itself deictic: something that can only be understood relationally, in terms of the reader's proximity to this novel or as a way of thinking about history itself. In turn, the novel insists that history, understood as "stories like these," must be understood in relationship to Trump.

The other time Trump's name is linked to financial fraud is when Maxine begins an investigation with Rocky Slagiatt, an investor behind some of Gabriel Ice's startups. She tells him that "Next invoice you can be Donald Trump or whatever, OK?" (Pynchon 2013, 65). Here, Trump's name represents financial extravagance: Rocky initially offers Maxine a retainer of $5,000, which she refuses in favor of a more modest $500. Maxine's comment likewise suggests the possibility of lying about that extravagance: Rocky could use a fake name for the next document about the investigation. Trump's name, then, signifies the exact opposite here of what it means later in the novel. If he then represents "blow[ing] off the small" contractors, here he is associated with paying them too much. Even so, Pynchon's phrasing still suggests the possibility of financial fraud, since "be[ing] Donald Trump" could equally mean paying generously (which seems unlikely, given our current situation) *or* using a false name on the invoice to hide Slagiatt's real identity. Maxine's "or whatever" emphasizes this ambivalence.

Trump's name is a signifier that allows us to understand texts, whether "stories like these" that we are reading or financial invoices, but only in

relation to that name as a signifier. (Trump makes everything about himself.) History as "stories like these" then becomes a matter of reading books
and understanding capitalist finance. And, unsurprisingly, in the third mention, Trump's name is used as a way of demarcating history. During one of
Maxine's excursions into the virtual reality program called DeepArcher, the
narrator describes the virtual scenery: "The old Hayden Planetarium, the pre-
Trump Commodore Hotel, upper-Broadway cafeterias that have not existed
for years" (Pynchon 2013, 428). The history and topology of New York City
can be understood in pre- and post-Trump terms, much in the same way
we can now begin to narrate the history of the twenty-first century. But the
building is part of a fake, virtual reality world. DeepArcher has its own, ever-
shifting topology and history, which is linked to the real but not in any consistent or essential way. In that sense, Trump's name here still is associated
with falsity, or at least with virtuality. Trump signifies a mere simulacrum of
reality.[10]

At first glance, the three references to Trump aren't particularly noteworthy in a novel obsessed with pop culture at the turn of the twenty-first
century. In fact, such references aren't surprising for Pynchon in general: for
example, Mickey Rooney appears as a character in *Gravity's Rainbow*. But
Pynchon's love of pop culture doesn't quite account for Trump as a politician; he appears in *Bleeding Edge* not as a presidential figure, but rather as a
figure of mockery from popular culture. Indeed, that was all Trump was when
Pynchon published the novel in 2013. To understand the politics of Trump's
inclusion, then, we must contextualize his character within one of Pynchon's
career-long interests: the activity of reading.[11]

Just like Oedipa Maas in Pynchon's *The Crying of Lot 49*, Maxine Tarnow is a reader. Already in that earlier text, Pynchon recognizes the dualism
of reading and politics: "Among them they had managed to turn the young
Oedipa into a rare creature indeed, unfit perhaps for marches and sit-ins, but
just a whiz at pursuing strange words in Jacobean texts" (Pynchon [1966]
1990, 104). Oedipa's reading seems to disqualify her from political praxis,
cloistering her in an ivory tower rather than in the "marches and sit-ins" of the
streets. Throughout the novel, her pursuit of texts eventually becomes indistinguishable from paranoid insanity. Maxine likewise seems aware of this
misfit between reading and politics. While she investigates Vip Epperdew's
alleged electronic cash register fraud, she recalls her mentor Professor Lavoof
and his saying: "There has to be a world off the books" (Pynchon 2013, 179).
Fraud investigation and, more broadly, politics seem to require something
beyond merely reading "the books" of financial transactions.[12]

And yet, Pynchon is working out these ideas about politics and reading in a
literal book: in an interaction with a real-world reader. And, as Trump's name
throughout the novel demonstrates, being "off the books" isn't necessarily in

the real. Indeed, we can now read Trump's infamous aversion to reading, and his preference for "alternative facts," as akin to the world of DeepArcher, which is an immersive, narrative world but one neither in books nor in the real. In other words, being "off the books" can still be either true or false: historical reality or "fake news."

This relationship—of reading to politics, of reality to paranoia—is an ongoing knot in Pynchon scholarship. Are reading and/as paranoia mere forms of escapism from the world "off the books," or does engaging with "the books" allow for real political interventions in the world, either in blocking capitalist fraud or in recovering lost histories?[13] In order to answer that question more definitively—at least as definitively as is ever possible with Pynchon—I now turn to Pynchon's earlier novel *Gravity's Rainbow*, and the way that novel also links reading, history, and the presence of authoritarian political figures.

"A FAITHFUL READER"

While Michiko Kakutani (2013) has famously referred to *Bleeding Edge* as "Pynchon Lite," the inclusion of Trump as a character directly links *Bleeding Edge*'s political concerns to *Gravity's Rainbow*, Pynchon's most acclaimed novel. As noted by both Weisenburger (2006, 322) and Krafft and Tölölyan (1983, 64), Pynchon revised the epigraph of Section 4 of *Gravity's Rainbow* late in the publication process; he changed it to be, simply, "What?", attributed to Richard M. Nixon (Pynchon [1973] 1995, 617).[14] Because of the lateness of that revision, Pynchon shows that he is interested in linking his writing to the politics of his contemporary moment. Furthermore, though *Bleeding Edge* is "about" 2001, the references to Trump demonstrate Pynchon's keen, almost anachronous, awareness of contemporary politics. The inclusion of political figures like Trump and Nixon likewise is linked to both novels' interest in the reading process: an interest central to the way Pynchon thinks about history, politics, and postmodernism. In other words, to understand Trump and *Bleeding Edge*, we have to look back at Nixon and *Gravity's Rainbow*.

At the end of *Gravity's Rainbow*, we are introduced to the figure of Richard M. Zhlubb through what appears to be a selection from a newspaper article. With his "chronic adenoidal condition, which affects his speech," "jowled" face, and "habit of throwing his arms up into an inverted 'peace sign;'" Zhlubb is usually read as a stand-in for Richard Nixon (Pynchon [1973] 1995, 754–55; Herman and Weisenburger 2013, 67, 143, 216–17). Zhlubb is the night manager of the Orpheus Theatre in Los Angeles, where the novel concludes. In the final pages, we realize that everything we have just read was part of a movie, and the projector has burned out as a rocket hurtles toward the theatre (seemingly a rocket launched in 1945). As we await our deaths, the narrator suggests we should sing a hymn from an out-of-print text by the protagonist Tyrone Slothrop's ancestor, and we are encouraged to "follow the bouncing ball"—that is, to read and then sing the hymn as it flashes up on the screen before us, though it's a hymn "They never taught anyone to sing" (Pynchon [1973] 1995, 760). The novel then concludes with that collective act of reading along and singing: "Now everybody—" (760). With the final dash, the novel suggests that the reading is unfinished—both of the hymn and the novel—and that future action might still remain.

While the scenes with Zhlubb/Nixon alternate between texts and film, the protagonist of the novel is also closely associated with reading. Before we ever meet Tyrone Slothrop, the narrator provides a genealogical description of the layers of junk cluttering his desk, ending with a copy of the sensationalist broadsheet the *News of The World*. The narrator remarks, "Slothrop's a faithful reader" (Pynchon [1973] 1995, 18).[15] If Trump in *Bleeding Edge* is a "tabloid figure," then Slothrop is a "faithful reader" of the tabloids.

Acts of reading thus bookend *Gravity's Rainbow*. Furthermore, Pynchon links the understanding of political history to those acts of reading. And, that reading, and the politics it elucidates, always already seems to be global for Pynchon. Slothrop's faithful reading takes the news of the *world* as its object. Like Maxine, whose investigation connects her to seemingly global conspiracies and to the virtual world of DeepArcher, Slothrop's readings are concerned with different types of "fake news." Both readers track either fraud or virtual reality or sensationalist tabloid stories. But at the same time, their readings involve a certain faith too: Slothrop's faithful reading or Maxine's willingness to experience the DeepArcher internet world *as if* it were real: to find a world "off the books." In fact, as *Bleeding Edge* progresses, it even starts to seem *more real* than the world: "reality" has a bleeding edge. Conspiracy as such suggests a certain kind of faith that, as the narrator of *Gravity's Rainbow* puts it, *"everything is connected"* (Pynchon [1973] 1995, 703; italics in the original), a faith which underscores our practice as literary critics: that the different parts of the texts add up to some coherent, meaningful whole.[16]

Like Trump's name as a historical marker, Slothrop's "faithful" reading is likewise linked to temporality. In addition to the association of reading and politics, Pynchon tends to associate reading with an anachronistic perspective. More to the point, Pynchon posits the relationship of reading and history to be an anachronous one that brings the past into the future, and vice versa. On the one hand, reading gestures to the future. We see this in the formal chronological shift from 1945 to 1973 that happens at the end of *Gravity's Rainbow*, or in the way Pynchon thematically links 2001 to 2013 in *Bleeding*

Edge. But, reading also obviously invokes the past, whether in the form of an out-of-print text by Slothrop's ancestor—since that text was associated with a heresy, perhaps it is also a form of "fake news"—or the financial records of the events that led up to the Dot Com burst and the September 11 attacks. When we think of how multiple timelines seem to exist at once in these texts, in particular the similarities between *Bleeding Edge's* 2001, *Gravity's Rainbow's* 1973, and our moment in 2019, it's impossible not to be reminded of the second line of *Gravity's Rainbow*: "It has happened before, but there is nothing to compare it to now" (Pynchon [1973] 1995, 3). This historical logic seems particularly apt in tracing Pynchon's oeuvre from the figure of Nixon to Trump: "It has happened before."

Gravity's Rainbow ends with a bouncing ball, and Pynchon's career as a whole bounces back and forth between Trump and Nixon. Both *Bleeding Edge* and *Gravity's Rainbow* dwell on historical repetition: of texts, authoritarian politicians, and so on. Indeed, the theme of "bouncing" itself models the necessity of reading additional texts, since it invokes the ending of Pynchon's *The Crying of Lot 49*. As Oedipa Maas tries to make sense of the vast conspiracy she may or may not have uncovered, she reflects on her late boyfriend Pierce Inverarity: "'Keep it bouncing,' he'd told her once, 'that's all the secret, keep it bouncing.' He must have known, writing the will, facing the spectre, how the bouncing would stop" (Pynchon [1966] 1990, 178). Casey Shoop and Kristin L. Matthews both have recently pointed out that Oedipa is a reader-character who models the real-world reader's own experience with the novel (Shoop 2012; Matthews 2012).[17] But whereas Oedipa likes the "book reviews in the latest *Scientific American*" and is "a whiz at pursuing strange words" (Pynchon [1966] 1990, 10, 104), Slothrop of course prefers the tabloids. (Although, contrary to Shoop and Matthews, we might note that Oedipa prefers the "book reviews" instead of the books themselves, and might not be as avid of a reader as many critics want her to be.) These different reading habits are often read as part of the mixture of high and low that is characteristic of postmodernism generally, and indeed in Pynchon's fiction specifically, which might mix Porky Pig and quantum mechanics in the same sentence. But what I'd like to highlight here is how postmodernity necessitates that one "keeps bouncing," moving from the *News of the World* to *Scientific American*, and then onwards to more Pynchon and maybe even Trump's latest tweet. Pynchon himself, his characters, and his real readers all must read a variety of real-world texts in order to read his fictional one. Bouncing means that, drawing on Jameson, we are not merely concerned with style here as parody or as pastiche, but rather as *practice* (Jameson 1991).[18] And, it is a practice that is enacted through reading, both as depicted in the text, and in our own interactions with it.

CODA: "NOW EVERYBODY—"

In one final act of "bouncing," I want to bring together the various threads of this essay: to dwell on the way Pynchon anchors his negotiation of global political and literary history, reading, and anachronous history to the figures of Nixon and Trump. It seems significant that, across forty years of his career, Pynchon would continue to both work on the same set of problems—reading, the global, and history—and see those problems through authoritarian politicians like Trump and Nixon. Far from being "Pynchon Lite," *Bleeding Edge* continues Pynchon's career-long mixture of postmodern stylistic experimentation as a way of speaking truth to the power of authoritarians like Trump.

Though Pynchon is far from a naive or sentimental writer, his frequent linkage of politics and reading—what we strive to do as professional literary critics—suggests that reading is more important than ever post-45. The characters of *Bleeding Edge* know Trump through reading the tabloids. And, maybe we can understand him a little better through reading Pynchon.[19]

NOTES

1. Nealon (2012) argues that post-postmodernism isn't a move "beyond" postmodernity, but rather an "intensification" of its processes (ix). In that sense, I view my project here as a continuation of his.

2. Though the term "fake news" dates to at least the nineteenth century, Trump popularized the phrase during the 2016 election, aided by a network of fake news websites in Macedonia (Silverman and Alexander 2016). "Alternative facts" was coined by Kellyanne Conway, in defense of then Press Secretary Sean Spicer's easily disprovable claims about Trump's inauguration crowd size (Blake 2017). "Post-truth" has a somewhat more complex history. It was coined by Serbian-American playwright Steve Tesich in 1992, though, like "fake news," it became popularized during the 2016 election. Oxford Dictionaries even named the term its word of the year for 2016 (Flood 2016). For postmodernism as "incredulity toward metanarratives," see Lyotard (1993, xxiv).

3. More accurately, continues to crumble. Critics like Barbara Christian and Kwame Anthony Appiah have long criticized mainstream postmodern literary theories for their inability to speak to lived experience or support actual political praxis. From a different intellectual tradition, Walter Benn Michaels is critical of postmodernism for its emphasis on identity politics, which he thinks is incoherent as an ideology and is only able to give causal historical accounts of present injustices without doing anything to actually address them. I've highlighted these thinkers, who no doubt would be horrified to be grouped together, only to show I am providing one narrative of postmodern thinking, and not the only one available. For more, see Christian (1987), Appiah (1991), and Michaels (2006).

4. Nixon and Trump knew each other in the 1980s, and according to Roger Stone, Nixon was "downright impressed" by Trump (Kruse 2018).

5. This episode premiered about two months after the 9/11 attacks.

6. For a discussion of the "out of joint-ness" of modernity, see Deleuze (1984, vii–viii). While Jameson characterizes postmodernism as a "waning of affect" (1991, 10), the collective We Are Plan C argues that there are three phases of capitalism, each with its own dominant affect. They associate the postmodern phase with boredom, and the contemporary phase with anxiety (We Are Plan C 2014).

7. For an earlier account of Pynchon's political engagement, see Ashe (1991).

8. For more, see Moretti (2013), Hungerford (2016, 141–67), and Love (2010). Of course, Moretti, Hungerford, and Love are all excellent close readers. I mention them here not so much as critics of close reading, but rather as representative of a contemporary discourse in the humanities that tries to reframe close reading in order to reenergize critical practice, after the waning of the political energies of postmodernism.

9. The quote that gives this section its title was uttered by another celebrity turned fictional president, Arnold Schwarzenegger, in *The Simpsons Movie* (2007).

10. As simulacra, both Trump's sense of "fake news" and the novel's portrayal of DeepArcher align with what Harry Frankfurt calls "bullshit" as opposed to "lying." The "bullshitter" refuses any distinction between true and false, and as is often the case with Trump, can't be lying because "the truth-values of his statements are of no central interest to him" (Frankfurt 2005, 55).

11. This is one of the main arguments of my larger project, out of which this essay grows. I argue that Ishmael Reed, Thomas Pynchon, Toni Morrison, and Leslie Marmon Silko have portrayed the act of reading in their fiction in order to envision, and sometimes push back against, an anachronous sense of history. That sense of history, in turn, enables them to reconcile their moment's contradictory ideas about race, politics, and literary innovation. My main contention is that these writers strive to *imagine the present as if it were already history*. The project demonstrates how their portrayals of reading enable a sense of anachrony which helps them conceptualize what that perspective might look like. In turn, I apply that perspective to contemporary critical conversations in the humanities. While prevailing accounts of the postwar period tend to focus on either historical or aesthetic problems, my account shows how these writers thought of those issues as inseparable. That is, a stylistic issue (like irony) and a historical problem (like racism) must be understood together. Understanding how these authors use reading to create an anachronous viewpoint on the history of those issues thus provides a new narrative for reconciling the competing literary and political impulses of their moment.

12. The anonymous collective CrimethInc. makes this critique of an apathetic Left who has given up on actual politics in the streets while they wait for Robert Mueller to save them by "reading the books" of Trump's financial records. Their critique seems even more on point after the release of that report, and the various misreadings and refusals of readings that followed (CrimethInc. 2019).

13. For example, Deleuzian Pynchon critic Stefan Mattessich thinks of reading as having real political possibilities (Mattessich 2002). Frederick Ashe reads Pynchon

as responding to the Left's privileging of praxis over theory/reading in the 1960s and 1970s (Ashe 1991). For another reading of the ambivalent politics of reading, see Meinel (2013). For more on Oedipa as a reader, see Hall (1991). For more on Pynchon's relationship to Right politics, see Shoop (2012).

14. The uncorrected galley sheets originally used lyrics from Joni Mitchell's song "Cactus Tree" as the epigraph.

15. Amy Hungerford has argued that postmodernism doesn't dispel faith as a meaningful form of belief, but merely shifts its object from the divine to the material. Postmodern texts manifest belief for the sake of belief, like Moe's "weird for the sake of weird," and often locate that belief in literary texts (Hungerford 2010).

16. Heather Love is critical of that underlying faith in her project on "close but not deep" reading practices. She suggests that close reading, and its faith in coherent wholes, ultimately maintains a humanist practice even in allegedly anti-humanist practices like postmodernism. Instead, she attempts to imagine a way of reading that is "flat" and "descriptive" as opposed to "deep" or "rich" (Love 2010).

17. For an earlier version of this claim, see the influential Levine (1986). Though these readings are all insightful, they sometimes collapse reading with interpretation more generally: a conflation I am attempting to avoid in this project, though not without difficulty.

18. See also Freer (2014, 158–63). Freer links Pynchon's countercultural stances to the rise of multiculturalism, so that rather than writing and reading being opposed to politics, as many 1960s radical groups believed, Pynchon's writing *is* his politics.

19. I'd like to thank everyone who helped me with this essay, including Stephen Hock, David Kurnick, Michelle Stephens, Jeffrey Lawrence, Lynn Festa, Moyang Li, Elizabeth Greeniaus, and many others. And last but not least, my wife Valerie, who bought a copy of *Gravity's Rainbow* after our first date.

REFERENCES

Appiah, Kwame Anthony. 1991. "Is the Post- in Postmodernism the Post- in Postcolonial?" *Critical Inquiry* 17 (2): 336–57.

Ashe, Frederick. 1991. "Anachronism Intended: *Gravity's Rainbow* in the Sociopolitical Sixties." *Pynchon Notes*, nos. 28–29, 59–75.

Blake, Aaron. 2017. "Kellyanne Conway Says Donald Trump's Team Has 'Alternative Facts.' Which Pretty Much Says It All." *Washington Post*. January 22, 2017. https://www.washingtonpost.com/news/the-fix/wp/2017/01/22/kellyanne-conway-says-donald-trumps-team-has-alternate-facts-which-pretty-much-says-it-all/?noredirect=on&utm_term=.2fe8bfa87f2e.

Christian, Barbara. 1987. "The Race for Theory." *Cultural Critique*, no. 6, 51–63.

CrimethInc. 2019. "Life in 'Mueller Time': The Politics of Waiting and the Spectacle of Investigation." *CrimethInc.* February 26, 2019. https://crimethinc.com/2019/02/26/life-in-mueller-time-the-politics-of-waiting-and-the-spectacle-of-investigation.

Deleuze, Gilles. 1984. *Kant's Critical Philosophy: The Doctrine of the Faculties.* Translated by Hugh Tomlinson and Barbara Habberjam. Minneapolis: University of Minnesota Press.

Flood, Alison. 2016. "'Post-truth' Named Word of the Year by Oxford Dictionaries." *Guardian*. November 15, 2016. https://www.theguardian.com/books/2016/nov/15/post-truth-named-word-of-the-year-by-oxford-dictionaries.

Frankfurt, Harry G. 2005. *On Bullshit*. Princeton: Princeton University Press.

Freer, Joanna. 2014. *Thomas Pynchon and the American Counterculture*. New York: Cambridge University Press.

Hall, Chris. 1991. "'Behind the Hieroglyphic Streets': Pynchon's Oedipa Maas and the Dialectics of Reading." *Critique* 33 (1): 63–77.

Herman, Luc, and Steven Weisenburger. 2013. *"Gravity's Rainbow", Domination, and Freedom*. Athens: University of Georgia Press.

Hungerford, Amy. 2010. *Postmodern Belief: American Literature and Religion since 1960*. Princeton: Princeton University Press.

———. 2016. *Making Literature Now*. Stanford: Stanford University Press.

Hutcheon, Linda. 1989. *The Politics of Postmodernism*. London: Routledge.

Jameson, Fredric. 1991. *Postmodernism, or, The Cultural Logic of Late Capitalism*. Durham: Duke University Press.

Kakutani, Michiko. 2013. "A Calamity Tailor-Made for Internet Conspiracy Theories." *New York Times*. September 10, 2013. https://www.nytimes.com/2013/09/11/books/bleeding-edge-a-9-11-novel-by-thomas-pynchon.html.

Kenny, Caroline. 2018. "Rudy Giuliani Says 'Truth Isn't Truth.'" *CNN*. August 19, 2018. https://www.cnn.com/2018/08/19/politics/rudy-giuliani-truth-isnt-truth/index.html.

Krafft, John M, and Khachig Tölölyan. 1983. "Notes." *Pynchon Notes*, no. 11, 63–64.

Kruse, Michael. 2018. "Trump Reclaims the Word 'Elite' with Vengeful Pride." *Politico*. November/December 2018. https://www.politico.com/magazine/story/2018/11/01/donald-trump-elite-trumpology-221953.

Lacan, Jacques. 2007. "The Subversion of the Subject and the Dialectic of Desire in the Freudian Unconscious." In *Écrits: The First Complete Edition in English*, translated by Bruce Fink in collaboration with Héloïse Fink and Russell Grigg, 671–702. New York: W. W. Norton.

Levine, George. 1986. "Risking the Moment." In *Thomas Pynchon*, edited by Harold Bloom, 59–77. New York: Chelsea House.

Love, Heather. 2010. "Close but Not Deep: Literary Ethics and the Descriptive Turn." *New Literary History* 41 (2): 371–91.

Lyotard, Jean-François. 1984. *The Postmodern Condition: A Report on Knowledge*. Translated by Geoff Bennington and Brian Massumi. Minneapolis: University of Minnesota Press.

Marantz, Andrew. 2016. "Trolls for Trump." *New Yorker*. October 24, 2016. https://www.newyorker.com/magazine/2016/10/31/trolls-for-trump.

Masciotra, David. 2017. "Donald Trump and the Hobbling of Shame: David Foster Wallace Warned Us about Reality TV and We Didn't Listen." *Salon*. January 8, 2017. https://www.salon.com/2017/01/08/donald-trump-and-the-hobbling-of-shame-david-foster-wallace-warned-us-about-reality-tv-and-we-didnt-listen/.

Mattessich, Stefan. 2002. *Lines of Flight: Discursive Time and Countercultural Desire in the Work of Thomas Pynchon*. Durham: Duke University Press.

McHale, Brian. 1992. *Constructing Postmodernism*. London: Routledge.

―――. 2012. "Pynchon's Postmodernism." In *The Cambridge Companion to Thomas Pynchon*, edited by Inger H. Dalsgaard, Luc Herman, and Brian McHale, 97–111. Cambridge: Cambridge University Press.

Meinel, Tobias. 2013. "A Deculturated Pynchon? Thomas Pynchon's *Vineland* and Reading in the Age of Television." *Amerikastudien/American Studies* 58 (3): 451–64.

Michaels, Walter Benn. 2006. *The Shape of the Signifier: 1967 to the End of History*. Princeton: Princeton University Press.

Moretti, Franco. 2013. *Distant Reading*. London: Verso.

Nealon, Jeffrey. 2012. *Post-Postmodernism, or, The Cultural Logic of Just-In-Time Capitalism*. Stanford: Stanford University Press.

Pynchon, Thomas. (1966) 1990. *The Crying of Lot 49*. New York: Perennial.

―――. (1973) 1995. *Gravity's Rainbow*. New York: Penguin.

―――. 2013. *Bleeding Edge*. New York: Penguin.

Shoop, Casey. 2012. "Thomas Pynchon, Postmodernism, and the Rise of the New Right in California." *Contemporary Literature* 53 (1): 51–86.

Silverman, Craig, and Lawrence Alexander. 2016. "How Teens in the Balkans Are Duping Trump Supporters with Fake News." *BuzzFeed News*. November 3, 2016. https://www.buzzfeednews.com/article/craigsilverman/how-macedonia-became-a-global-hub-for-pro-trump-misinfo#.op95xv35M.

The Simpsons. 2001. "Homer the Moe." Season 13, episode 3. Directed by Jen Kamerman. Written by Dana Gould. November 18, 2001. Fox.

The Simpsons Movie. 2007. Directed by David Silverman. Los Angeles: Twentieth Century Fox.

We Are Plan C. 2014. "We Are All Very Anxious." *Plan C*. April 4, 2014. https://www.weareplanc.org/blog/we-are-all-very-anxious/.

Weisenburger, Steven C. 2006. *A "Gravity's Rainbow" Companion*. 2nd edition. Athens: University of Georgia Press.

Welty, William G. 2018. "Towards a Politics of Stupidity." *Politics/Letters*. March 30, 2018. http://politicsslashletters.org/features/towards-politics-stupidity/.

White, Duncan. 2016. "The 5 Impressive Ways David Foster Wallace's *Infinite Jest* Predicted the Future." *Telegraph*. February 1, 2016. https://www.telegraph.co.uk/books/authors/the-5-impressive-ways-david-foster-wallaces-infinite-jest-predic.

Williams, Raymond. 1977. *Marxism and Literature*. Oxford: Oxford University Press.

Witzling, David. 2008. *Everybody's America: Thomas Pynchon, Race, and the Cultures of Postmodernism*. New York: Routledge.

Chapter 8

Trump Traces

Examining Donald Trump's Film and Television Cameos (1990–2004)

Ashleigh Hardin

Two weeks before the 2016 election, *Newsweek* published an article entitled "The Ridiculous Stories behind Donald Trump's Movie and TV Cameos," including interviews with screenwriters, producers, actors, and other crew members who interacted with the Republican nominee for president throughout the 1990s and early 2000s in his numerous cameo appearances (Schonfeld 2016). This article is the most exhaustive of a few pieces published online during the election, dating back as early as October 2015,[1] in which writers were rediscovering Trump's cameos. They occur in network television and premium cable shows, B movies and blockbusters; some remain and some have been deleted from the theatrical release and/or the DVD version. Occurring primarily in the hazy period between Trump's prime in the 1980s and his rebirth in *The Apprentice*, the cameos represent Trump's own flailing attempts to stay relevant. However, looking back on them, whether as stars with stories to tell about Trump on set or as YouTubers piecing together Trump's "filmography" in an attempt to find patterns and signs, the cameos do function as more than Trump-brand promotion. In the relative incoherency of his star persona and in the anti-narrativizing tendency of the cameo as vehicle, the outline of Trump's candidacy and presidency becomes legible. Similarly, the traces of Trump left in films where he filmed a cameo that ultimately was cut suggest popular culture's complicity in the creation of the Trump presidency.

The cameo appearance is an under-examined concept in film and star studies. Perhaps because they must be obvious (and thus somewhat impervious to close reading) and are typically the province of popular culture, cameo appearances have evaded much general theorizing. A high-art and preferably hidden cameo may be more appealing for critical analysis. Unsurprisingly, then, studies of Alfred Hitchcock's cameos in particular comprise a significant portion of the scholarly work on cameo appearances in film.[2] Hitchcock, inserting himself in cameos large and small into the majority of his films, provides rich fodder for analysis of the director's relationship to his body of work. D. A. Miller alludes to the basic assumption that cameo appearances function (and perhaps exist solely) to provide pleasure to the viewer: "The communal gloating is as definitive of the cameo as is Hitchcock's own flesh and blood" (Miller 2010, 107). Hitchcock's cameos allow the viewer to feel not only pleasure but superiority over the diegetic characters who remain ignorant of the significance of his presence; however, within the film, Hitchcock's presence is not significant—he has "no part to play, no narrative pertinence" (108). Miller's essay outlines the basic functions of the cameo, and its slipperiness for scholars, but Hitchcock's cameos are deeply idiosyncratic: certainly not all cameos have no relation to the narrative, and many are far more obvious than Hitchcock's, arguably providing less pleasure to the recognizing viewer.

When the cameo is not the director, when the cameo is not a part of a pattern, new interpretive questions arise. A few scholars have explored special cases of the cameo in order to understand the functions and attendant meanings it relays. In an article on fame and celebrity, Judith Roof argues for the centrality of the cameo to an understanding of fame as an ambivalent entity that "always misrecognizes" the famous subject (Roof 2009, 122). Like Hitchcock's cameos, the conventional cameo appearance is predicated on the subject already being famous and recognizable. Unlike Hitchcock's cameos, however, the conventional cameo appearance features a celebrity playing him- or herself rather than a nameless, often speechless character. By "embedding a famous person in a fictional vehicle as him- or herself," cameos bring pleasure to audiences when they recognize both the celebrity and the ruse that allows them to be both fictional and "real" at the same time (126–27). Though famous, in some sense, a celebrity's career must also be "complete" for the cameo to succeed. For this reason, perhaps, many of the best-known cameo appearances (not in the Alfred Hitchcock or, more recently, Stan Lee vein) are made by older celebrities and politicians. Roof's example, Neil Patrick Harris's cameo in *Harold and Kumar Go to White Castle*, follows this logic. Harris had been a child star whose career was stalling when he appeared as himself in the 2004 film. In *Harold and Kumar Go to White Castle*, Harris plays himself, but that self is only recognizable through Harold's and Kumar's recognition: the character "Neil Patrick Harris" in the film is very much at odds with the public persona Harris had cultivated over the previous two decades. The "real" Harris is known for his wholesomeness (in this way he is not unlike the innocent character he first achieved fame for playing, the precocious teenage doctor, Doogie Howser). In the film, he reveals that "real" self to be a fiction; the "real real" Harris of the film, apparently under the influence and obsessed with sex, shocks Harold and Kumar but amuses the audience. According to Roof, the cameo explicates the nature of fame: there is no "Neil Patrick Harris," at least not one the viewer has access to. Instead, there is "only a series of ever-enframing fictions, growing from and receding to a point that does not exist except as a fiction" (128). As Hitchcock's cameos remind us that the fictional world has an author who leaves his mark, Harris's cameo, Roof argues, reminds us that "fiction . . . is an effect of fame" (128).

Harris's cameo works, however, in part because of his acting ability. A significant portion of cameos, Trump's included, are done by celebrities who are not working actors. Kirsten Pullen examines the cameos of Zsa Zsa Gabor in this light; though also an actor, Gabor was arguably better known simply for being famous, making her an interesting corollary for Trump, who also kept himself in the public eye through personal scandals and romantic entanglements against a backdrop of opulence. In her chapter on Gabor, Pullen defines celebrities as "those who trade on their personality and persona for fame," noting that acting role and personality are increasingly "collapse[d]," suggesting that for the celebrity, both the role and the personality require public performance (Pullen 2014, 170). For a marginalized celebrity such as Gabor, cameos "indicate how playing oneself enables a kind of agency for performers otherwise imbricated within representational and institutional systems of domination" (200). Cameos not only gesture to the fictional nature of fame itself but also allow the performer to participate in a constant act of self-making. One need not be a skilled actor to be a skilled cameo player, if the goal is not a pleasurable performance for the audience but instead one's own desire to maintain celebrity and counter other circulating "fictions" about one's "real" self.

Though Trump clearly engaged in this sort of self-making, his cameos can be considered neither skillful nor revolutionary exercises of agency by a marginalized person. It is also debatable whether the cameos breathed new life into Trump's career, as Harris's did in *Harold and Kumar*. The cameos only seem to have become significant (and in some cases, legible) in the wake of his run for president. A screenwriter for the film *Zoolander*, in which Trump is "interviewed" on the red carpet by an E! News reporter, told *Newsweek* he couldn't remember Trump being in the film and explains that when a script calls for multiple cameos, as the red-carpet scene did, casting is simply "a matter of who we can get to show up on that day" (quoted in Schonfeld 2016). Trump did not appear to carefully select his cameos to optimize his self-promotion. He was hungry to be on camera and willing to appear in disastrously bad films. One such film, 1996's *Eddie*, was lampooned by the

Washington Post as an "alleged sports comedy" (B. Walker 1996) that features "a slew of shameless self-promoters" including Fabio and former New York City mayors Rudy Giuliani and Ed Koch (Kempley 1996). Nonetheless, the anecdotes of producers and stars who worked with Trump suggest that he was difficult to direct, arrogant and demanding. The executive producer of the aforementioned *Eddie* relayed to *Newsweek* that Trump was "aloof" about his attempts to offer feedback (Schonfeld 2016). For an episode of *The Nanny*, Trump requested that one of Fran Drescher's lines be rewritten to reflect that he is a billionaire, not a millionaire as the script indicated. A crew member on *The Fresh Prince of Bel-Air* claims that he threw a script at then-wife Marla Maples when she reached for it, scattering the pages everywhere (Schonfeld 2016).[3] These stories of an impetuous and irritable Trump only became part of mainstream Trump lore when the cameos became a subject of interest; the cameos only became interesting when Trump became an impetuous and irritable candidate for president of the United States, but in retrospect it seems there must have been something significant about the cameos all along. In a 2018 *Politico* article, Derek Robertson argues that "by imprinting himself in the cultural consciousness, against all empirical evidence, as a near-omniscient mogul, Trump carved out a space that would lead to his *Apprentice* run and, ultimately, the White House" (Robertson 2018). While I agree that Trump's self-presentation worked to counter narratives about his failing marriages and crumbling business empire, I hasten to add that the creation of a stable persona (the "near-omniscient mogul") is secondary to the creation of an incoherent, anti-narrativist space in which Trump operates. In examining Trump's cameo appearances from 1990 until 2004 (when *The Apprentice* premiered), I delineate patterns of meaning in his appearances, but also demonstrate the ways in which Trump's particular brand of cameo-playing foreshadows a presidential candidate whose celebrity persona lacks continuity.

"YOU JUST DON'T GET MORE NEW YORK THAN THAT": TRUMP THE BENEFICENT SYMBOL OF NEW YORK

A few things can be observed about Trump's cameo appearances in general. In television shows, most of Trump's cameos take place in the beginning of the series, in the first or second season. For two of the series, *The Fresh Prince of Bel-Air* and *The Nanny*, Trump appears in the fourth season. These two series began in the early and mid-1990s whereas the others began in the mid- and late 1990s, placing the median Donald Trump cameo TV appearance in 1997. His film cameos begin a little earlier, 1989, and end later, 2011. During this time, Trump also made many appearances on World Wrestling Entertainment shows, documentaries, and news and talk shows. However, by focusing on Trump within the context of fictional film and television cameos before the creation of his reality TV show *The Apprentice*, I wish to emphasize the performative aspect of Trump's developing persona. Within these constraints, a few trends can be noted. In a series of the cameos, Trump appears as a symbol of the high life in New York City (figure 8.1). In these cameos, Trump is mostly portrayed positively, though there are a few outliers discussed below. Turning to the cameos themselves for closer analysis, it appears that not even these New York City-centric cameos are uncomplicated.

One variety of these cameos features non-New Yorkers coming into contact with Trump while they are lost or otherwise marooned. For these characters, the appearance of Trump is a form of being welcomed to the metropolis. In *Home Alone 2: Lost in New York* (1992), perhaps the most famous of Trump's cameos, Kevin McAllister runs into Trump in the lobby of the Plaza Hotel, the opulent lodgings Kevin has chosen for his stay. Trump's quick directions to Kevin display what Robertson calls a "beneficence that's both understated and comically overblown at the same time" (Robertson 2018).

Figure 8.1   Trump's Cameo Appearance in *Sex and the City* (1999), "The Man, the Myth, the Viagra" (season 2, episode 8), Signifies the Wealth and Power of Samantha's Next Conquest. Screen capture.

Because Kevin is an anonymous, vulnerable Midwestern child colliding with a powerful New York celebrity, Trump's mere act of providing directions seems especially kind. Kevin does not recognize Trump as the owner of the magnificent hotel, but even if the 1992 viewer does not either, it is clear that Trump is in the right place while Kevin is "lost." In a 1997 episode of *The Drew Carey Show*, a show whose theme song celebrates the virtues of Cleveland, Drew Carey and his friends are stuck in a traffic jam while visiting New York City; Donald Trump hails them (because they're driving an ice cream truck) and, hearing their predicament, offers them his box seats at Yankee Stadium. In this case, Trump serves not only as a prop that helps create the atmosphere of New York City but as a counter to stereotypes about its impatient or unkind citizens. As an especially rich and powerful New Yorker, Trump's extraordinary beneficence in this case marks these unlucky Midwesterners as worthy.

Another type of New York City cameo features characters who are native New Yorkers but who are playing out a "fish out of water" narrative, often because they are female protagonists attempting to cross into male-dominated areas. In these cameos, Trump signifies that the protagonist has finally arrived. Whoopi Goldberg's two 1996 films *The Associate* and *Eddie*, Woody Allen's *Celebrity* (1998), and (to a lesser extent) the Sandra Bullock/Hugh Grant rom-com *Two Weeks Notice* (2002) fit into this category. In *The Associate*, Laurel Ayres (Goldberg) poses as a white man to start her own investment firm, as her mid-1990s Wall Street clientele would not take seriously an African American woman on her own. Trump appears with one of Laurel's business rivals, waiting for a table at a posh restaurant. When Trump ditches the rival and decides to sit at "Cutty's" (Laurel's fictitious male alter ego) table instead, his decision signifies that the momentum of the narrative has shifted strongly in Laurel's favor. In *Eddie*, Goldberg plays Eddie Franklin, the widow of a New York City police officer who drives a limousine by day and roots for the struggling New York Knicks by night. When a new owner hires Eddie as head coach (initially as part of a fan participation competition), she encounters resistance from fans, assistant coaches, and players alike. Through a series of personal interventions, she wins the goodwill of the players and coaching staff, and the team begins to win games. The film bookends her ascension from struggling imposter to successful head coach with two "news segments." The first features a "hardhat" blue-collar fan making sexist comments about Eddie's coaching followed by sound bites from then-current mayor Rudy Giuliani and former mayor Ed Koch. The second segment shows local retailers selling Eddie merchandise; the same construction worker from the beginning, now contrite about his earlier dismissal of Eddie; and Donald Trump, who quickly declares, "Actually, hiring Eddie was my idea from the beginning." The viewer knows there's no truth to his claim, but it introduces a theme of the Trump candidacy: taking credit for the success of others, and apparently suffering no consequences for it.

The *Eddie* cameo introduces an ambivalence about Trump that is noticeable in other cameos as well. In his 1998 cameo in the political sitcom *Spin City*, Trump appears at the intersection between subplots involving Mike's (Michael J. Fox) prostate problems and the mayor's writer's block. The exact nature of Trump's business with the mayor is unclear, but Mike solicits his help in advising the mayor on overcoming his writer's block. Trump arrogantly boasts that he wrote "nine chapters" of his book in a single day.[4] Mike quips he should call his next book *"The Art of Not Helping."* Adjacent to these two male characters struggling with metaphorical impotence (the inability to produce words or urine), Trump appears powerful, but only superficially. Mike calls him out quickly when he becomes unhelpful, and though Trump usurps the mayor's chair at the beginning of his cameo, the viewer knows that it is Deputy Mayor Mike, not the mayor, who wields the real power in the office.

In *Two Weeks Notice*, Trump could rightly be considered the villain of the plot. The film's protagonist, Lucy Kelson (Sandra Bullock), is a caricature liberal lawyer-activist fighting with caricature business tycoons to prevent the destruction of a community center. Hugh Grant plays George Wade, a hapless, womanizing real estate heir who seems like a handsome, British stand-in for Trump. In fact, Lucy only agrees to work with George because she is unable to "get in to see Trump." (*Two Weeks Notice* is the only Trump cameo in a feature film I am aware of in which Trump is invoked by name long before he appears on the screen.) The rest of the film leading up to Trump's cameo features Lucy continuing to do George's dirty work (including dealing with the fallout from his brief affairs with other women) in the hopes that he will preserve her community center. Ultimately, Lucy puts in her titular notice and offers to train her younger, more accommodating replacement. As Lucy realizes her attraction to George, Trump appears at a party, telling George he heard Lucy is leaving and that if his new chief counsel is any good, Trump will steal her away. Trump's comment is a proverbial kick to George while he is already down; it also shows that the high-level business dealings Lucy has attempted to infiltrate have an extremely petty undercurrent. The film concludes with the community center saved and Lucy and George united, but it is not clear how George was able to save the community center simply by stepping down from the company. Lucy is labeled "too perfect" for refusing to compromise her political beliefs; George on the other hand is "human" and unable to "control the economy" when he initially breaks his promise to save the community center. With the business part of the plot's resolution murky, the viewer must assume that the union of George and Lucy is what actually saves the community center: their mutual compromises giving birth to some caveat that allows the community center to survive. Unlike Trump's cameos in *Eddie* and *The Associate*, his appearance does not signify Lucy's success or arrival. Had she run into Trump at the beginning of the film, her endeavors would have been even less successful. Trump's collision with the male lead is likewise an indication of George's nadir. Thus, though Trump arguably makes more sense in this film than in several other cameo appearances, he has shed his role as benefactor and become, at best, a bit of a nuisance.

Thus, in some of the New York City-centric cameos, Trump carries the weight of the changing cultural significance of the city itself in the public imagination. As a symbol of the big city for outsiders, Trump is relatively uncomplicated: powerful, but welcoming and kind. When the TV show or film attempts to tell a New York story, however, Trump can become a quasi-villain. In Woody Allen's *Celebrity* (1998), Trump appears when the female lead, Robin (Judy Davis), interviews him for her TV show, *Luncheon at La Bijou*. She asks him what he is working on, and he responds that he is think-ing of buying Saint Patrick's Cathedral and putting up in its place "a very, very tall and beautiful building." Robin responds to his proposed destruction of a New York City landmark with "Well, that's just wonderful." Though Trump suggests he has enormous influence and power to be able to negotiate the purchase of the cathedral, he is the emblem of the empty celebrity that the film examines throughout. He is famous because he exists at a time when "everyone is celebrated." Robin's response to his threat to tear down Saint Patrick's Cathedral foreshadows the response of popular culture to some of Trump's other outrageous claims: deferential but meaningless acknowledg-ment of the "progress" Trump can make as a businessman.

One final example of the superficially positive but deeply ambivalent Trump cameo comes from his *Sex and the City* appearance in an episode entitled "The Man, The Myth, The Viagra" (1999). Donald Trump happens to be at the bar where Samantha enjoys an after-work cocktail. She looks at him, pleased by his presence, but not starstruck; her glance invites the advances of Trump's companion, Ed, an elderly millionaire who proceeds to spoil Samantha with gifts. Samantha has to consider whether to accept Ed's offer of financial support in exchange for sexual companionship. The gulf between Samantha and Ed is not just one of years, but class. Though Saman-tha herself is a wealthy white-collar professional, Ed's riches put him in an altogether different category: he lives in a mansion, has a servant, and can afford to give diamonds to a woman he just met. Though Trump's appearance with Ed seems to suggest and reinforce Ed's wealth, Ed's first comments to Samantha reference Trump's potential failings as a businessman. Ed sidles up to Samantha and says, "I was so distracted by your beauty, I think I just agreed to finance Mr. Trump's new project. You owe me $150 million." The remark is an ostentatious display of Ed's wealth (which appears to be his only opening gambit), but the implication is either that he does not have the money to finance Trump's project (an idea that would undermine his whole attempt) or that he expects to lose money on this project. Trump may be a symbol of New York, but New Yorkers are apparently cautious around him.

The appearance of Trump in this episode is further complicated by the context of the other subplots. Miranda, the show's cynic, begins a cross-class relationship as well. Unlike Samantha's, Miranda's new relationship with the blue-collar bartender Steve lasts in some form through the rest of the show and the two feature films. Both Samantha's and Miranda's encounters are described as "fairy tales" or "myths" in the episode, but the resolution of both forces each woman to incorporate the real "Man" into their narratives. Samantha discovers no amount of Viagra or cash can compel her attraction to Ed, and Miranda comes to believe that relationships can have a "happily ever after." Their experiences with both of these men also color their reactions to Carrie, the show's focalizing narrator, and her recent reunion with the nameless Mr. Big. As Lord mentions in the article cited above, the first reference to Trump is actually in the pilot episode of *Sex and the City* (1998), when Samantha describes Mr. Big to Carrie as "the next Donald Trump, except he's younger and much better looking." After a painful break-up with Mr. Big, Carrie reconciles with him, though her friends, especially Miranda, are skeptical he can change. Trump's appearance in this episode underscores the pessimism the women have about the relationship, and Mr. Big will only finally be recuperated enough for Carrie to settle down with after he leaves New York and gets his own name (John Preston). If Mr. Big is an avatar for Trump, he is not suitable for companionship until he is un-Trumped. While not a villain, Trump is a less than savory element of New York life that needs to be made over (made younger, hotter, and more emotionally vulnerable).

"I'VE NEVER CALLED HIM IN MY LIFE, OKAY?" TRUMP THE VILLAIN

In the early 1990s, Trump's infamous treatment of his first wife, Ivana Trump, during their divorce, and the subsequent jilting of fiancée Marla Maples, earned him scorn from multiple corners. The former Mrs. Trump herself made a cameo in the 1996 movie *The First Wives Club*, in which she encourages the mistreated ex-wives by advising, "Don't get mad, get everything." In a 1991 episode of *Designing Women*, Marla Maples also has a cameo appearance to comfort another jilted bride. At the end of the episode, Julia Sugarbaker (Dixie Carter) calls Trump on the phone and lambasts him, telling him, "on behalf of the American public . . . we no longer care *who* you date. . . . I repeat. We. Don't. Care!" Given his vindictive tendency to engage with critics of all kinds on Twitter, it seems possible that Trump's onslaught of cameos, most of which occurred during his short marriage to Maples, may have been a response to the negative publicity surrounding his affairs and divorces. Nonetheless, Trump did not pass up the occasional cameo where he played a straightforward bad guy.

In *The Little Rascals* (1994), Trump is the father of Alfalfa's arch-rival Waldo. Here he is taken out of his New York City milieu and his wealth represents the antithesis of the Rascals' small-town earnestness. Waldo calls Trump on a cell phone while piloting his soapbox derby car; Trump answers on his cell phone from the bleachers. While Waldo is a scheming and spoiled brat, he is made sympathetic for a moment when he tells Trump (who is a nameless oil tycoon) that he hopes he will make him proud by winning the race. Trump responds, "You're the best son money can buy." Waldo and his father's wealth are ultimately rebuked by the gang, who win the derby and learn to accept girls in their "He-Man Woman-Haters Club." Though Trump is again aligned with money and power, he is at odds with small-town values.

An even more stringent use of Trump appears in the second episode (2001) of the short-lived Denis Leary sitcom, *The Job* (figure 8.2). Leary plays Mike,

Figure 8.2 Trump in *The Job* (2001), "Elizabeth" (season 1, episode 2), Is a Lecherous and Unwelcome Presence for the Protagonist (Denis Leary) and Elizabeth Hurley, Herself Playing a Cameo Role as Well. Screen capture.

a hard-living New York City police officer; he crosses paths with Elizabeth Hurley (playing herself in a cameo role) when she calls the police about a harassment claim. Though Mike is married and has a live-in girlfriend as well (in a separate apartment), when he senses Liz is interested in him, he accepts an invitation to dinner with her. It is during this dinner that they encounter Trump, who apparently owns the upscale restaurant Liz has chosen. Within seconds of being introduced, Trump turns to Mike and says, "Listen, are you banging her?" Even Mike, who professes his worst nightmare is finding out "John Wayne was gay" and who flaunts not only his girlfriend but his possible relationship with Liz in front of his wife, is stunned by Trump's crassness. Liz tolerates Trump's presence for a few more seconds before he slinks off, flashing an awkward peace sign and saying, "Well, call me, Liz." As soon as he has left, Liz assures Mike, "I've never called him in my life, okay?" Though Mike and Liz never consummate their flirtation (as Liz is using Mike to make her boyfriend jealous), it seems clear that Mike was a more feasible candidate for Liz's attention than Trump himself.

Trump's cameo in *The Job* is unique for several reasons. First, Trump is usually the only cameo appearance in a television show. Even in a movie, if other cameo players are present, Trump does not interact with them. For example, in the case of *Eddie*, which is filled with cameos, Trump does not share the screen with Giuliani, Koch, or Fabio. The only "celebrities" Trump shares the screen with in his cameo appearances are his real-life romantic partners (Marla Maples in his *Fresh Prince of Bel-Air* [1994] cameo and Melania Knauss in his *Zoolander* [2001] appearance). To have an independent celebrity share the screen with Trump is intriguing; to use that celebrity to insult and negate Trump is far outside the norm. The cameo is also interesting because *The Job* uses New York City not only as its setting but as part of its ethos: the relative diversity of the cast, the range of crimes they respond to, the grittiness of the humor all trade on assumptions and stereotypes about the city. Trump is not needed to make the place. The episode in which he appears, titled "Elizabeth," does not need him for opulence and wealth either: Hurley supplies those qualities with her lavish apartment, her star power, and her younger and more attractive appearance. The interaction between Liz and Trump functions to disprove any claim to virility Trump might be able to make on the strength of his wealth and power alone. In doing so, Liz also undercuts his New York City ethos as well: Trump comes across as a pretender, one who is out of place with Liz even more so than Mike. Worse, he would undermine the efforts of the protagonist, Mike, who for all his faults, remains mostly sympathetic because he is an underdog.

Trump's negative cameos do something more complicated than just perpetuate the myth of his persona. Robertson argues that cameo Trump is "both a meticulously curated yet paper-thin idealization of a businessman, and a simple black hole of attention and celebrity" (Robertson 2018). Certainly, in the period of time right before *The Apprentice*, Trump's celebrity superseded any legitimate reputation he had a businessman. However, the negative cameos did not only contribute to this accumulation of celebrity—they prepare the audience to accept multiple, competing versions of Trump the person. They allow viewers to excuse "locker-room talk"[5] as an instant in a specific context, not part of a pattern, not a characterizing event in a narrative about who Trump is.

THE MISSING TRUMP TRACE: ERASED CAMEOS

One final type of Trump cameo deserves scrutiny, though it is arguably the most difficult to analyze. There are a significant number of Trump cameos that were cut from the final film. In fact, a great deal of the post-election conversation around Trump's cameos appears to have been instigated by remarks made by Chris O'Donnell on *Conan* in April 2017. In this interview, O'Donnell revealed that Trump may have requested a walk-on part in *Scent of a Woman* (1992) in exchange for permission to film at the Plaza Hotel. This piece of Trump trivia was repeated by Matt Damon in a September 2017 interview with *The Hollywood Reporter* (Galloway 2017). By the time Ben Affleck repeated it on a November 2017 episode of *The Late Show with Stephen Colbert*, nearly all Trump cameos had been reduced to erased cameos: "I heard that in order to get permission to film at his properties, he insisted on being put in the movie as an extra. So you had to go through this whole ritual of, like, pretending, 'Okay, now's the scene, Donald. Action.' And then they'd say cut and he'd go home, you know, and never ended up in any of the movies. I think actually, there is one movie." In Affleck's retelling, Hollywood used Trump for access to his properties and then quickly distanced itself from him.[6] However, in reality, Hollywood is more complicit in perpetuating Trump's celebrity than this narrative admits. It is worth examining briefly the films where Trump's cameo has been deleted to try to determine the cameo's meaning.

In addition to *Scent of a Woman*, Trump shot cameos for *54* (1998) and *Wall Street: Money Never Sleeps* (2010) that were deleted. The latter film falls outside the scope of my analysis, but it is particularly interesting because it was not lost to the proverbial cutting room floor, but is viewable on YouTube as a deleted scene.[7] Accounts of the cameo suggest that it was cut because Trump made too many demands and too little effort to justify his presence in the scene. The scene takes place in a London barber shop, but Trump apparently did not allow anyone to touch his hair, perhaps leading director Oliver Stone to cut the scene from the film and blame it on "'structural' issues"

("Donald Trump Filming 'Wall Street' Sequel" 2015). In this cameo, Trump is removed from his New York City context, but otherwise seems a natural fit for a film exploring the second act of a disgraced businessman whose heyday was in the 1980s. Though Trump's eccentricities prevented the cameo appearance from making it to the film, he is ultimately unnecessary. Gordon Gekko *is* Trump, to some extent, and audiences remain as confused in the twenty-first century as they were twenty years earlier about his status as the villain of the series.

The *Scent of a Woman* cameo appears to be the purely transactional kind that Affleck mentions. In the telling by Chris O'Donnell, Conan O'Brien suggests that director Martin Brest likely never intended for Trump's appearance to be in the film, which O'Donnell politely shrugs off. Though Trump owned the Plaza Hotel at the time, the location is not central to the film's plot, nor do the two main characters spend much time there. According to O'Donnell, Trump and Marla Maples would have appeared briefly getting out of a limousine on location. As far as Trump cameos go, this would have been one of the most fleeting and least Trump-aggrandizing. That no one mentioned it for twenty-five years also lends credence to O'Brien's hypothesis that it was never intended to appear in the film in the first place.

The same cannot be said for Trump's appearance in *54*, Mark Christopher's homage to disco and the nightclub of the same name. The fabled cameo would have run during the end credits, where celebrities walk a red carpet to return to the recently reopened Studio 54. According to Schonfeld, the cameo did appear in the theatrical release of the film, which was universally panned by critics, but does not appear in the DVD release or the "more lauded director's cut" (Schonfeld 2016). The editor of the film told Schonfeld he was not sure why Trump's cameo was cut (other cameos were not). Christopher claims he "doesn't remember much about filming Trump," but that he remembers the after-party: "The image that is burned into my memory is looking across the table and seeing Donald between two young women. He had one hand on one young woman's thigh and his other hand on the other's thigh. I thought, Hmm, how Studio 54" (Schonfeld 2016). As with *Wall Street: Money Never Sleeps*, the Trump cameo made narrative sense in *54*, a movie about a New York landmark, featuring cameos by all sorts of celebrities, including Ron Jeremy. The director's cut of the film, which emphasizes the bisexuality of its main characters (played by Mike Myers and Ryan Phillippe) has achieved cult status; this is not the kind of film we would expect to find Trump in, but even the director and editor themselves are not sure why. This Trump deletion gestures to a central truth about the Trump cameos, and, I would argue, his presidency: there is no simple explanation, but we should not be surprised to find Trump in any situation that affords him attention. In feeding that desire for attention through the use of Trump in cameos, as shorthand for successful businessman or spokesperson for New York, mainstream popular culture permitted the proliferation of a persona sufficiently incoherent to allow his insertion into any plot. In playing cameos rather than more substantial roles, Trump usurps narrative, preventing an understanding of the "story" of Trump in favor of easily meme-able Trump events.

In *Understanding Celebrity*, Graeme Turner argues that a person becomes a celebrity when the media is more interested in their private life than their public life. Trump's affair and relationship with Marla Maples, then, mark Trump's turn into celebrity. However, Turner further explains that the public role provides the excuse for elevating the person to celebrity status on the basis of their private life (Turner 2004, 8). In other words, Trump's marital problems and the celebrity that they evoked required a reassessment of Trump's activities as a businessman. To justify interest in Trump's affairs, we remember him as the quintessential businessman, smart, savvy, urbane. Trump's cameo appearances fictionalized his background and his family, erasing the scandal that had given birth to his celebrity. In doing so, the cameos enable a campaign rhetoric that might be most charitably described as episodic: lacking the consistency even of a formulaic reality TV show, Trump's words change radically from one context to the next as he tries to "steal the scene." According to several people he worked with on multiple cameos, Trump arrived on set like royalty and expected to be treated like an A-lister. It was apparently hard to convince him he was only playing a bit part. Now, as president, he retains the thirsty, ambitious ethos that powered his cameo appearances, and perhaps for that reason he still appears to many supporters as an accessible figure, a lucky allusion that is just at home in the Midwest as he is in Trump Tower. The cameo Trump is the Trump we know. He may be the only Trump that we can ever know.

NOTES

1. Other pre-election articles about Trump's cameos include Jason Russell's (2015) "Donald Trump's Tremendous Acting Career in 14 Clips," Adrienne LaFrance's (2015) "Three Decades of Donald Trump Film and TV Cameos," Meena Jang and Natalie Stone's (2016) "Donald Trump: 18 Memorable Cameos, From 'Home Alone 2' to 'Sex and the City,'" and Emma Lord's (2016) "Two Cringeworthy Donald Trump References in 'Sex and the City' You Forgot About."

2. Michael Walker (2005) lists Hitchcock's cameo appearances and provides a useful overview of scholarship on Hitchcock's cameos in *Hitchcock's Motifs*.

3. For discussion of Trump's cameo in *The Fresh Prince of Bel-Air*, see Peter Kragh Jensen's chapter in the present volume.—Ed.

4. Trump's ghostwriter Tony Schwartz told the *New Yorker* in 2016 that Trump did not write any portion of *The Art of the Deal*. In response to Trump's claims of

authorship, "Howard Kaminsky, the former Random House head, laughed and said, 'Trump didn't write a postcard for us!'" (Mayer 2016). Candace Bushnell's (1997) account of her friend Kate Bohner's work as Trump's ghostwriter on *The Art of the Comeback* (1997) suggests he did not write much of that book either.

5. During the October 9, 2016, presidential debate, Donald Trump used the phrase "locker-room talk" to dismiss comments he made during the filming of a 2005 episode of *Access Hollywood* (Healy and Martin 2016). Included among these comments were the infamous lines, "And when you're a star, they let you do it. You can do anything. . . . Grab 'em by the pussy" ("Transcript: Donald Trump's Taped Comments About Women" 2016).

6. The lore that Trump demands a cameo in every film and television production that shoots on his properties has become so widespread that it became the basis of a plot point in the FX series *Pose*. For discussion of *Pose*, see Meredith James's chapter in the present volume.—Ed.

7. See "Donald Trump & Gordon Gekko Get a Hair Cut!" (2016).

REFERENCES

54. 1998. Directed by Mark Christopher. Los Angeles: Miramax.

The Associate. 1996. Directed by Donald Petrie. Burbank: Buena Vista Pictures.

Bushnell, Candace. 1997. "A Leggy Stunner of Page Six Becomes Trump's Sexy Ghost." *Observer*. November 3, 1997. https://observer.com/1997/11/a-leggy-stunner-of-page-six-becomes-trumps-sexy-ghost-2/.

Celebrity. 1998. Directed by Woody Allen. Los Angeles: Miramax.

Conan. 2017. Season 7, episode 74. Written by Levi MacDougall. April 19, 2017. TBS.

Designing Women. 1991. "Marriage Most Foul." Season 6, episode 5. Directed by David Steinberg. Written by Mark Alton Brown and Dee LaDuke. October 7, 1991. CBS.

"Donald Trump & Gordon Gekko Get a Hair Cut!" 2016. YouTube video. *Coeptis Zero*. November 12, 2016. https://www.youtube.com/watch?v=cKZp-V1Uwtk.

"Donald Trump Filming 'Wall Street' Sequel: Hands Off the Hair!" 2015. *New York Daily News*. September 7, 2015. https://www.nydailynews.com/entertainment/gossip/confidential/donald-trump-wall-street-sequel-don-touch-hair-article-1.2350777.

The Drew Carey Show. 1997. "New York and Queens." Season 2, episode 24. Directed by Brian K. Roberts. Written by Christy Snell and Terry Mulroy. May 14, 1997. ABC.

Eddie. 1996. Directed by Steve Rash. Burbank: Buena Vista Pictures.

Galloway, Stephen. 2017. "Matt Damon Talks Clooney, Trump, 'Suburbicon' and Racism in America." *Hollywood Reporter*. September 1, 2017. https://www.hollywoodreporter.com/news/matt-damon-george-clooney-trump-suburbicon-racism-america-1034503.

Healy, Patrick, and Jonathan Martin. 2016. "In Second Debate, Donald Trump and Hillary Clinton Spar in Bitter, Personal Terms." *New York Times*. October 9, 2016. https://www.nytimes.com/2016/10/10/us/politics/presidential-debate.html.

Home Alone 2: Lost in New York. 1992. Directed by Chris Columbus. Los Angeles: Twentieth Century Fox.

Jang, Meena, and Natalie Stone. 2016. "Donald Trump: 18 Memorable Cameos, from 'Home Alone 2' to 'Sex and the City.'" *Hollywood Reporter*. March 10, 2016. https://www.hollywoodreporter.com/lists/donald-trump-18-memorable-cameos-873520/item/century-21-donald-trump-cameos-873659.

The Job. 2001. "Elizabeth." Season 1, episode 2. Directed by Tucker Gates. Written by Peter Tolan and Denis Leary. March 21, 2001. ABC.

Kempley, Rita. 1996. "'Eddie': No. 1 in Offense." *Washington Post*. June 1, 1996. http://www.washingtonpost.com/wp-srv/style/longterm/movies/videos/eddie.htm#kempley.

LaFrance, Adrienne. 2015. "Three Decades of Donald Trump Film and TV Cameos." *Atlantic*. December 21, 2015. https://www.theatlantic.com/entertainment/archive/2015/12/three-decades-of-donald-trump-film-and-tv-cameos/421257/.

The Late Show with Stephen Colbert. 2017. Season 3, episode 43. Written by Michael Pielocik. November 16, 2017. CBS.

The Little Rascals. 1994. Directed by Penelope Spheeris. Hollywood: Universal.

Lord, Emma. 2016. "Two Cringeworthy Donald Trump References in 'Sex and the City' You Forgot About." *Bustle*. March 29, 2016. https://www.bustle.com/articles/149234-two-cringeworthy-donald-trump-references-in-sex-and-the-city-you-forgot-about.

Mayer, Jane. 2016. "Donald Trump's Ghostwriter Tells All." *New Yorker*. July 18, 2016. https://www.newyorker.com/magazine/2016/07/25/donald-trumps-ghostwriter-tells-all.

Miller, D. A. 2010. "Hitchcock's Hidden Pictures." *Critical Inquiry* 37 (1): 106–30.

Pullen, Kirsten. 2014. *Like a Natural Woman: Spectacular Female Performance in Classical Hollywood*. New Brunswick: Rutgers University Press.

Robertson, Derek. 2018. "The Donald Trump Cinematic Universe." *Politico Magazine*. August 12, 2018. https://www.politico.com/magazine/story/2018/08/12/movies-donald-trump-cinematic-universe-219348.

Roof, Judith. 2009. "Fame's Ambivalents." *Journal of the Midwest Modern Language Association* 42 (2): 121–36.

Russell, Jason. 2015. "Donald Trump's Tremendous Acting Career in 14 Clips." *Washington Examiner*. October 7, 2015. https://www.washingtonexaminer.com/donald-trumps-tremendous-acting-career-in-14-clips.

Scent of a Woman. 1992. Directed by Martin Brest. Hollywood: Universal.

Schonfeld, Zach. 2016. "The Ridiculous Stories behind Donald Trump's Movie and TV Cameos." *Newsweek*. October 21, 2016. http://www.newsweek.com/ridiculous-stories-behind-donald-trumps-film-and-tv-cameos-511713.

Sex and the City. 1998. "Sex and the City." Season 1, episode 1. Directed by Susan Seidelman. Written by Darren Star. June 6, 1998. HBO.

Sex and the City. 1999. "The Man, the Myth, the Viagra." Season 2, episode 8. Directed by Victoria Hochberg. Written by Michael Patrick King. July 25, 1999. HBO.

Spin City. 1998. "The Paul Lassiter Story." Season 2, episode 14. Directed by Andy Cadiff. Written by Bill Lawrence. January 21, 1998. ABC.

"Transcript: Donald Trump's Taped Comments about Women." 2016. *New York Times.* October 8, 2016. https://www.nytimes.com/2016/10/08/us/donald-trump-tape-transcript.html.

Turner, Graeme. 2004. *Understanding Celebrity.* London: SAGE.

Two Weeks Notice. 2002. Directed by Marc Lawrence. Burbank: Warner Bros.

Walker, Bruce. 1996. "'Eddie': Air Ball." *Washington Post.* May 31, 1996. http://www.washingtonpost.com/wp-srv/style/longterm/movies/videos/eddie.htm#walker.

Walker, Michael. 2005. *Hitchcock's Motifs.* Amsterdam: Amsterdam University Press.

Wall Street: Money Never Sleeps. 2010. Directed by Oliver Stone. Los Angeles: Twentieth Century Fox.

Chapter 9

Entitlement and Wealth

The Whiteness of Donald Trump

Peter Kragh Jensen

Few could neglect to notice the crucial role that race played in Donald Trump's electoral campaign and continues to play in his presidency. As several observers (for instance, Cooper [2015]) have noted, Trump has on a diversity of issues from immigration and crime to anti-terrorism catered to a group of aggrieved white working-class and middle-class voters who feel that their stewardship of a primarily Christian Anglo-Saxon/Germanic chore culture is threatened by multiculturalism, globalization and PC culture. Trump's appointment of the cofounder of Breitbart News Stephen Bannon as White House chief strategist supports historian Nell Irvin Painter's (2016) contention that the election and presidency signify the changing stature of whiteness in the United States, where it has become marked as one distinct racial category among many and no longer passes as the silently assumed default. To some, taking a place in the proverbial racial tapestry of the United States may register as a demotion.

Barack Obama's blackness also made race a defining issue in the previous two election cycles, but while whiteness in the form of a backlash from an aggrieved electorate has continued to be subject of much rumination since Donald Trump announced his candidacy, few have addressed the issue of how Trump appears as a racialized figure—apart from his role as a spearhead of a predominantly white political movement. This perhaps speaks to the limits of the public discourse on whiteness, as whiteness is often articulated in connection with fading group privilege, but rarely invoked to describe how it specifically manifests as an instrument to accrue and wield power. Richard Dyer (1997, 3) notes that "the invisibility of whiteness as a racial position" is part and parcel of its power as it historically has situated white people outside of limiting race discourses and imbued the white race with a universality to speak for all of humankind.

As a man of German heritage, Trump represents many of the paradoxes of privilege in white American identity. David Roediger (2005) has documented the history of the discourses of race surrounding the immigrants that entered the United States in the late nineteenth and early twentieth centuries. He notes how many southern and eastern European immigrants were regarded as existing in a racial "in-between" state and only gradually attained the label of white that was entwined with being American. In comparison, the racial identity of immigrants from the "favored nations" (53) of northern Europe was on firmer ground. Prior to Trump, several Americans of German heritage have occupied the presidency, including Herbert Hoover, Dwight D. Eisenhower, Richard Nixon—and Barack Obama. However, as J. B. Burnell argues in a 1982 paper, on account of wartime hysteria, "No other North American ethnic group, past or present, has attempted so forcefully to officially conceal their ethnic origins. One must attribute this reaction to the wave of repression that swept the continent and enveloped anyone with a German past" (quoted in Thompson 2018, 3). In a study of American ethnic identity in the 1980s, Mary Waters (1990, 84–85) notes that the specter of Nazism still moved some Americans of German heritage to only acknowledge the non-German part of their ancestry. The shadow of this fraught negotiation with national identity loomed over Trump in 1987, when he claimed Swedish ancestry in *The Art of the Deal* although his grandfather Friedrich Trump emigrated from Kallstadt, Bavaria. Trump family historian and cousin of the president, John Walter, notes that the danger of offending Jewish tenants had a part to play in the family secrecy (Hansler 2017). Trump took steps to publicly embrace his German roots in 1999 when he served as Grand Marshal of the annual German-American Steuben Parade in New York City (Hansler 2017). A satirical campaign launched in 2016 by the late-night talk show *Last Week Tonight with John Oliver* under the name "Make Donald Drumpf Again" was aimed to remind the public of Trump's German ancestry. The campaign proved to be very popular, but also drew criticism for potentially playing into old anti-German resentment and mirroring Trump's own xenophobia by drawing into question his nationality with reference to a foreign-sounding name (Rosenbaum 2016). During the previous presidential cycle, Trump had notoriously turned the thorny relationship between American nationality and origins to his advantage by being the most visible person in the "birther" conspiracy movement that labeled Obama an undercover Kenyan citizen, ineligible to serve as president of the United States. The campaign to make the White House produce Obama's birth certificate allowed Trump to assume the role of an arbiter of American identity and exemplified how whiteness can be wielded as a political weapon.

Lieven (2016, 13) argues that Trump continues a Jacksonian strain of nationalism, which, in theory, upholds universalist values such as rule of law and democracy, but regards the white population of the republic as the only worthy guardians of these values. Further, Trump has repeatedly promoted the meritocratic aspects of his success and spoken of his career as reflective of a vertical continuity between classes in American society, while ignoring the obvious enabling factors of inherited wealth, as well as race and gender. In 1988 Trump said: "The fact is I go down the streets of New York and the people that really like me are the taxi drivers and the workers, etc." (Lewandowski and Bossie 2017, 73). Further, during the presidential campaign Trump and public supporters promoted the paradoxical image of a "blue-collar billionaire" (Colvin 2016) who stands apart from New York high society and who feels a greater kinship with the working people who voted for him.

Through much of his life in the public eye, Donald Trump has retained significant control over his image and has cultivated stardom by grandiose displays of conspicuous consumption and a decades-long public presence across genres and media. This presence includes cameos in television and film; appearances in news interviews, talk shows, and Vince McMahon's *WrestleMania* franchise; ownership of the *Miss Universe* beauty pageant; and hosting the reality shows *The Apprentice* (2004–2007, 2010) and *The Celebrity Apprentice* (2008–2015). Richard Dyer has described stardoms as a "structured polysemy" (1998, 3) that exists in a tension between the ordinary and the special (43). Through close reading, I will focus on Donald Trump's "extraordinariness" in a few popular media appearances and tease out how it materializes as a racially charged structure of meanings. I will argue that Trump's star persona has been constructed in a manner that casts him as a member of a benign, pseudo-royal white elite, both with respect to his appearances with black actors and in terms of an aesthetic tradition that presupposes the global centrality of the European/American white male. While it is beyond the scope of this essay to speculate about the political ramifications of these representations of a Caucasian regal stardom, it would seem relevant to invoke them to contextualize Trump's claims to a racially nonspecific "ordinariness" and detail how the class-transcending aspect of his star identity is saturated with notions of race.

Trump's rise to stardom coincided with what historians have broadly termed "The Reagan Era," named after President Ronald Reagan, who became the spearhead of a "conservative revolution" that ushered in economic deregulation and reduced fiscal spending on the background of a general weakened faith in the liberalism of the 1960s and 1970s. Historian Gil Troy argues that Trump became a symbol of the changing notions of commitment to public life in the Reagan Era: "The entrepreneurs of the moment such as Lee Iacocca, Donald Trump, and Ted Turner would join president Reagan in elevating the pursuit of wealth, the compulsion to consume, and the desperation to succeed from selfish acts of individualism into altruistic acts of patriotism. This brazen ethos, along with the slick sensibility and colorful graphics of an increasingly wired world, would be part of the Big Chillers' 'yuppie' package" (2005, 117).

The fascination with power displayed in flashy conspicuous consumption was mirrored in the popular culture of the era, in which soap operas like *Dynasty* and *Dallas* competed for the top slot in the prime-time schedule. Both shows featured families that had come to wealth through investments in oil drilling and, as the title *Dynasty* would suggest, dramatized fantasies of inherited privilege that echoed family structures in feudal systems. Co-creator of *Dynasty* Esther Shapiro pointed to the novel *I, Claudius* (1934), about intrigue and danger in the Roman courts of the Julio-Claudian Dynasty, as a key source of inspiration (Sturges 2011). As a side note, Joan Collins, who played the scheming femme fatale Alexis Carrington in *Dynasty*, has stated that Donald Trump's "no-holds-barred attitude" served as a model for the development of her character (Freeman 2016).[1]

TRUMP AND BLACKNESS

These references mark Donald Trump as an icon for the time who captured something crucial about the dreams and desires in the cultural imaginary by inhabiting a specific vision of wealth, power, and masculinity. I would argue that this vision also evinced notions of white supremacy. These can be difficult to discern in a predominantly white media culture, and Richard Dyer notices how "the structures, tropes and perceptual habits of whiteness" are most apparent in visual culture "when non-white (and above all black) people are also represented" (1997, 13). In these contexts it is also apparent that whiteness does not signify in a vacuum, but that it performs semiotic work on the nonwhite bodies in its vicinity. Sara Ahmed notes how whiteness manifests by orienting bodies in space (2007, 150). Trump's cameo in the sitcom *The Fresh Prince of Bel-Air* (1990–1996) is significant in this regard as the show features black actors in all leading parts and foregrounds themes of black upward social mobility. The cameo is very brief, spanning a little under two minutes of screen time, but the briefness serves as a testament to how established Trump's stardom was at the time, and how it connoted a relatively stable set of meanings. Trump functions as a rich signifier and a cultural shorthand as much as he plays a specific part in the plot of the episode. In this regard, an attempt to delineate Trump's role in the text must also consider its racial politics.

Fresh Prince tells the story of Will, a Philadelphia kid played by Will Smith, who gets in a scrape with street thugs, whereupon his mother sends him to live with his wealthy relatives in Bel-Air, the Banks family. The fish-out-of-water scenario features class collisions as the primary comedic mechanism, and the division is loaded with notions of race and masculinity. In this respect, Will's run-ins with his uncle Phil and his cousin Carlton provide much of the comedic fodder. Havens (2013, 102) notes how *Fresh Prince* "celebrated the hairstyles, clothing, speech, movement, and, above all, the music of black youth culture," while *The Cosby Show* (1984–1992), which featured a similar black nuclear family dynamic, treated it with greater apprehension and as something that "threatened to lure Theo Huxtable away from his studies and material success."

Carlton, who in his diction, mannerisms, and tastes leans toward preppy white upper-class culture, supports the Republican Party, and represents a comedic racial homelessness. He dreams of being accepted to study at Princeton, and his favorite musical artist is Welsh lounge singer Tom Jones. As noted by Havens (2013, 103), Will's uncle Phil represents an "older civil rights generation" whose insistence on respectability, material success, and social ascent sometimes clashes with the carefreeness of the younger hip-hop generation as personified by Will. Phil and Carlton are often the butt of Will's mockery, and their materialism and conservatism are consistently portrayed as laughable "racial inauthenticity" (Havens 2013, 104).

Trump makes a cameo in "For Sale by Owner" (1994), episode 25 in season 4. Most of the episode runs as a clip show, as Donald Trump has (anonymously) expressed interest in buying the Banks estate for a large sum of money. This puts the family in a dilemma and leads them to reflect on the good times they have had in the house. Despite rising bids from Trump, youngest daughter Ashley is reluctant to move out and, as the innocent, anti-materialist, conflicted moral center of the family, values memories over money.

Trump and his second wife, Marla, enter the episode toward the end when the Bankses' butler, Geoffrey, solemnly announces his arrival: "Sir, it is my esteemed pleasure to introduce Mr. and Mrs. Donald Trump." There is a brief silence, as the couple enters the door, which is broken by customary studio audience applause for the celebrity guest. Geoffrey is Oxford-educated and speaks with an upper-class British accent. Despite his servant status, he belittles and mocks the Banks family throughout the series and consistently marks his relative superiority. He has previously worked for British aristocrats and, though he is black, serves as an authentic remnant of the genteel white, European class society that upwardly mobile American capitalists like the Bankses are unsuccessfully trying to imitate. The last name of the family indicates the source for their status, signaling a bourgeois vision of social ascent.

Geoffrey tilts back his head and smiles as he makes the announcement. The volume and urgency of the delivery indicate the arrival of a very special guest (whose presence has even upset the familiar narrative continuity).

Though the show establishes a class conflict between working-class Will and the Banks family, the elegant, poised, and snarky Geoffrey serves to relativize the family's status as nouveau riche and delineate an upper limit for their social ascent.

Geoffrey outranks the family as he is a signifier of a system where status equals breeding. In this manner, as Geoffrey's announcement would indicate, Trump is the only character who is truly worthy of his esteem. This is interesting as Trump's status is only tied to material accrual, which a snobbish character such as Geoffrey could be expected to scoff at. However, the scene seems to place Geoffrey and Trump in the same political order of class privilege, in which Trump's whiteness is his only distinguishing feature. In *S/Z*, Roland Barthes (1974, 40) remarks that in the feudal order wealth stood an index of something, namely land ownership and familial ties, while in the bourgeois order wealth was shed of origin and became a standalone sign that can enter into circulation with other signs. In the semiotic economy of the episode, wealth remains a flexible sign that can evoke privilege with echoes of feudal entitlement under certain conditions, one being an association with whiteness.

When the Trumps appear in the doorway, Carlton lets out a scream of excitement, "It's the Donald! Oh my God!" and faints into the arms of Phil, who tosses him onto the living room couch (figure 9.1). Trump is an idol to

Figure 9.1 *The Fresh Prince of Bel-Air,* "For Sale by Owner," season 4, episode 25 (1994). Screen capture.

Carlton, who wishes to emulate adult white Republicans and is the family's most outspoken capitalist—he has also been the most vocal proponent of selling the house. This illustrates how the clash between Carlton and Will is also a clash between masculinities, and how Carlton's inauthentic upper-class blackness also betrays traces of effeminacy. In the episode, Carlton has been dismissive of nostalgia and sentimentality, as represented by Ashley. However, as Trump arrives, Carlton's longing for acceptance by the white moneyed classes is expressed as a stereotypically feminine loss of composure. Trump's masculine presence and status reduces Carlton to the caricature of a pearl-clutching white woman.

Phil proceeds to welcome Trump and shake his hand. The other Banks daughter, Hilary, who is a parody of a "valley girl," edges her way toward Trump to greet him. She says, "You look much richer in person," and laughs, which prompts mother Vivian to motion her away in embarrassment. It is a recurring joke throughout the series that Hilary sustains her glamorous lifestyle through promiscuity, and the inappropriate flirtatiousness marks her as a social climber. Will interrupts and gives a sales pitch for the house, finishing it with an offer to mow the lawn every Saturday for an extra $50,000 (figure 9.2). Will is also a social climber, but as a testament to his working-class background he offers his services as a low-rung employee to Trump.

Figure 9.2 *The Fresh Prince of Bel-Air*, **"For Sale by Owner," season 4, episode 25 (1994).** Screen capture.

Ashley completes Trump's introduction to the family by promptly accusing him of ruining her life and walking off. Trump turns to Marla and shrugs: "Everybody's always blaming me for everything." Trump's presence moves everyone else to stake out their position in the social order in relation to him. Like Geoffrey, he constitutes a ceiling, barring off the family members from further social ascent. He serves to underline the ridiculousness of the family's aspirations, which are presented as racially inauthentic. While this could also be understood as satire against a complacency of the civil rights generation and their children, the episode simultaneously serves to authenticate white male wealth and solidify the bond between race and class, the net message being that the Banks family may dream of being white, but Donald Trump is the genuine article.

The Bankses' agitated sycophancy and lack of professionalism in business dealings are a contrast to Trump, who remains calm and composed despite the commotion around him. He moves and speaks slowly with deliberation and restraint, while the range of his facial expressions is limited to polite smiles and the signature Clint Eastwood Squint. The family members are loud, animated, and move nervously, while there appears to be a relaxed honorability to Trump's conduct. It is only toward the end of the scene, when it is made known that Trump's agent has confused addresses, and Trump reveals a briefcase full of cash, that his character behaves with some decadence that could be read as self-parody. The entry of Trump into the Banks residence has a distinct corporeal aspect. His composure carries echoes of a whiteness that remains invisible and disembodied, as he disinterestedly observes the nonwhite people whose clumsiness and slapstick single them out as racially marked bodies.

It is worth noting that, although his identity is unknown for the major part of the episode, Trump is the character who acts with agency. He introduces the narrative conflict, but also functions as the deus ex machina who restores harmony while the intentions of the family members leave no mark on the storyline. Their disagreements render them inefficient in bargaining over the house, in which they live, and Trump's plans to establish ownership ultimately stand uncontested. Racial difference is therefore marked by the ability to claim spatial dominion.

AESTHETICS OF DISTANCE

The notion of a whiteness (or rather white masculinity) that is naturally imbued with the properties of disembodied and disinterested vision recalls Dyer's description of landscape traditions within European painting: "The idea of a landscape, framed and perspectively organised, suggests a position from which to view the world, one that is distant and separate. Moreover, the very grasping and ordering of the land on canvas or in a photograph suggests a knowledge of it, bringing it under human control" (1997, 36–37). Dyer connects this aesthetics of distance to a specific vision of the Western white man as born with a certain brilliance, ambition, and expansive energy that finds its clearest expression in the acquirement and management of land, which is discernible in the visual imaginary of Western painting. He also invokes *The Ryberg Family Portrait* (1796–1797) by Danish painter Jens Juel as an ideological specimen, in which a young nobleman with outstretched arm gestures toward the landscape in his possession.

Focusing on the urban landscape, literary historian Adrienne Brown has documented the conflicting and shifting roles that skyscrapers have played in the perception of race in America. In the decades after its invention in the 1880s, white writers tended to regard the appearance of the new architectural structure in the urban space as symptomatic of a growing threat to whiteness in modernity. The skyscrapers contributed to a disorienting crowding of the cityscape, in which ethnic difference was harder to perceive, and the white metropolitans could disappear as a visibly distinct group (2017, 40). On the other hand, urban architecture was another domain in which the United States could exhibit its exceptional entrepreneurial spirit, and the rural Western frontier found its parallel on the "eastern urban frontier" in the cities (161–62). Thus, the skyscraper became an emblem of American nationalism through its discursive ties to the same virtues of virility and initiative that allowed the white man to conquer the west.

While the skyscrapers' aura of distinctly American exceptionalism may have faded, I would argue that it is possible to see traces of this traditional racialized "aesthetics of distance" in Trump's own empire-building ventures, literally claiming visible urban space with skyscrapers carrying his name all over the world. The majestic stature of the buildings means that they are best appreciated from afar. Thus, if one stands on N. Wabash Avenue south of the Chicago River, the Trump Tower seems to block off the north end of the street. The tower rises from the ground and claims the horizon, making the Trump logo visible from the south and from the bridge crossing the river. Although Trump does not own all the buildings carrying his name, which he also loans out for licensing purposes, the branding of Trump has entwined the architecture with the man. His arcane aesthetic of grandness and gaudy glamour celebrates the building ventures as manifestations of his larger-than-life personality.

Beauty in expansion and renewal as expression of boundless initiative supports the personal brand of stardom that Trump has self-consciously manufactured throughout his career: a can-do entrepreneurialist who continues to excel in spite of frequent run-ins with people of overwhelming mediocrity. In this regard, 1986 proved to be a key year, as Trump gained significant clout in the public sphere of New York by taking charge of finishing the renovation of the Wollman Skating Rink in Central Park. Trump took six months to complete what the city's Parks Department had failed to get done for six years. Not surprisingly, the benefactor insisted that the rink should be adorned with his name. Trump transformed the construction process into a media spectacle by openly antagonizing city officials and Mayor Ed Koch, who he dismissed as "losers" (Kula and Hatkoff 2015). The publicity stunt managed to put him on the radar of chief federal prosecutor and future mayor Rudy Giuliani, who would become one of Trump's most trusted associates and currently serves as public attack dog on the president's legal team.

The sound and fury of Trump's brand of boundless entrepreneurialism has also served as a distraction from his less-than-genteel reputation in some areas of New York real estate, a reputation which has been also underpinned by racial tensions. In 1973, a group of prospective renters brought a lawsuit against Trump and his father Fred, according to which they were "accused of violating the Fair Housing Act by discriminating against potential minority renters" (Desjardins 2017). In 1989, Trump leveraged the weight of his public image against five black and Latino men in the case of the Central Park Five, who were accused and imprisoned for the rape of a twenty-eight-year-old woman. After the men had been arrested, Trump placed several full-page newspaper ads, in which he called for the restoration of the death penalty in New York. Although the men were exonerated on the basis of DNA evidence in 2002, Trump maintained their guilt as late as 2016.[2]

The connection between the "aesthetics of distance" and claims to space is made tangible in the intro to *The Celebrity Apprentice* season 4 and onwards. The opulent sequence is set to "For the Love of Money" (1973) by the Philadelphia band the O'Jays, a funk song, which, ironically, condemns the sin of avarice in a manner that depicts it as a threat to the urban poor. The opening sequence features a disjointed mixture of shots that can be grouped into five categories: shots of Trump, his family and his helicopter; shots of monuments and structures in New York; shots of the New York skyline; shots that introduce the celebrity participants who pose for the camera and hint at their claim to fame by interacting with props; and symbolic shots such as what seems to be an upward gaze at the sky from the center of an ancient amphitheater (hinting at the gladiatorial brutality of the competition). The sequence ends when a monochrome graphic of Trump and the show title is emblazoned on skyscrapers in the New York skyline.

The shots of New York, close-up and from afar, anchor the show geographically and thematize the show's ties to New York on three levels: as a center of world finance that the participants aspire to join in the image of Donald Trump; as a setting for the competitions, several of which take place in the open space of the city; and as The City of Donald Trump. New York has played a central part in Trump's career: he was born in Queens and made a large share of his fortune through real estate development in the city. However, the show stages the relationship with reverse emphasis: Donald Trump's importance to New York.

The intro sequence hints at this relationship with the continual intercutting between the city's iconography and slow-motion shots set on an airstrip, where Trump plays the part of the ever-busy mogul, walking in the foreground away from his helicopter in the background, rotor spinning, adorned with the logo of his brand (figure 9.3). The matching of skyline shots and close-ups of architecture suggests the importance of Trump's enterprise for New York at micro and macro levels. This impression is cemented at the end when Trump's face is projected on the New York skyline. It serves as a punctuation to the preceding sequence, summarizing the disjointed visual fragments of the city by giving them a unified identity under Trump.

The logo is reflected in the harbor water below, enhancing the effect of it being stamped on the architecture. The effect serves to promote Trump as a successful real estate developer but is also a metaphor for how he has played a key role in fashioning "the face" of contemporary New York, styling him as integral to the city's character. Further, whereas the removed point of view in Western visual culture only implied a controlling gaze through its aloofness, the intro goes a step further by literally inscribing the owner's visage on the urban vista (figure 9.4).

This visual celebration of Trump's expansive dominance as a real estate mogul leans on a tradition of Western imperialist image-making, which is

Figure 9.3 *The Celebrity Apprentice*, **seasons 4–7 (2011–2015).** Screen capture.

Figure 9.4 *The Celebrity Apprentice*, **seasons 4–7 (2011–2015).** Screen capture.

fueled by the enthusiasm for the Western man's conquest of space. Dyer notes that "the history of colonialism as popularly imagined and promulgated could be conveyed in terms of the excitement of advance, of forward movement through time, and of the conquest and control of space" (1997, 31). This marketing of Trump brings the aesthetics of imperialist art into the digital age, but (obviously) does not explicitly propagate white dominion. However, the aesthetic belongs to a narrative in which the white man is the world's dynamic, industrious center, and intimates that the horizon is his for the taking. As different instances of Trump's star text, the intro sequence and the cameo are in harmony: the imperial aesthetic of the intro sequence, which celebrates Trump's building ventures as expansion in space propelled by his unique genius, offers a justification for why the Banks family would idolize Trump and submit to his will.

CONCLUSION

While the candidacy of Donald Trump made whiteness more distinct as a racial category, public discourse has rarely touched on how Trump himself is portrayed in racializing discourses. The two textual examples in question are explicitly designed to maintain his stardom as extraordinary, and both texts cement his extraordinariness as intrinsically white. In *Fresh Prince* the black upper-class family's ridiculous aspirations, veneration for Trump, and awkward corporeality serve to naturalize Trump's stature as a member of an American hypercapitalist gentry. Trump's cultivation of a horizon-gazing aesthetic and the symbolic demarcation of the landscape as property in *The*

Celebrity Apprentice place Trump in an old narrative tradition that celebrates the Western man as the light of civilization who is naturally gifted for entrepreneurialism and conquest. Both presentations of Trump's brand play upon cultural tropes that refer to old systems of heritage-bound dominion, in which the white man is the center of the world.

NOTES

1. Fittingly, Salman Rushdie's novel *The Golden House* presents an avatar of Trump in the form of a would-be Roman dynast who styles himself "Nero Golden." For discussion of *The Golden House*, see Jaclyn Partyka's chapter in the present volume.—Ed.

2. For further discussion of Trump's involvement in the Central Park Five case, see Caitlin Duffy's chapter in the present volume.—Ed.

REFERENCES

Ahmed, Sara. 2007. "A Phenomenology of Whiteness." *Feminist Theory* 8 (2): 149–68. https://doi.org/10.1177/1464700107078139.

Barthes, Roland. 1974. *S/Z: An Essay*. Translated by Richard Miller. New York: Hill and Wang.

Brown, Adrienne. 2017. *The Black Skyscraper: Architecture and the Perception of Race*. Baltimore: Johns Hopkins University Press.

The Celebrity Apprentice. 2011–15. Seasons 4–7. March 6, 2011–February 16, 2015. NBC.

Colvin, Jill. 2016. "Donald Trump a 'Blue-Collar Billionaire' with a Lot of Money." *AP News*. July 18, 2016. https://apnews.com/24939b966d8942cd8f82e1b6234368ef.

Cooper, Matthew. 2015. "Donald Trump: The Billionaire for Blue-Collars." *Newsweek*. June 23, 2015. https://www.newsweek.com/2015/07/03/donald-trump-billionaire-blue-collars-345677.html.

Desjardins, Lisa. 2017. "How Trump Talks about Race." *PBS*. August 22, 2017. https://www.pbs.org/newshour/politics/every-moment-donald-trumps-long-complicated-history-race.

Dyer, Richard. 1997. *White*. London: Routledge.

———. 1998. *Stars*. New edition. London: British Film Institute.

Freeman, Anna. 2016. "Joan Collins Says Donald Trump Was Her Inspiration for *Dynasty* Legend Alexis Carrington." *Express*. July 27, 2016. https://www.express.co.uk/celebrity-news/694035/Joan-Collins-Donald-Trump-inspiration-Dynasty-legend-Alexis-Carrington-US-president.

The Fresh Prince of Bel-Air. 1994. "For Sale by Owner." Season 4, episode 25. Directed by Shelley Jensen. Written by Harrison Boyd. May 16, 1994. NBC.

Hansler, Jennifer. 2017. "Trump's Family Denied German Heritage for Years." *CNN*. November 28, 2017. https://www.cnn.com/2017/11/28/politics/trump-family-heritage/.

Havens, Timothy. 2013. *Black Television Travels: African American Media around the Globe*. New York: New York University Press.

Kula, Irwin, and Craig Hatkoff. 2015. "Donald Trump and the Wollman Rinking of American Politics." *Forbes*. August 24, 2015. https://www.forbes.com/sites/ offwhitepapers/2015/08/24/donald-trump-and-the-wollman-rinking-of-american-politics/.

Lewandowski, Corey R., and David N. Bossie. 2017. *Let Trump Be Trump: The Inside Story of His Rise to the Presidency*. New York: Center Street.

Lieven, Anatol. 2016. "Clinton and Trump: Two Faces of American Nationalism." *Survival* 58 (5): 7–22. https://doi.org/10.1080/00396338.2016.1231526.

Painter, Nell Irvin. 2016. "What Whiteness Means in the Trump Era." *New York Times*. November 12, 2016. https://www.nytimes.com/2016/11/13/opinion/wh at-whiteness-means-in-the-trump-era.html.

Roediger, David R. 2005. *Working toward Whiteness: How America's Immigrants Became White: The Strange Journey from Ellis Island to the Suburbs*. New York: Basic Books.

Rosenbaum, S. I. 2016. "John Oliver's 'Donald Drumpf' Jokes Play on the Same Ugly Xenophobia Trump Does." *Washington Post*. March 3, 2016. https://ww w.washingtonpost.com/posteverything/wp/2016/03/03/john-olivers-donald-drump f-jokes-play-on-the-same-ugly-xenophobia-trump-does/.

Sturges, Fiona. 2011. "The Good, the Bad and the Wildly Bitchy." *Independent*. January 24, 2011. http://www.independent.co.uk/arts-entertainment/tv/features/the-good-the-bad-and-the-wildly-bitchy-2192378.html.

Thompson, Maris R. 2018. *Narratives of Immigration and Language Loss: Lessons from the German American Midwest*. Lanham: Lexington Books.

Troy, Gil. 2005. *Morning in America: How Ronald Reagan Invented the 1980s*. Princeton: Princeton University Press.

Waters, Mary C. 1990. *Ethnic Options: Choosing Identities in America*. Berkeley: University of California Press.

Chapter 10

Trump for Kids

Can You Tell Us How to Get a Grump off Sesame Street?

Susan Gilmore

"Maybe [he] doesn't know how much good stuff has happened here?" "Maybe he *does* know. That's why he's tearing it down!" This snippet of dialogue, though it may sound like former administration officials performing last rites for the Obama legacy, is spoken by "Celina" and "Benny Rabbit" as they debate, along with their Sesame Street neighbors, the perverse machinations of mogul "Ronald Grump." *Sesame Street All-Star 25th Birthday: Stars and Street Forever!*, which aired on ABC in 1994 and was hosted by Barbara Walters, builds this anniversary special entirely around "speculator or terminator" Ronald Grump's plans to displace the denizens of 123 Sesame Street and build Grump Tower on hallowed children's television ground. Early in this special aimed at celebrating *Sesame Street*'s staying power, Ronald Grump (Joe Pesci) unveils his dastardly plans to hasten its demise. With the push of a button, a scale-model tower springs from his briefcase, replacing 123 Sesame Street with what Grump promises will be "a luxurious boutique called 'If You Have to Ask, You Cannot Afford It.'"

Though Joe Pesci plays Grump in this special with *Goodfellas* aplomb, delivering his signature Tommy DeVito line, "I amuse you?" (1990), straight at Children's Television Workshop cameras, the special hardly veils the satiric proximity between Ronald Grump and Donald Trump. Neither does it mark Grump's first nor his last appearance on *Sesame Street*. Grump first appears in 1988 (episode 2399) as a Grouch Muppet in a rumpled suit and hat who cons Oscar out of his trash can to make way for his "duplex candominium" ("Ronald Grump Builds the Grump Tower" [1988] 2015). He returns in 2005 (episode 4104) with an orange toupee and a slight name change from "Ronald" to "Donald" for a spoof of *The Apprentice*, featuring Oscar;

159

Grundgetta; two additional, aptly named Grouch contestants, "Swampy" and "Omagrossa"; and Elmo all competing to become Grump's "helpah" and chief sorter-of-trash ("Grouch Apprentice" [2005] 2017). Taken together, this trio of shows[1] serves as a prescient primer for how those Grump calls "the little people" (*Sesame Street All-Star* 1994) can contend with seemingly unmitigable executive power.

In the wake of Trump's presidential election, Elizabeth Weinreb Fishman, Sesame Workshop's Vice President of Strategic Communications, has insisted, "It's been over ten years since we featured the Donald Grump character and we have no plans to bring him back. . . . As you know, our content has always been politically agnostic" (Selk 2017). It is nonetheless tempting to read Trump's ongoing efforts to defund PBS as payback for what *Washington Post* reporter Avi Selk describes as "'Sesame Street's' surprisingly vicious takedowns of Donald Trump" (2017). Trump is not the first president to set his sights on PBS. Fred Rogers, the creator and mild-mannered star of *Mister Rogers' Neighborhood*, famously and movingly testified to a Senate Committee on behalf of Corporation for Public Broadcasting funding in the face of cuts proposed by the Nixon administration in 1969 (Harris 2012), and the popularity of *Won't You Be My Neighbor?*, the 2018 documentary devoted to Rogers's work, seems a fitting rejoinder to Trump-era budgetary bullying and meanness. When Newt Gingrich vowed in 1994 to "'zero out' the federal budget for the public broadcasting," as Robert W. Morrow chronicles this showdown in *"Sesame Street" and the Reform of Children's Television*, "Democratic Congresswoman Nita Lowey brought *Sesame Street* puppets to a committee hearing to speak out against the cuts: 'Make no mistake about it, this debate is about Big Bird and Oscar the Grouch and Barney and Kermit and the new Republican majority that would put them on the chopping block'" (2006, 165). Big Bird has become the synecdochical icon for *Sesame Street* and Public Broadcasting at large in more recent attempts to defund or support PBS. Mitt Romney appeared to do both at once during his 2012 campaign debate against Barack Obama in Denver, in which Romney defended plans to cut government subsidies to PBS while insisting, "I love Big Bird!" ("Mitt Romney Loves Big Bird" 2012). By contrast, Laura Bradley ascribes a murderous intent to Trump, writing in *Vanity Fair* that Trump's 2018 budget "seems to be taking a second stab at killing Big Bird's erstwhile home" (2018). Joshua Benton likewise gives Trump's proposed 2019 cuts to PBS (and NPR) a violent spin: "Trump wants to kill federal funding for PBS and NPR (again)" (2019).

In his survey of *Sesame Street* pre-presidential Trump parodies, Avi Selk casts doubt on any causal relationship between these depictions and the axes Trump has periodically thrown at PBS funding: "We know of nothing to suggest any link between these skits and Trump's budget proposal" (2017).

Moreover, Selk downplays the likelihood that Trump will do any lasting damage to the series: "Because the show now airs on HBO, Trump's plan is unlikely to destroy 'Sesame Street,' as Grump tried so hard to do" (2017). I read the series' send-ups less for the way *Sesame Street* defends itself than for the way it instructs and empowers its youngest and most vulnerable residents and viewers: children, who have arguably grown increasingly vulnerable under Trump. What interests me here are these parodies' pedagogical designs and the ways in which they anticipate Trump's "zero-tolerance"[2] antipathy toward children—particularly the "disadvantaged" (Adler [1972] n.d.) children of immigrants and the urban poor whom *Sesame Street* has most vitally served—and a multicultural America, for which *Sesame Street* serves as a microcosm.

THE ART OF THE PAIL

Ronald Grump first sets foot on *Sesame Street* in episode 2399 of season 19, airing on January 14, 1988—just two-and-a-half months after Donald J. Trump first published his businessman's bio, *Trump: The Art of the Deal*. "Ronald Grump Builds the Grump Tower" is almost certainly inspired by Trump's failed battle to evict the longtime residents of rent-controlled Central Park South, a "showdown" Trump spins as ultimately victorious in *The Art of the Deal*: "Sometimes by losing a battle you find a new way to win the war" (Trump 1987, 165). Reviewing *The Art of the Deal* for the *New York Times* in 1987, Christopher Lehmann-Haupt characterizes Trump as "disingenuous when he asserts that he never harassed the tenants of 100 Central Park South, but merely wanted to help the downtrodden when he threatened to move homeless people into the building's empty apartments." Jonathan Mahler gives the victory decidedly to the tenants, titling his *New York Times* April 2016 recap of the standoff, "Tenants Thwarted Donald Trump's Central Park Real Estate Ambitions," and observing that "on the eve of Tuesday's New York Republican primary, one can see Mr. Trump waging a much different sort of campaign, but with many of the same tactics—the threats, the theatrics, the penchant for hyperbole—that he has deployed in his quest for the Republican presidential nomination."

Joanne Mattern elides these tactics in *President Donald Trump*, her 2017 contribution to Scholastic's Rookie Biographies Series for beginning readers (grades 1–2), garnering harsh reviews from organizations such as Teaching for Change for the acritical, "celebratory" (Nganga and Cornelius 2018) portrait of Trump it delivers in prose and in a poem which rhymes Trump's economic success ("His businesses just grew and grew") with his political appeal ("people wanted something new") (Mattern 2017, 30). In his statement in response to the controversy surrounding the Trump Rookie biography, Scholastic Chairman and CEO Richard Robinson insists that "most of the teachers and librarians we serve would agree that discussing controversial aspects of any public figure's life isn't appropriate for our youngest readers" (Scholastic 2018) and redirects critics to Scholastic's "True Books biography of Trump for readers in grades 3–5" and its "*Junior Scholastic* and *Upfront* . . . magazines for middle school and high school readers" for age-appropriate accounts which "delve deeper into the controversial aspects of the Trump campaign and presidency," including "his views on immigration and Islam" (Scholastic 2018). Challenging Robinson in their review for Teaching for Change, Kathleen Nganga and Sarah Cornelius (2018) contend that "first and second graders are at an age when their perspectives about social change and citizenship begin forming. In presenting a simplified, positive narrative Mattern fails to expose young readers to critical thinking practices."

"Ronald Grump Builds the Grump Tower" ([1988] 2015) counters Trump's *Art of the Deal* and Mattern's Rookie Biography deficits. In introducing its young viewers to Ronald Grump, *Sesame Street* gives kids a lesson in critical thinking by exposing Grump as a developer who would level far more than he would build. Ronald Grump presents himself as a "Grouch builder," but his checkered sports jacket and his clashing, dilapidated camouflage fishing hat (its top flapping fittingly like a garbage pail lid) suggest a street-corner con artist whose trashcan school aesthetics and ethics make fellow Grouch Oscar an easy mark. Grump's reputation precedes his arrival on *Sesame Street*, duly impressing Oscar and summoning, in retrospect, an uncanny reversal of Trump's "drain the swamp" mantra-to-come: "Why, you're the Grouch who built a swamp in a day!"[3] When Grump offers Oscar a duplex in Grump Tower (figure 10.1) and three bonus bags of trash in exchange for Oscar's stoop, Maria declares Grump's ploy "a rotten deal," which is all that Oscar—"the contrarian in a can" (Davis 2009, 20)—needs to hear to exclaim, "Okay, I'll do it!"

If, in each of his visits to *Sesame Street*, Ronald Grump plays "the villain in a moral allegory" (Selk 2017), then perhaps the moral of the story in episode 2399 is "read the fine print." Renata Adler detects a buyer beware theme in early *Sesame Street* sketches, reading Ernie's refusal to buy an "8" from a trenchcoated "Muppet salesman" as evidence that "'Sesame Street's' attitudes toward consumerism are skeptical" ([1972] n.d.). The deal between Grump and Oscar turns ugly when Grump spots Oscar's elephant-in-the-can, "Fluffy," and best friend, "Slimey the Worm," and points to a "no pets" clause in the lease as grounds for their eviction ("Ronald Grump Builds the Grump Tower" [1988] 2015). Oscar's showdown with Grump becomes a surprising lesson in loyalty, given Michael Davis's description of Oscar's "positively misanthropic" character: "With his elongated neck and arch attitude, Oscar

Figure 10.1   Oscar and Ronald Grump Occupy Grump Tower. "Ronald Grump Builds the Grump Tower" ([1988] 2015). Screen capture.

seems like the kind of neighbor who would keep your baseball if it landed in his yard" (2008, 193). Oscar routinely chases his neighbors from his stoop with his signature "Scram!" (Borgenicht 1998, 106). And he out-Trumps Grump at name-calling, hurling insulting "pet names" such as "Feather Face" and "Overgrown Bag of Giblets" at Big Bird (Borgenicht 1998, 111). Yet even Oscar won't trade his pets for a gleaming "candominium" and surplus trash. As Caroll Spinney, Oscar's Muppeteer and voice, notes, "A lot of grouchy people really are not evil or bad in their heart. Oscar has a heart of gold" (Borgenicht 1998, 107). Not all Grouches are Grumps.

Avi Selk links *Sesame Street*'s first 1988 Trump send-up back to the 1970s, when "the Justice Department sued him and his father for allegedly refusing to rent to black people" (2017). African American viewers' initially uneasy identification with Oscar makes Selk's reading more plausible. According to Robert W. Morrow, "Some African-American adults perceived a degrading stereotype in a puppet—one that the workshop did not even consider African-American" (2006, 153). Morrow documents objections to not only Oscar's rudeness but also his complacency: "Some black viewers, however, complained that Oscar represented 'the inner-city character,' who passively accepted poverty and social injustice. One day care center director asserted:

'That cat who lives in the garbage can should be out demonstrating and turning over every institution, even *Sesame Street*, to get out of it'" (2006, 153). Ultimately, it takes a village or, in this case, a *Street* to get Oscar out of his contract with Grump. Grump's price is forty bags of trash, providing *Sesame Street* with an opportunity to fulfill two of its "original educational objectives": helping children understand "Symbolic Representation" and their "Social Environment" (Borgenicht 1998, 14). The residents of *Sesame Street*, including a parade of children, pitch in by pitching their trash Oscar's way, combining social action with practice counting out loud to forty ("Ronald Grump Builds the Grump Tower" [1988] 2015). Interspersed with these scenes featuring Grump, Oscar, and other *Sesame Street* regulars in the original broadcast episode are films that bolster this episode's communal values. One clip features children sharing swings, while another features a cartoon man counting forty stars—a warm-up, perhaps, for the program's trash-counting finale and a sign of its higher stakes and reach.

"SAVE OUR STREET"

When Ronald Grump returns to *Sesame Street* in 1994, he comes up against a neighborhood that is ever more populous and thoroughly diverse. By the 1990s, *Sesame Street* had "become a familiar and beloved face of multi-culturalism" (Morrow 2006, 164) and, as Mary Maddeve notes in 1999, the "poster show for respect of every race, creed and color that exists (and several—such as the blue and green cast members—that don't)" (quoted in Morrow 2006, 164). In *Sesame Street All-Star 25th Birthday: Stars and Street Forever!* (1994), despite this title's resolve, *Sesame Street*'s idyllic, inclusive urban habitat is threatened with extinction. Reporter "Kathie Lee Kathie" (Julia Louis-Dreyfus) questions whether Ronald Grump's tower plans spell the imminent destruction of a cross-cultural, cross-generational, and even cross-species utopia: "Unlike any other street in America, this has been a magical community of kids, grown-ups, and furry monsters, of learning, spirit, and joy, but now will Sesame Street become just a footnote in America's history?" To this canned-for-the-cameras query, Elmo provides a frank, out-of-the-mouths-of-babes answer: "If we don't do something about Mr. Grump, Elmo thinks we *will* be history." Those who find the prospect of one of *Sesame Street*'s most innocent Muppets delivering such dire news to daytime-television-viewing preschoolers and toddlers distressing will be somewhat relieved that *Stars and Street Forever!* aired at night on May 18, 1994, as an ABC special featuring Barbara Walters, the anchor for ABC's *20/20*, as the host of *25/25*, its metatheatrical spoof. *Sesame Street*'s ABC primetime special suits a grownup audience more likely to recognize and enjoy its roast of 1990s infotainment. Its in-jokes appeal to adults in a way Malcolm Gladwell argues *Sesame Street* was always "intended to appeal": "That's why the show is loaded with so many 'adult' elements, the constant punning and pop culture references" (2000, 112). In "The Stickiness Factor: *Sesame Street, Blue's Clues*, and the Educational Virus," Gladwell describes *Sesame Street* as "a magazine show" (2000, 116), suggesting its format's compatibility with that of television news magazines. Its Muppet correspondents deliver their exposé of Trump/Grump more sweetly *and* more bitingly than a strictly human press corps possibly could. Recalling his conversations on *The Morning Show* with Bil Baird's lion puppet, "Charlemane," Walter Cronkite admits in his 1996 autobiography, *A Reporter's Life*, that "a puppet can render opinions on people and things that a human commentator would not feel free to utter" (quoted in Davis 2008, 40).

Channeling "Goodfella" DeVito as much as Trump, Joe Pesci plays Grump as a mobster builder, making the residents of *Sesame Street* an offer they can't refuse (figure 10.2). Pesci's Grump begins by pitching "shiny new apartments" and the views from "the Grump Sky Café—did I mention it rotates?" and by protesting too much: "Look, I love you people! You deserve some of

Figure 10.2   An Offer They Can't Refuse: Grump (Joe Pesci) Presents Grump Tower to "The Little People." *Sesame Street All-Star 25th Birthday: Stars and Street Forever!* (1994). Screen capture.

the finer things, trust me! You won't miss all this" (*Sesame Street All-Star 25th Birthday: Stars and Street Forever!* 1994). But when the men, women, children, and Muppets of *Sesame Street* insist "*this*" is "*home*," Grump's gloves come off: "Okay, okay, that's it! I tried to be nice to you people, but you don't wanna listen. That's it, you got two weeks. Pack up and get out!" Well into the hour-long program, in an interview with reporter Kathie, Grump still condescendingly maintains, "I only want to do what's best for the people of Sesame Street—the little people—the little furry people." Grump's motives in this scene seem less philanthropic than philandering, as he charms the cameras and tells Kathie, "I always have time for a beautiful lady of the press." On and off the record, Pesci's Grump projects a predatory Trump. Grump goes beyond womanizing in a homophobic outtake in which he assaults and propositions Benny Rabbit: "Yeah, you little fag, do what you really want to do" ("Joe Pesci Assaults Muppet on Sesame Street [1994]" 2009).

ABC's *All-Star* special bolsters *Sesame Street*'s cast corps in their battle against Grump with celebrity guest reinforcements. In addition to Barbara Walters and Julia Louis-Dreyfus, Regis Philbin and Kathie Lee Gifford lend their journalistic hands while, in cameo appearances as an attorney, a "Tough Guy Helpline" operator, and the "Spirit of Hope," Corbin Bernsen, John Goodman, and Rosie O'Donnell, respectively, all share their expertise. Their ranks are further increased, via archival film clips, by a host of notables including Ray Charles, Jodie Foster, Marlee Matlin, Maya Angelou, Robin Williams, Paul Simon, and Marilyn Horne. By 1994, *Sesame Street's* regulars had expanded to include tap-dancing sensation Savion Glover and Ruth Buzzi. Older viewers may wish Buzzi would reprise one of her prior roles as "Gladys" on *Laugh-In* (1968–1973) by whipping out her purse and walloping Grump,[4] while just about everyone would enjoy watching Glover nimbly step-kick Grump to the curb; however, *Street* people and monsters tremble alike at the prospect of fighting a Goliath: "He's so rich!" "And powerful!" "And *mean*!" (*Sesame Street All-Star 25th Birthday: Stars and Street Forever!* 1994). Grump comes to *Sesame Street* slinging insults and vows to build, on 123 Sesame Street's "ruins," his "magnificent glass and steel edifice." Yet *Sesame Street* arms its Muppets with moral might. Though Grump rejects emotional appeals and dismisses one rites-of-passage montage as "cheap sentiment," the archival clips interspersed throughout the special document the power of knowing not just your numbers and letters but also when to sing, dance, laugh, hug, apologize, help, or simply look ridiculous. The last of these song-and-dance sequences takes us through the alphabet. (Without these letters, after all, we cannot spell *r-e-s-i-s-t*.) It is all the convincing Big Bird needs to conclude, "Sesame Street *is* worth fighting for! Let's let the world know how we feel about our home. Let's have a march, make a sign. Let's march on Ronald Grump!"

With their love of numbers, *Sesame Street*'s residents are readily mobilized to stand up and be counted, chiming in when Big Bird leads the cheer, "1, 2, 3, 4, Sesame Street forevermore!" It's unclear whether Grump's plans are ultimately derailed by this demonstration en masse or by Oscar's stubbornness and what Selk describes as "a deus-ex-machina twist": "Oscar reveals that his can is government property, and so Trump [*sic*] can't force him out" (2017). Along the way, there are smaller but no less instructive victories. "Chaz" (Charles Grodin) and "Bitsy" (Susan Sarandon), a wealthy-snob couple and prospective Grump penthouse tenants ("We love looking down on things"), reluctantly consider *Sesame Street*'s urban charm. Chaz finds the neighborhood "fascinating . . . it's like watching a vanishing culture PBS special" and pronounces its "cityscape . . . visually interesting in a we-the-people, wretched-refuse kind of way," but Oscar's pet worm, Slimey, puts the deal on ice by crawling on Bitsy and sending a literal chill down her spine. Benny Rabbit's first response to Grump's plan is defeatist and opportunistic: he tells Big Bird, "You can't fight City Hall" (ignoring Gordon's rejoinder, "You sure can try") and brownnoses Grump, laughing at his own expense when Grump calls him "Buckteeth" while hoping to land a job as Grump Tower's doorman. When Grump informs Benny that Grump Tower will have "a robotic doorman: no wages, no overtime, no attitude," Benny is radicalized and runs off hollering, "We've got to stop Ronald Grump! Sesame Street must be saved!" Perhaps it is Grump himself who travels the furthest distance. He finds a friend in Oscar, whom he has name-called "Fuzzball" and "Fuzzmop" throughout the program, when they discover their mutual aversion to happy endings. Grump gives Oscar a handshake and a *Casablanca* conclusion: "Oscar, this could be the start of a really rotten relationship." The full cast celebrates the global scope and staying power of a street become a "world" that is "ours for good," singing Joe Raposo's "Sing" (Borgenicht 1998, 145) in medley with Robby Merkin and Mark Saltzman's "Our Favorite Street" as their finale. Accepting defeat, even Grump joins in.

GROUCH APPRENTICES

Grump returns to *Sesame Street* in 2005 restored to Grouch-Muppet form but with a name change from "Ronald" to "Donald" and a bright orange toupee ("Grouch Apprentice" [2005] 2017) that make his resemblance to Trump unmistakable. Airing on September 28, 2005, "Grouch Apprentice" takes satirical aim less at Trump the unscrupulous developer than at Trump the celebrity CEO of *The Apprentice* (not yet two years into its 2004–2017 television run). "Grouch Apprentice" sends up many trademark features of *The Apprentice*: its Grouch contestants gather around a boardroom table laden with trash; Grump hails a taxi and (blending Oscar's and Trump's catchphrases) sends Grouch contestants "Omagrossa" and "Swampy" packing with "Scram—you're fired!" Above all the other satirical targets in this episode and beyond prior episodes featuring Grump, "Grouch Apprentice" skewers Trump's narcissism. Grump shares Trump's predilection for boasting, superlatives, and posting his name in all caps just about everywhere, including on the trash can he pops out of at the start of the show. *Sesame Street* delivers a one-two punch to Grump's notoriety: when Maria asks, "Who's Donald Grump?" unaware of his celebrity, Oscar informs her, "Donald Grump happens to have the most trash of any Grouch in the world. . . . His name is on every piece of trash in town!" Grump may be vainly flattered by Oscar and company's serenade, "Whose name equals trash, to you and to me?" but this episode trashes Trump relentlessly.

Sesame Street's "Grouch Apprentice" anticipates Trump's toxic cultural impact as Grump's Grouch contestants parrot his taunts and devolve into a table full of "nyah-nyah" chanting "deplorables"—to borrow Hillary Clinton's infamous description of Trump's base (Reilly 2016)—far too embroiled in arguing with each other to stay on task when Grump issues a challenge. One of these contestants, however, is not like the others.[5] They are bested by Elmo, Grump's best apprentice by virtue of his tireless aptitude for counting rotten fish and sorting sneakers full of holes *and* Grump's best foil by virtue of his indefatigable cheer (figure 10.3). In *Street Gang: The Complete History of "Sesame Street"*, Michael Davis describes Elmo as the "embodiment" of

Figure 10.3   Grump and Apprentice Elmo. "Grouch Apprentice" ([2005] 2017). Screen capture.

Sesame Street: "He's an exuberant, inquisitive, trusting, embracing, innocent, playful, life-affirming star" (2008, 349). Elmo is also a powerful proxy and role model for impressionable young viewers, as David Borgenicht insists in *Sesame Street Unpaved*: "He's simplicity incarnate, but he's not simple-minded. Elmo's the eternal child" (1998, 85).

In the end, Elmo and Oscar alike refuse to feed Grump's ego. When Grump rejects Elmo for being "too good," Elmo is unfazed. He's not in it for Grump's trash prizes (a neat play on "cash prizes") but for altruistic reasons—"Elmo just likes to help!"—although when Grump exclaims, "But everyone wants my trash! There must be something here you want!" Elmo mischievously grabs Grump's toupee. Oscar and Grundgetta win "Grouch Apprentice" as Grump declares them *both* the worst helpers I have ever seen," but when Grump reminds them that they must help sort his trash in order to keep their winnings ("that's the deal—remember?"), they turn Grump down: "Forget it! We're Grouches! We don't help! . . . We don't want your trash—not if we have to help. . . . Besides, it's got your name all over it. . . . We can get our own trash! . . . You better fire us." Grump refuses, so Oscar and Grundgetta turn his tagline on Grump, "Scram—you're fired!" and, wearing his spare toupee, Grump hastily gathers up his trash, hails a taxi, and leaves *Sesame Street*.

"OPEN SESAME"

The inspiration for the title *Sesame Street* and the lyrics to the program's theme song reveal a high-stakes quest for directions to "where the air is sweet" (Davis 2008, 160). As writer-producer Jon Stone recounts,

> I told Bruce [Hart] to include "Every door will open wide." This was also an oblique reference to the title of the program, embodying the idea of "Open Sesame," or the opening of the minds. More important, I insisted that the recurring theme in the lyric be "Can you tell me how to get to Sesame Street?" The opening I envisioned was one of children—real peer-group children—running happily, tumbling, playing along the way, but always intent on getting to Sesame Street, perhaps occasionally pausing to ask an adult this recurring question. (Davis 2008, 160)

Getting to Sesame Street seems all the more pressing today in light of Trump's efforts to close borders and incarcerate children who try to cross them. Christopher Lehmann-Haupt concludes his 1987 review of *Trump: The Art of the Deal* by calling it "a fairy tale." In 2018, autobiographer Trump's most memorable slogan, "Sometimes by losing a battle you find a new way to win the war," resurfaced nightmarishly on a mural in Casa Padre, a children's immigration detention center in Brownsville, Texas (Martinez 2018). In English and Spanish, Trump's winning words flank his portrait and float over a White House flying a "huge" American flag. What combative and conflicting lessons do they teach the children and Border Patrol agents converging at Casa Padre?[6]

Trump's border battle has walled him off as well, but there are signs PBS has breached Trump's barriers on at least one occasion. In a January 2, 2019, cabinet meeting during the budget standoff and government shutdown, Trump described himself watching *PBS NewsHour* while holed up and "lonely" in the White House over the holidays "just in case people wanted to come and negotiate the border security" and being pleasantly surprised by *NewsHour*'s accurate coverage of his negotiations with North Korean leader Kim Jong-un: "I was surprised, based on everything I've heard about them. I'll have to start watching PBS much more" (Barajas 2019). *Sesame Street* continues to give children avenues for empowerment. While Trump watches and tweets, Sesame Workshop has made Big Bird the mascot for its "Yellow Feather Fund," expanding its educational programming to reach refugee children worldwide (America's Charities, n.d.) and closer to home through its *Plaza Sésamo* contributions to Mexico's Children's Rights campaign (Sesame Workshop, n.d.). Sesame Workshop explains, "We started the Yellow Feather Fund as a grassroots avenue for fans and supporters to contribute—and to make a meaningful difference in the lives of children" (America's Charities, n.d.). Today's donors and tomorrow's voters may be yesterday's audience for Ronald/Donald Grump. While "rookie" bios and border murals school our youngest readers in Trump's sky's-the-limit power, *Sesame Street*'s millennials are coming of age well trained in the art of undoing the deal.

NOTES

1. "Mr. Trump" makes an additional, nominal appearance in episode 2704, first broadcast March 15, 1990, phoning in an offer to buy Mr. Hooper's store.

2. "Attorney General Announces Zero-Tolerance Policy for Criminal Illegal Entry" (Department of Justice 2018).

3. Trump didn't coin "drain the swamp" but made it his mantra beginning with a press release and a campaign speech in Green Bay, Wisconsin, on October 17, 2016 (Nazaryan 2017). Swamp-builder Ronald Grump and "Grouch Apprentice" contestant "Swampy" provide two prescient parodies decades ahead of Trump's "drain the swamp" promise.

4. For an example, see the YouTube video "*Rowan and Martin's Laugh-In*: Gladys and Tyrone" (2017).

5. Thanks and apologies to Jon Stone and Joe Raposo for this paraphrase of their classic *Sesame Street* song "One of These Things" (Davis 2008, 162).

6. Trump has adopted pedagogical tactics to stir up anti-immigrant fears. On the campaign trail and, since taking office, in speeches for events such as CPAC (the

Conservative Political Action Conference), Trump routinely recites Oscar Brown Jr.'s lyrics to "The Snake" (based on Aesop's fable "The Farmer and the Viper") despite Brown Jr.'s daughters' objections (Oppenheim 2018).

REFERENCES

Adler, Renata. (1972) n.d. "Cookie, Oscar, Grover, Herry, Ernie, and Company: The Invention of 'Sesame Street.'" *New Yorker*. Accessed June 10, 2019. https://www.new yorker.com/magazine/1972/06/03/cookie-oscar-grover-herry-ernie-and-company.

America's Charities. n.d. "The Sesame Street Yellow Feather Fund." *America's Charities*. Accessed May 1, 2019. https://www.charities.org/charities/sesame-st reet-yellow-feather-fund.

Barajas, Joshua. 2019. "Trump Says He'll 'Have to Start Watching PBS Much More.'" *PBS*. January 3, 2019. https://www.pbs.org/newshour/politics/watch-t rump-says-hell-have-to-start-watching-pbs-much-more.

Benton, Joshua. 2019. "Trump Wants to Kill Federal Funding for PBS and NPR (Again); It Won't Happen, but It's Still Damaging." *NiemanLab*. March 11, 2019. https://www.niemanlab.org/2019/03/trump-wants-to-kill-federal-funding-for-p bs-and-npr-again-it-wont-happen-but-its-still-damaging/.

Borgenicht, David. 1998. *Sesame Street Unpaved: Scripts, Stories, Secrets, and Songs*. New York: Hyperion.

Bradley, Laura. 2018. "Why Are Trump and the G.O.P. So Determined to Kill PBS?" *Vanity Fair*. February 12, 2018. https://www.vanityfair.com/hollywood/2018/02/ donald-trump-budget-pbs-public-media-spending-cuts.

Davis, Michael. 2008. *Street Gang: The Complete History of "Sesame Street"*. New York: Viking.

———. 2009. "Street Smarts." *American Way*, August 15, 2009. Reprint, *36th Daytime Emmy Awards* program, 2009, 17–20. http://cdn.emmyonline.org/day_36th_ program_telecast.pdf. Citations refer to the reprint.

Department of Justice. 2018. "Attorney General Announces Zero-Tolerance Policy for Criminal Illegal Entry." United States Department of Justice, Office of Public Affairs. April 6, 2018. https://www.justice.gov/opa/pr/attorney-general-announc es-zero-tolerance-policy-criminal-illegal-entry.

Gladwell, Malcolm. 2000. "The Stickiness Factor: *Sesame Street, Blue's Clues*, and the Educational Virus." In *The Tipping Point: How Little Things Can Make a Big Difference*, 89–132. New York: Little, Brown.

Goodfellas. 1990. Directed by Martin Scorsese. Burbank: Warner Bros.

"Grouch Apprentice." (2005) 2017. YouTube video. *Children Shows*. June 11, 2017. https://www.youtube.com/watch?v=y7Riu16AC18&t=606s.

Harris, Aisha. 2012. "When Mister Rogers Defended Public TV." *Slate*. October 5, 2012. https://slate.com/culture/2012/10/mister-rogers-senate-testimony-defending-pbs-watch-video.html.

"Joe Pesci Assaults Muppet on Sesame Street (1994)." 2009. YouTube video. *Mat Baxt*. November 24, 2009. https://www.youtube.com/watch?v=Gl3evXJqb54.

Lehmann-Haupt, Christopher. 1987. Review of *Trump: The Art of the Deal*, by Donald J. Trump with Tony Schwartz. *New York Times*, December 7, 1987.

Mahler, Jonathan. 2016. "Tenants Thwarted Donald Trump's Central Park Real Estate Ambitions." *New York Times*, April 18, 2016. https://www.nytimes.com/2016/04/19/us/politics/donald-trump-central-park-south.html.

Martinez, Gina. 2018. "There's a Mural of President Trump with an *Art of the Deal* Quote at the Shelter Housing 1,500 Immigrant Children." *Time*. June 14, 2018. http://time.com/5312226/donald-trump-mural-immigrant-kids-center/.

Mattern, Joanne. 2017. *President Donald Trump*. Children's Press Rookie Biographies. New York: Scholastic.

"Mitt Romney Loves Big Bird—Presidential Debate." 2012. YouTube video. *Wall Street Journal*. October 3, 2012. https://www.youtube.com/watch?v=Ilv3VLIGJzE.

Morrow, Robert W. 2006. *"Sesame Street" and the Reform of Children's Television*. Baltimore: Johns Hopkins University Press.

Nazaryan, Alexander. 2017. "Drain the Swamp, One Year Later: Is Trump Draining or Drowning?" *Newsweek*. October 16, 2017. https://www.newsweek.com/trump-white-house-has-become-swamp-he-promised-drain-686000.

Nganga, Kathleen, and Sarah Cornelius. 2018. "Scholastic Tells Children: Trump is Great." *Social Justice Books: A Teaching for Change Project*. June 12, 2018. www.socialjusticebooks.org/scholastic-childrens-book-on-trump/.

Oppenheim, Maya. 2018. "Daughters of Man Who Wrote 'The Snake' Tell Trump to Stop Using Poem to Smear Immigrants." *Independent*. February 27, 2018. https://www.independent.co.uk/news/world/americas/trump-the-snake-lyrics-immigration-policy-daughters-anger-us-president-a8230771.html.

Reilly, Katie. 2016. "Read Hillary Clinton's 'Basket of Deplorables' Remarks about Donald Trump Supporters." *Time*. September 10, 2016. http://time.com/4486502/hillary-clinton-basket-of-deplorables-transcript/.

"Ronald Grump Builds the Grump Tower." (1988) 2015. YouTube video. *Sesame Maniac*. March 22, 2015. www.youtube.com/watch?v=5FeyDm4vrFo&t=529s.

"Rowan and Martin's Laugh-In: Gladys and Tyrone." 2017. YouTube video. *Time Life*. May 9, 2017. https://www.youtube.com/watch?v=QQtQ4Nsja_8.

Scholastic. 2018. "A Statement from Our Chairman and CEO, Richard Robinson, about the Rookie Biography of Donald Trump." *Scholastic*. June 16, 2018. http://mediaroom.scholastic.com/press-release/statement-our-chairman-and-ceo-richard-robinson-about-rookie-biography-donald-trump.

Selk, Avi. 2017. "Trump Wants to Defund PBS. 'Sesame Street' Brutally Parodied Him for Decades." *Washington Post*. March 21, 2017. www.washingtonpost.com/news/arts-and-entertainment/wp/2017/03/20/trump-wants-to-defund-pbs-sesame-street-brutally-parodied-him-for-decades/?utm_term=.43d710308966.

Sesame Street All-Star 25th Birthday: Stars and Street Forever! 1994. Directed by Chuck Vinson. Written by Mark Saltzman. May 18, 1994. ABC.

Sesame Workshop. n.d. "Latin America." *Sesame Workshop*. Accessed May 1, 2019. https://www.sesameworkshop.org/where-we-work/latin-america.

Trump, Donald J. 1987. *Trump: The Art of the Deal*. With Tony Schwartz. New York: Random House.

Won't You Be My Neighbor? 2018. Directed by Morgan Neville. Universal City: Focus Features.

Part II

TRUMPOCALYPSE NOW

Chapter 11

Howard Jacobson's *Pussy* and the Literary Hot Take

Tim Lanzendörfer

Donald Trump is an inescapable presence in Howard Jacobson's 2017 novel *Pussy*. The novel narrates the rise of Fracassus, the heir of the Grand Duchy of Origen in the country of Urbs-Ludus, from spoiled brat to spoiled candidate for Prime Mover of All the Republics. Fracassus is, in Jacobson's non-too-subtle description—and even more so in Chris Riddell's less-subtle illustrations—a set of key memes about Trump. He has "spun gold hair" (2017a, 19), is a born misogynist (23), an inveterate Twitter user, a child and then man of "no interests" who "notices nothing" (11). "He lacks charm, he lacks looks, he lacks humour, he lack quickness, he lacks companionableness, and yet he's arrogant" (22), Fracassus's father thinks early on, and yet believes that Fracassus should, indeed would, climb, would go on "to Muck Out the Pig-Pen, seize the levers of power, and win for the House of Origen the mystical respect which had so far eluded it" (18). But, fifteen years into his life, Fracassus turns out to be anything but a born leader: "He had grown somnolent, podgy, ill-mannered and, even by his own standards, uncommunicative" (34). Faced with the crisis of turning this youth into a future leader, the Grand Duke hires two tutors to turn him into a viable future Prime Mover. As the novel progresses, we follow Fracassus as he gets taught how to tweet, falls in love with a liberal, and finally may have become—the novel isn't entirely clear about it—the Prime Mover himself. On the way to this goal—which is his father's more than his own, it must be said—Fracassus encounters a host of figures in various places: his tutors, the well-meaning former university professor, Kolskeggur Probrius, and Probrius's colleague and later lover, Dr. Yoni Cobalt; Caleb Hopsack, leader of the "Ordinary People's Party" (82), who becomes Fracassus's teacher at tweeting; Sojjourner Heminway, a radical activist who becomes the only person Fracassus ever loves, and who ends up running against him in the book-ending election for

175

Prime Mover. He crosses the Wall that separates Urbs-Ludus from its sister republics to meet the president of Gnossia and later Vozzek Spravchik, the foreign secretary, minister of home affairs, and culture secretary of Cholm, who is also a game-show host who "arm-wrestles bears" (126), and takes a short look at liberal democracy in Plasentza and discovers he does not like it. He becomes a reality television star himself, Grand Duke in his own right when his father dies, and finally begins the political campaign for Prime Mover whose end the novel leaves tantalizingly dangling.

Two things about *Pussy* are striking (at least). The first is the rapid pace in which the novel was written, published, and even translated, in the wake of Donald Trump's November 2016 election victory: "The fastest writing the British author has ever committed to print and was vomited out in the two months following the US elections" (White 2017). This genesis is well-enough documented: it was announced in newspapers as early as January 2017, and published by Jonathan Cape in April 2017; a Dutch translation was published in April 2017, an Italian one in October 2017, and a German in February 2018. This speed reflects, on the one hand, the immediacy of Jacobson's reaction. As Jacobson himself has averred, it was written in "a fury of disbelief" (Kean 2017), a literary hot take on the 2016 election and the politics beyond it.[1] Besides being a novel with a remarkably fast genesis, however, it is also one that despite what appears to be its obviousness—as William Leith (2017) points out in the *Evening Standard*'s review, "You don't have to spend any time wondering who the satire is aimed at"—also appears to defy, at least within the narrow bounds of its comedic endeavor, easy generic categorization. Leith calls it a satire; Danuta Kean (2017), with some help from Jacobson himself, says it is a "fairytale"; Mark Lawson (2017), in *The Guardian*, suggests that it is an allegory; and *The Guardian*'s Andrew Anthony (2017), somewhat complicatedly, calls it "a pastiche of the 18th-century satirical novel"—again, possibly with some input from Jacobson himself, though Jacobson himself also found that it was impossible to categorize, "this satire, this fable, this parable" (Jacobson 2017b). For most of the novel's reviewers, these terms are ways to address the overt Trump parallels which, in most reviewers' opinion, equal the novel's "raison d'être" (Scholes 2017). Whatever else it does needs to be read against its specific engagement with Trump, and the 2016 election: in such a reading, as Philip Collins (2017) of the *Times* suggests, "Fracassus is Trump, Sojjourner . . . is Hillary Clinton . . . Spravchik . . . is Vladimir Putin." But as the summary above should indicate, it is in fact quite complicated to make sense of *Pussy* as a straightforward Trump parody: Jacobson's looking-glass world has as many obvious parallels to Trump as it has obvious differences, differences which are key to understanding the novel's work. Collins suggests that it "feels . . . like a sermon to the converted"—something Jacobson is well aware of—but in many ways, this is a reading that hinges (too) strongly on foregrounding the Trump figure Fracassus, rather than the surrounding apparatus of description that highlights the workings of the world in which he acts. Several commentators on the novel have noted that for all the overtness of its satirical imagination it appears to defy an easily allegorical reading. As Lawson says, Jacobson's "caricature is confused": as the heir to a family of rulers, Fracassus seems more Clintonian than Trumpy, and while many of the more minor characters of the novel appear fully as stand-ins for real-life counterparts, others just as clearly do not. Against the backdrop of this limited availability of a straightforward reading of itself as chiefly a parody of Trump, *Pussy* emerges as something more. If we have to give it a name, *Pussy* is a satire of an age more than of a single person: of "an age grown weary of making informed judgements" (Jacobson 2017a, 15) specifically.

This, too, is a point not lost on many of the commentators (Douglas Kennedy [2017], reviewing the novel in the *New Statesman*, says that "it also captures, with chilling accuracy, the way Trumpism is a reflection of the post-literate world we increasingly inhabit"). I would like to expand somewhat on this, departing from the two observations made above: its generic malleability and its hot-take nature. In what appears to me a revealing line, Lawson in *The Guardian* suggests that Fracassus's election opponent and erstwhile love interest—another obvious incongruity between Jacobson's novel and the real world—Sojjourner Heminway is "obviously a proxy for Hillary Clinton but allocated no satire of the dynastic, personality or reputation complications of Trump's actual final opponent" (2017). Lawson, clearly, understands this as a failure of the novel, both politically and representationally: its obvious satire of Clinton is also an obviously limited, not to say bad satire, because it does not actually satirize the actual Hillary Clinton. But this may be precisely the point: Jacobson's novel thrives on its effort to make readers reflexively draw onto the "obvious" allegorical content of his characters before withdrawing this obvious allegory from them. To understand *Pussy* as allegorical means to take its often complex system of reference and non-reference seriously as an attempt, perhaps incidental, to discover a more than superficial truth about the contemporary moment. In so doing, *Pussy* reflects, too, on the allegorical mode itself. Speaking on the political use of allegory, Tara Mendola and Jacques Lezra have suggested that allegory has lately come to be a conservative mode: "Allegory is the mode of alt-news" ([2017] 2015, 2), they argue. In deconstructing allegory as such, then, *Pussy* does more than offer a "mere" satire of Donald Trump: it suggests, first, that any genuine allegorical mode must necessarily leave room for interpretation in the contemporary moment, and second, that whatever lessons are to be drawn from the rise of Trumpism must be drawn far more broadly than with easy reference to the concrete moment and mode of

Trump's own rise. Fracassus is, and is not, Donald Trump: but his story suggests how Trumps rise everywhere.

I want to pursue this argument in two ways. First, I want to relate the notion of allegory to the formal work of Jacobson's novel, suggesting that it becomes accessible as allegory in part through its immediacy of writing, and through precisely those passages that complicate easy equivalencies between the novel's characters and its external referents. This argument, that is, understands the novel's nature as a literary hot take as fundamentally productive. Reviewers have, if they have commented, been somewhat critical of the haste with which *Pussy* saw publication: as Lucy Scholes (2017) has it, "I'm inclined to wonder what the hurry was." Scholes means to suggest that Jacobson's hot take does not add significantly to what we know about Trump: the authorial desire to be in print quickly is equated with what, in a different era, Jonathan Franzen called "the burden of newsbringing" (1996, 44), a heroic version of authorship that not even Jacobson apparently subscribes to. Yet the question, if framed like that, may be wrong: the point may not be what the authorial desire was, but rather what this hurry allows us to see. As I will discuss in the first section of this chapter, we may be within our rights to see the very speed of Jacobson's response as productive of allegory, meaningfully understood.

There is, however, a corollary to this point that I want to pursue—a bit more shortly—later on: namely, the fact that such speed of publication is possible only in a particular market situation, a situation which Jacobson himself has participated in before in writing to order the second installment of Hogarth's "Hogarth Shakespeare" series, prose reimaginations of several Shakespearian plays, in his case a version of *The Merchant of Venice* entitled *Shylock Is My Name* (2016). Understanding Jacobson's role as a prestigious and commercially successful name in the literary market will form a necessary part of the first argument insofar as the novel's apparent critique of easy allegory may also be understood as a critique of what may be called a superficiality of the wider system of the literary market.

PUSSY'S ALLEGORY AND THE
AGE OF DONALD TRUMP

Pussy self-identifies as allegory and asks us to perform allegoresis, allegorical interpretation. The former it does through the overt way in which it sometimes seeks to identify its characters with real-world counterparts, and, again, not least among the different instances of this are the various paratextual suggestions that this is, chiefly, a satire on Donald Trump: the cover illustration and the frontispiece (both by Chris Riddell), both of which "clearly" are caricatures of Trump, for instance, and certainly the overt title, which asks us to recall the most infamous of pre-election Trump quotes. The latter it does precisely by the way in which its system of allegorical referents remains fundamentally irresolvable if understood as a matter of simple substitution.

The work of allegory requires some initial observations, if only to tease out the inherent complications between academic and more run-of-the-mill understandings of it. As Rita Copeland and Peter T. Struck point out, "The nature of allegorical writing is elusive" (2010, 2) and it is always intimately related to allegorical interpretation. While writers may vest their works with an allegorical load, so readers may attempt to read texts allegorically no matter what, the kind of reading for concealed truths which literary interpretation excels at. Given allegory's "often indeterminate" reference (Copeland and Struck 2010, 2), these aspects of allegory are necessarily complementary: allegorical reading must frequently do much of the heavy lifting. Fredric Jameson notes that "the allegorical spirit is profoundly discontinuous, a matter of breaks and heterogeneities" that require us not just to read whatever equivalencies allegories appear to produce "at each perpetual present of the text"—not a problem for us, now, in reading *Pussy*—but also to understand that this is a form (in Jameson's moment) now-available, and to us still perceptible as being "somehow congenial for us today" (1986, 73).[2] The allegorical mode—which may find its home in parody, satire, and any number of other textual genres—appears contemporary in a number of ways—"closer to our experience of representative politics today," as Mendola and Lezra have it ([2017] 2015, 1), suggesting that the this-for-that of contemporary elective politics, including the set of political slogans, argumentative and rhetorical displacements, and other ways in which unspoken belief in white supremacy, say, gets coded as fair anxiety for a "Great" America, is deeply allegorical itself. For Mendola and Lezra, this makes allegory a deeply problematical mode: one which appears to require the return of "heroic interpretation," in Rita Felski's doubting formulation (2015, 55), in order to unmask the actual referents of the often-innocuous allegorical cover. But this, as both Mendola and Lezra and Felski argue, also seems limited, reducing allegory (or, in Felski's case, all literature) to an always reactionary, ideologically compromised form, suitable only for the singular critical gesture of hermeneutical suspicion. Much like Felski argues for the critical practice at large, Mendola and Lezra suggest that allegory is also a necessarily positive force, one which can "help cultures struggle with the egregiously aggressive and self-destructive forms of politics the last years have brought to the fore" ([2017] 2015, 9).

Allegory, then, is tied complicatedly into the contemporary moment, both in literature and politics: on the one hand, it serves the ends of conservative and reactionary politics, and in this form, requires decoding; on the other, it serves as grounds for working through the same complex political forces.

Both of these issues speak to a third: the way in which a renewed interest in allegory is also tied to a worry about realism as a useful literary mode. As Jeremy Tambling argues, "Allegory demonstrates its substitutive nature, its inability to complete, but it also questions the adequacy of those forms of writing that it is imagined can achieve 'totality'" (2010, 168)—meaning, especially, a Lukács-derived understanding of realism. Something similar is argued by Alison Shonkwiler and Leigh Claire La Berge in their introduction to *Reading Capitalist Realism* when they note that the contemporary sway of neoliberalism signally complicates the capacity of realism to genuinely represent a social totality (2014, 16–17). They approvingly quote Jeffrey Williams's (2013) argument that the contemporary, neoliberal novel "shifts from moral allegory to a resigned realism" in which "the machinations of the powerful are no longer hidden," but rather on full, and naked, display.[3]

Against this background, when Mendola and Lezra say that "we take allegory to have replaced realism as an explicitly, even vulgarly, *political* mode" ([2017] 2015, 3), the idea of the "political" here must signal the belief in the possibility of some form of resistance: it does so, I would argue, by offering a better sense of the contemporary than realism could. I want to pick up Jameson's idea of the "national allegory" here, if in somewhat theoretically reduced and slightly shifted form. In his ground-breaking essay "Third-World Literature in the Era of Multinational Capitalism," Jameson suggests that in third-world writing, *"The story of the private individual destiny is always an allegory of the embattled situation of the public third-world culture and society"* (1986, 69). Characters' allegorical relationship to the world at large is understood by Jameson (and this is what I want to emphasize over the details of his argument for a specific class of writing) as "a form of . . . mapping of the [social] totality" (88n26). Allegory, the contemporary critical understanding has it, in what we could cobble together from the above, simultaneously resists the notion that any realistic depiction of the world can ever grasp it fully while offering a mediated, "mapped" version of precisely this totality itself.

The point of this excursion may only become clear when we return, again, to the public reactions to Jacobson's novel. To understand *Pussy* as allegorical in the way I have sketched above, especially as derived from Jameson and Tambling, "solves," as it were, several problems which commentators, including Jacobson himself, have pointed out. The first, perhaps, is the fundamental problem with writing a satire on Trump, a problem very much connected to the idea of realism as such. As Lucy Scholes (2017) has it, "The problem with any attempt to satirise Trump's improbable but very real presidency is that he's already so outrageous as to be beyond parody." If reality can trump the fictional depiction of it, if the purchase of satire is limited, then the purchase of realism is also limited: the means by which it is possible to offer a literary engagement with the rise of Donald Trump cannot be realist. It is certainly necessary to point out again that to read *Pussy* as a satire of Trump or his presidency alone is already a bit of a misreading: as Jacobson himself notes, "It's the people who are the object of the satire" (2017b), as authorially conceived, and as I will sketch out in more detail below. More expansively, however, we need not limit ourselves to this, either. I have emphasized the "critical" understanding of allegory above—and I mean this to be a term that designates the academy more than literary critics writing for newspapers—for a reason. I do so in order to set off a "better" understanding of what allegory is from the version which I have faulted Mark Lawson for, and return to the second problem with *Pussy* that critics have noted, the way in which its allegory appears to be difficult to parse. This is not the contemporary academic way of reading allegory; it is a public, faintly conservative way of doing so, in which easy equivalencies between characters and their real-life counterparts form a readily intelligible, but fundamentally simple, allegorical meaning: this is the allegory of John Bunyan's *The Pilgrim's Progress* (1678). The fundamental problem that many critics have seen with reading Jacobson's novel as allegory is best caught in the brief entry the term rates in *The Penguin Dictionary of Critical Theory*: "A successful allegory is consistent and coherent at all levels" (Macey 2001, 9). Jacobson's *Pussy* is not: it cannot easily be parsed accurately onto real-world characters. But that, I would argue, is its greatest value. Indeed, it is what I would argue makes it almost meta-allegorical: it is as much about our expectations for an allegory as it is about its chosen topic, as much about the things we think literature can do as about the things that it satirically depicts. This, too, is a relation to realism, in a way: for what Lawson is looking for is, we might say, a realistic allegory, a way to read as directly as possible from the text to the real world. Allegory is all fine and good, as long as it remains obvious: allegory *as* resigned realism, as it were. Jacobson's novel challenges this very notion: it suggests, in no uncertain terms, that what makes an allegory worthwhile is the need to interpret it, a clear acknowledgment of the form's demand on readers to come to their own conclusions about its meaning.

The second point, however, is more complex, in part because it involves the novel's own apparent—but again, not fully realized—politics. Jacobson's novel is widely, but deeply conservatively, scathing, satirizing everything from the contemporary university's liberal politics and political inefficacy (2017a, 49) to the financial market (15) to liberal democracy (137) and direct democracy (67–68), to a generalized despair for the contemporary moment:

> Technological advance that had so far outstripped any human use for it that people were sending high-definition images of their faeces to imaginary acquaintances on the moon and watching others doing the same on screens they

at all times carried in the palms of their hands. A belief in the free market of
goods and ideas that concealed a profound reluctance to trade freely in either. A
delight in what was gaudy that concealed a contempt for the wealth that made
the gaudy possible. A contempt for wealth that concealed a veneration for it. A
sense, that is to say, of universal futility and despair. (158)

Such observations function as burlesque, as Douglas Kennedy points out
(2017), but simultaneously as precisely the kind of attempt at sketching in a
social totality that is the contemporary function of allegory, exceeding con-
siderably the narrow focus on Trump that many reviews, and in interviews
Jacobson himself, highlighted. *Pussy*'s allegory is impossible to resolve
simply: indeed, even its politics are impossibly convoluted. Are the people,
"pinioned between moralists and apologists all their lives" (165), as the
novel has it, themselves righteous victims of overbearing discourses? But at
the same time, it holds these people in contempt, suggesting that Sojjourner
Heminway's decision to focus on "serious politics" is "her first mistake"
(186). And earlier, one of Fracassus's interlocutors claims that the people just
don't "know what's best for them . . . because their besetting weakness is that
they love a fraudster" (110). The decentering of Fracassus in these moments
is also a useful decentering of Trump: it requires serious engagement with the
novel's wider claim that there is a systemic problem in the world that permits
the rise of Trumpism, suggesting that Fracassus is as much a result of societal
developments as himself to blame.

    As the novel wears on, this increasingly comes to the fore. Fracassus, a
product of his upbringing and malleable under a variety of influences, remains
crude, vulgar, misogynistic, intellectually uncurious—subject of influences,
but no shaping force himself. Between the various pressures exerted on him
by his Twitter-teacher Caleb Hopsack and the glamorous Putin-soundalike
Spravchik, he becomes ever more recognizably Trumpian in his campaign
for Prime Mover, but at the same time ever less obviously his own force. In
its overt depiction of the various ways in which the world of Urbs-Ludus is
congenial to the growth of Fracassus, and Fracassus himself congenial to the
production of a political machine geared to his ascendancy, *Pussy* produces
an utterly overdetermined version of the contemporary: one which cannot
coherently explain even as it seems insistent on the idea of explanation, and
thereby allegorical of a contemporary moment (unfortunately still our own,
but certainly Jacobson's moment of writing) that similarly sought to explain,
and similarly found explanation impossible.

    This work of Jacobson's allegory is tied in interesting ways to the speed
with which Jacobson wrote the novel—indeed, its allegorical character stems
in no small way from the speed with which it was written, and for that I want
to turn a different passage, in the middle of the novel. Fracassus, in a surprise

twist, has met a woman he genuinely likes: Sojjourner Heminway, a "coat-check girl at his father's club" (2017a, 91). She is "a dark-haired feminist graduate with trousers and her own views" (91), a dire threat to Urbs-Ludus's ruling classes and, what is more, an ill fit for Fracassus. So, his mother and father stage an intervention: they note that she is "a Rational Progressivist of the School of Condorcet" before haranguing him with a survey of her progressive politics' alleged roots and history,

> starting with the *populares* of ancient Rome . . . through Rousseau, Diderot, Kant, Hegel, pausing for support at Nietzsche's attack on Hebrew Socialism—and ending up, via Marx and Lenin, with the brutal charismatic revolutionism of Castroism, the murderous, killing-them-softly quietism of Corbynism, and the blood-soaked rice fields of Pol Pot. (96)

I want to focus on the mention of Corbyn here: Andrew Anthony, reporting on an interview with Jacobson, notes first that among all the real-life contemporary politicians that appear to take their turns as characters, only Corbyn gets a mention under his own name (between Castro and Pol Pot, no less), and says of Jacobson: "He is surprised when I remind him of [the] quote. He thought he hadn't referred to any real British politicians directly" (Anthony 2017). Jacobson's answer bespeaks the haste with which the novel was produced, but also the almost unconsciously allegorical nature of his novel. On the one hand, clearly, no one saw fit to question Jacobson's use of Corbyn here in the editing process, and Jacobson did not review the manuscript carefully enough to catch it. On the other, it is also clear from this exchange that Jacobson did not, as it were, consciously write about Corbyn: the British Labour Party leader's inclusion is a slip of the typewriter. I don't mean to say that we have anything like unmediated access to the authorial stream of consciousness, and with that, to something like a "political unconscious" of the writing process itself, thanks to the speed with which it was written. But at the same time, I also mean to not wholly disavow the possibility that a literary hot take of the kind *Pussy* is allows us far more interpretative leeway, and requires more work from us, than a fully worked-out quasi-allegory might have. The authorial oversight which leaves Jeremy Corbyn in the novel is also a call to reconsider the remaining figures as more than just simple analogues of their real-world counterparts: it almost explicitly asks what the difference might be between Corbyn and Putin, between Corbyn and Hillary Clinton, that one might rate direct mention and the others are allegorized into complicated representations. From an author known for his displeasure with Corbyn, such an overt attack takes on added importance when read against the various moves to mask and alienate all the other quasi-identifiable characters. It's a moment of authorial revelation that throws into relief the work of the novel: a scathing critique of the entirety of the political and social contemporary.

BRIEFLY, *PUSSY*, THE LITERARY, THE MARKET

Reading *Pussy* requires us to take seriously the nexus between a formal matter (the writing of allegory as a critique of allegories), a conditioned response from public readers (a too-simple allegoresis), and its essential nature as what I have been calling a "hot take." I have suggested above how we may read the practice's immediacy interpretively. Let me now offer a few, tentative, thoughts about the novel's relationship with the market, and the idea of the literary, both of which, again, I want to read as inseparable from its hot-take nature. By extension, of course, given what I have said about this above, that also means that its place in the market is irreducibly part of its meaning.

The question of *Pussy*'s literariness, and more importantly of its thinking about literariness, may appear a bit off the beaten path: an explicitly Swiftian satire, expertly if speedily wrought by a recognized writer, and reviewed in all major newspapers, must immediately appear to have some cachet. This is certainly true, but *Pussy* is also interested in speaking about the question of what good literature should look like, even if it does so as ambivalently as its take on the world's politics. It does so through explicit if not sustained reference to reading as a cultural good.

Pussy includes explicit discussion of at least two readers: the first, the Grand Duchess, Fracassus's mother, in fact is said to do little but read, most especially when compared to how much time she spends with Fracassus. Yet her choices come under what appears to be sustained satirical attack.

> The leaves of her favourite novels fluttered between her fingers and as they did she could hear the wind blow through the enchanted forest. Sometimes she would turn only to turn back again, letting the pages sigh to her of danger then of rescue, rescue then of danger, back and forth. The books she loved best were printed on the finest paper, as diaphanous as fairy wings. They might float from her they were so slight. But when she snapped a volume shut she could hear the castle gates crash closed. (Jacobson 2017a, 21–22)

For the Grand Duchess, reading is both a material experience and an escape: a way to leave behind the confines of the castle within which she is stuck, and something that is sensory, rather than emotional or intellectual—"susurrating fairy stories," as the novel has it once (61). It is this kind of reading, too, which she has been hoping Fracassus would engage in: early on, the novel indicates that the Grand Duchess has asked his earliest tutors to allow him to "read about wizards and dragons like other children," which do not interest Fracassus. Defeatedly, the tutors then suggest "there is little literature of any other sort available to a person his age" (35). It is this kind of reading which the novel tells us the second explicitly identified reader engaged in, Fracassus's ill-fated but mysterious older brother Jago, whose "defection" (36) and apparent abandonment of a future as a leader in Urbs-Ludus the Grand Duchess fears is partially her fault. The Grand Duchess had "read to him of chocolate factories and magic schoolboys. His tutors had worried that he was still reading about the chocolate factories and magic schoolboys he'd loved at the age of nine or ten when he was nineteen or twenty, but Demanska Origen hadn't minded that. She was still reading about them herself" (36–37). Whatever purpose reading serves in the novel, then, it is obviously not a reading that is geared toward difficulty and literary experience, something to bear in mind, especially when the novel occasionally appears to slide into a greater critique of a failure to read as the basis of Fracassus's intellectual incapacity. When, for instance, during the first meeting with Professor Probrius, the Grand Duke comments to the Grand Duchess that Fracassus is a brute "because he doesn't read," the Duchess replies that he does read the Duke's selection of comics, after all (45). And indeed, a little later the novel picks this up. Fracassus tweets, "My mother still nagging me about reading so my father buys me a comic. *The Prince* by Mantovani" (86), in which, over a week, he manages to read one page and then gives up. The several satirical levels aside—Mantovani, a reference to a British-Italian band leader, as a confusion for Machiavelli; the idea of reading as short an essay as *The Prince* in comic-book form; and of course Fracassus's failure to even finish that—reading as such does not come off very well in this, either.

At first glance, then, the point of *Pussy*'s complaint is not about reading as such, it is about "good" reading: not Dale Carnegie or Adam Smith (authors we are told the Grand Duke reads to Fracassus [Jacobson 2017a, 60]), but not, either, the fantasy stories which clearly do form Jago's, and apparently his mother's, reading experience. *Pussy*'s fundamental and straightforward argument appears to be that in a society where all childhood reading is about fairies and dragons, and readers do not really outgrow such reading, fundamental critical and intellectual faculties cannot be developed: such reading, pure escapism, is a waste of time. But the literary politics of the novel, like much of its political argument, seems somewhat confusing. Advocates of reading *in principle*, the Grand Duke and Duchess fail to make Fracassus do it, and fail to instill in Jago the kind of reading the novel—but not the Grand Duke and Duchess—would appear to prefer, the kind of literary fiction which Jacobson's novels are themselves part of. But, complicatedly, Jago's abandonment of his family, read against what happens to heirs to the Grand Duchy in Fracassus's case, appears to be understandable as a good choice.

The Grand Duchess's worry that her choice of reading material for Jago had played a part in it, that fantasy had motivated Jago to escape, in a way the Grand Duchess can't, suggests that it has a positive role to play, even if that positive role is not positive to the Grand Duchess. Indeed, the novel never quite spells out what should be so terrible about reading this kind of fiction; rather, it appears to assume a more general, civilization-critical stance that it never manages to solidify into a clear argument for any kind of fiction. In part, the novel seems confused because it abandons much of this subplot as it reaches its half-way point: its late references to Jago as voting for Fracassus's opponent and to their mother in her reading room (189) are not tied to a sustained engagement with the question of (fiction) reading, and again appear to ask us to consider what exactly should be deplorable about fantasy literature when it produces voters for Sojjourner Heminway. Like most everything else in the novel, then, genre reading is tapped as an apparent marker of cultural decline whose final purpose within the novel is more complicated.

The uneasy relationship between different value regimes of reading may also speak to Jacobson's own position in the literary market. Jacobson, a comic novelist first and foremost, became a "literary" writer very much in the wake of winning the Man Booker Prize in 2010 for his novel *The Finkler Question*. As Jeremy Rosen (forthcoming) points out, the simple conjunction "Man Booker Prize winner Howard Jacobson" now names a "brand in the literary market place," one identified not merely with a particular writer and his oeuvre, but with the recognition of the entire literary establishment. There can be little doubt that *Pussy*'s publication process is possible only because Jacobson is one of those "esteemed contemporary writers," and indeed perhaps one of the "canonical literary authors" whose "brands" make possible the expectation of sales very much no matter what (Rosen, forthcoming). Indeed, *Pussy* rides on this expectation doubled, since it must also bank on the belief that a literary readership, or perhaps even more precisely, Jacobson's usual readership, is unlikely to include Trump voters, and for them, a Trump satire (which the title page, again, clearly suggests *Pussy* is) by Jacobson, in the wake of the traumatizing 2016 election, is a far more certain purchase than any other random novel. Jacobson's name makes the novel possible as an object in the world: a literary hot take that can, as it were, only ever be "literary," with all the cachet that the notion brings with it.[4] But at the same time, Jacobson's relationship to the idea of the "literary" is uneasy. He is, for example, one of the writers recruited to write for the Hogarth Shakespeare series: a hack, indeed one who ended up, by some reporting, forced to write his Shakespeare novel, *Shylock Is My Name*, a take on *The Merchant of Venice*, despite having preferred other texts (Alter 2015)—a patently straightforward effort on the part of Hogarth to associate one of the best-known writers on Jewish life with the play best known for being about a Jew.

This is not to denigrate Jacobson's writing—either in *Shylock Is My Name* or in *Pussy*—or to suggest that in writing to order, and in writing to an immediately obvious market such as *Pussy*'s, he abandons some mystical notion of literary autonomy. Rather, I want to think through what *Pussy*'s relation to the literary market can tell us about the novel, especially against the backdrop of the novel's own engagement with less highbrow forms of fiction and reading. And this means to highlight again the uncertain footing of its own position, very much as with its allegorical take on Trump. *Pussy* is already generically suspect, as we have seen; and one of the things it might be, and one of the few things that it is authorially argued to be, is a "fairytale" (Kean 2017), a "moral fable" (Jacobson 2017b) in the vein of Swift or Samuel Johnson. But being a fairy tale, of course, highlights again the generic difficulty with which Jacobson has to cope: How is this different from the fairy stories of the Grand Duchess, after all? What relation does *Pussy* have to the escapism of the Grand Duchess's reading—or to Jago's physical escape from the confines of a future in the Origen family? *Pussy*, again, is not sure: it simultaneously recognizes its tenuous position as a marginally literary, marginally useful text, even as it avows for itself greater ability to work in the world. But as far as the market is concerned, it is also not really a fairy tale: nothing in its paratext suggests anything of the sort. The market pitch for *Pussy* is for a novel-satire of Trump—a description of a version of *Pussy*, but perhaps not the best. There is, then, a fundamental contradiction between the various things *Pussy* tries to be, authorially and as a product for the market, that mirrors its formal, text-internal contradictions.

What remains is the point that Jacobson's hot-take novel is very much conditioned by his previous success, by the recognition that as a writer, he is a saleable brand; but also that he understands himself as in competition with other, similarly saleable writers. As he confessed to Sophie Gilbert, "I actually imagined that all across the English-speaking world, other novelists were writing books similar to this, getting it off their chests, out of their systems" (Jacobson 2017b). Jacobson, clearly, may not see this as a commercial decision—does not, indeed could not, suggest that his writerly hurry was in part an attempt to write and publish, as the interview's title announces it, "the first Trump-era novel" (Jacobson 2017b)—but I think we need to take the hint. Between the possibility of writing a hot take (which, arguably, is open to anybody) and the strictures of the market, the extensive publicity campaign to which the various interviews and newspaper and magazine reviews and pre-review reports speak, *Pussy* is a novel for the market: a novel for a market that only has a market when it is a hot take. But in as much as it is this hot-take nature that makes it interpretatively useful, an accidentally successful allegory, we may go so far as to claim that it is the market's strictures that produce a commercially and literarily viable product-artwork. To all of this, the novel's nature as a hot take is crucial.

CONCLUSION

Allegory, if what I have argued above makes any sense, is certainly the form which best describes the relationship between *Pussy* and the real world; but it is barely an allegory *of* anything in particular. It is an allegory *as*, specifically, an allegory as totality of the post-election moment: a moment of a deep desire to explain and a deep impossibility to obtain explanations, a moment in which it was not even possible to fully grasp what was to be explained. In so being, it is also a take on the idea of simple political explanation, suggesting that our collective desire for explanation will shape our reaction to the provision of an open allegory. We may easily imagine the culture-in-crisis moments of the narrative, the despair over identity politics, dumbed-down universities, people reading fantasy, and other marks of (cultural) upper-class disdain and nostalgia to be an authorial take, of course: Jacobson's own stance, as it were. But that is neither here nor there: the novel is more complicated than that, offering in its very indeterminacy, and in its being read as far more simple-minded than it itself is, an allegorical take on the impossible moment of Trump, a working-through of everything about the contemporary situation that may have played a role in his rise. Everything else, it leaves to the reader, mocking him only when he turns to simple answers.

Much of this, like the novel itself, may seem unsatisfying. The politics of *Pussy* are, at times, desperately astute; at others, they sound eerily like the nostalgic yearning for a better, more cultured past—one without smartphones or 140-character policy statements, with student populations willing to be intellectually challenged and voters willing to make considerate choices based on the public weal. What redeems this potential jeremiad is the fact that it does not make this point consistently, that it meanders easily between readings of the people as dupers and duped, between the possibility of reading it beyond simple cause-and-effect declension narratives, to become a complex, and timely, allegorical take on the present. Indeed, it is a deeply challenging allegory: *Pussy* plays with the convention of allegory, and readers attempting to find easy equivalencies are themselves part of the joke. But it is also an accidental allegory: an allegory whose full force stems from what we may suggest is the fundamentally rushed working through that it provides. It is a literary hot take on a desperately complicated political situation, one which, with greater time for reflection, Jacobson might have been able to shape more carefully into an allegory of the sort many reviewers expected, one in which the substitutions of one character for one real-world analogue are easier to accurately parse. But that is not the book we have; what we have, instead, is a confused mess of a book that leaves us no wiser, and only horrifiedly amused. In this, at the very least, it is an obviously successful literary registration of the totality of the post-2016 moment.

NOTES

1. Not, incidentally, the only one: Scott Kenemore's *Zombie-in-Chief: Eater of the Free World; A Novel Take on a Brain-Dead Election* was published in August 2017, and features a recognizable Donald-Trump-like zombie winning election, despite being revealed to be a zombie, to the presidency.

2. Indeed, the fact that allegory is always pointing at something different from what is obviously there appears to involve it immediately in the very contemporary debate around the value and valence of surface reading, and of critique.

3. See Jaclyn Partyka's chapter in the present volume for discussion of Salman Rushdie's *The Golden House* in terms of questions about the value of realism in the contemporary "post-truth" moment.—Ed.

4. A point reinforced, rather than counteracted, by a return to my earlier reference to Scott Kenemore's *Zombie-in-Chief* (2017). While this novel may appear to argue for the possibility of many Trump hot takes to be published by any writer, within the limited canon of zombie fiction, and for his publisher, Talos, Kenemore may be a Jacobson-analogue of sorts, a ready sale where other—and, especially, new—authors would not be. The one caveat that would appear to work here, is that overall, zombie fiction's readership is liable to be more conservative than Jacobson's readership.

REFERENCES

Alter, Alexandra. 2015. "Novelists Reimagine and Update Shakespeare's Plays." *New York Times*. October 5, 2015. https://www.nytimes.com/2015/10/06/books/novelists-reimagine-and-update-shakespeares-plays.html.

Anthony, Andrew. 2017. "Howard Jacobson: 'Trump in the White House—That Must Never Feel Normal.'" *Guardian*, April 2, 2017. https://www.theguard ian.com/books/2017/apr/02/howard-jacobson-pussy-interview-trump-in-white-ho use-must-never-feel-normal.

Collins, Philip. 2017. Review of *Pussy*, by Howard Jacobson. *Times* (London). April 8, 2017. https://www.thetimes.co.uk/article/pussy-by-howard-jacobson-wtr6g 9xm9.

Copeland, Rita, and Peter T. Struck. 2010. Introduction. *The Cambridge Companion to Allegory*, edited by Rita Copeland and Peter T. Struck, 1–11. Cambridge: Cambridge University Press.

Felski, Rita. 2015. *The Limits of Critique*. Chicago: University of Chicago Press.

Franzen, Jonathan. 1996. "Perchance to Dream." *Harper's*, April 1996, 35–54.

Jacobson, Howard. 2017a. *Pussy*. London: Jonathan Cape.

———. 2017b. "*Pussy*, the First Trump-Era Novel, Is a Brutal Satire." Interview by Sophie Gilbert. *Atlantic*. May 9, 2017. https://www.theatlantic.com/entertainment/archive/2017/05/howard-jacobson-pussy-donald-trump-brexit/525852/.

Jameson, Fredric. 1986. "Third-World Literature in the Era of Multinational Capitalism." *Social Text*, no. 15, 65–88.

Kean, Danuta. 2017. "Howard Jacobson Writes Donald Trump Novella *Pussy* in 'a Fury of Disbelief.'" *Guardian*. January 24, 2017. https://www.theguardian.com/books/2017/jan/24/howard-jacobson-writes-donald-trump-novella-pussy.

Kenemore, Scott. 2017. *Zombie-in-Chief: Eater of the Free World; A Novel Take on a Brain-Dead Election*. New York: Talos.

Kennedy, Douglas. 2017. "Ode to a Philistine: Howard Jacobson's *Pussy*." *New Statesman*. April 26, 2017. https://www.newstatesman.com/culture/books/2017/04/ode-philistine-howard-jacobsons-pussy.

Lawson, Mark. 2017. "*Pussy* by Howard Jacobson Review—Quickfire Satire of Trump." *Guardian*. April 13, 2017. https://www.theguardian.com/books/2017/apr/13/pussy-howard-jacobson-review-trump.

Leith, William. 2017. Review of *Pussy*, by Howard Jacobson. *Evening Standard*. April 13, 2017. https://www.standard.co.uk/lifestyle/books/pussy-by-howard-jacobson-review-a3515046.html.

Macey, David. 2001. *The Penguin Dictionary of Critical Theory*. London: Penguin.

Mendola, Tara, and Jacques Lezra. (2017) 2015. "Introduction: Allegory and Political Representation." *Yearbook of Comparative Literature*, no. 61, 1–9.

Rosen, Jeremy. Forthcoming. "Shakespeare Novelized: Hogarth, Symbolic Capital, and the Literary Market." In *The Novel as Network: Literary Form, Idea, Commodity*, edited by Tim Lanzendörfer and Corinna Norrick-Rühl. Basingstoke: Palgrave Macmillan.

Scholes, Lucy. 2017. "*Pussy* by Howard Jacobson Review: The Problem with Satirising Trump's Improbable Presidency Is That He's So Outrageous as to Be Beyond Parody." *Independent*. April 12, 2017. https://www.independent.co.uk/arts-entertainment/books/reviews/pussy-howard-jacobson-book-review-a7679821.html.

Shonkwiler, Alison, and Leigh Claire La Berge. 2014. "Introduction: A Theory of Capitalist Realism." In *Reading Capitalist Realism*, edited by Alison Shonkwiler and Leigh Claire La Berge, 1–25. Iowa City: University of Iowa Press.

Tambling, Jeremy. 2010. *Allegory*. The New Critical Idiom. London: Routledge.

White, Hilary A. 2017. "Seething Satire of Trump's Rise." *Independent.ie*. April 16, 2017. https://www.independent.ie/entertainment/books/book-reviews/seething-satire-of-trumps-rise-35621409.html.

Williams, Jeffrey J. 2013. "The Plutocratic Imagination." *Dissent*. Winter 2013. https://www.dissentmagazine.org/article/the-plutocratic-imagination.

Chapter 12

"Terminal Stupidity"

Graft Zeppelin and Trump Sky Alpha

Bruce Krajewski

Why does Mark Doten's *Trump Sky Alpha* (2019) matter?[1] In assessing the novel in the Age of Trump, Ali Smith declares, "The novel matters because Donald Trump" (2017, 40). *Trump Sky Alpha* is a novel from a genre—satire, so it makes sense on the topic of mattering also to turn to Justin E. H. Smith's "Why Satire Matters" (2015). If Smith is correct, "Satirists detest the present age, not only in view of the horrible people in power, but also in view of the plainly unimpressive record of all of us who have failed to do anything about it." That unimpressive record applies to the characters in *Trump Sky Alpha*. The novel's narrator admits that the characters missed the moment for successful rebellion: "There might have been a chance, once, to resist, there must have been, but that moment was lost somewhere, it had slipped away—where had all the little moments been? there must have been so many chances to not be where we were—but this is where we were" (22). Ultimately, however, Doten the satirist uses his novel to move satire outside Smith's frame.

Trump Sky Alpha bends to the Zeitgeist, ordaining the global internet as the novel's main malefactor, displacing perhaps the more popular choice, Donald Trump.[2] As the novel has it, Trump is a consequence of the global internet: "Trump is a symptom of the internet, of American sickness on the internet" (Doten 2019, 65). Like Google itself, we internet users couldn't live up to a code of conduct as simple as "Do No Evil!" We might as well have been given paradise and told we could have paradise forever as long as we didn't touch that one fruit on that tree over there.

Doten's novel suggests that Trump is not the worst that the "American sickness" with the internet has in store for us: *The universe has been fine-tuned for the internet in its forty years to set the conditions of totalization to make the world's end possible. To circumvent the controls of the bilateral mutually assured destruction through distribution, through the insertion of the network into everything*" (Doten 2019, 39). Instead of anticipating the apocalypse heading toward us with the spread of the global internet, academics, librarians, and businesspeople embrace Second Life, Amazon, distributed networks, cryptocurrencies, maker culture, and the Internet of Things as harbingers of a glorious, politically enlightened, future. Some think paradise is just on the other side of the motherboard. *Trump Sky Alpha* speaks to an audience "who saw the internet as a new utopian space that would . . . usher in new forms of being, or restore the old ways we'd lost" (30). It's only after the apocalypse in the novel that one of the characters, Rachel, realizes she has been wrong about the internet: "I should have spent less time on the internet while I still had my girls. . . . Less here in this noise, more time with those people I had loved" (101).

As touching as it sounds, that bleak lesson from Rachel isn't going to sell books. We need cray-cray, explosions, war, drama, intrigue, bombast. Enter Trump Sky Alpha, the zeppelin. Let's address the zeppelin in the room, the dirigible stalking Mark Doten's novel, which is as unforgettable as the worst line in cinema history from *Southland Tales* (2007): "Move to the rear of the Mega-Zeppelin!" Doten's perfecto-cigar-shaped airship is unmissable as a vehicle for surplus meaning in *Trump Sky Alpha*, beyond associations to Germans with visions of world domination dancing in their heads. Remember "tenor and vehicle" from Lit 101 in high school. Our author knows about metaphors. One of Doten's characters says, *"There is so much metaphor"* (2019, 202). That line could have been a publicity blurb for this book.

Readers won't need Freud to figure out the dirigible's symbolism, any more than Richard Klein's *Cigarettes Are Sublime* (1993) is required to understand the linkage between sex and cigars/cigarettes. If you've seen the film *Now, Voyager*, with Bette Davis smoking up a storm, you'll get it; you can't help but get it. It's in your face, that smoke, that meaning, from the cigarette.[3]

Freud cautioned his readers not to place too much trust in universal symbols, so it seems important to attend to the specific context of *Trump Sky Alpha* and its airship that seats 224 at a starting price of $50,000 (Doten 2009, 5). It's a vehicle for graft of epic proportions, with price increases designed to appeal to the wealthy's lust for exclusivity and branding. Thus, the ticket price on the zeppelin jumps with "ultradeluxe packages" like meals that feature "lobsters with **TRUMP** embossed on tail fin and right claw" (5).[4]

Trump Sky Alpha is published by an esteemed press in Minneapolis, where much of the novel's action takes place. The origin of the zeppelin also has roots in Minnesota. Ergo, when anyone wishes to construct the mise-en-scène for the history of transportation, the Midwest figures prominently. Orville Wright was born in Ohio, and he and his brother opened their bicycle shop in Dayton where they sold "Wright Flyers." Before the Wright Brothers, military men in the Civil War began using balloons for reconnaissance. That activity captured the imagination of Count Ferdinand von Zeppelin, who made his way as a German military man to the United States during the Civil War to participate in balloon exercises at Fort Snelling in St. Paul, Minnesota. In fact, Zeppelin's first balloon ride was at Fort Snelling around 1863, according to the 1931 biography of Zeppelin by Margaret Goldsmith (45). In a 1915 newspaper article in the *St. Paul Pioneer Press* Zeppelin describes his experience: "I contracted for several hundred cubic feet of gas, all that the St. Paul Gas Works would let me have. I arose to a height of several hundred feet but the gas was of such poor quality that I could not attempt a long flight. But it was while over St. Paul in the balloon that the idea came to me that successful dirigible flights could be made" (Goldsmith 1931, 46). Zeppelin took what he learned in St. Paul back to Germany, specifically to Lake Konstanz. The hangar for the first zeppelin was almost directly across the lake from where the University of Konstanz now stands, near Friedrichshafen, on the eastern shore of the lake. There with a group of engineers and other helpers, Count Zeppelin designed and put together the first zeppelin that had its initial flight in 1900 above the lake, lined with curious locals waiting to see what the "crazy count" had done (Goldsmith 1931, 96–113).

The zeppelin's military genesis played a key role in its survival as a form of transportation. Zeppelin, an aristocrat, exhausted his own considerable funds on the initial prototypes, the materials, and the employees needed to get the project off the ground. A career military person, Zeppelin exploited his military and governmental connections to persuade Germany's leaders to finance more airships. The persuasion worked only because Germany's leaders foresaw the advantages such airships would have in war. Those working in the literary realm around that time did not miss the decisive strategic importance of air power, such as H. G. Wells in 1908 with *The War in the Air*.

Adhering to this history linking airships and the military, which could easily include drone warfare, Doten has the US military controlling *hors scène* Trump's zeppelin, until Trump, after a smack to Mike Pence's face that floors Pence and briefly paralyzes the onlookers at the White House, boards the zeppelin alone as the Third World War is about to break out. Trump escapes his handlers and manages to get on the zeppelin when no one else is there. Trump resides on the zeppelin "for the duration of his presidency" (Doten 2019, 7), floating between New York City and Mar-a-Lago. The narrator ridicules those who try to stop Trump's escape: "Three more agents actually grabbing onto mooring cables as the zeppelin lifted off, struggling up their respective cables for a few seconds before plummeting to their deaths like losers—and that's what they were, *total losers*—Trump in his glassed-in enclosure firing off a few quick tweets ('Happy to be flying back to NYC! Beautiful night! Fake News Media WRONG as usual!!!')" (11).[5] Doten has Trump's topoi, cadences, and punctuation down. Doten has mastered Trumpspeak. The first Trump-centric section of the novel dazzles.

A key moment in the first section (subsequent chapters are devoted to other characters) is Ivanka's reaction in Columbus Circle to casualties in a nuclear attack—some members of her family. This episode raises brilliantly the satire's stakes by putting flesh on what could have been a haute couture cartoon character. That scene of Ivanka in grief alters the emotional dynamic, and introduces a powerful question: Will the father (Trump) turn against the daughter (Ivanka)? "It was after Ivanka went on TV, after she said *No*, after she said *no no no*, after the first small and very restrained US nuclear launch, and Trump wouldn't say a word, the screens all showed her kneeling or crouching there, vomit running down her blouse, and he was silent, which they realized later was a warning, a sign of things to come" (Doten 2019, 8). The fictional fireworks in the first chapter almost guarantee that the subsequent sections seem monochrome by comparison, despite a *Clockwork Orange + Pi* scenario later in the novel with a character called Birdcrash. Anyone could have guessed that Trump's zeppelin would suck all the air out of the book's room, degrading in several senses the story's other elements.

Still, the opening section with the president permits Doten to make hay with the imagery connected to Trump's zeppelin. The zeppelin transforms Trump into a celestial figure, with "the people of America pointing up, saying things like *Wow* and *Look, Dad*" (Doten 2019, 7). Doubtless Doten knows the opening images of *Triumph of the Will*, with Hitler, god-like, descending from the clouds in a plane that lands among adoring masses in Nuremberg (Sennett 2014, 51). Similarly, it's no accident that Count Zeppelin was honored by the people of Konstanz with a monument depicting him as Icarus, figure of high-flying ambition. The philosopher Slavoj Žižek notes the same spatial phenomenon taking place in São Paulo, "which boasts 250 heliports in its central downtown area. To insulate themselves from the dangers of mingling with ordinary people, the rich of São Paulo prefer to use helicopters." For Žižek, it's like "*Blade Runner* or *The Fifth Element*, with ordinary people swarming through the dangerous streets down below, whilst the rich float around on a higher level, up in the air" (Žižek 2009, 5).

While the zeppelin casts a shadow over the novel's other themes, Doten keeps topics and themes intertwined, if only by association. Icarus, Birdman, Birdcrash, flying things, missiles, birds, tweets, the Aviary. The narrative apart from Trump involves an intensive effort by military and government officials to use journalists to hunt down a crucial password, supposedly known by the character Birdcrash. The government officials give Rachel, a journalist, access to a working archive of the internet's remnants, where she uncovers references to a little-known book by a man named Sebastian de Rosales who inspired a shadowy hacktivist group called the Aviary. That group has a role in the internet's downfall, an outage that lasts for several days and seems to precipitate the first nuclear strike. The Aviary has a strong interest in the enigmatic presence of a figure known only as Birdcrash. Rachel tracks down Birdcrash and learns from him that the lulz had more meaning to the hacktivists than activities that supported the common good. As part of her investigation, Rachel is reminded of an interview she did with de Rosales. In the interview, de Rosales confesses he doesn't see an alternative to capitalism, because the internet serves capitalism's consumptive nature: *"Everything* has to be consumed, that's the logic of capitalism, and that's the same logic that's accelerated by the internet" (Doten 2019, 121).

The tone in the passages above appears less satirical than flatly descriptive. As the *Onion* discovered, the gap separating reality and satire has mostly evaporated. Nonetheless, Doten's reputation is as a satirist, and much of the advance publicity for this book sought to reinforce that view. Doten's book comes from a press with the self-declared mission "to foster new thinking about what it means to live in the world today" ("Graywolf Press," n.d.). Satire isn't meant to be explanatory; it aims for change. Satire's capacity as a weapon for political change has a recent troubling history, starting with Hugo Rifkind's influential February 2017 piece in the London *Times*, "Laugh All You Like but Satire Changes Nothing," the essence of which is in the subheader: "Liberals need to realise that however good they make them feel, comedy sketches about Trump are self-indulgent." The month before Rifkind's essay appeared, *McSweeney's* published Jeff Loveness's "This is the Political Satire That Finally Stops Trump," a self-defeating piece about the futility of satire. Loveness's narrator goes to the White House to meet Trump:

> "Well, 'Mr. President,' you may have outsmarted everyone else, but there's one thing you forgot about."
> " . . . The power of comedy. How could I have been so blind?" (Loveness 2017; ellipsis in the original)

Loveness wants to hurl a cream pie into the face of people who imagine that satire has any impact on Realpolitik. Despite Rifkind and Loveness, producers of satire, like Doten, persist.

Doten's book belongs to the growing genre of Trumplit, which runs from the Swiftian exemplar that is Howard Jacobson's *Pussy* (2017) to writer Jill Twiss and illustrator E. G. Keller's *A Day in the Life of Marlon Bundo* (2018) to John Lanchester's *The Wall* (2019) to the comedian Elijah Daniel's 2016 gay erotica contribution, "Trump Temptations: The Billionaire & the Bellboy," containing lines like: "His gorgeous ass flapped behind him like a mouthwatering stack of pancakes in his pants. My hunger for pancakes had never been stronger" (Daniel n.d.). Jacobson's prose strikes less a RuPaul pose, and more a posh literary stance, suitable for the classroom. Elijah Daniel's work, which he seems to have disowned after its surprising success, eschews the subtleties and allegorical window dressing of *The Wall* for a full-frontal assault on the coarse linkages among lust, money, politics, and power.

While Rifkind and Loveness insist on satire's failures, they do not seem to be addressing the kind of satire offered by Elijah Daniel. This difference seems akin to Žižek's point in *Absolute Recoil* about what is revealed during what Ivana Novak and Jela Krečič describe as "a collapse into mere vulgarity" (quoted in Žižek 2014, 293). Žižek's example comes from Ernst Lubitsch's *Ninotchka* (1939), a scene that turns away from "an exemplary case of sophisticated Hegelian humor" (Žižek 2014, 293) toward the moment a character (Leon) in the film "falls on his ass in the most embarrassing and clumsy way" (Novak and Krečič quoted in Žižek 2014, 293). The political success of this "exemplary instance of what Lacan calls 'subjective destitution'" (Novak and Krečič quoted in Žižek 2014, 293) is to expand the laughing audience, as happens in *Ninotchka*. Ninotchka's laugh is not "the laughter of wisdom," the conformist laughter that comes from appreciating sophisticated satirical points in a clever joke, but "a laughter into which we fall," a laughter of solidarity in which everyone in the restaurant participates when Leon leans a little too far back and crashes (Žižek 2014, 294).

Doten's satiric contribution to Trumplit suggests a third way between Jacobson and Daniel, a way satire can offer more than an all-or-nothing prospect, either a form of performance able to shame politicians into conformity or a delusional and futile, if entertaining, exercise in significant political reform. Georg Lukács, the famed Hungarian literary critic and philosopher, worked out satire's third possibility. A fine description of what Lukács had in mind appears in an article entitled "Anticapitalist Affect" by Jakob Norberg:

> Lukács assigns a political function to the affect, informed by his Marxist conception of class struggles in history. The politically oriented satirist, he claims, discerns the unsustainable character of society with perfect clarity and detects its corruption through the medium of a hatred that nobody and nothing can mitigate. To hate means to be clear-eyed and focused on unavoidable political battles, and to write satire is to attack society explicitly and publicly, an enterprise that can only be strengthened by hate. Satire animated by hate can function as a vehicle of revolution. (2018, 156)

Satire can foreground the anxiety of the seeming impossibility of intervention, much as Doten's novel underscores that sense—"There must have been so many chances to not be where we were" (2019, 22). Think of hate as the fuel for overcoming Newton's first law of political inertia—citizens who have stayed at rest continue to do nothing. Readers might recoil from anyone endorsing hate, especially given the recent attention to hate speech, and the policing of social media for anything that deviates from civil discourse. It will have to be *our* hate, however. As Doten points out in *Trump Sky Alpha*, *"We love his [Trump's] hate"* (104). The end of Trump's hate, as the novel has it, is dire: *"Trump . . . the most hated man in the history of the world, hated twenty-four hours a day by more living humans than anyone has ever been hated by, is ending the world that hates him"* (104). Doten's spotlight on what more there is to hate about Trump and his politics expands the audience that should be fed up, that wants its hate to energize change before Trump's hate achieves its goals, one of which seems to be a perpetual state of mutual hostility. This key feature of Doten's novel, an inflation of what should be despicable and a call to would-be despisers to insert themselves into a cause propelled by the hatred of hate, means Doten has entered a territory within satire for which Rifkind and Loveness lack an account, rooted as their views are in a kind of satire suitable to a court jester, the singular outsider (not a collective movement) *approved by the authorities* to mock vices, incompetent rulers, and so on. Often the jester's role reminds everyone of the artist's subservience to the ruler. The jester performs to relieve tension, and to "humanize" the people with power and position, not do away with them in favor of egalitarianism (Otto 2001, 262).[6]

Early in *Trump Sky Alpha*, Rachel complains that "things in the world over which I had no control were taking on too much meaning" (Doten 2019, 33). This is the end point of Hans Blumenberg's insight: "Perhaps we should cultivate not only a rage at the meaninglessness of the world, but also a bit of fear in the face of the possibility that some day it could be replete with meaning" (2010, 55). My sense is that Doten might agree to switch the verbs in Blumenberg's quotation: we should fear meaninglessness, and rage that the world is replete with meaning. Replete with meaning describes Doten's novel well. There is so much metaphor. Rachel is a character, who, for example, ponders "the symbolism of Renaissance paintings" (Doten 2019, 33), making her a suitable pursuer of puzzles and internet conspiracy theories.

In a review of Agatha Christie's work, John Lanchester (2018) juxtaposes the prose and handling of characters among Christie, Margery Allingham, and Dorothy Sayers. Lanchester describes Christie's prose as "flat and functional" compared to her rivals. That phrasing fits Doten's characters (except for Trump, of course, who is conjured via mimesis, and Doten can do mimesis as well as Stephen Colbert). What compensates for "flat and functional" characters in Doten's novel is Doten's capacity for summoning an emotional attachment by choosing brief visceral episodes, scenes in which dramatic and vivid things happen to *his* characters that then make them *my* characters.

For example, Rachel is taken prisoner by a source she hunted down for her internet humor story. A power drill is involved, which compelled me earlier to mention *Pi*. What happens to Rachel isn't akin to the Ramsay Bolton torture scenes in *Game of Thrones*, but it is memorably gruesome and extended.

As sometimes happens in high-concept satire, complex character development takes a back seat to big-picture ideas—the role of the internet in our lives, global politics, the internet as a tool of capitalists, the siren song of esotericism, one or another pending apocalypse. To gauge how high the satirical concepts are in this case, readers can turn to the acknowledgments, where Doten cites, among others, Fredric Jameson (Doten 2019, 287). Jameson's view of allegory, explicitly attached to ideology, "The construction and constitution of individual subjectivities and their susceptibility to *revolutionary change*" (2019, xi; my emphasis), performs a key interpretive function for Doten's novel. Allegory is a means for reenacting the premise that "the human adventure is one" (Jameson 1981, 19).[7] Jameson's take on allegory gives readers the tools to gloss one of the rhetorical triumphs in *Trump Sky Alpha*, Trump's unsettling Heron of Alexandria dream, which appears toward the end of the novel, and counts as a prime example of Doten's modus operandi: "I dreamed of Heron of Alexandria, who boiled his daughter's body and chopped up the corpse into little bits, and he made a fabulous new family of clockwork and bone and gold, and set it free in the world" (Doten 2019, 264).[8] Doten has placed two pages earlier a gloss on this dream worthy of Greek mythology (the story of Cronus): "A father could cut open his daughter or really just open like a door in her side and find the beauty inside, and find that everything is gold in there, like clockwork. They say a king touches his food and it becomes gold, and he can't eat it, but I can. I can eat gold" (262).[9] Respectability might call for Ivanka's "*no no no*." But, as writerly figuration, this dream is gold.[10]

NOTES

1. The quotation "terminal stupidity" comes from Doten (2019, 86). A version of this chapter first appeared in the *Cleveland Review of Books*.
2. Doten avoids the frequent mistake of resorting to individualism as a means for explicating an enormously complex political period. As a historian of National Socialism, Tim Mason, warns, "Methodological individualism simply cannot work as a way of giving a coherent account of social, economic and political change. . . . 'Hitler' *cannot* be a full or adequate explanation, not even of himself" (1995, 219). Likewise, "Trump" is not an adequate explanation of the current political crisis in the United States.
3. See also Lynn Barber's "I Smoke, Therefore I Am" (2006).
4. It happens that a membership at Mar-a-Lago doubled to $200,000 after Trump's election, so Doten's attention to profiteering by a president barely counts as fiction. See Robert Frank, "Mar-a-Lago Membership Fee Doubles to $200,000" (2017).

5. For the importance of Twitter to Trump's presidency, it's important to recall Trump's own claim that he wouldn't have won the presidency without Twitter, which led the co-founder of Twitter to apologize for having made Trump's presidency possible. See Avi Selk, "Twitter Co-founder: I'm Sorry if We Made Trump's Presidency Possible" (2017). Furthermore, Brian Ott and Greg Dickinson assert, "We are willing to . . . say that Trump's manner of speaking and Twitter's underlying logic, as a modality or medium of communication, are virtually homologous." See Brian Ott and Greg Dickinson, *The Twitter Presidency: Donald J. Trump and the Politics of White Rage* (2019, 59).

6. See Steven Rosendale and Laura Gray-Rosendale's chapter in the present volume for a reading of Showtime's animated series *Our Cartoon President* as a Trump satire that serves this "humanizing" function.—Ed.

7. Allegory's and, in general, literature's interactions beyond the individual are also emphasized in *Allegory and Ideology*: "Ideology . . . as that intersection between the biological individual and the collective which is at stake in thinking" (Jameson 2019, xiii). Of course, not everyone agrees with Jameson that "the four levels [of allegory] essentially exhaust the various terrains on which ideology must perform its work" (Jameson 2019, xvi). Geoff Waite, for example, warns readers of Nietzsche about the dangers of sticking with the usual interpretive channels (1996, 91–92).

8. The detail about the boiled bits looks to be a Doten invention, though there was a Heron of Alexandria who was a kind of ancient Count Zeppelin: Heron built a wind-powered machine.

9. Salman Rushdie's *The Golden House* resonates with this passage in *Trump Sky Alpha* by presenting an avatar of Trump in the form of a would-be classical figure who styles himself "Nero Golden." For discussion of *The Golden House*, see Jaclyn Partyka's chapter in the present volume.—Ed.

10. My thanks to the librarians at the University of Texas at Arlington and at Texas A&M-College Station for assisting with the research for this essay.

REFERENCES

Barber, Lynn. 2006. "I Smoke, Therefore I Am." *Guardian*. February 5, 2006. https://www.theguardian.com/film/2006/feb/05/features.review2.
Blumenberg, Hans. 2010. *Care Crosses the River*. Translated by Paul Fleming. Stanford: Stanford University Press.
Daniel, Elijah. n.d. "Trump Temptations: The Billionaire & the Bellboy." *Wattpad*. Accessed June 3, 2019. https://www.wattpad.com/story/63074949-trump-temptations-the-billionaire-the-bellboy.
Doten, Mark. 2019. *Trump Sky Alpha*. Minneapolis: Graywolf.
Frank, Robert. 2017. "Mar-a-Lago Membership Fee Doubles to $200,000." *CNBC*. January 25, 2017. https://www.cnbc.com/2017/01/25/mar-a-lago-membership-fee-doubles-to-200000.html.
Goldsmith, Margaret. 1931. *Zeppelin: A Biography*. New York: William Morrow.
"Graywolf Press." n.d. *Graywolf Press*. Accessed June 3, 2019. https://www.graywolfpress.org/.

Jacobson, Howard. 2017. *Pussy*. London: Jonathan Cape.

Jameson, Fredric. 1981. *The Political Unconscious: Narrative as a Socially Symbolic Act*. Ithaca: Cornell University Press.

———. 2019. *Allegory and Ideology*. London: Verso.

Klein, Richard. 1993. *Cigarettes Are Sublime*. Durham: Duke University Press.

Lanchester, John. 2018. "The Case of Agatha Christie." *London Review of Books*. December 20, 2018. https://www.lrb.co.uk/v40/n24/john-lanchester/the-case-of-agatha-christie.

———. 2019. *The Wall*. New York: W.W. Norton.

Loveness, Jeff. 2017. "This Is the Political Satire That Finally Stops Trump." *McSweeney's Internet Tendency*. January 23, 2017. https://www.mcsweeneys.net/articles/this-is-the-political-satire-that-finally-stops-trump.

Mason, Tim. 1995. "Intention and Explanation: A Current Controversy about the Interpretation of National Socialism." In *Nazism, Fascism and the Working Class: Essays by Tim Mason*, edited by Jane Caplan, 212–30. Cambridge: Cambridge University Press.

Norberg, Jakob. 2018. "Anticapitalist Affect: Georg Lukács on Satire and Hate." *New German Critique* 45 (3): 155–74.

Ott, Brian L., and Greg Dickinson. 2019. *The Twitter Presidency: Donald J. Trump and the Politics of White Rage*. New York: Routledge.

Otto, Beatrice K. 2001. *Fools Are Everywhere: The Court Jester around the World*. Chicago: University of Chicago Press.

Rifkind, Hugo. 2017. "Laugh All You Like but Satire Changes Nothing." *Times* (London). February 7, 2017. https://www.thetimes.co.uk/article/laugh-all-you-like-but-satire-changes-nothing-bpqlgm72x.

Selk, Avi. 2017. "Twitter Co-founder: I'm Sorry if We Made Trump's Presidency Possible." *Washington Post*. May 21, 2017. https://www.washingtonpost.com/news/the-switch/wp/2017/05/21/twitter-co-founder-im-sorry-if-we-made-trumps-presidency-possible/?utm_term=.8e3dbda434e7.

Sennett, Alan. 2014. "Film Propaganda: *Triumph of the Will* as a Case Study," *Framework* 55 (1): 45–65.

Smith, Ali. 2017. "The Novel in the Age of Trump." *New Statesman*, October 13–19, 2017, 40–45.

Smith, Justin E. H. 2015. "Why Satire Matters." *Chronicle of Higher Education*. February 23, 2015. https://www.chronicle.com/article/Why-Satire-Matters/190149.

Southland Tales. 2007. Directed by Richard Kelly. Culver City: Samuel Goldwyn Films.

Twiss, Jill. 2018. *A Day in the Life of Marlon Bundo*. Illustrated by E. G. Keller. San Francisco: Chronicle Books.

Waite, Geoff. 1996. *Nietzsche's Corps/e: Aesthetics, Politics, Prophecy, or, The Spectacular Technoculture of Everyday Life*. Durham: Duke University Press.

Žižek, Slavoj. 2009. *First as Tragedy, Then as Farce*. London: Verso.

———. 2014. *Absolute Recoil: Towards a New Foundation of Dialectical Materialism*. London: Verso.

Chapter 13

Our Cartoon President and the Politics of Laughter

Steven Rosendale and Laura Gray-Rosendale

No watcher of the Showtime animated series *Our Cartoon President* can miss the derisive rebuke of the Trump administration that lies at the show's heart. The series, which was created by veteran comedian Stephen Colbert along with his *Late Show* executive producer Chris Licht, happily spoofs everyone from liberal media icons like Rachel Maddow and Anderson Cooper to Democratic politicians like Nancy Pelosi and Chuck Schumer, but it's clear throughout the seventeen episodes of the show's first season (2018) that the show's real targets of ridicule are the president and his allies and family. The show is a spinoff of a recurring *Late Show* segment in which Colbert interviews a cartoon Trump who inevitably comes off like a buffoon (whether the *Late Show* writers have written his lines, or, as sometimes happened, the segment attributed only actual Trump quotes to the cartoon president).

The rhetorical strategy of *Our Cartoon President* follows along similar lines, heavily shaping the representation of the president and his key allies in exaggerated terms that openly declare the show's contempt for them, all the while maintaining a topicality that keeps the satire rooted in reality. The cartoon president's very first words in the early release version of the first episode of the series, "State of the Union," addressed directly to the audience, leave little doubt of the show's producers' stance regarding the administration: "My fellow Americans and temporarily unfurloughed nonessential federal dead weight, we are one year into my presidency, and it's time to finally admit I am absolutely crushing it. These past few weeks alone, I've achieved headlines with words like 'porn star,' 'shithole,' and 'cognitive function.'"[1]

From this starting point, the episode and series develop a consistent portrait of Trump that emphasizes the themes articulated in his opening statement: narcissism and self-aggrandizement, questions about Trump's sexism and moral character, questions about his politics of race and poverty, and—especially—questions about Trump's mental capabilities. Later in the first episode, for example, Trump reveals that he'll announce the national bird during the State of the Union: when he is surprised by the news that the country already has a national bird, he commands that the bald eagle be made into the national flower. In a gag that runs through the episode, Trump repeatedly tries—unsuccessfully—to grab the nuclear "football" from the officer protecting it. He continuously makes unintentionally self-damaging remarks ("Hey, I didn't get three women to marry me by breaking promises") that simultaneously reveal the dark nature of his character and his oblivious-ness to that dark nature. Excitedly referring to his planned military parade, for example, Trump says, "Finally, like those lucky foreigners, Americans will get to see our military march through their streets." Trump's allies fare no better (and sometimes worse). Treasury Secretary Steven Mnuchin is introduced as a character with such contempt for the poor that he openly articulates a desire to put smallpox on pennies. We first meet Senior Adviser Stephen Miller as he prays to a demon to help him write Trump's State of the Union address—while hanging from meat hooks in his underpants. Other key figures are similarly caricatured: Vice President Mike Pence and his wife Karen, Ivanka and Jared, Jeff Sessions, Sarah Huckabee Sanders, Don Jr. and Eric, and others are each ridiculed as characters too dumb or blind or evil to understand how detestable their own politics are (figure 13.1).

That Colbert's newest show takes such an open and sharply critical stance regarding the Trump administration is hardly surprising: Colbert has been well known as one of the nation's most biting and controversial political satirists

Figure 13.1   Stephen Miller. *Our Cartoon President,* "State of the Union," season 1, episode 1 (2018). Screen capture.

since his notorious 2006 White House Correspondents' Dinner address, and those familiar with his parody of Bill O'Reilly on *The Colbert Report*, or with Colbert's frequent mockery of the president on *The Late Show with Stephen Colbert* are already well acquainted with Colbert's strident satiric stances. As Colbert himself has said, "People ask me all the time, do you get tired of mocking the president? . . . and this is a complicated answer: No and hell no" (Gibbons and Eggerton 2018). As a stunned Colbert intoned at the close of his 2016 election special, "the devil cannot stand mockery" (*Stephen Colbert's Live Election* 2016).

Although the meanness of *Our Cartoon President* is easy to recognize, it's much more difficult to properly fix just what the rhetorical effect of all of this mockery is. In the primary division of satire that differentiates between a gentle and wry Horatian sort of attitude and the more invective Juvenalian form, a key element is the delicate negotiation between the demands of entertainment and criticism. Horatian satire is generally recognized to emphasize the comfort and entertainment of its audience: the primary response to the target of satire is a wry amusement in which the audience is encouraged to smile and think, "what a world!" Juvenalian satire, by contrast, drives harder at substantive criticism designed not to elicit wry smiles, but outrage and change. The idea of Horatian satire is to not go too far in the direction of direct critique or to put off audience members too much. By contrast, as Holbert et al. put it, "Juvenalian laughter is meant not to heal but to wound" (2011, 192).

At first glance, *Our Cartoon President* seems clearly Juvenalian because of the stridency of its attacks on the president. But is it really? It is one thing to notice that a text establishes an antagonistic stance toward the president, and quite another to be able to claim that that antagonism has the likelihood of creating meaningful rhetorical effects that can lead to change or even simply anger—the usual Juvenalian convention. In this essay, we examine precisely this issue, offering brief analyses of a few scenes from the first season of the series that illuminate some interesting difficulties in placing the show with regard to its satirical effect, to suggest that *Our Cartoon President* represents a kind of mixing of satiric genres—a mixing that carries implications for the show's ultimate rhetorical effects. Ultimately, we argue that some of the satiric techniques employed by *Our Cartoon President* work to minimize critical reflection and may even encourage the audience to adopt ideas the satire is apparently intended to criticize.[2]

While the show employs a variety of comedic techniques, perhaps the most striking is a kind of critical ventriloquism, in which Trump and his allies are made to utter what are essentially critical conclusions long ago reached by Trump opponents regarding the administration's character, real beliefs, and behavior. In episode 1, for example, a hapless Mitch McConnell says openly,

"I've agreed to value political expediency over my conscience," a conclusion about him shared, no doubt, by many, but hardly something we could realistically expect to hear him say out loud. In episode 5, "State Dinner," Steve Mnuchin is made to say this about himself: "I once paid to have a cow pushed off a cliff by a big shovel. Thought it would be funny. It was just OK." The self-revelation of Trump himself is especially striking in this regard. In episode 4, "Family Leave," he struggles to come up with ways to keep from offending Ivanka, who may disagree with some of his policies. After some discussion, Trump announces that "there comes a time in every presidency when he must choose between the love of his daughter and the satisfaction of making an incendiary nationalist powder keg go kaboom. It's a choice I must make alone." When Trump visits the Lincoln Memorial to commune with the former president, he implores, "Tell me what to do. Tell me how a president balances his family life with his obligation to demonize the margins of society" (as he deliberates, two thought bubbles pop up representing the interests competing in his mind: on the one hand, Ivanka saying, "I love you, Daddy," and in the other, a crowd of Nazis chanting, "Jews will not replace us!"). Earlier in the same episode, Trump goes even further in his embrace of white supremacy: informed by General Kelly that a Turkish terrorist group is seeking to obtain nuclear materials, Trump replies, "Hey, so long as they don't hit Skokie and Charlottesville, we're good." This kind of moment, in which Trump and those in his orbit blandly and openly attribute to themselves the darker motives that Trump opponents have already concluded exist, can feel like a kind of truth-telling because it seems like evidence of a conclusion long suspected, as if Trump—finally!—is telling us the straightforward truth about himself.

This central comedic gambit comes into play repeatedly as *Our Cartoon President* develops its principal stances on how Trump should be understood with regard to not only race and racism but also economic inequality and classism, and sexism. It's important, however, to pause over such moments to take stock of their self-confirming qualities, not only in the sense that the ventriloquistic technique is inherently self-confirming but also in that the rhetorical goal of such moments appears to be the confirmation of already-held conclusions about the administration. It is difficult, for example, to imagine a nonpartisan viewer being convinced that Trump's racial ideology is problematic by having Trump openly say, as he does in episode 16, "I am racist": the purpose of such moments appears to be structured, not around a persuasive goal directed to an as-yet-unconvinced audience, but rather around the goal of confirming the beliefs of an already antagonistic one. What the creators of *Our Cartoon President* have the president say certainly treats Trump with contempt, but the goal of the ventriloquism itself appears to be to evoke satisfaction, not outrage, in the audience.

Indeed, the more one pores over the episodes, the less it appears that the show adheres to strictly Juvenalian goals. Certainly, political analysis and the close consideration of social issues that might be expected of a truly Juvenalian text are nowhere to be found in the first season's seventeen episodes. Depictions of white supremacy and racism, for instance, are largely associated with punchlines. Episode 15, "The Wall," features many such moments, including a segment representing a Trump rally during which people are shouting, "Build the wall!" When rally members complain about the lack of an actual wall being built, Trump explains, "We can't do a wall right now. We spent a lot of money on baby cages, and a wall would just keep us from getting enough babies to fill 'em up." The dark frankness of the term "baby cages" works in the same manner as the rest of the cartoon president's self-damaging statements: stirring outrage about the truly tragic situation of immigrant child separation isn't the point, but rather the quick confirmation of a contemptuous stance regarding Trump himself. The issue of child separation is quickly dismissed in favor of a new joke about replacing the wall with an ice skating rink, and there's scarcely time for the viewer to register the real problem here, engage in critical analysis, or arrive at a new or enhanced sense of outrage—let alone arrive at a resolve to work toward change.

Occasionally, the show's creators allow the cartoon president to utter what can initially feel like social analyses, but even in these cases, opportunities to offer information, develop criticism, or stir the wrath of the audience are passed up in favor of the satisfactions of caricature, name-calling, and jokes. Addressing CPAC in episode 4, Trump calls out, "Speaking of reptiles, NRA sweetheart Wayne LaPierre is here. Waiter, bring Wayne a Wet-Nap. He's got blood all over his hands. Do you know how complicit Wayne LaPierre is? ['How complicit is he?' the CPAC crowd chants.] Wayne LaPierre is so complicit, Poland just made it illegal to talk about him!" In "The Wall," after being convinced that he has to keep his promise to his constituents, Trump instead decides to build just a small piece of the wall. He states, "We're not building the whole wall. We need just enough to fill a camera lens. Length: 100 feet. Height: taller than a man in search of freedom. Width: one sixth of a six-foot party sub." Similarly, Trump's answer to questions about why the real wall isn't being built would be a clever retort if delivered by someone else: "Where is it? You'll never see it unless you wander this desert on the brink of death. You see, America is the land of empty, symbolic gestures, like the inscription on the Statue of Liberty, Black History Month, and recycling." The wall, Trump suggests, is simply an idea, moving on, in a perverse evocation of Tom Joad's famous soliloquy in *The Grapes of Wrath*, to incisively point out that the ideology that calls for the wall is already well embodied in American society. "The real wall," the cartoon president says, "the wall that keeps people from ever assimilating in our society, is in here [points to his head]—our hearts. Every time we sneer at a Mexican woman ahead of us in line at the grocery store, that's the wall. Every time we blame affirmative action for our dumb kids not getting into Rutgers, that's the wall." The moment has an easily imagined critical potential regarding the president's comfort with racism that is only partially undermined by the buffoonery of his heart-missing gesture, but here again, the potential to foster outrage is quickly dissipated as the episode moves on to standard gags about the stupidity of the Trump children, Stephen Miller, and Sean Hannity, who praises the cartoon president for being "the only one who knows where to find my racism g-spot." The main point, clearly, is to confirm the audience's belief that Hannity might be a racist, rather than to develop analysis or push an audience toward anger and a desire for change. Here again, the comedic gambit of having characters themselves exaggeratedly acknowledge the most damning things already believed about them may actually soften their characters by making them agents of the text's way of revealing its stance and associating them with the audience's pleasure at being confirmed in its beliefs (figure 13.2).

The show's failure—or refusal—to sustain critical analysis or keep its attention trained on promoting anger and a desire for change is striking, extending to all of the ostensibly critical issues activated by the show as the cartoon president bumbles his way through scenarios charged with sexism and class struggle in addition to the themes of racism and white supremacy just discussed. In episode 4, "Family Leave," for example, Ivanka's struggle to promote gender equity could provide abundant opportunities to stimulate outrage and analysis, as the cartoon Trump remains focused on his daughter's

Figure 13.2 The Wall. *Our Cartoon President*, "The Wall," season 1, episode 15 (2018). Screen capture.

appearance throughout the episode: "Isn't she beautiful, folks?" he interjects as Ivanka tries to articulate her desire to promote gender equity, "Give 'em a twirl, honey! C'mon!" The juxtaposition articulates a stance (Trump is a sexist), but the potential for developing more than the most basic critique isn't seized upon. In similar fashion, the Mnuchin character is often portrayed in terms that could open analyses of the administration's class ideology, but labeling Mnuchin an elite classist is more nearly the point than illuminating the audience on class issues. In this way, *Our Cartoon President* differs substantially from educational satire like *The Daily Show*, or from the work of fellow *The Daily Show* alums John Oliver or Lewis Black—or some of the other work of Colbert himself.

If the show's failure to integrate analysis or foster critical reflection means that some of its Juvenalian efficacy is lost, another feature of *Our Cartoon President* may undermine the show's political impact even more. As we've discussed, the show's way of characterizing Trump and others may appear especially severe—as if the show really were breaking new boundaries in terms of the level and uncompromising nature of invective against the administration. Eric is a special target for especially brutal ridicule emphasizing the extreme limitation of his intellectual abilities, but the critique goes so far that it loses nearly all sense of realism. "I don't think I can make the state dinner: I can't find a sitter for Eric," Trump quips in "State Dinner," while in "State of the Union," he treats Eric like a small child: "Eric, if you're ever in doubt, you just find a policeman and tell him you're lost," the cartoon president coos to him. In episode 2, "Disaster Response," we learn that "Eric can't do anything well! He didn't even learn to walk until he was seven. And even then it was more of an upright crawl." Trump later adds another set of details that, while cruel, are also so exaggerated that the sense of realistic critique is entirely lost: "Well, I miss the old Eric who never undermined me by being good at things. The old Eric would've met President Xi wearing one sock with his breath reeking of crickets." Donald Trump Jr. is similarly skewered as a clueless frat boy, who comments in "State Dinner" that Justin Trudeau is "the son of a world leader, like me, so he knows what it's like to live with strict rules, like don't do the jerking-off hand motion, don't leave your Oakleys on the Tomb of the Unknown Soldier." Stephen Miller is also represented as a subject of disdain, but the character is again presented in terms that leave most connections to reality behind—as in the repeated gag about his demon worship. In episode 2, Stephen is asked about how they might create a group of Trump lookalikes to take over some of his tasks, and his answer, while consistent with his character, also pushes his character beyond the reach of realism: "All I need is a cheek swab, sterile turkey baster, and coven of ovulating lesbian hyenas to create a horde of Trump super-beasts that will reign terror."

Trump's character itself is often also given to us in similarly fantastic terms that may undermine the potential for political critique. While few but Trump's most ardent supporters would accuse him of legislative genius, cartoon Trump's ignorance is so spectacular that we might well question the purpose of the representation. In episode 6, "Media Strategy," the cartoon president lays out "signature legislation that will define my legacy," but the bill turns out to be devoted to "reduc[ing] the air in potato chip bags." The segment does imply a critique of the worth of Trump's actual legislative predictions, but even here, the critique is cursory and devolves into a fat joke: "If I let them derail my potato chip agenda," he laments, "I won't be able to look at the man I see in the two gigantic mirrors placed side by side!" In any case, if the cartoon president is himself too stupid to understand how inept at setting a legislative agenda he is, his chief of staff, John Kelly is not, but again, the terms in which the criticism is laid out stretch the reality of Trump's ignorance for the sake of humor rather than critique: when in episode 4 Ivanka's proposed Paid Family Leave Bill arrives at the White House, he says to his president, "I would have given it to you, but it only had one picture and due to its lack of cool spaceships, I chose not to share it."

The importance of this tendency to favor the entertainment of personal mockery over critique should not be underestimated as we attempt to assess the politics of *Our Cartoon President*. While cartoon General Kelly's reasons for not bothering to give cartoon Trump a copy of important legislation raise the issue of how troubling it is to have a president who is widely reputed to refuse to read even the most important intelligence briefs, this issue is quickly overwritten by the silliness of suggesting that Trump will only look at material with "cool spaceships" on it, and we are left to wonder what the purpose of raising the substantive issue was in the first place. As critic Sonia Saraiya (2018) suggests,

> In mapping out [Trump's] character, "Our Cartoon President" knows him very well; his doddering cluelessness makes him approachable, while cowardice, graft, and narcissism lurk at the edges of his jokes. (In one throwaway gag, Trump avoids a $35 per-person debt to a crowd of angry employees by ordering a drone strike on them.) And yet the humor about him posits that what is offensive about Trump is his fake tan, his belly, his overlong tie—instead of, you know, the litany of terrible things he has said and done.

The "approachable" nature of cartoon Trump and his family may be the most curious feature of the series, and also perhaps its most important rhetorical element. For amid the more withering attacks on the First Family that run throughout the series, another, softer portrait frequently comes through. In nearly every episode, viewers are treated to looks at imagined interfamily interactions the like of which are never seen in public. In these interactions, Trump often appears as a bumbling, inept, but ultimately loving father whose children adore him. "Disaster Response," for example, features the cartoon First Family enjoying a television feature about themselves (the president is frequently shown watching television about himself). The bit is full of barbs, as everyone takes turns insulting Eric and uttering their self-damaging admissions, but it also shows a family with affection for each other, that hangs out together, and that the cartoon president cares for—in his own way. The cartoon president, of course, misses the jokes about his family that air on the special feature, but the segment ends with the family together, celebrating itself, the children agreeing as Trump exclaims, "Wow! That's some family I've got, right? [applause] We like that, don't we? We like that! Let's watch it again at twice the volume!" As James Poniewozik (2018) puts it, the Trump of *Our Cartoon President* "is an oafish Peter Griffin type: a First Family Guy" who is "hapless but harmless." Julia Selinger (2018) agrees, suggesting that in the episode, "within their roles of neglected son and uncaring father, each man [Eric and Trump] feels as if he's been infantilized. It's a sympathetic portrayal of a family whose actual behavior errs on the side of fascistic. The series ultimately hinges on the premise that these people are innocuous doofuses and not insidious politicos" (figure 13.3).

Episodes like these begin to suggest strongly that there is something missing in the picture of the show as a particularly harsh criticism of Trump and those around him. In its apparent meanness, Colbert's show may look like a strong Juvenalian invective, but the rhetorical implications of the modes in

Figure 13.3   Trump TV Family. *Our Cartoon President*, "The Wall," season 1, episode 15 (2018). Screen capture.

which the invective is delivered pull the show in another direction, one in which the audience is amused and confirmed in a set of judgments, but without pushing the boundaries of understanding, and also without much opportunity for anger. As the cartoon president himself says in an oddly metafictional moment in "State of the Union," "Each and every one of you voted for me, and the ones who didn't, you kind of wanted to see what would happen, and it's happening more than you could have imagined. Now some are worried that this show might humanize me. Well, too late, folks." Deprived of his real menace—yes, humanized—cartoon Trump is likely to elicit little more than a wry smile from viewers, who may be encouraged to shake their heads and mutter, "what a president . . . ."

As the show enters into its second season, the fact that this Horatian element of the series may very well be unintentional will be of little comfort to those for whom "change the president!" is the only imaginable response to the current administration. In any case, the show's creators' intent is of less interest, ultimately, than the likely implications and impact of what they have actually achieved, and in the case of *Our Cartoon President*, the impact may be inimical to the show's creators' intent. As Saraiya (2018) complains, the show's "lighthearted humor about Trump displays a lack of anger so potent it is alienating. What president are they seeing," she wonders, "that they aren't tearing their hair out with rage? Surely, the stakes are too high to be following along with the latest constitutional crisis like it's an episode of 'South Park.' And yet 'Our Cartoon President' is so insistently breezy that one's own righteous anger seems irrelevant—as if the show is gaslighting outrage." And it is in this sense that the first season of *Our Cartoon President* might well be regarded not only as a Juvenalian failure but as something much worse. The cartoon president himself may appear harmless, but *Our Cartoon President* is not. In defusing outrage and even "gaslighting" it, Colbert's show does the president's work for him. The show may perform a task that the real Trump seems to be unable to accomplish—to lessen by some increment the outrage of those opposed to him: as Lisa Gring-Pemble and Martha Solomon Watson (2003) argue about the limits of satire, "Some forms of humor may facilitate audience acceptance of the very ideas the satirist intends to disparage" (132).

NOTES

1. These lines were pulled from the episode for the official premiere of *Our Cartoon President*, not because they were too strident, but because they weren't topical enough by the premiere date: Trump's "shithole countries" statement, for instance, already a month old by the February 11, 2018, premiere, was replaced in the premiere episode by a reference to Representative Devin Nunes, whose memo alleging FBI

surveillance abuses was released to the public on February 2. As of this writing, the early release version of the opening lines of the episode is still available online. See *"Our Cartoon President—My* Fellow Americans" (n.d.).

2. See Bruce Krajewski's chapter in the present volume for further discussion of the efficacy of satire as a response to Trump.—Ed.

REFERENCES

Gibbons, Kent, and John Eggerton. 2018. "'Our Cartoon President' and a Dog Day Evening." *Broadcasting & Cable*, February 5–12, 2018, 6.

Gring-Pemble, Lisa, and Martha Solomon Watson. 2003. "The Rhetorical Limits of Satire: An Analysis of James Finn Garner's *Politically Correct Bedtime Stories.*" *Quarterly Journal of Speech* 89 (2): 132–53.

Holbert, R. Lance, Jay Hmielowski, Parul Jain, Julie Lather, and Alyssa Morey. 2011. "Adding Nuance to the Study of Political Humor Effects: Experimental Research on Juvenalian Satire versus Horatian Satire." *American Behavioral Scientist* 55 (3): 187–211.

Our Cartoon President. 2018. Season 1. February 11–August 26, 2018. Showtime.

"Our Cartoon President—My Fellow Americans." n.d. *Showtime.* Accessed June 25, 2019. https://www.sho.com/video/60038/our-cartoon-president---my-fellow -americans.

Poniewozik, James. 2018. "An Animated Trump as First Family Guy." *New York Times*, February 10, 2018.

Saraiya, Sonia. 2018. Review of *Our Cartoon President. Variety.* February 9, 2018. https://variety.com/2018/tv/reviews/our-cartoon-president-stephen-colbert-showti me-tv-review-1202692370/.

Selinger, Julia. 2018. Review of *Our Cartoon President. Slant.* February 8, 2018. https://www.slantmagazine.com/tv/our-cartoon-president-season-one/.

Stephen Colbert's Live Election Night Democracy's Series Finale: Who's Going to Clean Up This Sh*T? 2016. Directed by Jim Hoskinson. November 8, 2016. Showtime.

Chapter 14

"Nobody Wants to See That Fuckhead"

Ball Culture and Donald Trump in FX's Pose

Meredith James

When *Pose* creator Ryan Murphy explained why he took the character Donald Trump out of the show, he replied, "Nobody wants to see that fuckhead" (Nussbaum 2018). "[James] Van Der Beek's part in the first draft was written to be a young Trump," Murphy notes (Stack 2018); however, Murphy changed his mind, instead casting Van Der Beek to play a Trump executive symbolic of excess and greed. Although Murphy's comment might seem to be in defiance of Trump's power, Murphy is conceding that Trump, in some ways, is a driving force in his show. The conspicuous invisibility of Trump in *Pose* articulates how the lives of people in liminal spaces are directly influenced by his ruling authority whether he is physically present or not. There are two worlds present in the show: Ball World and Trump World. The series depicts the story of the trans and queer communities struggling in 1980s New York and the ruthless, dog-eat-dog business world. *Pose* writers privilege the stories of the Ball World, creating sympathetic portrayals of marginalized people, whereas Trump World is depicted as hostile and cruel. Inspired by Jennie Livingston's 1990 documentary *Paris Is Burning*, *Pose* tells the stories of people recognizing and defying the dominant power's influence while upholding mainstream middle-class values, normalizing their stories and making these stories relatable to a largely non-LGBTQ+ audience.

Pose is definitely political, even in its production: "The show has 108 trans cast and crew members and 31 L.G.B.T.Q. characters, as well as several trans directors. In addition, Murphy is giving his profits from the show to causes that benefit trans communities. 'It's television as advocacy,' he said. 'I want to put my money where my mouth is'" (Desta 2018). This advocacy is urgently needed in the current political moment of Trump's presidency. *Pose* is a significant show; as co-creator Steven Canals points out, "We've never seen people like this occupy space in television, ever. We didn't want to create this bleak, baroque version of New York. . . . And yet we still wanted to be true to the time period. So we made sure that we centered and grounded the narrative in the theme of family and ambition and survival" (Kennedy 2018). The tender portrayals of the trans and queer communities create empathy, and their presence in such a well-scripted show gives voice to their humanity and their agency.

Pose reshapes thinking and gives more depth to understanding Ball World, picking up where *Paris Is Burning* left off. Many of the early reviews of *Paris Is Burning* regarded the documentary as being only about the disenfranchise- ment of the people performing in the Ball World. As Moe Meyer (1997) points out, "Where I saw displays of power, others were seeing powerless- ness; where I saw change and transformation manifested through the agency of the meaningful gesture, others were seeing deluded automatons hypnoti- cally following the siren call of consumer capitalism" (41). *Pose* makes clear that the members of the community have power and agency. Certain mem- bers of the Houses of Evangelista and Abundance certainly pursue luxury and material wealth, but they are hardly deluded. Esther Godfrey (2005) analyzes *Paris Is Burning* in light of Judith Butler's assertion that drag culture can be a destabilizing force that liberates gender: "The theatricality of drag . . . works to dislodge essentialized notions of gender identity and sexual difference." The first season of *Pose* (2018) does exactly this and as well destabilizes ruling-class authority represented by the 1980s and 2010s Trump eras.

The ball scenes help punctuate the action of the stories. In the first episode of season 1, "Pilot," for example, before Blanca leaves the House of Abun- dance, the House robs a museum for costumes they can wear to win the ball category Royalty. By robbing the museum and using the royal garments for the ball, they are at once undermining the world of affluent New York City with which Trump is clearly associated and upholding those Trump values of winning at all costs. "Mopping" or stealing is part of the ball culture so that the disenfranchised can participate in categories such as Rich Bitch. The House of Abundance is arrested after performing at the ball, however, and this establishes the liminal position of drag culture and transgender identities in 1980s New York City and that they do not get to participate in Trump World.

The series focuses on transwomen of color and not so much on Trump World. Janet Mock, who writes and directs *Pose*, says, "Kate Mara, Evan Peters, James Van Der Beek, they're not centered on this show. They are our supporting cast. These TV stars! They are our supporting to these women. They know that and they're conscious of that. They know they're there to help serve the themes of the show and give context to these women's lives, where usually it would be the opposite" (Fallon 2018). The characters of Matt

Bromley (James Van Der Beek), Stan Bowes (Evan Peters), and Patty Bowes (Kate Mara) are not the focus, but rather they only exist to contrast the values of the trans and queer communities.

Murphy's *Pose* asks the audience to explore Ball World and identify with the transgender Latinx character Blanca Evangelista (Mj Rodriguez) as she desires middle-class values and traditions and creates the House of Evangelista. She makes a safe home for her children, people who through different circumstances have found themselves struggling to survive the mean streets of 1987 New York City. In a reading of Harlem ball culture, Moe Meyer (1997) sees the Ball World in *Paris Is Burning* as a "discursive space opened up by the enunciations of the queen, a space of probable empowerment" and argues that "the body of the queen, of the Mother of the House, is not a metaphor but a necessity" (40). Blanca is the site of action and narrative movement, but although the show largely centers on Blanca, all of the other characters contribute to the creation of Ball World and Trump World. Through depicting Trump World as cruel, making the Ball World virtuous and family-oriented, and watching the worlds collide in the form of a relationship between Trump employee Stan and Angel Evangelista (Indya Moore), *Pose* creators are championing the trans and queer communities over Trump.

It is important to recognize Blanca is Latinx. In the case of the Central Park Five and over the last few years, Trump's comments about crime and immigration have largely targeted Latinx communities, particularly Mexicans, and at times he doesn't seem to realize Puerto Rico is part of the United States (see, for instance, Karni and Mazzei [2019]). As Lindsay Pérez Huber (2016) points out in the *Charleston Law Review*, the US Census Bureau has "found that 2015 marks the first time in U.S. history that more than 50% of children under the age of 5 are non-white" and that "in November 2015, a national poll found 50% of people, regardless of political affiliation, were 'mainly worried' about the recent changes in 'cultural diversity' in the U.S." (232, 233). Pérez Huber suggests that "white elites, like Trump, are reacting to the inevitability of a non-white U.S. majority where their power and status are threatened" (241). Blanca's and other characters' mere presence on television can be read as a threat to this white elitism. Trump in his presidency has elicited fear of marginalized Others through his many speeches on immigration, but he takes it further: "Trump now vows to 'make America *safe* again' with a new emphasis on the collective threat of 'violent' African Americans, 'dangerous' undocumented Latina and Latino immigrants, and 'treacherous' Muslims. In just a few short months, what was an undocumented Latina/o immigrant stance in Trump's campaign has evolved to an anti-People of Color stance" (Pérez Huber 2016, 244).

In all of this, Trump, although he is only referred to in the show, is symbolic of the hegemonic forces at play, especially through the characters of Matt Bromley, Stan Bowes, and sometimes Elektra Abundance (Dominique Jackson). Matt, a Trump devotee, represents all that is morally reprehensible in the sphere of New York City's ruling elite. He mentors Stan, who later in the series refuses to wholly identify with him. In episode 1, ball emcee Pray Tell (Billy Porter) introduces the drag competition category, describing Executive Realness as "high-powered businessmen of the eighties! The suit! The 401(k)! . . . At the Russian Tea Room! . . . Don't scare the white people!" Shortly thereafter, we see Stan Bowes walk into the opulent Trump Tower, where he is interviewed by Matt. This interview anchors the show in many ways. Not only does this scene establish our ruthless villain Matt, but it also sets up the elitist values and the lure of material wealth that Blanca fights against. As Stan is visibly nervous, the dialogue proceeds as follows:

Matt: What do you want?
Stan: Well, I want to be you.
Matt: That's a very good answer.
Stan: I want what you have—I want a view of the river or the park or both. I want to be able to walk by a shop on Fifth, see something in the window for my wife and just go buy it.
Matt: The new American Dream. For the first time in American history, it's considered a good thing to flaunt your success. Right? Let people know how rich you are. This watch? Patek Philippe rose gold, nine grand. I've got four of them. I've watched a Met game from the owner's box and partied with Gooden and Strawberry afterwards. Just the other day I was backstage at a Cyndi Lauper concert. I drive a Mercedes 350 and the suit is bespoke. God bless Ronald Reagan.

This interview scene is punctuated by Matt snorting cocaine, emphasizing the grotesque nature of the 1980s, which Trump represents in this show. The symbolism of each of the items and people Matt references is pretty obvious: the ostentatious Patek Phillippe and Mercedes, the notorious partying of Mets Gooden and Strawberry, the Lauper bubblegum pop anthem "Girls Just Want to Have Fun." All of this condenses the worst ideal of the 1980s: excess. Also important in this scene is Matt's love of Ronald Reagan, a president often criticized as merely acting the role of the presidency.

Trump World is fake and inauthentic. As Fallon (2018) notes, "Peters' and Van Der Beek's characters and the world they occupy put into harsher perspective the world in which Angel and her community struggle, a world in which AIDS, poverty, homelessness, and abuse isn't a haunting specter, but the dark reality." However, not everyone agrees that Trump's inclusion in *Pose* is even necessary. Critic Ariana Romero (2018) argues, "Stan, a closeted queer man with a wife and kids, doesn't have to work for Trump for us to understand who he is as a character and the problems he faces as someone climbing the corporate ladder in the 1980s. *Wall Street*, *Glengarry Glen Ross*, and *The Wolf of Wall Street*, which begins in the exact year *Pose* takes place, have all frozen the pinstripe-suited, cutthroat, hair-slicked business culture of the era forever." However, it's hard not to agree with the show's co-creator Brad Falchuk, who describes Trump as "the biggest fraud of all time. . . . If the show is called *Pose*, he poses as someone who is much richer than he is, much smarter than he is, much more educated than he is. He is the representation in terms of all that is wrong in terms of inauthenticity. But the contrast between someone like Blanca . . . and someone like him could not be greater. I think it was important we felt that contrast" (Stack 2018). Henry A. Giroux (2017) seconds Falchuk's assessment of Trump: "Emulating the fascist embrace of the cultural spectacle, Trump language became a vehicle for producing sensationalism, emotions, shock and effects that mimicked the performances of tawdry Reality TV. He spoke and continues to speak from a discursive space in which anything can be said, the truth is irrelevant, and informed judgment becomes a liability" (890). Like Reagan, Trump is lampooned as a presidential poseur.

Trump World is similarly portrayed in *Pose* as being vapid and dangerous. In episode 3, "Giving and Receiving," Matt, the avatar of Trump World, becomes jealous of Stan's participation at an executive board meeting which Trump attends. We don't see Trump, but his presence looms. Stan tells Matt he has pitched an idea that Trump should get a cameo in all of the television shows and films that shoot on Trump properties, which is humorous since Trump has no cameo in *Pose* despite its use of exterior shots of Trump Tower. However, it does reinforce the idea of Trump as spectacle and manipulator, especially when we recall that Matt refers to Trump as "a master of the publicity machine" in episode 2, "Access."[1]

In episode 6, "Love Is the Message," while Matt is sexually harassing a secretary, Stan confronts Matt about exposing his affair with Angel to his wife Patty and they fistfight. Stan asks Matt, "Why do you hate me?" To which Matt replies, "I don't care enough about you to hate you. I resent you. You think you deserve what I have. Well, you don't, New Jersey. I was born better than you. You don't take what I have. I take what's yours. . . . The guy you're pretending to be doesn't exist." Matt, who is the Trump representative, makes clear that capital is all that matters. Matt doesn't even know at this point in the series that Angel is transgender. He is judging Stan solely based on class, not sexuality. Even though Stan is the aggressor in the fight, he is not punished at work but instead lauded. In episode 7, "Pink Slip," he tells Angel, "Apparently that kind of expression of manliness is encouraged there.

Now everyone thinks I'm a rock star for leaving my wife for my mistress."
Trump World not only allows aggressive competition but rewards it, making
the ruling-class values seem without humanity.

In stark contrast to Matt is Blanca Evangelista, the heart of the show.
Blanca, in episode 1, reveals to ball emcee Pray Tell she is HIV-positive, and
that she wants to leave a legacy, a House that values kindness, generosity, and
love, unlike her current House of Abundance. As she says about the House of
Evangelista in "Mother of the Year," the eighth and final episode of season
1, "We may not be a House of numbers, but we are a House of love." Her
split from her Mother Elektra and the House of Abundance in episode 1 does
not go smoothly. Blanca asks Elektra for her blessing to strike out and begin
her own House. Elektra insults Blanca, saying, "Look at me. Look at you. I
can pass. I can strut down Fifth Avenue when the sun is sitting high as my
cheekbones and be waited on at Bergdorf's same as any white woman while
you hide away in the shadows." Elektra uses her position of Mother and her
financial wealth, which helps her to pass not only as a woman but also as a
wealthy woman, to intimidate Blanca. Elektra Abundance is Blanca's foil in
the first season of the series as she desires the values of the ruling class, and
because of this, she is punished in several ways.

One of the ways Blanca represents virtuous middle-class values is that she
works as a nail technician while Elektra relies on her sugar daddy Dick Ford
(Christopher Meloni). Blanca wants her children to attend school or work
legitimate jobs, though she does make an allowance for her daughter Angel to
be a prostitute and to work in the peep show theater, saying she can do with
her body what she pleases. Blanca uses "tough love" to keep her children in
line. In episode 3, Damon (Ryan Jamaal Swain) gets into trouble at dance
school and Blanca punishes him by not allowing him to perform in the Snow
Ball. In episode 7, Blanca admonishes Papi (Angel Bismark Curiel) for selling drugs and ejects him from the House of Evangelista. There are numerous
examples in which the audience can identify with Blanca as she navigates
the world of child-rearing. Blanca struggles financially, but the audience can
admire and identify with her struggle to make ends meet. For example, in
episode 5, "Mother's Day," while Elektra treats her unhappy children to a
feast paid for by Mr. Ford, Blanca serves her happy children sloppy joes. This
juxtaposition signals who we as an audience should root for—the underdog.

Blanca also desires to create traditions with her children. In episode 3,
Blanca creates a traditional Christmas setting down to the popcorn string
decoration. Although the House of Evangelista doesn't have much, it's hard
not to be moved to tears during the gift-giving scene at the Chinese restaurant.
Her foil Elektra, however, takes her children mopping Salvation Army buck-
ets, explaining their actions by saying: "That's why we hit the bucket up on
Madison. Every dollar one of those rich Upper East Side bitches put in that

bucket is a gift back to themselves. Wipes away all the guilt they feel about spending all that money on silliness to put under their tree." Elektra, who often likens herself to the "rich Upper East Side bitches," justifies stealing in the same way the rich women justify their conspicuous consumption. Plus, Elektra's intentions are not to give her children an extravagant Christmas as she promises, but to use the money as a down payment for her gender confirmation surgery. Even as "through surgical procedures, gestures, and clothing, perceived essentialized biological formulations of a sex/gender system are disrupted" (Godfrey 2005), these juxtapositions call into question the concept of motherhood. As an audience, we can simultaneously feel happy for Elektra and disappointed by her actions. This complicates not only perceptions of sex/gender systems but moral codes.

In episode 7, after Mr. Ford dumps Elektra, she goes out on a search for a new sugar daddy, advertising in papers. She meets a potential suitor at a dingy bar, and as she assesses his wealth, she makes a list of demands, trying to strike an artful deal: "I will need an apartment, fully furnished. Nothing south of Sixtieth or east of Third Avenue. I will know that I am loved when I receive gifts. Expensive ones. I also expect a weekly allowance. In cash. And only after I feel looked after will I even consider a kiss on the cheek. I am a lady, after all." He agrees and makes his demands about her looks, but when he finds out she no longer has a penis, he chastises her for not including that in her advertisement. Of course, this is a negotiation, rather than a love connection. While Blanca privileges love, Elektra is unmotivated by emotion. Elektra has to go back to working at a peep show, becoming once again an object rather than a subject.

Episode 8, the final episode of the first season, opens with a tired and aged Elektra working at the peep show until the virtuous Blanca comes to save her. When Elektra tells Blanca, "I don't like being needy," Blanca comforts her: "You got a lot to hate yourself for, but needing help ain't one of them." This episode wraps up neatly as Blanca takes Elektra off the streets and gets Elektra a restaurant job as a hostess. Blanca's sons get professional dancing jobs, and she fixes Pray Tell up with bartender Keenan. Blanca is vindicated in the season finale as she is crowned Mother of the Year. Unlike Elektra, Blanca's work and rugged pragmatism pay off. Elektra learns her lesson, joins the House of Evangelista, and tells Blanca, "You taught me what a real Mother is." Blanca becomes what Moe Meyer (1997) describes as an ideal drag Mother who "makes her appearance as a self-reflexive play with identities, with instruments of dominance turned against themselves" (40).

Ball World and Trump World collide in the series when one of Blanca's children, Angel, and her Trump employee boyfriend, Stan, fall in love and strive to live in a traditional, heteronormative fantasy though she is transgender and he is attracted to her transgenderness. After the interview with

Matt in episode 1, an empowered Stan looks to satiate his sexual desire with a transgender prostitute. Stan and Angel spot each other, and at first Angel refers to Stan as a "window shopper," but quickly she begins to see an opportunity for love when she realizes Stan doesn't necessarily want sex, but wants to talk. And so begins the love affair between Stan and Angel. Angel is also impressed that Stan works for Trump, admiring Trump's legendary and garish gold toilet, saying, "Now that's living in style." Angel's admiration reflects America's fascination with Trump World: "Trump's brand, as a crystallization of his entire life story, is an ode to a particular form of mass consumption. . . . Trump's opulence invokes desire in his followers: his acquisition of now infamous golden toilets; his 'success' in having three marriages to beautiful women; his influential branding of architecture, wine, golf courses, and endless luxury items with his name. In short, Trump embodies revolutionary hedonism" (Goldstein and Hall 2017, 401–02). This revolutionary hedonism in the show is a dangerous and unwelcoming world of crass self-indulgence, but the pursuit of pleasure at all costs is tempting to both Angel and Stan.

Early in the series, Angel's character is reminiscent of the tragic Venus Xtravaganza from Livingston's *Paris Is Burning*, who wants to be a "spoiled rich white girl" (1990). But unlike Venus, Angel survives because she adopts Blanca's worldview. Angel confides to Stan that she wants "a home of my own, I want a family, I want to take care of someone, and I want someone to take care of me. I want to be treated like any other woman." Although their relationship is perceived by the outside world as abnormal, they desire a conventional relationship, one that does not necessarily need gaudy material wealth. Their relationship crashes stock gender-binary and racial anxieties; however, there are reminders throughout the first episode and throughout the first season that the odds are against them. Not only that, but Angel's full rejection of Stan at the end of episode 8, the first-season finale, indicates her desires have shifted from aspiring to be part of Trump World and solidifies her allegiance to the Ball World. She no longer wants to pretend and pose. Rather, she realizes her authentic self.

Stan's presence in the show represents posing in all of the wrong ways. In episode 2, Stan reveals to Angel that he is merely performing in Trump World:

I'm no one. I want what I'm supposed to want, I wear what I'm supposed to wear, and I work where I'm supposed to work. I stand for nothing. I've never fought in a war and I probably won't ever have to because the next one's gonna kill us all. I can buy things I can't afford, which means they're never really mine. I don't live. I don't believe. I accumulate. I'm a brand. A middle-class white guy. But you're who you are even though the price you pay for it is being disinvited from the rest of the world. I'm the one playing dress-up. Is it wrong to wanna be with one of the few people in the world who isn't? To have one person in my life who I know is real?

Stan at once validates Angel's subject position and also criticizes the Trump World to which he belongs. As Murphy told the *New York Times*, "It was in the Reagan era, the Trump era in New York City, when you could pretend to be money and be seen as wealthy. You could pretend to be anything and be accepted, whereas before that, you really had to have the background and education and breeding. It was the beginning of surface passing" (Galanes 2018). Stan, like Trump, is "surface passing," and lacks the depth of Angel, Blanca, and even Elektra.

In episode 3, Stan surprises Angel with her own beautiful apartment. At first, Angel is happy and excited, but when Stan chooses to spend Christmas with his family, Angel destroys the special Christmas treats she made. Angel's epiphany about the loneliness of being kept like a possession shifts her perspective on what her true desires are. In episode 5, she moves out of the apartment back to the modest home of the House of Evangelista. Angel explains to Blanca that she is "playing hard to get." To which Blanca replies, "Let me get this straight. To prove how mad you are, you moved out of your luxury co-op to come back here in this creaky-ass apartment." Blanca, despite disbelief, is proud that her daughter has returned home. All of this supports the championing of middle-class, family-oriented values over the values of Trump World that Blanca despises (promiscuity, drug use, stealing, etc.).

Stan is also rejected by his wife Patty when she discovers the affair. Patty is a stable New Jersey housewife who understands the line between the Trump-like life Stan promises her and the life she actually leads. At the end of the first episode, Stan takes Patty to the Rainbow Room as he feels guilty for spending time with Angel, but Patty recognizes she is merely performing this extravagant lifestyle. Later, in episode 5, Matt is getting his revenge by telling her about Stan's affair while simultaneously hitting on her. He invites her to come to him if she "need[s] to make [her] own money," saying, "I'm always looking to hire new talent." His attempted seduction of her is framed in the economic logic of Trump World. Patty tells him, "I believe you; I just don't trust you. . . . I'm not just some dopey Jersey housewife. I'm not trapped in this life. I choose it." Like Blanca, Patty is concerned with upholding traditional middle-class values and is not tempted by the Trump World that Matt represents. In episode 8, Patty declares her independence from Stan, telling him he is not allowed back in the house unless he quits his job. She will not allow Trump World in her house, whether in the form of Matt or Stan.

After Patty finds out about the affair, Stan moves into the luxury apartment with Angel and they set up house, eating homecooked meals and watching

TV, but when Angel brings Stan to a ball, Stan is allowed in but he is not embraced by the community. These scenes show how clearly delineated these worlds can be. Trump World and Ball World are not compatible, and this is something Stan must come to realize:

Angel: You didn't like it?
Stan: No, it just didn't like me. I'm never gonna fit in a place like that.
Angel: You don't have to come. We can go get salads. Or stay at home, or go see movies. The balls are not my whole life.
Stan: But they're a huge part of it. And so is my office, so are my kids. We've been in a bubble. This whole time we've been together, I thought the secrecy was the thing holding us back, but maybe it was what was keeping us together. I don't fit in anywhere.
Angel: You thought living on the fringes of society was gonna be some kind of picnic and roses?
Stan: I just thought it would be easier than being a fraud.
Angel: That's 'cause you're a white boy from the suburbs.
Stan: I just wanted a taste of what you have. One moment of being true in my whole goddamn life. But I can't. I do love you.

Stan breaks Angel's heart, but Angel ultimately rejects Stan when he comes back. Stan is not "real" enough to belong to Ball World. At the end of the first season, Stan is left floundering while Angel stands strong. Ball World is legitimate, while Trump World has no validity, and to belong to it is being a fraud.

Trump is no stranger to drag culture, since he motorboated Rudy Giuliani in a drag comedy skit for the Mayor's Inner Circle Press Roast in 2000. This video has reemerged many times with millions of views and "reappears routinely to baffle the internet as the lives of its two protagonists take stranger and stranger turns" (Corcoran 2018). No surprise, Giuliani and Trump miss the point of drag culture, and in the video they come off as frat boys out on a lark, pretending to do drag. Conversely, the drag critique of Trump in *RuPaul's Drag Race* season 11, episode 4, "Trump: The Rusical" (2019) is far more sophisticated and fun, and certainly less creepy. During this competition, contestants are asked to perform a parody of *Grease*, making Trump seem to be a womanizing buffoon and an unstable leader with songs like "Cheese Frightening." As Kate Kulzick (2019) writes in her review of this episode, "Trump parody is a very saturated market, so while a drag performance centered on the president may seem like a solid jumping off point, it could easily retread very well-worn territory. Thankfully, the *Drag Race* producers and the writers of 'Trump: The Rusical' find just the right balance between pointed political satire, campy excess, and self-aware silliness."

Much like *Pose*, Trump is not the most important character of this critique (though Ginger Minj's performance as Trump is fabulous), and his displacement gives power to the drag queens playing the women in his life. Though not satirical, *Pose*, too, is good at displacing and dismantling Trump's power. His power is more of a nuisance than the ideal.

However, as Giroux (2017) notes, "With Donald Trump's election as president of the United States, the scourge of authoritarianism has returned not only in the toxic language of hate, humiliation and bigotry, but also in the emergence of a culture of war and violence that looms over society like a plague" (887–88). The actual power of Trump as commander in chief is a scary reality for people in the LGBTQ+ community and People of Color, given his transgender military ban and his internment of people at the Mexican border. Sadly, he isn't without a devoted base: "Trump's spectacle of sexual transgression, civil lawlessness, and excessive opulence is exactly what is being embraced" (Goldstein and Hall 2017, 402). At the New York premiere of *Pose*, Ryan Murphy said, "Our community is under such attack from this administration. . . . I wanted to put something optimistic and uplifting out there" (Tacher 2018). *Pose* is a necessary cultural artifact because it succeeds in uplifting the communities which Trump is currently vilifying, and because it is calling Trump World out as the inauthentic pose that it is. Ball World is the authentic voice in the series. As of this writing, *Pose* season 2 has not yet premiered, but it will be interesting to see if the Trump critiques continue. But if the goal for the creators of *Pose* was to educate, they pass.

NOTE

1. For discussion of Trump's cameos, including the lore that he demands a cameo in every film and television production that shoots on his properties, see Ashleigh Hardin's chapter in the present volume.—Ed.

REFERENCES

Corcoran, Kieran. 2018. "Donald Trump Once Stuck His Face into Rudy Giuliani's Chest for a Drag-Queen Comedy Skit—and the Video Refuses to Die." *Business Insider.* May 8, 2018. https://www.businessinsider.com/trump-stuck-his-face-in-rudy-guilianis-chest-in-2000-drag-comedy-skit-2018-5.
Desta, Yohana. 2018. "Why Ryan Murphy Kicked Trump Out of *Pose*: 'Nobody Wants to See That F—khead.'" *Vanity Fair.* May 7, 2018. https://www.vanityfair.com/hollywood/2018/05/ryan-murphy-donald-trump-character-pose-show.

Fallon, Kevin. 2018. "Donald Trump's Presence Looms Large in 'Pose,' FX's Transgender Drama Series." *Daily Beast*. June 2, 2018. https://www.thedailybeast.com/donald-trumps-presence-looms-large-in-pose-fxs-transgender-drama-series.

Galanes, Philip. 2018. "Ryan Murphy and Janet Mock on 'Pose,' Diversity and Netflix." *New York Times*. May 23, 2018. https://www.nytimes.com/2018/05/23/arts/television/pose-ryan-murphy-janet-mock.html.

Giroux, Henry A. 2017. "White Nationalism, Armed Culture and State Violence in the Age of Donald Trump." *Philosophy and Social Criticism* 43 (9): 887–910.

Godfrey, Esther. 2005. "'To Be Real': Drag, Minstrelsy and Identity in the New Millennium." *Genders*. February 1, 2005. https://www.colorado.edu/gendersarchive1998-2013/2005/02/01/be-real-drag-minstrelsy-and-identity-new-millennium.

Goldstein, Donna M., and Kira Hall. 2017. "Postelection Surrealism and Nostalgic Racism in the Hands of Donald Trump." *HAU: Journal of Ethnographic Theory* 7 (1): 397–406.

Karni, Annie, and Patricia Mazzei. 2019. "Trump Lashes Out Again at Puerto Rico, Bewildering the Island." *New York Times*. April 2, 2019. https://www.nytimes.com/2019/04/02/us/trump-puerto-rico.html.

Kennedy, Mark. 2018. "Creator of 'Pose' Says FX Show Celebrates 'Incredible Souls.'" *AP News*. June 5, 2018. https://www.apnews.com/526762da194745db8264d7dbd50a34fd.

Kulzick, Kate. 2019. "The Political Gets Personal as *RuPaul's Drag Race* Tackles 'Trump: The Rusical.'" *A. V. Club*. March 21, 2019. https://tv.avclub.com/the-political-gets-personal-as-rupauls-drag-race-tackle-1833481248.

Meyer, Moe. 1997. "Rethinking *Paris Is Burning*: Performing Social Geography in Harlem Drag Balls." *Theatre Annual*, no. 50, 40–71.

Nussbaum, Emily. 2018. "How Ryan Murphy Became the Most Powerful Man in TV." *New Yorker*. May 7, 2018. https://www.newyorker.com/magazine/2018/05/14/how-ryan-murphy-became-the-most-powerful-man-in-tv.

Paris Is Burning. 1990. Directed by Jennie Livingston. Off White Productions.

Pérez Huber, Lindsay. 2016. "'Make America Great Again!': Donald Trump, Racist Nativism and the Virulent Adherence to White Supremacy amid U.S. Demographic Change." *Charleston Law Review* 10 (2): 215–48.

Pose. 2018. Season 1. June 3–July 22, 2018. FX.

Romero, Ariana. 2018. "*Pose* Doesn't Need Its Donald Trump References." *Refinery29*. June 4, 2018. https://www.refinery29.com/en-us/2018/06/200893/pose-episode-1-donald-trump-building-references.

RuPaul's Drag Race. 2019. "Trump: The Rusical." Season 11, episode 4. March 21, 2019. VH1.

Stack, Tim. 2018. "James Van Der Beek's Role in *Pose* Was Originally Donald Trump." *Entertainment Weekly*. June 7, 2018. https://ew.com/tv/2018/06/07/pose-james-van-der-beek-donald-trump/.

Tacher, Taryn. 2018. "Ryan Murphy Wants 'Pose' to Be 'Uplifting' for LGBTQ Community in Trump Era." *Variety*. May 18, 2018. https://variety.com/2018/scene/vpage/ryan-murphy-pose-premiere-lgbtq-1202815745/.

Chapter 15

Exhausting the Present

Twitter, Trump, and Engagement Fatigue in Olivia Laing's Crudo

Shannon Finck

The jacket synopsis of Olivia Laing's *Crudo* (2018a) positions the novel to answer a weighty question: "How do you make art, let alone a life, when one rogue tweet could end it all?" The notion of the world-ending tweet is a relatively new apocalypse scenario, entering the cultural imagination at a time when public and political figures have begun to participate in social media more and more, for better or worse, in order to reach and grow their constituencies. Perhaps no one is more notorious for this mode of address than the forty-fifth president of the United States, Donald Trump, whose late-night hot takes and @s of world leaders on Twitter have held both the press and the populace in their digital thrall since he took office in 2017. Despite the perceived triviality of the form, Trump's tweets have gone beyond shock and offense to cause real harm, threatening human rights, due process, and national security. But rather than ending the world—for instance by triggering nuclear war with North Korea or Iran—these brief and frequent communiqués appear, to the distress of many, to be constructing it, entangling our digital and lived experience like nothing before. As evinced by the 2012 tweet that serves as the novel's epigraph—wherein Trump invites himself to remodel the UN General Assembly in the opulent style of its hulking neighbor, Trump World Tower—140 characters that were once merely obnoxious have lately taken on a darker significance as Trump rebuilds the nation in his own looming image.[1]

In response, *Crudo* takes shape around tweets and headlines, moves at the pace of a newsfeed, and resounds with the rhetoric of crisis. Though its protagonist, Kathy, spends the entire novel at a comfortable remove from the troubling events she reads about online—first, vacationing in Italy in advance of her wedding; afterward, idling around pools, patios, and estates in the UK—these events affect her emotionally and psychologically as she peers in on US and global news via "her scrying glass, Twitter" (Laing 2018a, 35). Kathy is an amalgam of the autobiographical Laing in the summer of 2017, entering her forties, preparing for her own wedding against a backdrop of perplexing current events, and punk postmodernist Kathy Acker, who was a decade older than this novel's central character when she died in 1997. In addition to views conceivably belonging to Laing, Kathy's narration, in the style of Acker, borrows from an array of media and cultural texts and incorporates these verbatim, unattributed, and decontextualized.[2] The effect is a stream-of-consciousness narrative pieced together from the detritus of modern democracy as it crumbles in "real time" in push notifications, SMS, and the president's tweets. The following extended passage contains two of Trump's tweets from August 2017, illustrating how the novel mimics Acker's wry tone and makes use of its contemporary intertexts, and it captures Kathy's harried state of mind as she writes:

> She decided to look at Twitter, to check it out. It was worse than she'd expected. He was retweeting Fox News about jets in Guam that could fight tonight, but he was also taking time out to trashtalk the FailingNewYorkTimes. My first order as President was to renovate and modernize our nuclear arsenal. It is now far stronger and more powerful than ever before . . . . . . Hopefully we will never have to use this power, but there will never be a time that we are not the most powerful nation in the world! When? When had he done that? (42–43; ellipsis in the original)

Crudo's privileged narrator, who finds "Armageddon" taking place inside her laptop (48), is both safe from all this turmoil and not entirely safe, fine and not entirely fine. She scrolls in awe of "how consequences mount up with the minutes, invisible invisible and then overwhelming" (47). Overwhelmed as she claims to be, she remains hesitant to disconnect from life on the screen.

Trump's tweets intrude on the novel's diegesis in the same way Laing admits they invaded her thoughts and surmises they have invaded readers' thoughts as well, provoking a range of feelings from anxiety to despair, maybe on occasion resulting in affective outbursts of our own. Chris Kraus describes the process by which *Crudo* "erupted" from Laing "breathlessly" over just seven weeks, "captur[ing] the psychic effect of living in the perpetual state of remote emergency that defines the present" (2018). Confronting a feeling of unreality shared by many Westerners after the 2016 general election, Kathy immerses herself in "the hyper-acceleration of the story" available via platforms like Twitter and Instagram (Laing 2018a, 87). She grows accustomed to the "queasy" satisfaction of "reliable shots of 10am and 3pm and 7pm outrage" provided by the daily news (87), though she fears the way it numbs her, "making her incapable of action, a beached somnolent whale" (90). Like Acker, her namesake, this fictional Kathy aims to make sense of confounding circumstances by closing the distance between herself and others in person, in writing, and online. Like Acker, her interest in other lives, bodies, and texts lies somewhere between praxis and compulsion. Simultaneously Laing and not Laing, Kathy Acker and not Kathy Acker, us and not us, *Crudo*'s Kathy navigates this "permanent present of the id" with her smartphone in hand and her heart on her sleeve (43). She is neither hero nor sage chronicler of this moment in history. She is not a particularly likable character. Laing explains that when she sought "a character that could observe the turbulence" rather than suffer it, as she was, she cast around and found Kathy (Kraus 2018). "Oh Kathy, nobody wanted you," Laing, or maybe Kathy herself, declares at one point in the novel; "Oh Kathy, now they do" (45). Of all the surprising features of the early twenty-first century surveyed in *Crudo*, the recovery of a complicated literary voice like Acker's to deal with a barrage of tweets and other such virtual noise grounds the work's most valuable insights and, I argue, its politics.[3]

Otherwise, the title—evoking delicate slivers of uncooked fish, lightly dressed—fittingly signals the rare, meaty tidbits delivered by the narrative as well as by micro-blogging services such as Twitter. Early reviews conveyed a general "sense that everything matters yet nothing does" in *Crudo*, a quality of the reading experience "that can make one feel a bit ill . . . the way that being online too long can do" (Garner 2018). But social media posts, like dishes *al crudo*, are meant to be consumed right away and in one bite. Their flavor depends upon serving them fresh; neither holds up to extensive processing. Composed of the raw material of digital ephemera, *Crudo* is not by design an enduring or in-depth cultural commentary. Rather, the novel is an experiment in temporarily neutralizing the threat of right-wing worldbuilding (or worldending) via social media by exhaustively documenting, thus staying in, the present—upsetting though the present may be. It is, in other words, a study in remaining engaged.

During the time Laing was writing *Crudo*—her first work of fiction—she was, she confesses, "failing to write a different book, a serious nonfiction book about the body and violence and protest" (Kraus 2018). She was also feeling exceptionally world-weary:

I was finding it impossible [to write], and I realized it was because the world was changing too rapidly. Because of Trump, because of Brexit, because of the rise of fascism and the attack on concepts like truth and democracy, I just couldn't write the kind of nonfiction I'd done in the past. To write from a stable point of view meant losing the feeling of chaos and perpetual disruption that was the signature of summer 2017. (Kraus 2018)

Enter Kathy. Drawing from Acker's personal brand of pastiche—and often enough, to wit, her words—Laing's polyphonic account of the first months of Trump's presidency, replete with the president's "full arsenal of exclamation marks" (Laing 2018a, 86), demonstrates how certain texts and tweets capture our attention and adhere to our perceptions of current events. Using Acker's voice and cut-up process to explore the unpleasant stickiness of these texts, Laing finds her own writing freed from the obligation to produce sublime and inspiring work about affairs she finds revolting and available to get down into the gutter with the other "opinionated little voice[s]" in the "indecently augmented chorus" that Kathy shrugs off as "the world talking" (33). Ever the provocateur, Acker could do things in prose "that you [You generally? You, Laing?] can't do anymore, short skirts but in sentences-form" (45). Acker "was no stranger to saying things so disgusting and repellent that everyone gagged" (47). Laing tells Kraus, "Writing as Kathy, as this hybrid Franken-stein composite of me and Acker, was immediately liberating" (Kraus 2018). Acker's work, she believes, "creates possibilities" (Kraus 2018). In a beauti-ful twist of fate, Pussy, King of the Pirates, becomes the unlikely challenger we need to take on the Pussy-Grabber-in-Chief.[4]

But Acker has also been Quixote, hacking away at giants who turned out to be mere men, and the Donald Trump whose online presence currently casts a long shadow over the whole of modern democracy, it turns out, is something of an illusion, too. That is not to say that Trump's words, or words in gen-eral, are not dangerous or that fighting damaging fictions is not a worthwhile endeavor. On the contrary, Acker dedicated her life's work to rewriting toxic narratives, "MALE TEXTS WHICH WEREN'T HERS" (Acker 1986, 39). She buried her voice in the literature she ravished and plundered until it emerged from the blood and guts that remained—the "fleshy, emotive frag-ments of female experience within a framework of formalist rigor" (Kraus 2017, 90). To brave such an authorial insurrection, she must have disbelieved that these texts were the cultural exemplars they purported to be or that they had the power to shape the world they seemed to have. At least, she was will-ing to find out. Laing's project takes a similar approach to the magnetism of the newsfeed, disrupting the gripping velocity at which news items appear, refresh, and update and lending to the novel a feeling of "the present being fed back in the past tense, as if we're living in history" (Kraus 2018). Kathy also recounts serious matters in a pointedly flippant tone, an earmark of Acker as well as the prevailing rhetorical mode of Twitter users. This strategy calls to attention contradictions in our thinking about social media participation as both frivolous and dangerous, a means by which otherwise "thoughtful people . . . slip comfortably into the permanent state of distractedness" (Carr 2010, 112). In either case, the prescription is generally avoidance—don't spend too much time online, don't take it too seriously, and definitely don't let it change your mind. Yet, it is changing our minds. From Maggie Jackson's thesis that the erosion of "our capacity for deep, sustained, perceptive attention" comes at the cost of "intimacy, wisdom, and cultural progress" (2008, 13), to Sven Birkerts's warnings that "too much information" transforms us in ways we cannot predict (2015, 4), scholarly consensus maintains that the internet and communications platforms, like e-mail and social media in particular, are rewiring our brains and rewriting our scripts for living. Acker's work, though it predates many of these technologies, insists that if we leave texts alone, either because we fear them or because we've deemed them unworthy of interest, we preserve them as artifacts. We must engage them to disempower them. Likewise, cultivating an intimate familiarity with other, different, new kinds of texts empowers our own voices. One of Quixote's timeless signifying functions is trolling those who believe the rise of new media forms spells the end of the world.[5]

Hand-wringing over the twin risks of information overload and endless distraction posed by digital media has a long history, but the conversation has evolved over the first part of the twenty-first century. In *Contemporary Fictions of Attention*, Alice Bennett describes the ways "reading and attention have . . . become part of a fraught collection of concerns about subjectivity and self-management manifested as a discourse of crisis surrounding readers' capacity for attention" (2018, 1). While many contemporary novelists reflect upon this crisis in their work and, Bennett argues, participate in a "culture of scrutinizing their own attention" (9), it may be useful to today's beleaguered readers and anxious Twitterers to find examples of attention to attention that challenge the dominant discourse. Laing's is one such contemporary novel that attends differently to the specific reading practice of social media use. *Crudo* is a "fiction of attention," the likes of which Bennett describes, in that it both offers a "meaningful representation" of attention to social news and media sharing and manipulates narrative conventions in order to "orchestrate or influence readers' attention" to their own habits (11). Its ludic narrative operates with a model of attention more complex and elastic than panic over a crisis admits, situating these dialogic transmission systems, first, within a history of formally experimental, polyvocal texts, and second, in relation to in-person encounters.

If it feels as though the virtual world is making the physical one less real or reliable, Laing's work proposes (re)turning to postmodern fiction's patterns and tropes to sort things out. It turns out this is a fairly modest proposal. Bennett reminds us, "Fiction's history is inseparable from realistic narratives that, as part of their verisimilitude, are sometimes long-winded or rambling; it has space for tangential flights of fancy, and developed techniques to accommodate the undirected associations of the stream of consciousness" (2018, 16). In practice, even long-form, realist fiction "is always interested in the speculative, the digressive and the iterative; it is, in itself, a distraction" (16). Fictional narratives and social media narratives—for example, threads, stories, or "filter bubbles"—share (at least) two things in common: they allow us to represent the world and to escape it. While digital/information literacy undeniably requires specific interpretive or hyperreading skills, reading, Bennett posits, has "*always* been inattentive . . . the play of attention and distraction is part of the structure of narrative itself" (16). Due to devices like metafiction, intertextuality, and pastiche, this interplay of oppositions is even more pronounced in postmodern fiction, drawing readers' attention to distraction/disruption and its constitutive possibilities. Rather than scolding readers for participating in narrative detours, postmodernism rewards us with layered meaning.

In elegant metaphorical terms, Paul North suggests that because diversions of focus introduce additional information to a particular context in an instant, they confirm "not just the possibility but the existence of an infinitely inclusive collective without the need to count out its members or represent itself" (2012, 183). This claim could easily describe a polyphonic novel—any Acker novel, in fact; they are all so crowded with voices. As Kraus notes, Acker used reading and writing as "technolog[ies] to access other ways of being" (Miller 2017). So has Laing, and so does Kathy. Acker, who read voraciously and wrote so much that her neighbors complained about the noise of her typewriter (Kraus 2017, 29), imagined transcending unpleasant circumstances in her life by entering texts—figuratively, of course, but often literally just copying lines into whatever she was drafting. Laing admits that inventing the Kathy persona and plugging her (Kathy) into the stream permitted her (Laing) to move forward, overcoming, as Kraus (2018) puts it, "the engineered exhaustion and numbness the news cycle inflicts" in order to get on with her next nonfiction book, *Funny Weather* (forthcoming), which addresses the stakes of art in a tempestuous political climate head-on. Similarly, at her most stressed, Kathy finds herself "writing everything down" and sharing it so that "she might exhaust the present" (Laing 2018a, 8). Plagiarizing, imitating, and sharing/retweeting are all ways of drawing or paying attention to written texts. At the same time, they can offer ways of distracting ourselves from our own limited points of view, magnifying others and offering their words up for appreciation or scrutiny. These reading/writing modalities build momentum, oddly, by letting things pile up—voices, texts, ideas, worries. In *Crudo*, attending to everything—Trump's tweets, Brexit, climate change, watermelon, dahlias, Comme des Garçons—becomes a strategy for "living at the end of the world" (18). At least, it enables Kathy to avoid becoming anesthetized to either life's little pleasures or the immensity of the world's suffering. In contrast to Trump's use of Twitter to manufacture confirmation bias and shore up the false impression of a unified party and nation with retweets of Fox News, the thread that links Acker to Laing to the fictional Kathy deconstructs the autocratic site figured by @realDonaldTrump. Moreover, scattering Trump's threats, lies, and aggrandizements among the minutiae of the everyday—moments as they pass—allows Kathy and her circle to collectively envision a future, so that even as "Twitter's ABLAZE" with the news of Trump's firing of James Comey, she and her friends can see through to a time when the smoke has cleared and they "know how it panned out" (28). The novel thus imagines, imperfectly, what it might look like to "exhaust the present," rather than letting it exhaust us, by doubling, compiling, or reproducing its forms in hopes of altering their effects, if not their functions.

There are those who find Laing's experiment insufficient to the problem of Trump, all for which he stands, and the stage at his disposal. Disappointment characterizes reviews of Trump-era novels by established writers. And while it may be easy to dismiss hyperbolic diatribes like Richard North Patterson's (2019) essay in the *Atlantic*, which argues that Donald Trump's lies have "rendered fiction redundant," others are more incisive in their claims. Gareth Watkins (2019), for example, delivers a scathing critique of the tendency for "Trump novels" to be populated by wealthy, white characters having nervous breakdowns. He writes,

> Nobody from the dead center of the political spectrum can get it right so long as they employ Trump as window dressing for stories of the same neurotic but ultimately good-hearted middle-to-upper-class coastal liberals that a good portion of literary fiction has always been about. They won't get it right as long as everything is reduced to the personal, to atomized individuals feeling just awful that bad things are happening somewhere else to someone else—seeing the world in terms of the actions of individuals, not systems, and definitely not in terms of class struggle.

His contention rings true of *Crudo*. Neither Kathy nor the novel seems to be "asking difficult questions about why authoritarianism is on the rise, and how their own class might be complicit with it" (Watkins 2019). It does not show us "a world where Trumps are no longer possible" (Watkins 2019). But Laing, or at least Kathy, seems to anticipate this criticism and counters it with a defense of what it feels like to be an individual, refusing to ignore "the tide of cruelty in the world" (Laing 2018a, 109). "Sometimes people say Kathy is not a realistic writer, that she is gratuitous in her effects," she writes, "but she can't help feeling they are walking with their eyes closed. She didn't make the dead girls up. Or the prisons" (100).

The most generous treatment of this and other Trump novels as literary fiction's latest lost causes comes from Erik Hane (2018). Hane would seem to understand what Laing is driving at in *Crudo* and even empathize with Kathy's altogether ordinary suffering to a degree. He writes,

> I do not need to describe for you, reader—a person with a conscience and a pulse—what this last year and a half has felt like. We're all anxious and addled and many of us have turned following the news into what amounts to a second full-time job. We're hitting refresh; we are clicking vigorously to See New Tweets; we're watching our fundamental notions of action and consequence fall away with each new revealed scandal, none of which have made much of a dent. . . . Something inside us has been knocked off its axis.

His sketch of the quotidian trauma of life after Trump echoes Kathy's observations about the misshapen relationship between truth and consequences, cause and effect, and the world and Web 2.0 applications:

> Some sort of cord between action and consequence had been severed. Things still happened, but not in any sensible order, it was hard to talk about truth because some bits were hidden, the result or maybe the cause, and anyway the space between them was full of misleading data, nonsense and lies. It was very dizzying, you wasted a lot of time figuring it out. . . . A lot had changed this year. (Laing 2018a, 62)

Affinity with Kathy aside, however, Hane's main criticism of experiments like *Crudo* is that they amplify the very platforms and sociopolitical positions their authors detest purely by representing them—or perhaps by representing them "purely." He finds "the proliferation of these literal story elements cribbed from a CNN chyron" more "troubling" than poignant because they reveal nothing beyond the basic fact that "writers are having the same problem everyone else is: an inability to look away" (Hane 2018). Implicit in this censure is the conviction that writers *should* be able to look away. They should, as they are specially endowed, "[write] the political moment"; instead, as Hane sees it, they are allowing the moment to write them (2018).

Like other forms of attention-policing, this line of argument situates attention within an economy of scarcity, in which we are obliged to direct the precious resource of our attention toward objects or endeavors that are worthwhile, transformative, or uplifting. It ignores the potential for shareable content such as tweets or memes to lay important groundwork for the production of such objects or the facilitation of such endeavors (Garber 2015). Nevertheless, Hane makes a compelling case for choosing not to attend to Trump's tweets, or exposés on Dylann Roof, or the *Daily Stormer*—all cited in *Crudo*. He uses Nazis:

> It is one of fascism's goals to monopolize our attention. It would like to shrink our imagination; it would like for us to peer wide-eyed at its harsh restrictions

and be able to think of nothing else. And it is tempting to stare like this, because fascism and its precursors are rife with contradictions that seem to beg to be pointed out by Reasonable People. But that's one of its tricks. Fascism welcomes our attempts to play logical "gotcha" with its inconsistencies because it knows we will lose—not because we won't find a fallacy but because the fallacy won't matter. (2018)

On this point, again, Hane and Kathy appear to concur: "Numbness," she reflects, "was what the Nazis did, made people feel like things were moving too fast to stop and though unpleasant and eventually terrifying and appalling, were probably impossible to do anything about" (Laing 2018a, 87). Examined side by side, we can see how anxieties about imperiled attention, and not ideological differences, found Hane's discomfort with works like Laing's, though he probably wouldn't much care for Kathy's appraisal of Nazi fashion at the Charlottesville protests either (53). Hane would prefer authors not squander emotional and intellectual reserves, or the broad reach that mainstream publishing affords them, by engaging fascism long enough to "write its story" (2018). Kathy, on the other hand, notes that Nazis killed "the people who had refused to engage" alongside everyone else (Laing 2018a, 63). Both stances recognize attention as political and call for attention with intention. Even if it's not in short supply, to what and how we pay attention matters in that it produces material effects.

Synonymous with other forms of close, sustained attention such as "commitment" and "involvement," the term "engagement," used in a twenty-first-century context to define a set of social reading behaviors online, connotes how seriously we take reading even when we find the texts wanting or troubling. Directives to engage in specific ways, to "raise awareness" or "stay woke," seem almost to outweigh action as benchmarks of "good" citizenship. In a similar vein, engagement can be monetized, gamified, meted out with apps, and even medicated (following diagnoses of attention deficit disorders). Because engagement online is often visible to others, it invites the risk of wedding one's avatar to the objects of one's interest (e.g., brands, particular websites, posts, political figures). In all these ways, engagement involves both attention and meta-attention, a hyper-awareness of the ways we invest our attention, who might be watching, and what they might be learning about us and the ways we interpret the world.[6]

According to Bennett, attention to attention disrupts attention itself. Not only can the delicate discursive bubble we inhabit digitally not "withstand rough handling or the scrutiny of a pointed gaze," we have come to believe that the "absorbed attention" that many reading experiences require is "only possible through a labour of disciplined focus"—difficult to keep up, become immersed in, or enjoy (2018, 1). Given these demands, it is easy to see how the various texts competing for our exclusive attention can quickly lead to a state of content saturation, or "engagement fatigue," the solution to which might seem to be to simply disengage.[7] On the other end of a spectrum of possible outcomes, however, deliberate engagement with a diverse range of texts can enact "a shift of attention out of a closed domestic unit or static situation into something less focused and more ambiguous" (Bennett 2018, 80), guiding readers/users toward empathy, creative thinking, and problem solving. That was certainly Acker's wager, tested by Laing in *Crudo*. Engagement in its numerous vicissitudes—labored, compulsory, distracting, disruptive, and so on—structures the novel as the inverse of nostalgia for an imagined time before attention was in such high demand and information so difficult to process.

Laing's engagement with unsettling texts strives, on the one hand, to settle them—not permanently or irrefutably, but within a time and place, as a form of bracketing or containment. These texts penetrate Kathy's narrative, but they do not dominate it. She takes them in, so they cannot consume her. Such was Acker's way; as she put it in an interview with Michael Silverblatt, she "need[ed] other texts" to react to in order to thrive and work (Silverblatt [1992] n.d.). On the other hand, engaging disquieting material teaches Laing to be more selectively and intensely unsettled by some pieces of information, and thereby more generous toward others, which, she tells Kraus, is "what [she] want[s] art to do" and what she believes Acker's work does (Kraus 2018). Readers can track this shifting dynamic in Kathy's attitude as the summer comes to an end and her reflections begin to sound more like resolutions to act: "If it was happening to someone, it being unspeakable violence, how could she be happy. . . . Kathy could not settle" (Laing 2018a, 112). Tensions between settling matters or scores, being, oneself, unsettled, and settling *for* certain things abound in *Crudo*, cleverly woven into the narrative by way of a double entendre using none other than the word "engagement."

Crudo represents Kathy's social media use frequently but comments on it indirectly, using antanaclasis; her youthful, modern engagement with online content competes for her attention with her very traditional engagement to an older man. Though it is this latter engagement that ostensibly invests the novel with a plot, it becomes clear that Kathy's relationship to her portable electronic devices is at least as important to the story. She exclaims, "If this was love she'd take it, lying next to him naked, both fiddling with their phones" (Laing 2018a, 23). Kathy's engagement to marry—her first; his third, a cliché—is not any less profound to this former wild child than world news. She marvels at bourgeois normativity; having "never spent much time with heterosexuals, she didn't know there were so many of them, and all so similar" (24). Neither is the matrimonial engagement less vexing. She worries about getting weighed down by marriage and "clanking around like tins tied to a car" (7). After a fight with her fiancé, she turns to Twitter for, of all things, solace (35). Later, she remarks, "Her husband's sad eyes upset her but also infuriated her, she detested being responsible for anyone else's happiness. . . . Finally she understood all the aloof boyfriends, the endless appeal of people who were only half there" (84–85). As the novel contemplates Kathy's ambivalent relationship to both her engagement to be married and her engagement with online content, readers observe how these compartmentalized features of her life evoke similar affective responses. They each, in turn, supplant Kathy's "old pals hankering and craving" with a nagging feeling of obligation toward other people—a very Ackeresque character arc (85). Laing stages these forms of engagement in the text in ways that demonstrate how the experience of "reading" one another and the world via digital media is no more inherently distressing or chaotic than the familiar contact we experience "IRL."

While many readers, as reviews demonstrate, find Kathy's engagement online no less vain or vapid than Trump's or anyone else's, I find more evidence to suggest that Kathy gleans from the acts of scrolling, clicking through, and checking in a set of literacy skills for interpreting the present. For instance, whenever things get too trying or circumstances feel too grim, Kathy toggles between her two most pressing engagements—the news and her nuptials—as one opens or shifts to a new window or tab when taking a break from mental labor or searching for new information online. In this fashion, she returns over and over again with renewed stamina to tasks and topics she previously found unmanageable or inconceivable. Many times, Laing signals Kathy's pivots using the adverb "anyway": "Anyway, she'd gone" (8); "Anyway they sorted it out" (35); "Anyway she painted her eyelids" (67). The entire first section of *Crudo* is titled "Anyway" (1), which gives it the impression of an extended aside, or, alternatively, an inevitability. The procession of "anyways" through which Kathy's summer progresses indicates both that ordinary life goes on in the present, with little regard to our historicizing, and that Kathy has created—stumbled upon, perhaps—a way to divide her attention long enough to abide within it.

Because the novel leaves Kathy in the present, boarding a flight back to the United States, we can't know her next move. Laing's next move was to resume work on *Funny Weather*. If her short essay in *Frieze* "The Intertwining of Art, Gardening, Filmmaking and Writing," published under the "Funny Weather" tag, is any clue, this book will examine art of all kinds, including gardening, as means of political resistance as well as ways of reclaiming or rethinking time and attention. In this short piece, Laing recounts a 1939 entry in Virginia Woolf's diary, which "records hearing Hitler on the radio" (Laing 2018b). It follows: "Her husband, Leonard, was in the garden he'd painstakingly constructed at Monk's House. . . . 'I shan't come in,' he shouted. 'I'm planting iris, and they will be flowering long after he is dead'" (Laing 2018b).

About halfway through *Crudo*, Kathy, mostly quoting Acker from *Don Quixote*, dismisses Donald Trump and elevates her art in the same sweeping gesture: "Now, sitting on her sofa, she wrote: how did America begin. To defeat America she had to learn who America is. She wrote: Trump, a minor factor in nature, no longer existed. She wrote: what are the myths of the beginning of America. She was beginning to excite herself" (Laing 2018a, 74). I don't think Laing's work is trending toward elaborate arguments for self-care, but it may be headed toward a politics of artistic engagement that staves off the end of the world by preserving in indiscriminate detail the daily minutiae of which history and our lives are composed. And while this narrative technique is not new, it must now be reworked and reworked again to include new and fleeting forms of minutiae—the texts, tweets, and Instagrams through which we attend to the world's bedlam and its beauty.

NOTES

1. The full text of this tweet reads: "The cheap 12 inch sq. marble tiles behind speaker at UN always bothered me. I will replace with beautiful large marble slabs if they ask me" (Trump 2012).

2. Laing does supply an exhaustive list of intertexts as sources at the end of the novel (2018a, 135–41), echoing Acker's disambiguated sources at the end of each chapter in *The Childlike Life of the Black Tarantula* ([1973] 1998). Citing them at once in this way simulates for readers the process of literary scrolling, by which Laing compiled *Crudo* out of bits of news, tweets, and passages from Acker's novels (Kraus 2018).

3. Laing is not the only artist recently interested in Acker. Chris Kraus's biography, *After Kathy Acker* (2017); Matias Viegener's edited collection of Acker's e-mail correspondence with McKenzie Wark, *I'm Very into You* (2015); and Kaucyila Brooke's continuously touring image installation, *Kathy Acker's Clothes* ([1998, 2004] n.d.) are just a few of several creative and critical projects demonstrating a resurgence of interest in Acker's life and work.

4. It's difficult to identify the first reference to Trump as "Pussy-Grabber-in-Chief," but the epithet originates from a recording of Trump's comments on women to television host Billy Bush, in 2005, stating that he could "grab 'em by the pussy" because he is "a star" ("Transcript: Donald Trump's Taped Comments About Women" 2016).

5. Of the many satirical themes in Cervantes's original work, *Don Quixote*'s treatment of seventeenth-century anxieties about the dangers of losing touch with reality as a result of reading too much or too exclusively in the fanciful genre of Romance is probably the one that resonates most with twenty-first-century concerns about new media and information literacy. As Rachel Nevins argues, the elderly Don Quixote figures the quintessentially untrained or "bad reader," whose undiscerning tastes and reading habits lead to an "inability to distinguish between fiction and nonfiction . . .

books [and] reality itself" that is not unlike the way "people on social media sites like Reddit are churning out a worldview that's dissociated from reality . . . in which reality nevertheless gets ensnared" (Nevins 2019). Where Nevins holds the classic novel up as "a cautionary tale for our age, in which misinformation and conspiracy theories proliferate" online, others before her have made similar arguments about Quixote and popular media—such as radio or television—ascendant in their times. For a thorough history of these sorts of readings, see West (2019).

6. Bennett discusses these and several other features of attention's relationship to technology in detail in the introduction to *Contemporary Fictions of Attention* (2018).

7. While no official definition of engagement fatigue prevails, medical and marketing professionals and social scientists alike share a set of similar concerns regarding the ways in which the pace and plethora of online content not only cause users to turn away but produce symptoms of burnout and other reaction disorders. In *Exhaustion: A History*, Anna Katharina Schaffner explains engagement fatigue as a psychosomatic illness in which "the ubiquity of new information and communication technologies, such as the Internet, e-mail, Twitter, social networks, and cell phones . . . no longer allow[s] us properly to disconnect and to relax, blurring the boundaries between work and life and thus causing chronic stress" (Schaffner 2016, 9). See, for a popular example, Michael Stoner's blog post arguing that the term be added to future iterations of the DSM (Stoner 2009).

REFERENCES

Acker, Kathy. 1986. *Don Quixote*. New York: Grove.

———. (1973) 1998. *The Childlike Life of the Black Tarantula*. In *Portrait of an Eye*, 1–90. New York: Grove.

Acker, Kathy, and McKenzie Wark. 2015. *I'm Very into You: Correspondence 1995–1996*. Edited by Matias Viegener. South Pasadena: Semiotext(e).

Bennett, Alice. 2018. *Contemporary Fictions of Attention: Reading and Distraction in the Twenty-First Century*. London: Bloomsbury.

Birkerts, Sven. 2015. *Changing the Subject: Art and Attention in the Internet Age*. Minneapolis: Graywolf.

Brooke, Kaucyila. (1998, 2004) n.d. *Kathy Acker's Clothes. Kaucyilabrooke.com*. Accessed May 21, 2019. http://kaucyilabrooke.com/index.php?/projects/archive--kathy-ackers-clothes/.

Carr, Nicholas. 2010. *The Shallows: What the Internet Is Doing to Our Brains*. New York: W.W. Norton.

Garber, Megan. 2015. "#TheDress and the Rise of Attention-Policing." *Atlantic*. February 27, 2015. https://www.theatlantic.com/technology/archive/2015/02/thedress-and-the-rise-of-attention-policing/386357/.

Garner, Dwight. 2018. "'Crudo' Is a Novel with a Real-Life Novelist in Thin Disguise." *New York Times*. September 24, 2018. https://www.nytimes.com/2018/09/24/books/review-crudo-olivia-laing.html.

Hane, Erik. 2018. "The Year in Trump Novel Pitches: An Agent's Lament." *Literary Hub*. March 30, 2018. https://lithub.com/the-year-in-trump-novel-pitches-an-agents-lament/.

Jackson, Maggie. 2008. *Distracted: The Erosion of Attention and the Coming Dark Age*. Amherst, NY: Prometheus Books.

Kraus, Chris. 2017. *After Kathy Acker*. South Pasadena: Semiotext(e).

———. 2018. "Becoming Kathy Acker: An Interview with Olivia Laing." *Paris Review*. September 11, 2018. https://www.theparisreview.org/blog/2018/09/11/becoming-kathy-acker-an-interview-with-olivia-laing/.

Laing, Olivia. 2018a. *Crudo*. New York: W. W. Norton.

———. 2018b. "The Intertwining of Art, Gardening, Filmmaking and Writing." *Frieze*. April 20, 2018. https://frieze.com/article/intertwining-art-gardening-filmmaking-and-writing?language=en.

———. Forthcoming. *Funny Weather: Art in an Emergency*. New York: Picador.

Miller, Nicole. 2017. "Chris Kraus: *After Kathy Acker*." *Guernica*. October 16, 2017. https://www.guernicamag.com/chris-kraus-kathy-acker/.

Nevins, Rachel. 2019. "*Don Quixote* or the Dangers of Reading Badly." *Ploughshares*. January 12, 2019. http://blog.pshares.org/index.php/don-quixote-or-the-dangers-of-reading-badly/.

North, Paul. 2012. *The Problem of Distraction*. Stanford: Stanford University Press.

Patterson, Richard North. 2019. "I Used to Write Novels. Then Trump Rendered Fiction Redundant." *Atlantic*. March 31, 2019. https://www.theatlantic.com/ideas/archive/2019/03/richard-north-patterson-i-quit-novels-cover-trump/585901/.

Schaffner, Anna Katharina. 2016. *Exhaustion: A History*. New York: Columbia University Press.

Silverblatt, Michael. (1992) n.d. "Kathy Acker." *KCRW*. Accessed June 17, 2019. https://www.kcrw.com/culture/shows/bookworm/kathy-acker.

Stoner, Michael. 2009. "Engagement Fatigue: The Ultimate Consumer Response to Irrelevant Engagement Marketing." *Mstoner.com*. October 17, 2009. https://www.mstoner.com/blog/marketing-communications/engagement_fatigue_the_ultimate_consumer_response_to_irrelevant_engagement_/.

"Transcript: Donald Trump's Taped Comments about Women." 2016. *New York Times*. October 8, 2016. https://www.nytimes.com/2016/10/08/us/donald-trump-tape-transcript.html.

Trump, Donald J. (@realDonaldTrump). 2012. "The cheap 12 inch sq. marble tiles behind speaker at UN always bothered me. I will replace with beautiful large marble slabs if they ask me." Twitter, October 3, 2012. https://twitter.com/realdonaldtrump/status/253488938264715264.

Watkins, Gareth. 2019. "The Disappointing Trump Novel." *Commune*. Spring 2019. https://communemag.com/the-disappointing-trump-novel/.

West, Kevin R. 2019. *Literary Depictions of Dangerous Reading*. Lanham: Lexington.

Chapter 16

"Be a Little *Genrequeer"*

Rushdie's The Golden House *in the Age of Post-Truth*

Jaclyn Partyka

When Salman Rushdie went on the press circuit following the publication of his novel *The Golden House* (2017), a number of headlines and reviews focused on the seemingly prescient nature of the novel's subject matter in regard to the rise of Donald Trump to the American presidency.[1] This sentiment is reinforced in an interview Rushdie did with poet Tishani Doshi at the 2018 Hay Festival, where he describes how he was constructing a Trumpian cast of characters for the novel before Trump became a serious figure on the national and political stage: "And all of this I had made up before I was ever thinking of Donald Trump. I invented him before he came up. And it was a little scary, when suddenly there they were" (India Today Web Desk 2018). Regardless of how much we trust this account from Rushdie, as many of the chapters preceding this one have demonstrated, Trump has been a figure of cultural imagination for decades. The question now is how this larger-than-life fictional caricature has become an intrusive political reality. I suggest that one way to conceptualize the kind of border-crossing Rushdie describes above is to take into account how discussions of genre and fictionality have become much more significant within a post-truth moment.

Dubbed the word of the year in 2016 by Oxford Dictionaries (Flood 2016), "post-truth" has become a somewhat slippery term, encompassing seemingly everything from the proliferation of maliciously constructed fake news and the willing spread of political lies, to the general frustration in the public's attempts to negotiate information across increasingly partisan information silos. There have also been a number of think pieces attempting to link the contemporary post-truth moment to a longer legacy of literary postmodernism.[2] Through the decentering of Enlightenment concepts such as the self, history, and knowledge, canonical considerations of postmodernism created skepticism about grand narratives and dominant structures. On the surface, this rendering of postmodernism seems to align well with what we have come to understand as the post-truth moment. However, while I concede that the postmodern project of deconstructing master narratives has led to a certain skepticism around established knowledge institutions, the motivations around the post-truth moment are more intentionally reactionary than intellectually deconstructive. Generally, while postmodernism uses irony and pastiche to self-reflexively appropriate institutions of knowledge and power, the post-truth moment "emphasizes discord, confusion, [and] polarized views" purposefully, and often for political gain (Harsin 2018, 3).

Thus, as the rhetoric of post-truth gains more dominance it opens up space for the rise of authoritarian power. As Lee McIntyre points out, the debate over the post-truth has significant stakes: "What is striking about the idea of post-truth is not just that truth is being challenged, *but that it is being challenged as a mechanism for asserting political dominance*" (2018, xiv; emphasis in the original). Though McIntyre cautions against a too-easy connection of the post-truth to Trump (15), there has certainly been a correlation in the way attacks on facts, reason, and sincerity often originate from Trump and his spokes-people, with Rudy Giuliani's claim that "truth isn't truth" as the most outright and blatant representative of discourse in this category (Phillips 2018). This sentiment is shared within the fictional world of *The Golden House*, with one character—the narrator's girlfriend, Suchitra—encapsulating the problematic ethos of the post-truth moment best: "*True* is such a twentieth-century concept. The question is, can I get you to believe it, can I get it repeated enough times to make it as good as true. The question is, can I lie better than the truth" (Rushdie 2017, 221). And so, in a world where "facts are less influential in shaping political debate or public opinion than appeals to emotion and personal belief" (*Oxford English Dictionary Online* 2017), I suggest that the stakes of artistic and imaginative representation seem more important.

What we have come to understand as the post-truth also has special implications for contemporary fiction. Using Rushdie's treatment of the proto-Trump era in *The Golden House* as a case study, this chapter demonstrates how navigating the rhetoric of post-truth must involve tactical gestures of fictionality. Much of my consideration of fictionality draws from the understanding that "fictionality in the form of the intentional use of invented stories and scenarios . . . is ubiquitous in our culture" (Nielsen, Phelan, and Walsh 2015, 62). Once believed to be siloed within the halls of literary institutions, fictionality has become a rhetorical strategy across a number of discourse communities, from politics to journalism. But learning how to negotiate the differences between these discourses takes special consideration of not only authorial intent but genre. While gestures of fictionality become disingenuous or malicious when applied to political speech, they can take on different rhetorical effects when relegated to literary genres.[3] Thus, literary fiction, in its ability to both resemble elements of the real world and yet remain distinct, operates as a useful battleground to contend with epistemological traumas related to our post-truth moment.

One way to understand how contemporary literary fiction has a rhetorical and substantive effect on our contemporary world is through Theodore Martin's definition of the contemporary. To Martin, the contemporary is "a *strategy of mediation*: a means of negotiating between experience and retrospection, immersion and explanation, closeness and distance" (2017, 5). In order to demonstrate this type of critical method, Martin suggests that a renewed attention to genre can be used to trace both "change and continuity" across literary history through shifts in aesthetic form (2017, 6). Applying this framework to a post-truth context, for instance, can help clarify distinctions between the satire and literary hoaxes of the past and today's iteration of fake news and alternative facts.[4] Within this context, I argue that what is intriguing about the post-truth moment for Rushdie's *The Golden House* is the way that it puts certain established literary genres into relief while simultaneously elevating marginalized and niche creative genres as more substantial rhetorical actors.

Rushdie is certainly no stranger to mingling generic categories in his treatment of fiction. Referring to *Midnight's Children* and the novel's supernaturally omniscient first-person narrator, Søren Frank identifies an "encyclopaedic" effect, that manifests in a "generic hybridity as it mixes elements of family saga, *Bildungsroman*, autobiography, national history, myth, legend, the picaresque, epic, slum-naturalism, magical realism, essay, prophecy, satire, comedy, tragedy and surrealism" (2010, 196). In *The Satanic Verses*, the effectiveness of this sort of panoramic narration is enabled by an omniscient and seemingly extradiegetic narrator, such that shifts across generic modes are more palatable since they are filtered through a god-like (or Satanic) figure. However, *The Golden House* employs an intradiegetic narrator, in the young filmmaker René, who, as I'll explain below, is less convincing in his ability to play with these genres on such a massive scale. Instead, the sections that follow demonstrate how René's search for a suitable genre to capture the story of Nero Golden[5] and his family functions as a meta-commentary on Rushdie's ongoing and somewhat stilted project to couch social commentary on Trump and the post-truth era in the platform of fiction.

REALISM

A renewed attention to realism—a literary genre inherently wound up in the project of verisimilitude and an accurate representation of reality—is especially relevant within the post-truth moment. The stakes of realism understandably rise when it seems like wide swathes of the population are living in completely separate realities. Perhaps for this reason, many initial reviews of Rushdie's *The Golden House* immediately position Rushdie's novel within the legacy of realist writing.[6] While this designation would be unremarkable for a number of contemporary novelists, Rushdie's relationship with realism has always been qualified alongside the author's canonical status as one of the originators of the subgenre of magical realism. As a representative mode of postcolonial writing, magical realism, from well-known authors like Rushdie, García Márquez, and others, collapses the boundaries between what is real and what is fantastic in a way that "generates a scrupulous equivalence between the two domains" (Quayson 2006, 728). In this way, magical realism became a dominant mode for postcolonial writing that concerned itself with creating non-Eurocentric visions of reality that call into question the dominant narratives through a method that Rushdie describes as "telling the truth by means of obvious untruth" (Rushdie 2018). Rushdie's *Midnight's Children*, for instance, relies on the conceit that all those born during the Partition of India are imbued with supernatural powers. However, while magical realism may have been the appropriate style for Rushdie to artfully weave Saleem Sinai's life story alongside the break between India and Pakistan, Rushdie asserts that *The Golden House* represents his "personal revolt against magic realism" (Tuttle 2017). Rushdie's affront to the subgenre of literary writing he helped to make mainstream suggests the need for a new version of qualified realism to respond to the age of post-truth and the proto-Trump era. But, what would that realism actually look like?

Rushdie's 1983 novel, *Shame*, is perhaps the most explicit frame to think about how the author has previously conceived of the function of realism to depict contemporary events. In a thinly veiled novel outlining the atrocities and power struggles afflicting Pakistan in the 1970s, *Shame* ambitiously juxtaposes contemporary events through a historical lens. As in *The Satanic Verses*, the narrator of *Shame* is an extradiegetic figure, above the fray of events, both historical and contemporary. It is this kind of distance that allows him to make the following distinction: "But suppose this were a realistic novel! Just think what else I might have to put in. . . . How much real-life material might become compulsory!" (Rushdie 1983, 71). What follows is a telescopic list of the social and political ills afflicting Pakistan and the wider world, including the execution of Zulfikar Ali Bhutto, the rise of global anti-Semitism, the increase in heroin exports, and the practice of bribing judges. Following this litany, the narrator laments that addressing the specifics of these actual political affairs of Pakistan in the 1970s in the novel would have little effect:

By now, if I had been writing a book of this nature, it would have done me no good to protest that I was writing universally, not only about Pakistan. The book would have been banned, dumped in the rubbish bin, burned. All that effort for nothing! Realism can break a writer's heart.

Fortunately, however, I am only telling a sort of modern fairy-tale, so that's all right; nobody need get upset, or take anything I say too seriously. No drastic action need be taken, either.

What a relief! (72)

What is most telling in this characterization of realism is how the bifurcation between the imaginative and real seems less secure under a realist rubric. The idea that the mantle of realism generates a "compulsory" addition of real-world material is especially troubling to *Shame*'s narrator. Additionally, the almost ironic aspect of this description of censorship in some ways presupposes the *Verses* Affair, where the stakes of fictional representation became a life and death scenario for Rushdie and his publishers after the Ayatollah Khomeini's Valentine's Day fatwa in 1988. Within this context of censorship, it makes sense that fiction, and other such "modern fairy-tales," should be distinct from nonfictional genres like history or journalism. And yet, this pronouncement is made with a tongue-in-cheek awareness of how the sharp lines between these genres are often an imaginary construction.

Thus, it's in *The Golden House* where Rushdie embraces new genres of representation to articulate their relationship with realism. By filtering its generic classification through the perspective of the novel's narrator, René, the novel takes a circuitous route to determine the most appropriate gesture for realism in this contemporary moment. In many ways, aspiring filmmaker René is positioned as a more intrusive Nick Carraway as he studies and speculates about his Greenwich Village neighbors, the titular Goldens of the novel. Prior to their hasty and mysterious arrival, on the date of Barack Obama's inauguration no less, the Goldens become a jolt of focus for what René imagines as "a mighty film . . . dealing with migration, transformation, fear, death, rationalism, romanticism, sexual change, the city, cowardice, and courage; nothing less than a panoramic portrait of [his] times" (Rushdie 2017, 28). Those acquainted with Rushdie's oeuvre would find this litany of foci somewhat familiar, recalling the epic and transformative elements of both the novel that sparked his literary star, *Midnight's Children*, and the book that placed him in the global crosshairs, *The Satanic Verses*. However, in articulating his grand design, René's aspirations here seem imbued with arrogance, such that we are left with a narrator who seems out of pace with the project he's presenting. Other characters also recognize that René does not seem equipped for the task. While a film student, René's intended project is panned by his professor due to lack of excitement or substance (28–29).

And it is here where the mysterious arrival of Nero Golden—the first of two Trumpian avatars Rushdie weaves into the novel—lends René the material necessary to construct his grand designs.

Defining his artistic vision as "Operatic Realism" (Rushdie 2017, 28), René seems to align himself with the *verismo* movement in the Italian opera. Containing an "excess of passion and emotion" and a rapid series of climaxes, *verismo* often exposes and juxtaposes societal and political extremes (Carner 1985, 7). This mode also correlates with the realist subgenre of naturalism, where characters function as societal types in order to portray a determinist sensibility. Thus, in many ways, this extreme and punctuated version of realism seems appropriate to tackle the increasingly divided years leading up to the Trump presidency.

And perhaps this is why in interviews Rushdie endorses René's vision of Operatic Realism, admitting that "that's kind of what I'm trying to do here" (Tuttle 2017). Within this context, René's artistic intentions seem more fitting if they function as a front for Rushdie's larger authorial aspirations to create a novel suitable for the post-truth moment. In an essay for the *New Yorker*, Rushdie outlines the difficulty of coping with a world in which "the breakdown in the old agreements about reality is now the most significant reality" (Rushdie 2018). Along these lines, the impetus behind literary realism has genuine stakes for both Rushdie and his literary colleagues: "We stand once again, though for different reasons, in the midst of the rubble of the truth. And it is for us—writers, thinkers, journalists, philosophers—to undertake the task of rebuilding our readers' belief in reality, their faith in the truth. And to do it with new language, from the ground up" (Rushdie 2018). I propose that the "new language" of reality that Rushdie seeks in *The Golden House* may actually be an amalgamation of a number of realistic subgenres. In this way, Rushdie veers close to Frederic Jameson's paradoxically modernist conception of realism as "a discovery process . . . with its emphasis on the new and the hitherto unreported, unrepresented, and unseen, and its notorious subversion of inherited ideas and genres" (Jameson 2012, 476). Thus, in constructing a novel in which these subgenres are elevated alongside each other, Rushdie creates a more realistic representation of how contemporary readers must constantly negotiate switching between nonfictional, fictional, and hybrid genres within the context of the post-truth moment. As Suchitra at one point suggests to René about his film project, "Maybe mix up the genres, be a little *genrequeer*" (Rushdie 2017, 222).[7] In what follows, I argue that *The Golden House* models how Rushdie strategically reimagines certain subgenres of realism to appropriately depict the difficulties and absurdities of the pre-Trump era. By artfully weaving together forms like the historical novel, hybrid genre forms like the mockumentary, and exaggerated representations found in comic books, Rushdie asks his readers to broaden their understanding of realism to better contend with this current historical moment.

HISTORICAL NOVEL

While on the surface the historical novel may seem out of step with my discussion of the contemporary post-truth moment, there is merit in exploring how this subgenre has reemerged as a means to reflect on the past in order to record our current moment. There has also been a resurgence of critical attention on the historical novel as a genre. Perry Anderson's (2011) retrospective on the form, for instance, connects the "second coming" of the historical novel with the stylistic mix-ups of counterfactuals, anachronisms, and temporal shifts characteristic of postmodernist styles. Anderson's survey follows in the legacy of Lukács's canonical study of the genre as a signifier of the rise of nationalism, where the tensions of social change ultimately led to an emerging historical consciousness (Lukács 1983, 19–30). Since then there has been a critical recognition of the form's dominance in both critical and popular literary markets. For instance, James English's computational study finds that novels with historical settings have dominated prize-nominated fiction since 1980 (2016, 407–08). But Alexander Manshel's recent update to the genre, through his overview of what he calls the "recent historical novel," is perhaps best to explain the kind of historical consciousness Rushdie engages with in *The Golden House*. Manshel's outline of this offshoot of the genre strategically embraces contemporary tensions, claiming that recent historical novels are often "grounded in catastrophe, mediated by the news, and marked by a particularly ambivalent politics" (Manshel 2017). In this way, Manshel's treatment of historical consciousness is especially attentive to anxieties relevant to the post-truth moment.

For instance, one of the most noteworthy consequences of the post-truth moment revolves around the struggle to break through an increasingly fragmented political sphere where a "prevalent nondialogue" between partisan groups results in the failure to achieve a common discourse or understanding (Harsin 2018, 5). Whereas Lukács's classical depiction of the historical novel, through Sir Walter Scott's *Waverley*, depicted a world in flux between ideologies of the past and social change, the concluding effect of the novel is one of progress and "future development" (Lukács 1983, 32).[8] However, the kind of middle distance between ideologies forged in *Waverley* around the Jacobite Revolution is troubled in *The Golden House*, where the novel's ambivalent treatment of political factions embraces conflict as an inevitable and seemingly insurmountable obstacle to political discourse. This stance is perhaps best articulated by René's late parents, expatriate Belgians and university professors, who cultivate an extreme affinity for the city of New York. As René's father at one point explains, "De point is, we like de bubble, and so do you. . . . We don't want to live in a red state, and you—you'd be done for in for example Kansas, where dey don't believe in *evolution*" (Rushdie 2017, 25). This description both echoes and reinforces conservative laments about the limited scope of urban coastal elites to acknowledge the political power of so-called flyover states, which is one of the dominant narratives for why Donald Trump won the 2016 election. Thus, the kind of political ambivalence Manshel highlights is embraced by René and his parents, who appear happy to exist in their bubble-within-a-bubble in Greenwich Village, even if the ideological underpinnings behind this perspective are difficult to pin down.

While these kinds of self-imposed information bubbles certainly contribute to how the atmosphere of post-truth can lead to political ambivalence, another significant factor is how the mass proliferation of news media creates a mediated experience of reality. In *Imagined Communities*, Benedict Anderson (2006) argues that the collective experience of reading the newspaper can lead to feelings of national belonging and community. This act of imagining recent history through the act of reading has since been amplified with the advent of digital media and the twenty-four-hour news cycle. However, as the scale of written information available, from sources both reputable and otherwise, increases beyond what Anderson originally conceived, it becomes more difficult to imagine a collective unity. Rather, what results is less a mediated understanding of recent history or the news than a detached experience. For example, René describes the beginnings of the 2016 primary season through language of both frustration and avoidance:

> The Joker was on TV, announcing a run for president. . . . Unable to watch the green-haired cackler make his improbable declaration, I turned to the crime pages and read about killings. . . . A police officer named Michael Slager shot and killed Walter Scott, an unarmed black man, in North Charleston, South Carolina. . . . There were floods and tornadoes across Texas and Arkansas, seventeen dead, forty missing. And it was only May. (Rushdie 2017, 220–21)

While I will address the characterization of Trump as a comic-book villain later in this chapter, what is most striking about this passage is the way in which the multiplicity of tragedies present in René's consumption of news seems to functionally overwrite each other to create an ambivalent effect. This effect works in opposition to Lukács's contention that in the wake of significant tragedy or mass global events, humans begin to see themselves as "historically conditioned"—where history becomes "something which deeply affects their daily lives and immediately concerns them" (Lukács 1983, 24). Rather, the commentary here intentionally cultivates disengagement. René seems ill-equipped to consciously engage with large-scale issues like systemic racial violence (Walter Scott) and global catastrophes related to climate change (tornadoes, floods), which is ironic because he chooses to consume this kind of news in opposition to the somehow more unpalatable 2016 primaries. The exhaustion inherent in this passage—"it was only May"—signifies a different kind of historical consciousness from what Lukács originally outlined. Rather than fostering an imagined sense of community, René's engagement with recent history only breeds insecurity and avoidance.

However, these specific references to real-world news stories also function to bolster the novel's aura of authenticity by virtue of using catastrophic events to tether the fictional storyline to history proper. In this way, "Contemporary fiction functions as both a currency by which historicity is measured, and the process through which it accrues" (Manshel 2017). Hyde and Wasserman contend that this attention toward historiography is also a dominant characteristic of many contemporary fictions, such that "they are consumed with time itself and, if not with historicity, then perhaps with historiography, with the telling and writing of history" (2017, 13). This tendency echoes discussions of the historical novel, such that there is a propensity in contemporary novels to "revisit and revise the past through explicitly formal means . . . to interrogate its continuities with the present" (Hyde and Wasserman 2017, 11). In this way, catastrophe functions as both a focus and an impetus in the recent historical novel, such that the act of writing through the state of emergency marks historical time, providing much-needed meaning in a contemporary moment characterized by slow disaster.

To read *The Golden House* as a recent historical novel is to recognize Rushdie's participation in the act of historicizing the proto-Trump era. However, some reviews read futility in this kind of project, asking, "With the news daily showing a changing American condition, how does the novel keep up, how does it do what journalism and the likes of Colbert and John Oliver can't?" (Fazli 2017). What is likely missing from Rushdie's representation of the contemporary moment is what Lukács would call "necessary anachronism," where fictional characters can better articulate and reflect on the historical situation than those living through the events (Lukács 1983, 63). Rather, René and Rushdie instead choose to filter their respective treatments of the Goldens and Trump indirectly by adopting exaggerated and satirical generic forms like the mockumentary and the comic book.

MOCKUMENTARY

Seemingly in response to the problem of historiography outlined above, René's film project wavers between the two poles of fiction and nonfiction

at various times. While initially positioning himself as an outside reporter
of the Goldens' story, he later admits that he fancies himself as more of an
"imagineer" rather than a "literalist" (Rushdie 2017, 24). René seems committed to a qualified and semi-imaginative treatment of realistic representation, even though his father reminds him that this mode no longer wields
the cultural capital it once did: "Maybe stop trying to make sings up. Ask
in any bookstore . . . iss de books on de nonfiction tables dat move while de
made-up stories languish" (29). The tension in René's artistic vision here
comes to a head after a conversation with his girlfriend surrounding the
epistemological traumas stemming from our post-truth moment. Suchitra
begins:

> "You need to become post-factual."
> "Is that the same as fictional?"
> "Fiction's elite. Nobody believes it. Post-factual is mass market, information-
> age, troll generated. It's what people want." (222)

What this exchange hinges on is the idea that generic categories that were
once thought to be straightforward are now troubled by the rise of post-
truth rhetoric. Fiction becomes a signifier for coastal elite cosmopolitans,
such that the act of disavowing the arts becomes a political strategy of the
conservative right. The irony is that the decline in value seen in literary fiction was accompanied by the popular and largely algorithmic rise of "post-
factual" forms of media, such as memes and viral online content. This nod
to troll-generated content circulated online fleshes out the atmosphere of
the novel by connecting it to key mechanisms and genres of post-truth that
have become ubiquitous in the time leading up to the Trumpian moment.
Thus, Suchitra's offhanded suggestion that perhaps "mockumentary is the
art form of the day" (222) inspires René to rethink his framing of his project to focus on a scripted faux-documentary for his study of the Goldens
(222). This genre choice allows René to harness a middle ground between
the popularity of mass-market nonfiction and his desire "to make the world
up" (29). In their survey of the subgenre, Roscoe and Hight describe the
mockumentary as a form that emerged at a historical moment "in which the
association between factual discourse and factual means of representation
is increasingly tenuous" (2001, 3). Essentially, as the documentary rose in
popularity, the tropes and styles of the genre begin to be co-opted by other,
largely fictional, genres as a means of subverting the documentary form's
cultural prestige (3–4). The ethos behind this strategy is characteristically
postmodern, where the mixing of genres and fictional signifiers creates an
experience both familiar and subversive, in a way that, according to Cynthia
Miller, is pointedly uncomfortable. Miller contends that "discomfort [is]

central to [the mockumentary's] mission—for it is through that discomfort that we, as both audience and subject, reflect on our norms, values, ideologies, and ways of being" (2012, xii). Thus, René's choice to pursue the mockumentary form puts a discomforting slant on the logic of truthful representation, favoring the partial-truth or satirical-truth over an explicit realism.

Additionally, the advantages René sees in using the mockumentary form solve a number of key problems for him as he continues to suss out the Goldens' story. For instance, as the plot of the novel develops, René becomes more personally invested in the family's narrative, such that he conspires with Nero Golden's new Russian wife, Vasilisa, to conceive a baby and pass the child off as Golden's heir and offspring.[9] In addition to his personal colluding with, or contaminating of, the object of his film, René is also periodically frustrated with his inability to conceive of the whole narrative since the family remains secretive in their conversation with him. Though initially wary of the idea of piecing together missing details in the story, René bolsters his commitment to the mockumentary form through another appropriately named literary tradition: "*A golden story.* . . . for the Romans, a tall tale, a wild conceit. A lie" (Rushdie 2017, 233; emphasis in original). Likely a reference to Apuleius and his stories of fantastic metamorphosis, this qualification allows René to harness the freedom of the mockumentary in order to depict a contemporary moment transformed by the ideological war between truth and lies waging around the upcoming election.

COMICS

While both the recent historical novel and the mockumentary have legitimate ties to nonfictional discourses, *The Golden House* is also peppered with comic-book tropes that present an extremist vision of post-truth reality. In co-opting the popularity of the symbiotic genres of superhero films and comic books, Rushdie is able to reframe the turmoil of the 2016 presidential election into a binary conflict between heroes and villains. The comic-treatment of this event provides a backdrop of impending disaster as a foil to the Golden family's litany of personal misfortunes: "To step outside [of the Golden House] was to discover that America had left reality behind and entered the comic-book universe; D.C. . . . was under attack by DC. It was the year of the Joker in Gotham and beyond" (Rushdie 2017, 248). While there are shades of Trump in the character of Nero Golden, the most explicit references to him are filtered through the adopted persona of Gary "Green" Gwynplaine, a real estate owner and "vulgarian" presidential hopeful who "made himself the mirror image of the notorious cartoon villain" the Joker (Rushdie 2017,

168). The Joker, in his pursuit of chaos and showmanship, is an apt cipher for Trump, who brandishes a larger-than-life personality that relies on shock-value more than substance. In his study of the Joker as a satirical figure, Johan Nilsson describes the character as "a very tragic . . . and violent figure at a psychological level, but he wears the face of comedy" (2015, 168). It is the dialectic between the horrific and the comedic that makes the Joker and Trump satirical figures under Paul Simpson's guidelines for satire, where the audience must mentally contend with contradictory narratives at the same time (2003, 8–10). However, problems arise when there is a failure to read the satirical nature of these figures as a skewed and extreme representation of existing discourses in reality.

For example, the information bubbles of post-truth partisan politics refer-enced earlier become reframed as a conflict between chaotic villains and a heroic metropolis committed to maintaining reality:

> It was a year of two bubbles. In one of those bubbles, the Joker shrieked and the laugh-track crowds laughed right on cue. In that bubble the climate was not changing and the end of the Arctic icecap was just a new real estate opportunity. In that bubble. . . . multiple bankruptcies would be understood to prove great business expertise. . . . In that bubble knowledge was ignorance, up was down, and the right person to hold the nuclear codes in his hand was the green-haired white-skinned red-slash-mouthed giggler who asked a military briefing team four times why using nuclear weapons was so bad. . . . In the other bubble . . . was the city of New York. (Rushdie 2017, 249–50)

This truncated excerpt of the Joker's platform includes multiple references to mythologies surrounding Trump—from his questionable acumen as a businessman, his willful ignorance about potentially dangerous topics like climate change and nuclear weapons, to his commitment to promoting vio-lent voices and ideologies. While under normal conditions these qualities effectively initiate a satirical reading of what it means to be presidential, René is surprised when the Joker is taken seriously: "What was astonishing, what made this an election year like no other, was that people backed him *because* he was insane, not in spite of it" (248; emphasis in the original). In this way, the Trump-Joker figure portrayed in *The Golden House* functions as a case of malicious metalepsis, where fictional and non-serious elements cross the invisible boundary between the real and the satirical. It's just this kind of border-crossing that makes post-truth rhetoric so alarming and dif-ficult to deal with. However, it's unlikely that the response René and other New Yorkers seem to take, to again recede into the bubble of perceived reality, is the solution. Rather, faced with the facts that malicious fictions are becoming real, René's final option is to embrace the power of overt fictionality.

CONCLUSION

In its final iteration René's film project abandons the generic ambiguity of the mockumentary form in favor of "a fully fledged fiction" (Rushdie 2017, 360). This return to fiction comes in the aftermath of the election and after René admits his infidelity and deceit surrounding the conception of Nero Golden's son. In confessing his wrongdoings and embracing the personal fallout, René recalibrates his relationship with the truth: "Lies can cause tragedies, both on the personal and the national scale. Lies can defeat the truth. But the truth is dangerous too" (359–60). And so, René returns to the project of telling stories, both personal and hopeful, as a means of both deflection and reassurance: "But the Republic remained more or less intact. Let me just set that down. . . . It's a fiction in a way, but I repeat it" (358–59). In a post-truth moment when many of our knowledge institutions seem less reliable as representatives of truth and facts, recognizing fiction for what it is—a way to shape a world—may be one of the best balms for our insecure times.

NOTES

1. See, for example, Ron Charles, "Salman Rushdie Launches a Novelistic Attack on Trump" (2017).

2. See Aaron Hanlon, "Postmodernism Didn't Cause Trump. It Explains Him" (2018).

3. However, a sharp distinction must be made between lies and fictional discourse since there is a significant difference between imagining a different state of affairs and deceiving in order to influence policy and opinion in the actual world (Nielsen, Phelan, and Walsh 2015, 63).

4. See, for example, Robert Darnton, "The True History of Fake News" (2017).

5. The fact that one of the avatars of Trump in *The Golden House* is a character who styles himself "Nero Golden" resonates with Mark Doten's *Trump Sky Alpha*, which at one point presents Trump as imagining himself in terms of a king eating gold. For discussion of *Trump Sky Alpha*, see Bruce Krajewski's chapter in the present volume.—Ed.

6. Random House explicitly markets the novel as the author's "triumphant and exciting return to realism" (*"The Golden House* by Salman Rushdie" n.d.).

7. The term "queer" is a not used lightly in the novel, since issues of queerness and nonbinary gender identity make up a significant part of Dionysus "D" Golden's storyline. While the scope of my focus in this chapter lies elsewhere, much could be said about how Rushdie grapples, successfully and unsuccessfully, with queer identity in the novel.

8. By contrast, Diana Wallace recognizes the misogynist limitations of Lukács's reliance on Scott as dismissive of important women writers also working within the form, both preceding and following Scott's supposedly "classical" model. For more, see Wallace, *The Woman's Historical Novel: British Women Writers, 1900–2000* (2005).

9. The details here, while fantastic, echo some of the more sensational news stories surrounding Trump, including the investigation into Russian hacking and involvement in the election and rumors about Trump's sexual proclivities while in Russia found in a commissioned dossier. Additionally, Vasilisa's character correlates well with Trump's tendency to wed beautiful women from Eastern Europe.

REFERENCES

Anderson, Benedict. 2006. *Imagined Communities*. Revised edition. New York: Verso Books.

Anderson, Perry. 2011. "From Progress to Catastrophe." *London Review of Books*. July 28, 2011. https://www.lrb.co.uk/v33/n15/perry-anderson/from-progress-to-catastrophe.

Carner, Mosco. 1985. *Giacomo Puccini: "Tosca"*. Cambridge: Cambridge University Press.

Charles, Ron. 2017. "Salman Rushdie Launches a Novelistic Attack on Trump." *Washington Post*. September 5, 2017. https://www.washingtonpost.com/entertainment/books/salman-rushdie-launches-a-novelistic-attack-on-trump/2017/09/05/9d871688-91d5-11e7-89fa-bb822a46da5b_story.html?noredirect=on&utm_term=.1c8b06bb2fe9.

Darnton, Robert. 2017. "The True History of Fake News." *New York Review of Books*. February 13, 2017. http://www.nybooks.com/daily/2017/02/13/the-true-history-of-fake-news/.

English, James F. 2016. "Now, Not Now: Counting Time in Contemporary Fiction Studies." *Modern Language Quarterly* 77 (3): 395–418.

Fazli, Shehryar. 2017. "Rushdie's Domus Aurea: 'The Golden House' by Salman Rushdie." *Los Angeles Review of Books*. September 13, 2017. https://lareviewofbooks.org/article/rushdies-domus-aurea-the-golden-house-by-salman-rushdie/.

Flood, Alison. 2016. "'Post-truth' Named Word of the Year by Oxford Dictionaries." *Guardian*. November 15, 2016. https://www.theguardian.com/books/2016/nov/15/post-truth-named-word-of-the-year-by-oxford-dictionaries.

Frank, Søren. 2010. "The Aesthetic of Elephantiasis: Rushdie's *Midnight's Children* as an Encyclopaedic Novel." *Journal of Postcolonial Writing* 46 (2): 187–98.

"The Golden House by Salman Rushdie." n.d. *PenguinRandomHouse.com*. Accessed March 4, 2019. https://www.penguinrandomhouse.com/books/558138/the-golden-house-by-salman-rushdie/9780399592829.

Hanlon, Aaron. 2018. "Postmodernism Didn't Cause Trump. It Explains Him." *Washington Post*. August 31, 2018. https://www.washingtonpost.com/outlook/postmodernism-didnt-cause-trump-it-explains-him/2018/08/30/0939f7c4-9b12-11e8-843b-36e177f3081c_story.html?noredirect=on&utm_term=.90f90fbf0347.

Harsin, Jayson. 2018. "Post-Truth and Critical Communication Studies." *Oxford Research Encyclopedia of Communication*. December 2018. https://doi.org/10.1093/acrefore/9780190228613.013.757.

Hyde, Emily, and Sarah Wasserman. 2017. "The Contemporary." *Literature Compass* 14 (9): e12411. https://doi.org/10.1111/lic3.12411.

India Today Web Desk. 2018. "I Am Responsible for Donald Trump: Salman Rushdie." *India Today.* June 4, 2018. https://www.indiatoday.in/fyi/story/salman-rushdie-says-he-is-responsible-for-donald-trump-1250201-2018-06-04.

Jameson, Fredric. 2012. "Antinomies of the Realism-Modernism Debate." *Modern Language Quarterly* 73 (3): 475–85.

Lukács, Georg. 1983. *The Historical Novel.* Translated by Hannah Mitchell and Stanley Mitchell. Lincoln: University of Nebraska Press.

Manshel, Alexander. 2017. "The Rise of the Recent Historical Novel." *Post45.* September 29, 2017. http://post45.research.yale.edu/2017/09/the-rise-of-the-recent-historical-novel/.

Martin, Theodore. 2017. *Contemporary Drift: Genre, Historicism, and the Problem of the Present.* New York: Columbia University Press.

McIntyre, Lee. 2018. *Post-Truth.* Cambridge: MIT Press.

Miller, Cynthia J. 2012. Introduction. *Too Bold for the Box Office: The Mockumentary from Big Screen to Small,* edited by Cynthia J. Miller, xi–xxi. Lanham: Scarecrow Press.

Nielsen, Henrik Skov, James Phelan, and Richard Walsh. 2015. "Ten Theses about Fictionality." *Narrative* 23 (1): 61–73.

Nilsson, Johan. 2015. "Rictus Grins and Glasgow Smiles: The Joker as Satirical Discourse." In *The Joker: A Serious Study of the Clown Prince of Crime,* edited by Robert Moses Peaslee and Robert G. Weiner, 165–78. Jackson: University Press of Mississippi.

Oxford English Dictionary Online. 2017. S.v. "post-truth."

Phillips, Kristine. 2018. "'Truth Isn't Truth': Rudy Giuliani's Flub Tops 2018's Quotes of the Year." *Washington Post.* December 11, 2018. https://www.washingtonpost.com/politics/2018/12/11/truth-isnt-truth-rudy-giulianis-flub-tops-s-quotes-year/.

Quayson, Ato. 2006. "Fecundities of the Unexpected: Magical Realism, Narrative, and History." In *The Novel.* Vol. 1, *History, Geography, and Culture,* edited by Franco Moretti, 726–56. Princeton: Princeton University Press.

Roscoe, Jane, and Craig Hight. 2001. *Faking It: Mock-Documentary and the Subversion of Factuality.* Manchester: Manchester University Press.

Rushdie, Salman. 1983. *Shame.* New York: Alfred A. Knopf.

———. 2017. *The Golden House.* New York: Random House.

———. 2018. "Truth, Lies, and Literature." *New Yorker.* May 31, 2018. http://www.newyorker.com/culture/cultural-comment/truth-lies-and-literature.

Simpson, Paul. 2003. *On the Discourse of Satire: Towards a Stylistic Model of Satirical Humour.* Amsterdam: John Benjamins.

Tuttle, Kate. 2017. "Salman Rushdie on the Opulent Realism of His New Novel, 'The Golden House.'" *Los Angeles Times.* September 14, 2017. https://www.latimes.com/books/jacketcopy/la-ca-jc-salman-rushdie-20170914-story.html.

Wallace, Diana. 2005. *The Woman's Historical Novel: British Women Writers, 1900–2000.* Hampshire, UK: Palgrave Macmillan.

Index

Page references for figures are italicized.

About the Contributors

Joseph M. Conte is Professor of English at the University at Buffalo. His latest book, *Transnational Politics in the Post-9/11 Novel*, is forthcoming from Routledge. He is the author of *Design & Debris: A Chaotics of Postmodern American Fiction*, which received the Agee Prize in American Literary Studies from the University of Alabama Press in 2002, and *Unending Design: The Forms of Postmodern Poetry*, which was released as an e-Book by Cornell University Press in 2016. Book chapters and articles on a wide range of contemporary literature and criticism have appeared in *American Literature in Transition: 1990–2000, Modern Fiction Studies, Twentieth-Century Literature, Critique: Studies in Contemporary Fiction, The Cambridge Companion to Don DeLillo*, and other venues.

Clinton J. Craig is a PhD candidate at University of Louisiana at Lafayette, where he studies creative writing and contemporary fiction. He has previously published academic work in *ANQ: A Quarterly Journal of Short Articles, Notes, and Reviews* and creative work in *Gravel, The Hunger, Tammy, Jelly Bucket*, and others. His current research focuses on nonhuman narrators and recursive fiction.

Caitlin R. Duffy is a doctoral candidate in the English Department at Stony Brook University. Her scholarly interests include nineteenth-century American gothic literature and American horror cinema. She is particularly interested in exploring how capitalism and liberalism influence and color gothic texts. Her work has been published in *The Journal of Dracula Studies* and *Poe Studies*. Caitlin currently teaches courses in film, literature, and writing at Stony Brook University.

Shannon Finck is Lecturer in English at the University of West Georgia. She earned her PhD in twentieth-century American literature with a secondary emphasis in global postmodern and contemporary literatures at Georgia State University in 2014. She also holds an MFA in creative nonfiction and narrative poetry from Georgia College (GCSU). Her work appears in *Angelaki, Miranda, a/b: Autobiography Studies, LIT: Literature Interpretation Theory, The Journal of Modern Literature, Lammergeier, The Florida Review, FUGUE*, and elsewhere. She is currently working on a book about postmodern and experimental life writing, entitled *Thin Skin: Autotheory & Resilience.*

Susan Gilmore is an associate professor of English at Central Connecticut State University. She is the editor of a special cluster on "Riot" for *Modern Language Studies* (Winter 2019) and is currently expanding this project into the critical anthology *"Language of the Unheard": Riot on the American Cultural Stage.* Her essay, "'Don't Let the Bastards Grind You Down' *Again*: Returning to *The Handmaid's Tale*," is included in *The Handmaid's Tale: Teaching Dystopia, Feminism, and Resistance across Disciplines and Borders*, eds. Karen A. Ritzenhoff and Janis L. Goldie (Lexington, 2019). Her poems and essays have appeared in the *Connecticut Review* and *Drunken Boat*, and in *Touches of Venus: An Anthology of Poems about Ava Gardner*, ed. Gilbert L. Gigliotti (Entasis Press, 2010). She has also published articles on the poetry and plays of Mina Loy, Sophie Treadwell, and Edna St. Vincent Millay, on Margaret Fuller's Native American encounters in *Summer on the Lakes*, and on Gwendolyn Brooks's verse journalism.

Laura Gray-Rosendale is a professor in Rhetoric, Writing, and Digital Media Studies, and President's Distinguished Teaching Fellow at Northern Arizona University. Her research and teaching interests focus on memoir and theories of autobiography, history of rhetoric and composition, literacy studies, and popular culture studies. She directs the STAR (Successful Transition and Academic Readiness) English Program, a curriculum that addresses the needs of students who are first generation and/or in economic need. Along with various articles and book chapters, she has published the following books: *Rethinking Basic Writing, Alternative Rhetorics* (with Sibylle Gruber), *Fractured Feminisms* (with Gil Harootunian), *Radical Relevance* (with Steven Rosendale), *Pop Perspectives, College Girl* (winner of the Gold Medal Independent Book Publisher's Award in Memoir), and *Getting Personal: Teaching Personal Writing in the Digital Age* (winner of the Silver Medal Independent Book Publisher's Award in Theory and Education). Currently she is the guest editor on two special volumes (on graduate education and basic writing) for the *Journal of Basic Writing.*

Ashleigh Hardin is an assistant professor of English at the University of Saint Francis in Fort Wayne, Indiana. Focusing on contemporary and twentieth-century American literature and culture, her dissertation examined narratives of addiction during the War on Drugs. She has presented at meetings of the International Society for the Study of Narrative, the American Literature Association, Popular Culture Association, and the Cultural Studies Association. Her work on race and narratives of addiction has appeared in *Arizona Quarterly*.

Stephen Hock is an associate professor of English at Virginia Wesleyan University. He is the coeditor (with Jeremy Braddock) of *Directed by Allen Smithee* (University of Minnesota Press, 2001), and his work has appeared in journals and edited collections including *Contemporary Literature*; *Italian Americana*; *Literature/Film Quarterly*; *Michael Chabon's America: Magical Words, Secret Worlds, and Sacred Spaces* (Rowman & Littlefield, 2014); *The Poetics of Genre in the Contemporary Novel* (Lexington Books, 2016); and *Pynchon's California* (University of Iowa Press, 2014).

Meredith James is an associate professor of English at Eastern Connecticut State University. Her research and teaching interests include Indigenous Studies and American Studies.

Peter Kragh Jensen is a doctoral student in Screen Cultures at Northwestern University. His research interests include contemporary political comedy, race, globalization, and digital culture.

Bruce Krajewski is a writer, translator, and editor living in Texas. His story "The Gravity of the Situation" is forthcoming in *The Anthology of Babel*.

Tim Lanzendörfer is Assistant Professor of American Studies at the University of Mainz. He is the author of *Books of the Dead: Reading the Zombie in Contemporary Literature* (University Press of Mississippi, 2018) and of a large number of essays on the contemporary novel, as well as the editor of *The Poetics of Genre in the Contemporary Novel* (Lanham: Lexington, 2016).

William Magrino is an associate director of the Writing Program at Rutgers, The State University of New Jersey, New Brunswick, and has served as Director of Business & Technical Writing since 2007. He holds a PhD in English Literature and frequently presents his research at international conferences on topics concerning literature, pedagogy, professionalism, and administration. William is the coauthor of two professional writing textbooks, now in their fourth editions. In addition, he coauthored two peer-reviewed articles examining the pedagogical implications of social media, both derived from previous MLA presentations: "Teaching the New Paradigm: Social Media Inside and Outside the Classroom" (2013) and "Professionalizing the Amateur: Social Media, the 'Myth of the Digital Native,' and the Graduate Assistant in the Composition Classroom" (2014). He is also a contributor to *New Paths to Raymond Carver: Critical Essays on His Life, Fiction, and Poetry* (University of South Carolina Press, 2008), and his current research is concerned with representations of youth culture in the fiction of Bret Easton Ellis.

David Markus is a language lecturer in the Expository Writing Program at New York University. He earned his PhD in Comparative Literature from the University of Chicago. His writing and research focuses on representations of dwelling and domesticity in late capitalist contexts, social practices in contemporary art, and the conflict between intimacy and artistic ambition in modern and contemporary literature and visual culture. His articles and reviews have appeared in publications such as *Art Journal, Frieze, Art in America*, and *Flash Art*.

Jaclyn Partyka is a lecturer in the Writing Arts Department at Rowan University. She holds a PhD in English, and her research focuses on authorship, genre, and contemporary multimodal literacies. Her writing has appeared in *Contemporary Literature* and *Metaliterate Learning for the Post-Truth World* (2018).

Steven Rosendale is a professor of Literature at Northern Arizona University. His research and teaching focuses on ecocriticism and literary modernism. In addition to a variety of articles and book chapters in those fields, he is coeditor (with Laura Gray-Rosendale) of *Radical Relevance: Toward a Scholarship of the Whole Left* (SUNY Press, 2005), and editor of *Dictionary of Literary Biography 303: American Radical and Reform Writers* (Gale, 2004) and *The Greening of Literary Scholarship: Literature, Theory, and the Environment* (U Iowa Press, 2002).

William G. Welty is completing his PhD in Literature in English at Rutgers University. His dissertation is entitled "'A Strange Course': Reading, Race, and the Anachronous Histories of Post-45 American Fiction." The project focuses on how Ishmael Reed, Thomas Pynchon, Toni Morrison, and Leslie Marmon Silko have portrayed reading as an activity within their novels. Its major claim is that these authors consistently link reading to a sense of anachronous history, in order to imagine a perspective that might reconcile the contradictory racial imaginaries and aesthetic impulses of the postmodern period. Welty has published on Ishmael Reed, Flannery O'Connor, Jim

Jarmusch, Jacques Lacan, and Slavoj Žižek. His work has been featured in *Textual Practice*; *Psychoanalysis, Culture, and Society*; *The Encyclopedia of the Black Arts Movement*; *Hypercultura*; and *Politics/Letters*. He is also the cofounder of the Rutgers Post-45 Research Group. When he isn't writing about race and anachronous futures, he enjoys home-brewed beer, kickboxing, and going for walks with his wife Valerie, and their dogs Baxter and Charley.

Ingram Content Group UK Ltd.
Milton Keynes UK
UKHW020710170423
420292UK00015B/728

9 781498 598064